DEMON SLAYER:
KIMETSU NO YAIBA
VOLUME 21
Shonen Jump Edition

Story and Art by
KOYOHARU GOTOUGE

KIMETSU NO YAIBA
© 2016 by Koyoharu Gotouge
All rights reserved. First published in Japan
in 2016 by SHUEISHA Inc., Tokyo. English
translation rights arranged by SHUEISHA Inc.

TRANSLATION John Werry
TOUCH-UP ART & LETTERING Evan Waldinger
DESIGN Jimmy Presler
SHONEN JUMP SERIES EDITOR Rae First
GRAPHIC NOVEL EDITOR Mike Montesa

The stories, characters and incidents mentioned
in this publication are entirely fictional.

No portion of this book may be reproduced or
transmitted in any form or by any means without
written permission from the copyright holders.

Printed in the U.S.A.

Published by VIZ Media, LLC
P.O. Box 77010
San Francisco, CA 94107

11
First printing, April 2021
Eleventh printing, April 2022

PARENTAL ADVISORY
DEMON SLAYER: KIMETSU NO YAIBA is rated T for
Teen and recommended for ages 13 and up. This
volume contains realistic and fantasy violence.

VIZ MEDIA

SHONEN JUMP

viz.com

KOYOHARU GOTOUGE

Hi, I'm Gotouge. Since the start of 2020, we've been stuck indoors listening to nothing but depressing news. Despite that, I hope you're doing well. There hasn't been a day without trouble since the start of my serialization. I feel like my soul is breaking into pieces every day, but I've been using duct tape to piece it back together so I can keep moving forward.

I think a lot of my readers feel the same way. We don't necessarily have an enemy, but we feel like we must fight and win. Those of us who've been holding on, repeating to ourselves that we can't lose, are courageous warriors. I hope fortune smiles upon you.

DEMON SLAYER

KIMETSU NO YAIBA

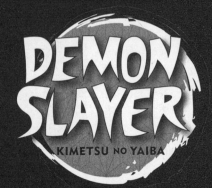

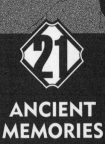

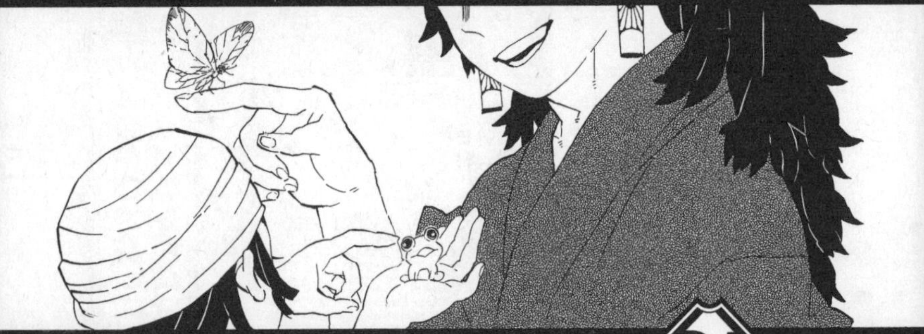

21

ANCIENT MEMORIES

KOYOHARU GOTOUGE

CHARACTERS

TANJIRO KAMADO

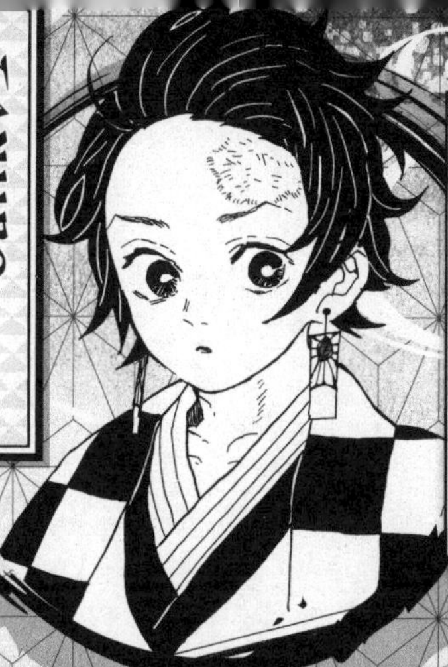

A kind boy who saved his sister when the rest of his family was killed. Now he seeks revenge. He can smell the scent of demons and his opponents' weaknesses.

NEZUKO KAMADO

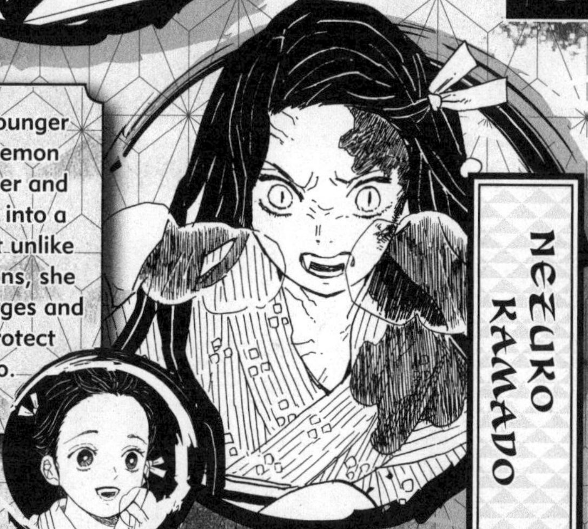

Tanjiro's younger sister. A demon attacked her and turned her into a demon. But unlike other demons, she fights her urges and tries to protect Tanjiro.

STORY

In Taisho-era Japan, young Tanjiro makes a living selling charcoal. One day, demons kill his family and turn his younger sister Nezuko into a demon. Tanjiro and Nezuko set out to find a way to return Nezuko to human form and defeat Kibutsuji, the demon who killed their family!

After joining the Demon Slayer Corps, Tanjiro meets Tamayo and Yushiro—demons who oppose Kibutsuji—who provide a clue to how Nezuko may regain her humanity.

Nezuko manifests the ability to withstand sunlight, so Kibutsuji comes for her and attacks Ubuyashiki Mansion. The Demon Slayers plunge into Infinity Castle and defeat the Upper Rank 2 and 3 demons!!

They eventually defeat the Upper Rank 1 demon but suffer many losses. Now Tanjiro and the remaining Hashira rush toward Kibutsuji.

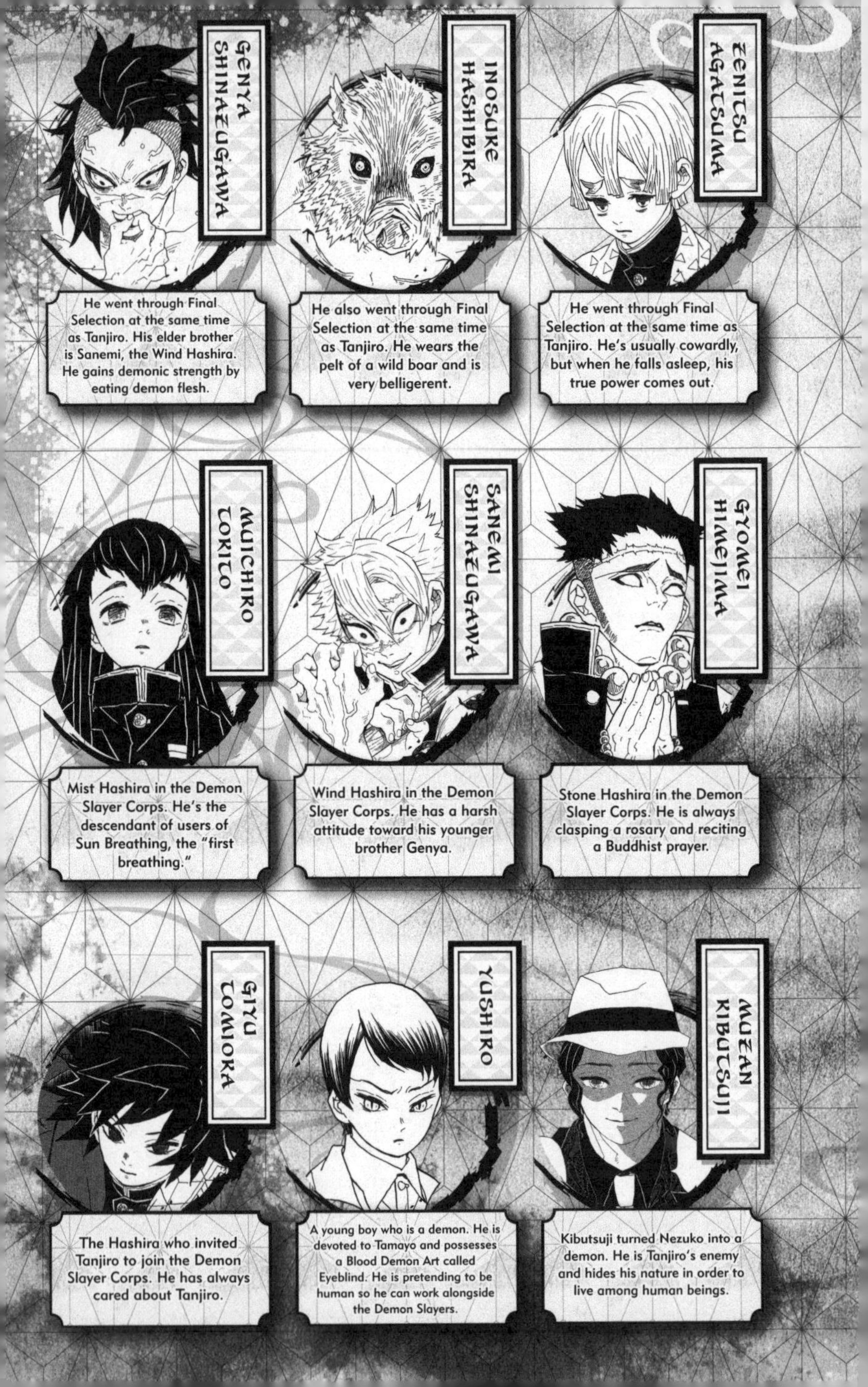

ZENITSU AGATSUMA
He went through Final Selection at the same time as Tanjiro. He's usually cowardly, but when he falls asleep, his true power comes out.
INOSUKE HASHIBIRA
He also went through Final Selection at the same time as Tanjiro. He wears the pelt of a wild boar and is very belligerent.
GENYA SHINAZUGAWA
He went through Final Selection at the same time as Tanjiro. His elder brother is Sanemi, the Wind Hashira. He gains demonic strength by eating demon flesh.
GYOMEI HIMEJIMA
Stone Hashira in the Demon Slayer Corps. He is always clasping a rosary and reciting a Buddhist prayer.
SANEMI SHINAZUGAWA
Wind Hashira in the Demon Slayer Corps. He has a harsh attitude toward his younger brother Genya.
MUICHIRO TOKITO
Mist Hashira in the Demon Slayer Corps. He's the descendant of users of Sun Breathing, the "first breathing."
MUZAN KIBUTSUJI
Kibutsuji turned Nezuko into a demon. He is Tanjiro's enemy and hides his nature in order to live among human beings.
YUSHIRO
A young boy who is a demon. He is devoted to Tamayo and possesses a Blood Demon Art called Eyeblind. He is pretending to be human so he can work alongside the Demon Slayers.
GIYU TOMIOKA
The Hashira who invited Tanjiro to join the Demon Slayer Corps. He has always cared about Tanjiro.

CONTENTS

DEMON SLAYER!
KIMETSU NO YAIBA

21

ANCIENT MEMORIES

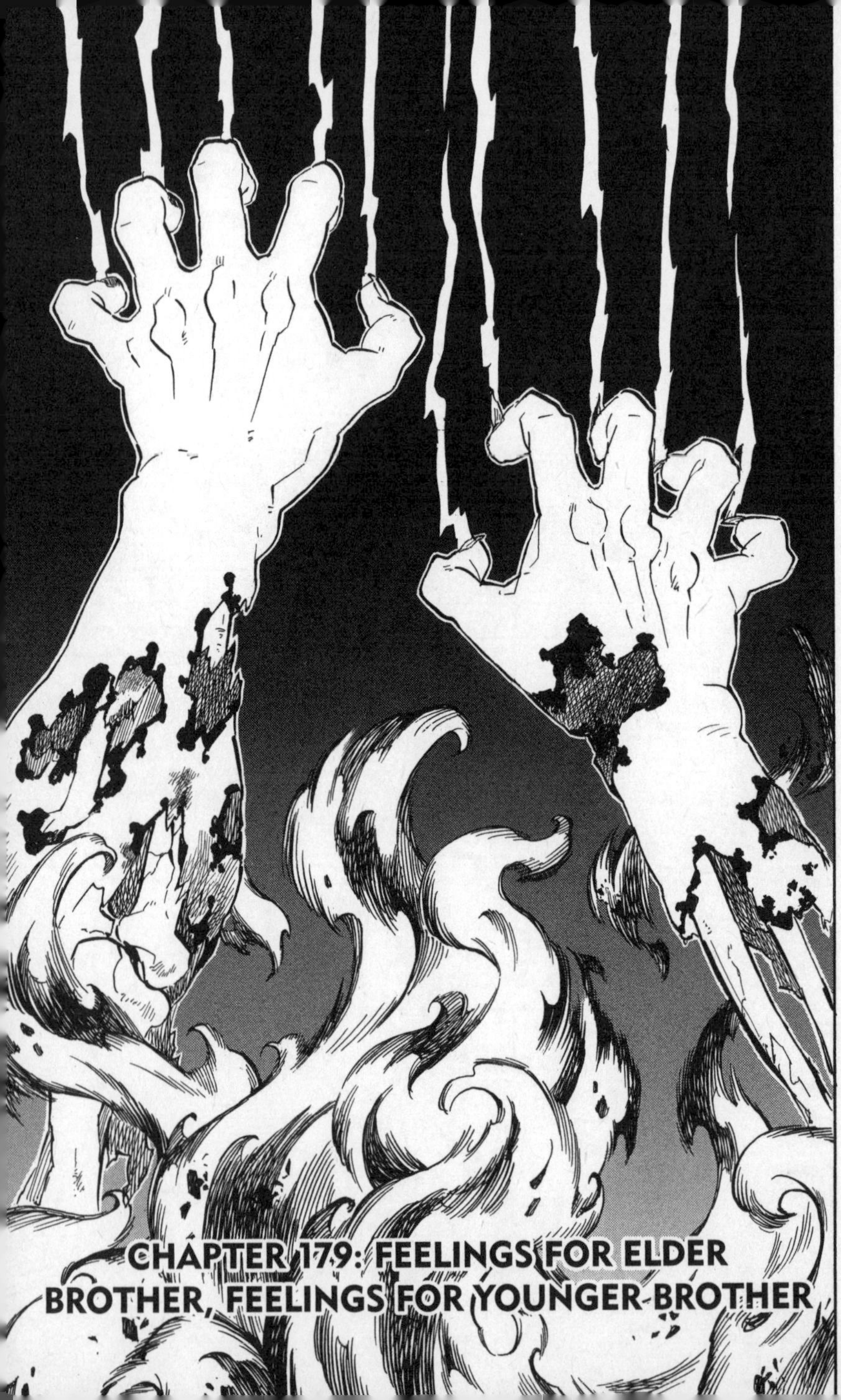
CHAPTER 179: FEELINGS FOR ELDER BROTHER, FEELINGS FOR YOUNGER BROTHER

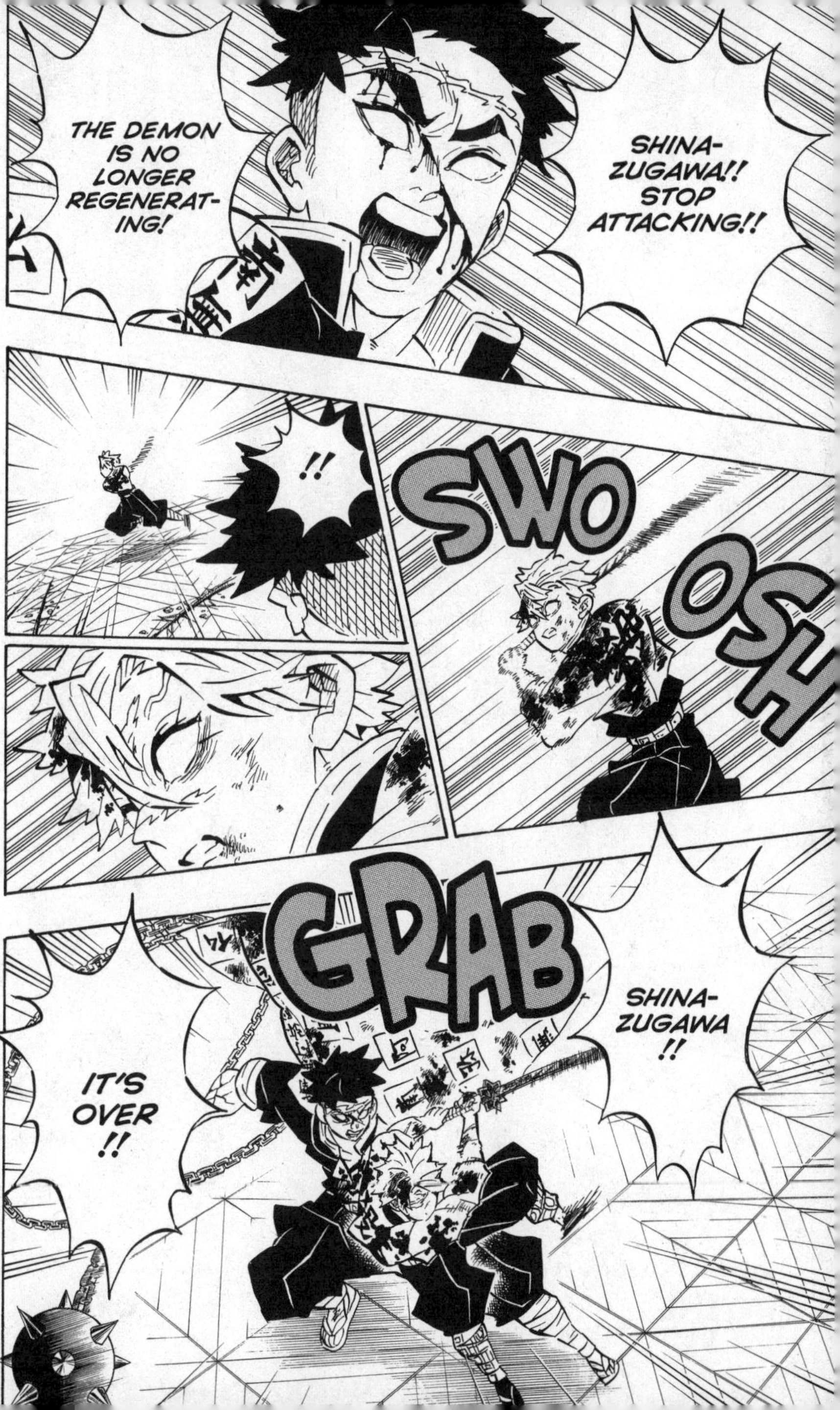
SHINA-ZUGAWA!! STOP ATTACKING!!
THE DEMON IS NO LONGER REGENERAT-ING!
SWOOSH
!!
GRAB
SHINA-ZUGAWA !!
IT'S OVER !!

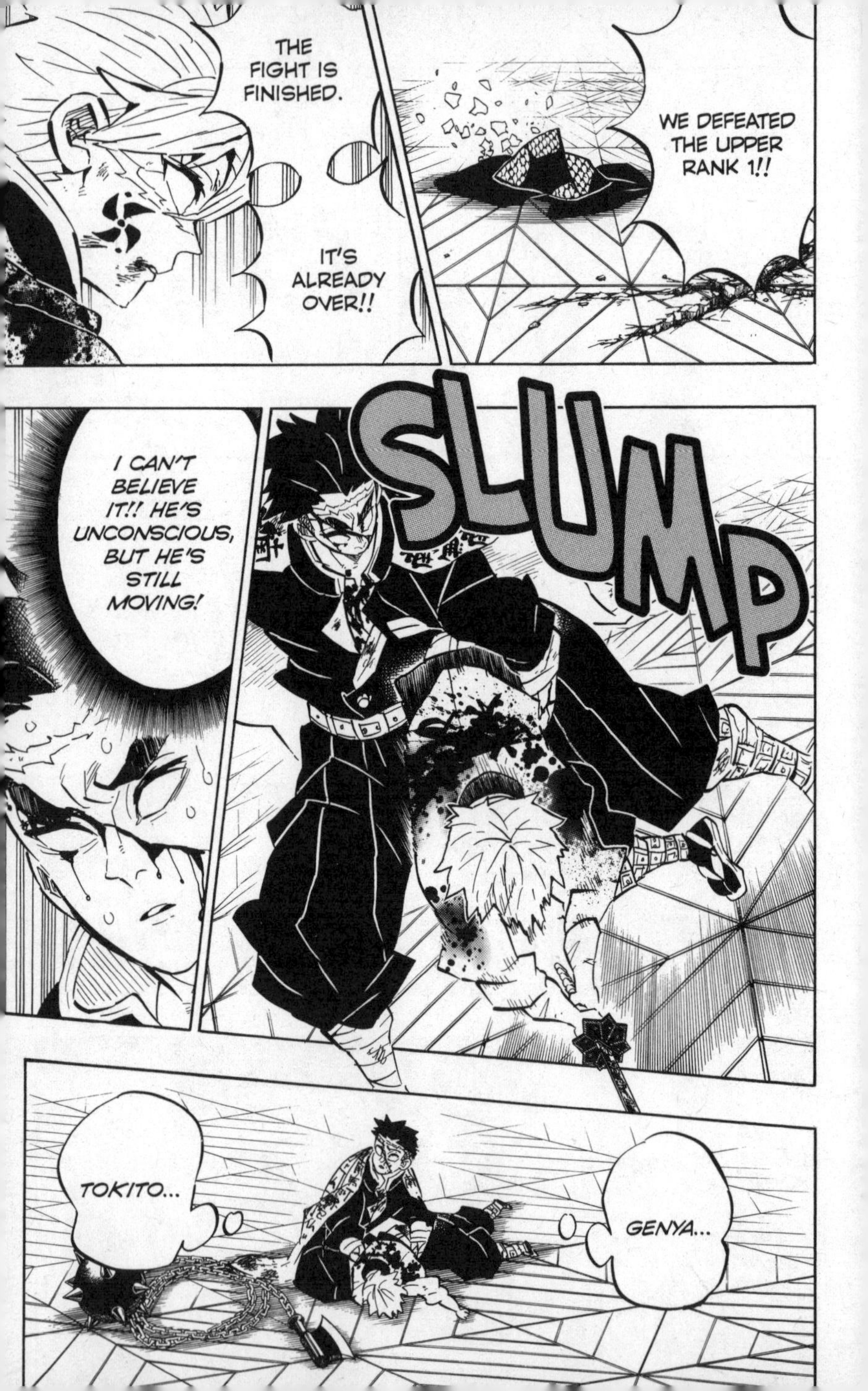
WE DEFEATED THE UPPER RANK 1!!
THE FIGHT IS FINISHED.
IT'S ALREADY OVER!!
SLUMP
I CAN'T BELIEVE IT!! HE'S UNCONSCIOUS, BUT HE'S STILL MOVING!
GENYA...
TOKITO...

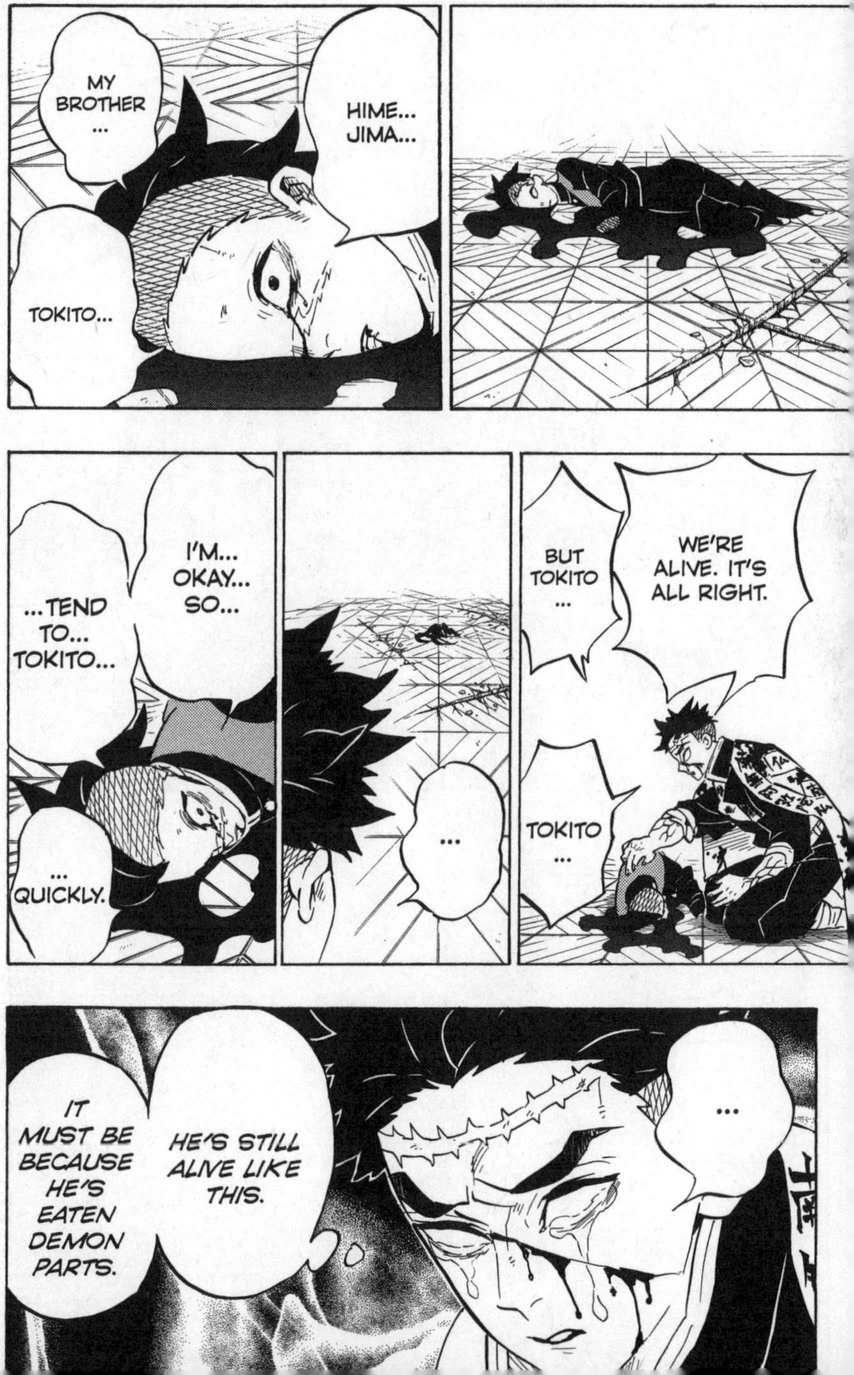
HIME... JIMA...
MY BROTHER ...
TOKITO...
WE'RE ALIVE. IT'S ALL RIGHT.
BUT TOKITO ...
TOKITO ...
...
I'M... OKAY... SO...
...TEND TO... TOKITO...
... QUICKLY.
...
HE'S STILL ALIVE LIKE THIS.
IT MUST BE BECAUSE HE'S EATEN DEMON PARTS.

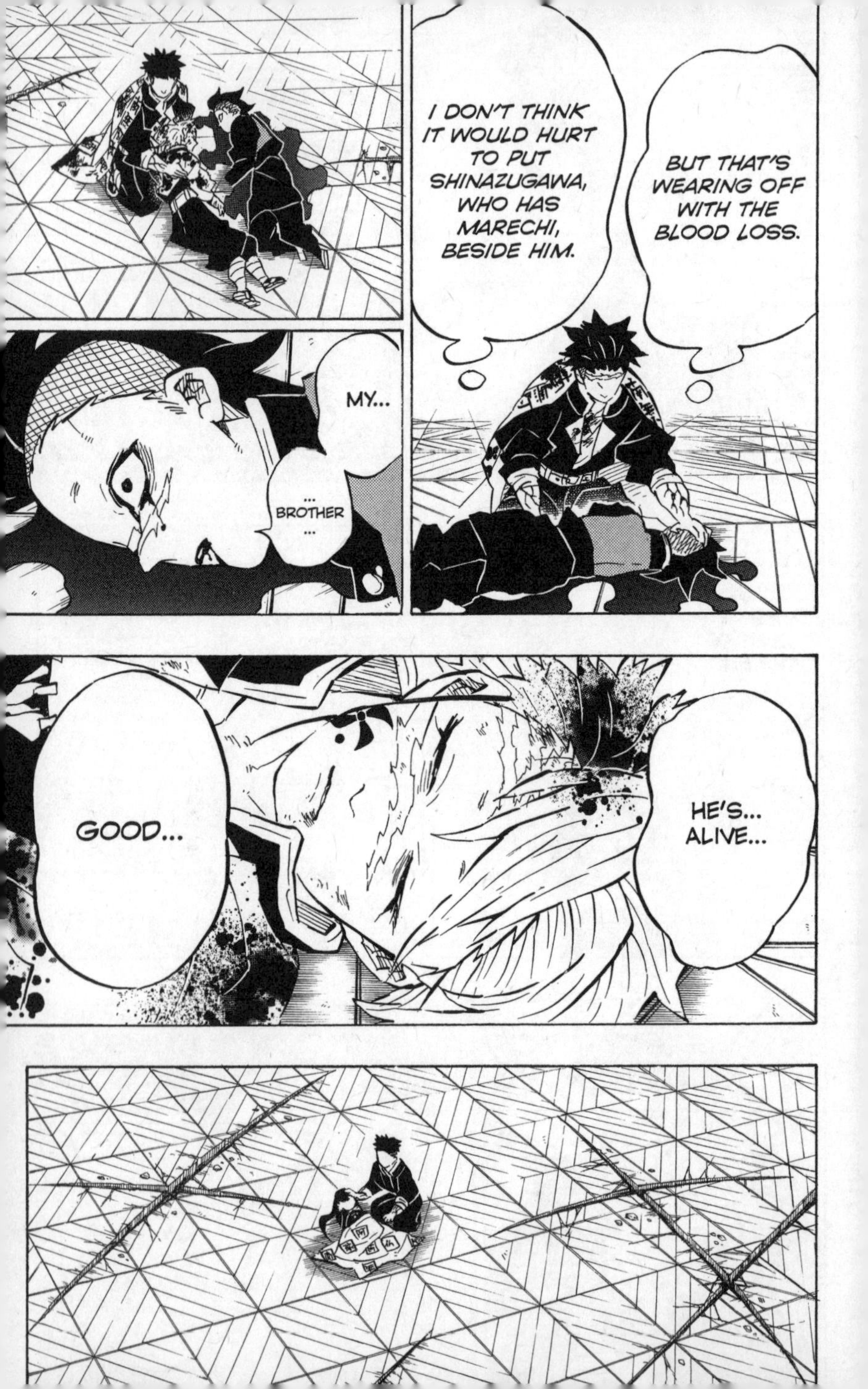
I DON'T THINK IT WOULD HURT TO PUT SHINAZUGAWA, WHO HAS MARECHI, BESIDE HIM.
BUT THAT'S WEARING OFF WITH THE BLOOD LOSS.
MY...
... BROTHER ...
HE'S... ALIVE...
GOOD...

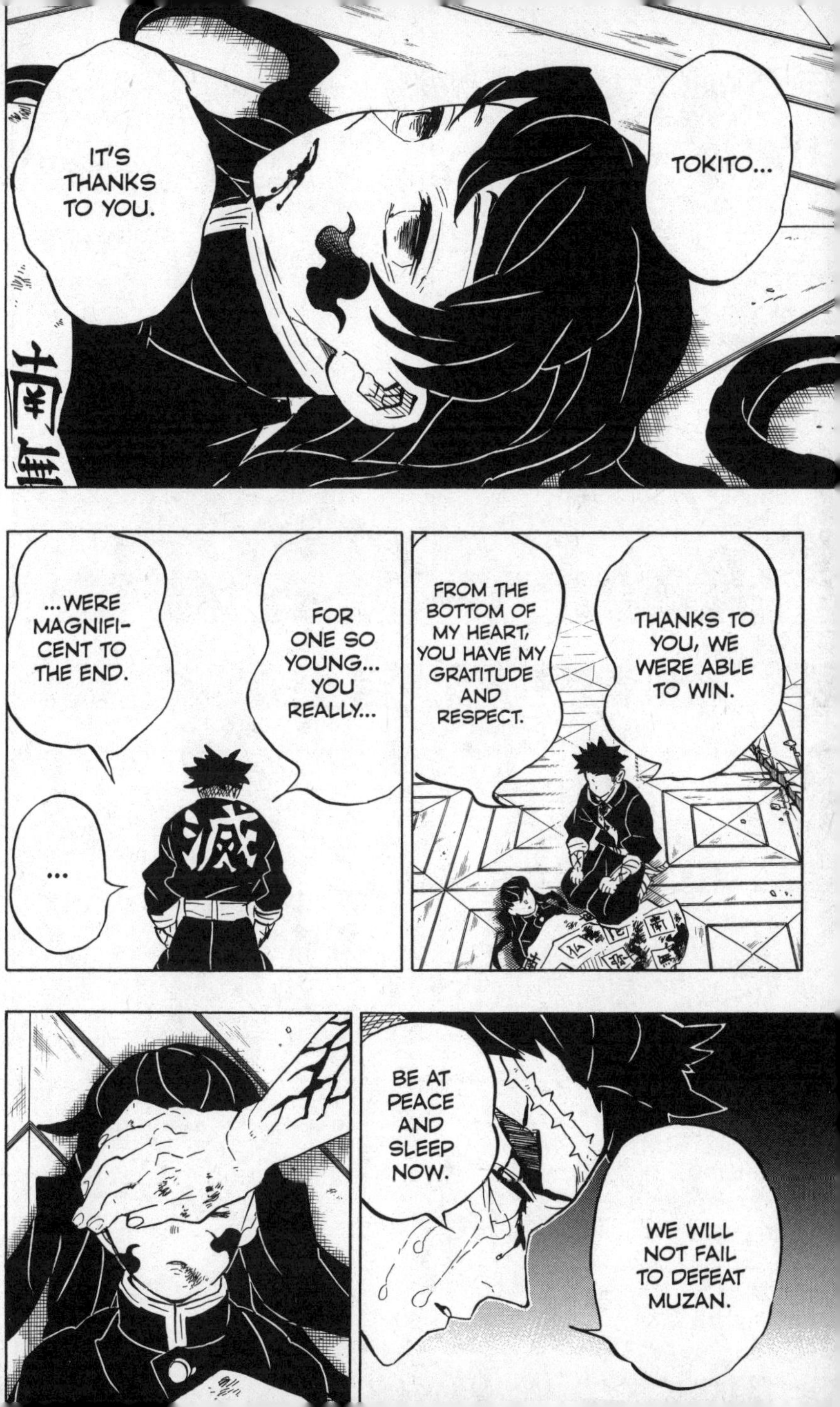
TOKITO...
IT'S THANKS TO YOU.
THANKS TO YOU, WE WERE ABLE TO WIN.
FROM THE BOTTOM OF MY HEART, YOU HAVE MY GRATITUDE AND RESPECT.
FOR ONE SO YOUNG... YOU REALLY...
...WERE MAGNIFICENT TO THE END.
...
BE AT PEACE AND SLEEP NOW.
WE WILL NOT FAIL TO DEFEAT MUZAN.

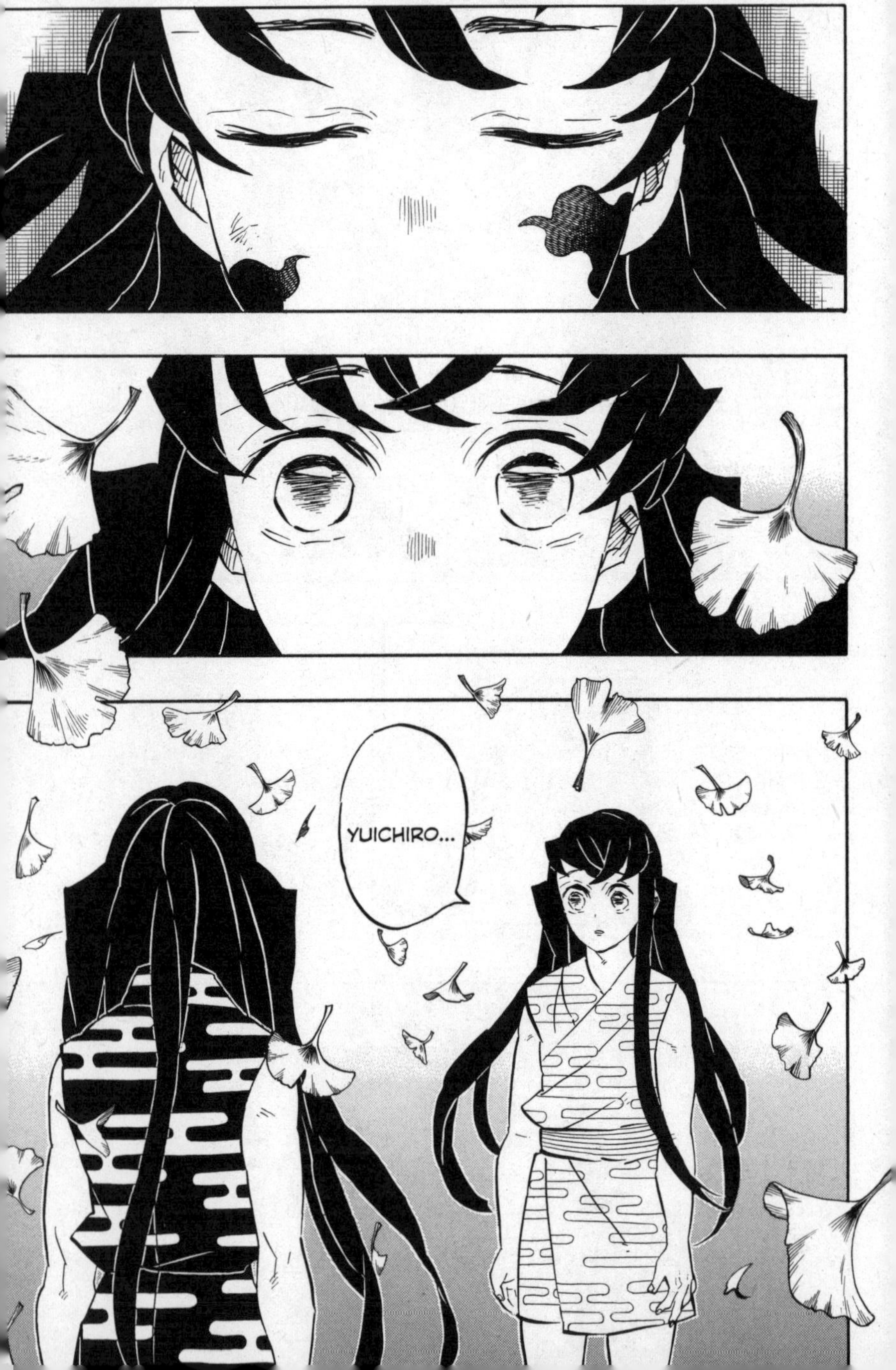
YUICHIRO...

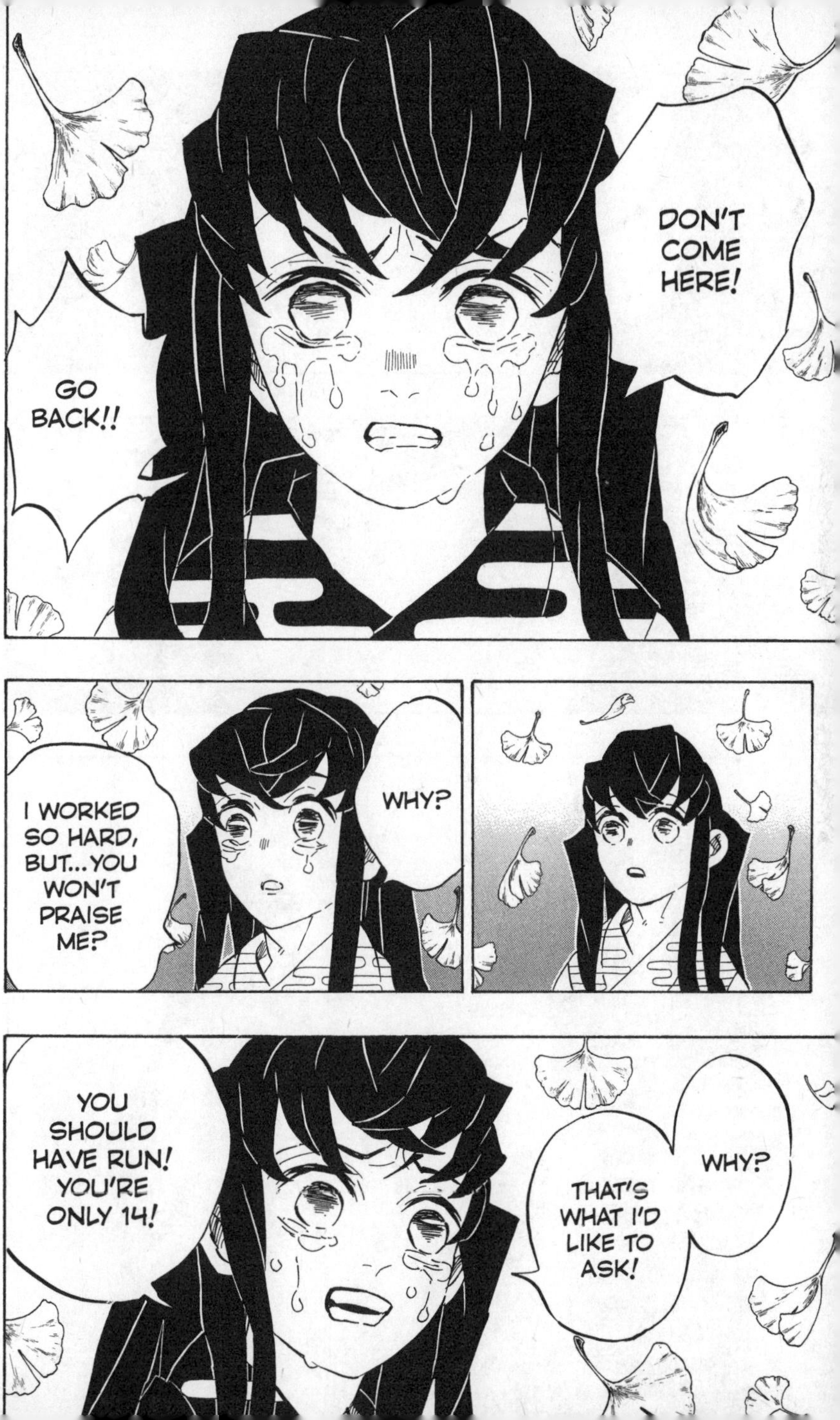
DON'T COME HERE!
GO BACK!!
WHY?
I WORKED SO HARD, BUT...YOU WON'T PRAISE ME?
WHY?
THAT'S WHAT I'D LIKE TO ASK!
YOU SHOULD HAVE RUN! YOU'RE ONLY 14!

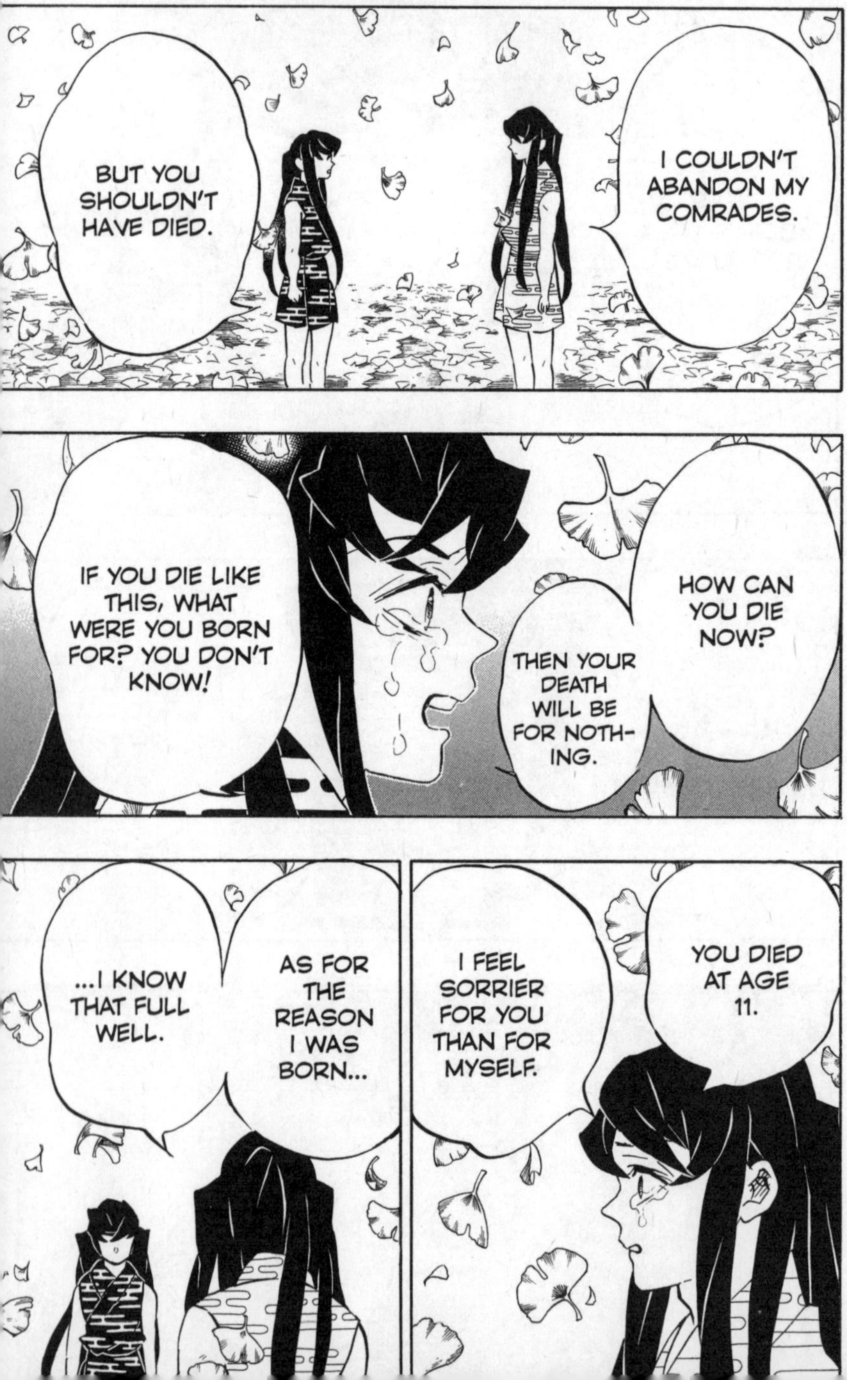
I COULDN'T ABANDON MY COMRADES.
BUT YOU SHOULDN'T HAVE DIED.
HOW CAN YOU DIE NOW?
THEN YOUR DEATH WILL BE FOR NOTH-ING.
IF YOU DIE LIKE THIS, WHAT WERE YOU BORN FOR? YOU DON'T KNOW!
YOU DIED AT AGE 11.
I FEEL SORRIER FOR YOU THAN FOR MYSELF.
AS FOR THE REASON I WAS BORN...
...I KNOW THAT FULL WELL.

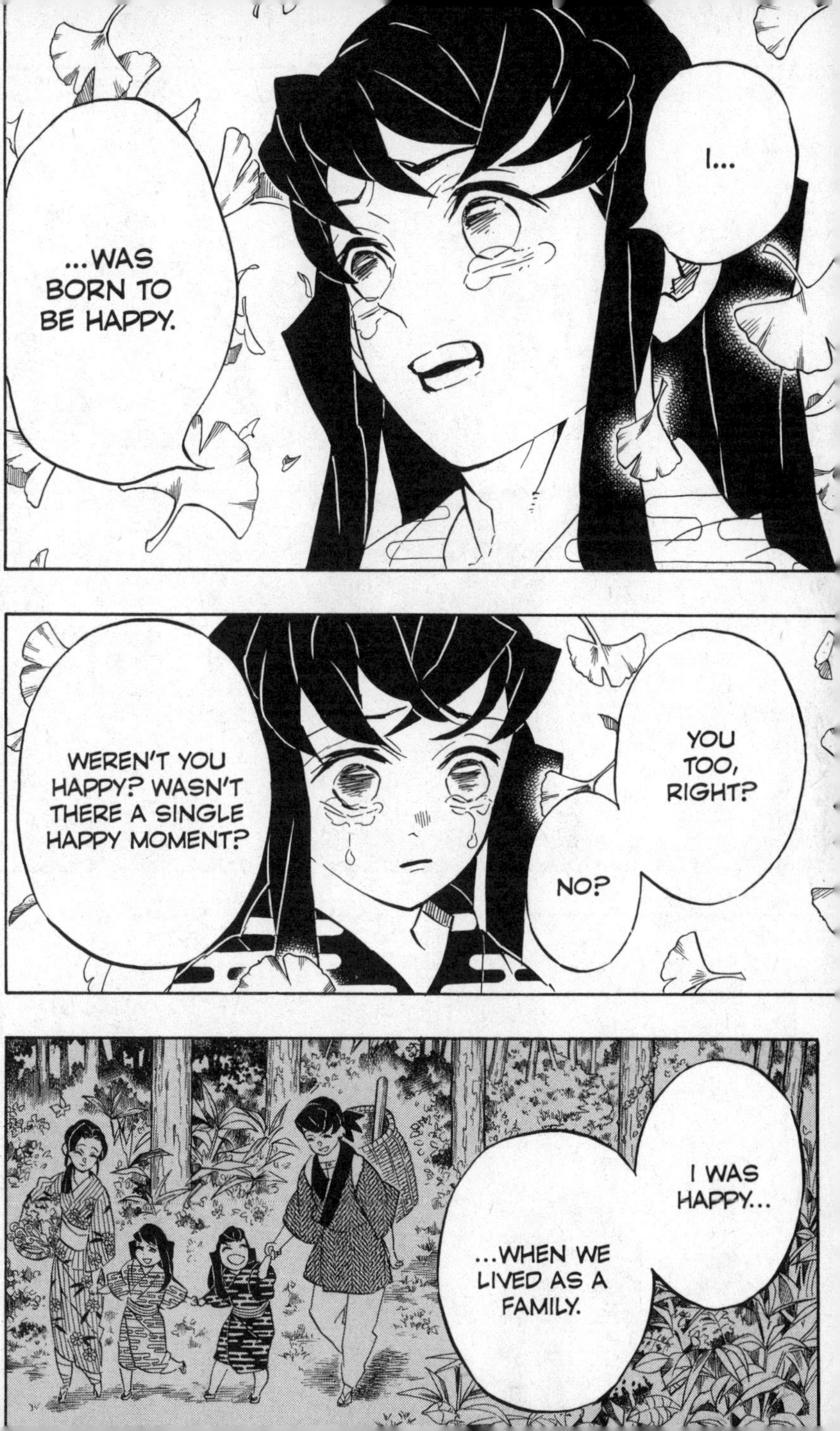
I...
...WAS BORN TO BE HAPPY.
YOU TOO, RIGHT?
NO?
WEREN'T YOU HAPPY? WASN'T THERE A SINGLE HAPPY MOMENT?
I WAS HAPPY...
...WHEN WE LIVED AS A FAMILY.

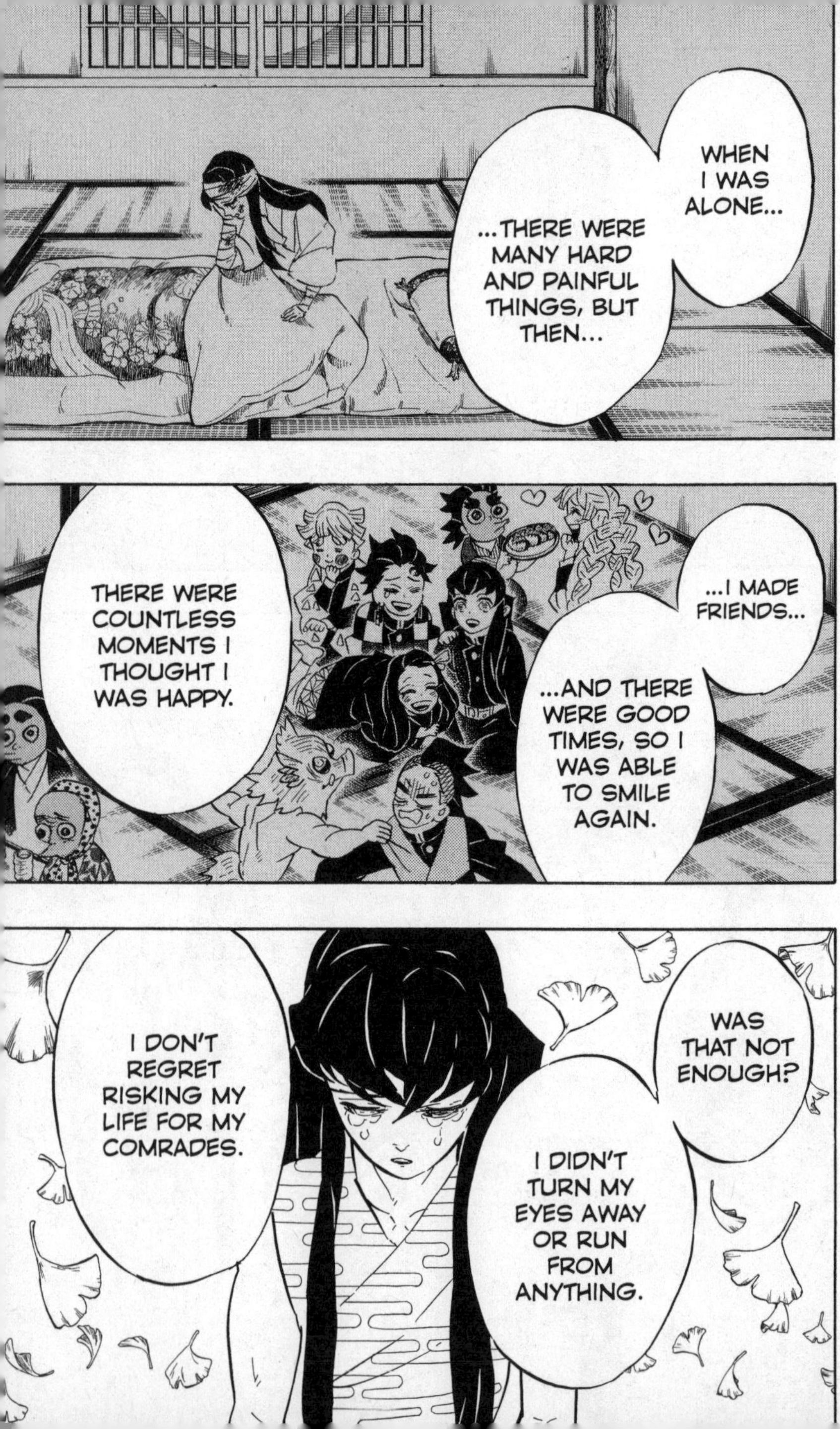
WHEN I WAS ALONE...
...THERE WERE MANY HARD AND PAINFUL THINGS, BUT THEN...
...I MADE FRIENDS...
...AND THERE WERE GOOD TIMES, SO I WAS ABLE TO SMILE AGAIN.
THERE WERE COUNTLESS MOMENTS I THOUGHT I WAS HAPPY.
WAS THAT NOT ENOUGH?
I DIDN'T TURN MY EYES AWAY OR RUN FROM ANYTHING.
I DON'T REGRET RISKING MY LIFE FOR MY COMRADES.

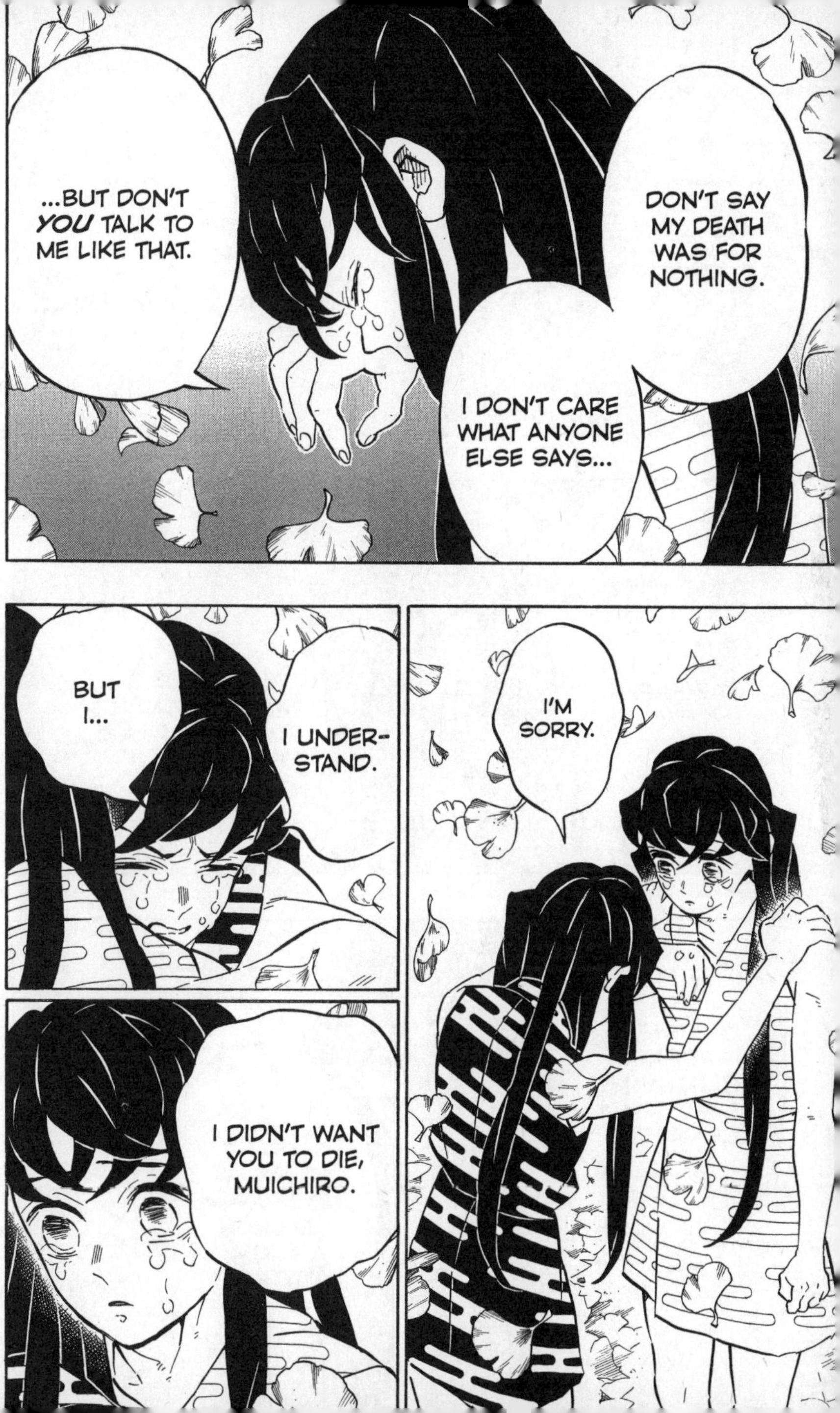
DON'T SAY MY DEATH WAS FOR NOTHING.
I DON'T CARE WHAT ANYONE ELSE SAYS...
...BUT DON'T *YOU* TALK TO ME LIKE THAT.
I'M SORRY.
I UNDER-STAND.
BUT I...
I DIDN'T WANT YOU TO DIE, MUICHIRO.

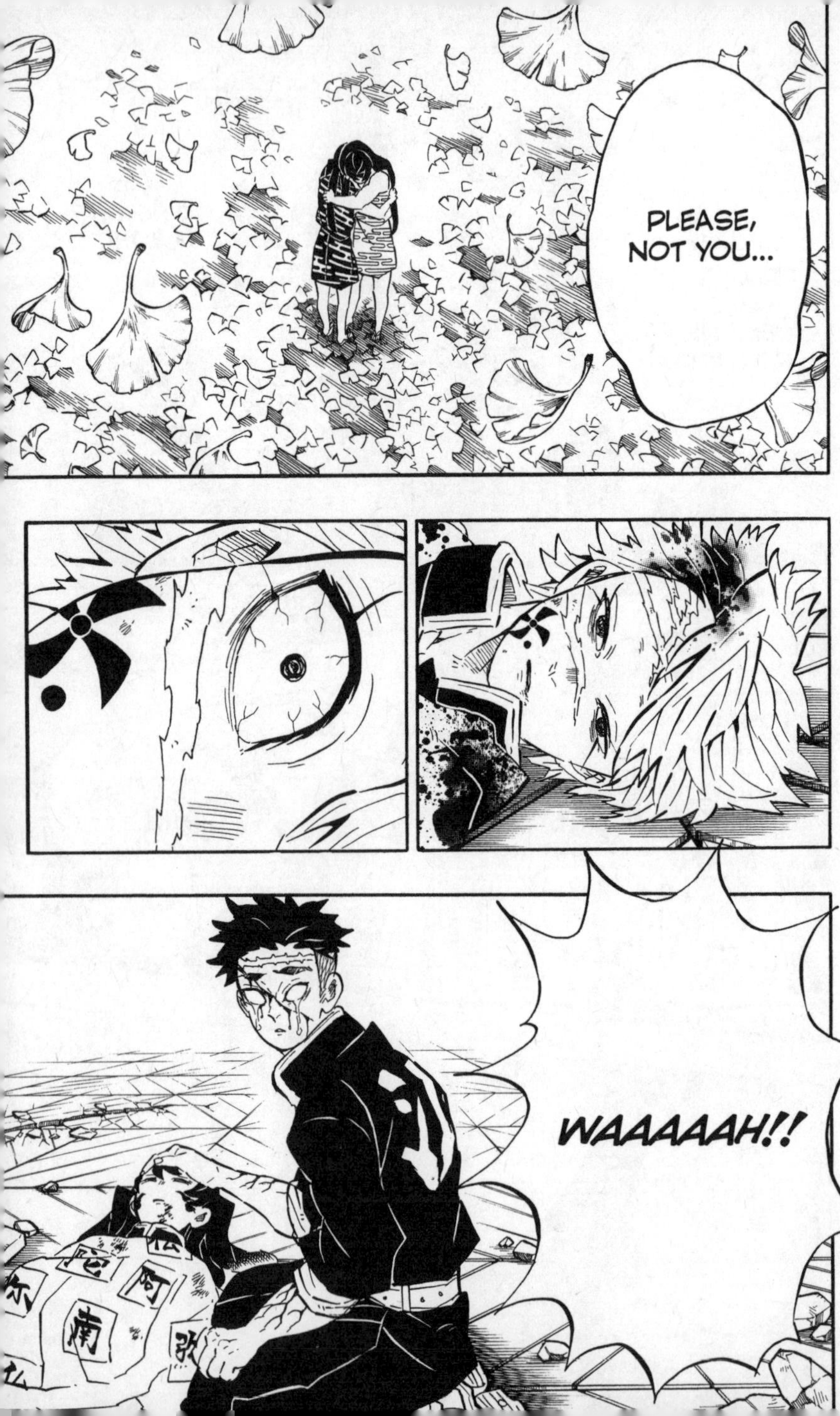
PLEASE, NOT YOU...
WAAAAAH!!

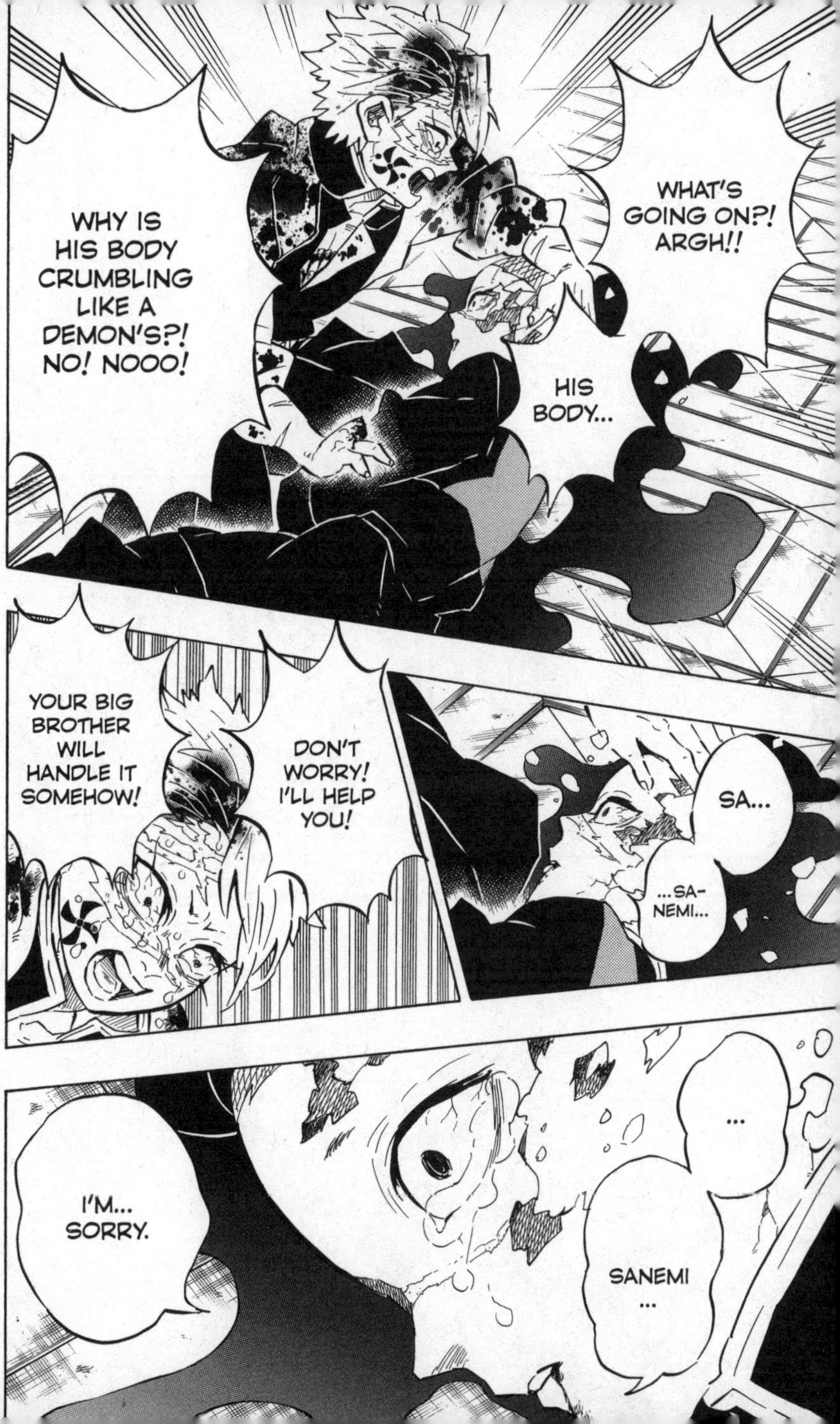
WHAT'S GOING ON?! ARGH!!
HIS BODY...
WHY IS HIS BODY CRUMBLING LIKE A DEMON'S?! NO! NOOO!
SA...
...SA-NEMI...
DON'T WORRY! I'LL HELP YOU!
YOUR BIG BROTHER WILL HANDLE IT SOMEHOW!
...
SANEMI ...
I'M... SORRY.

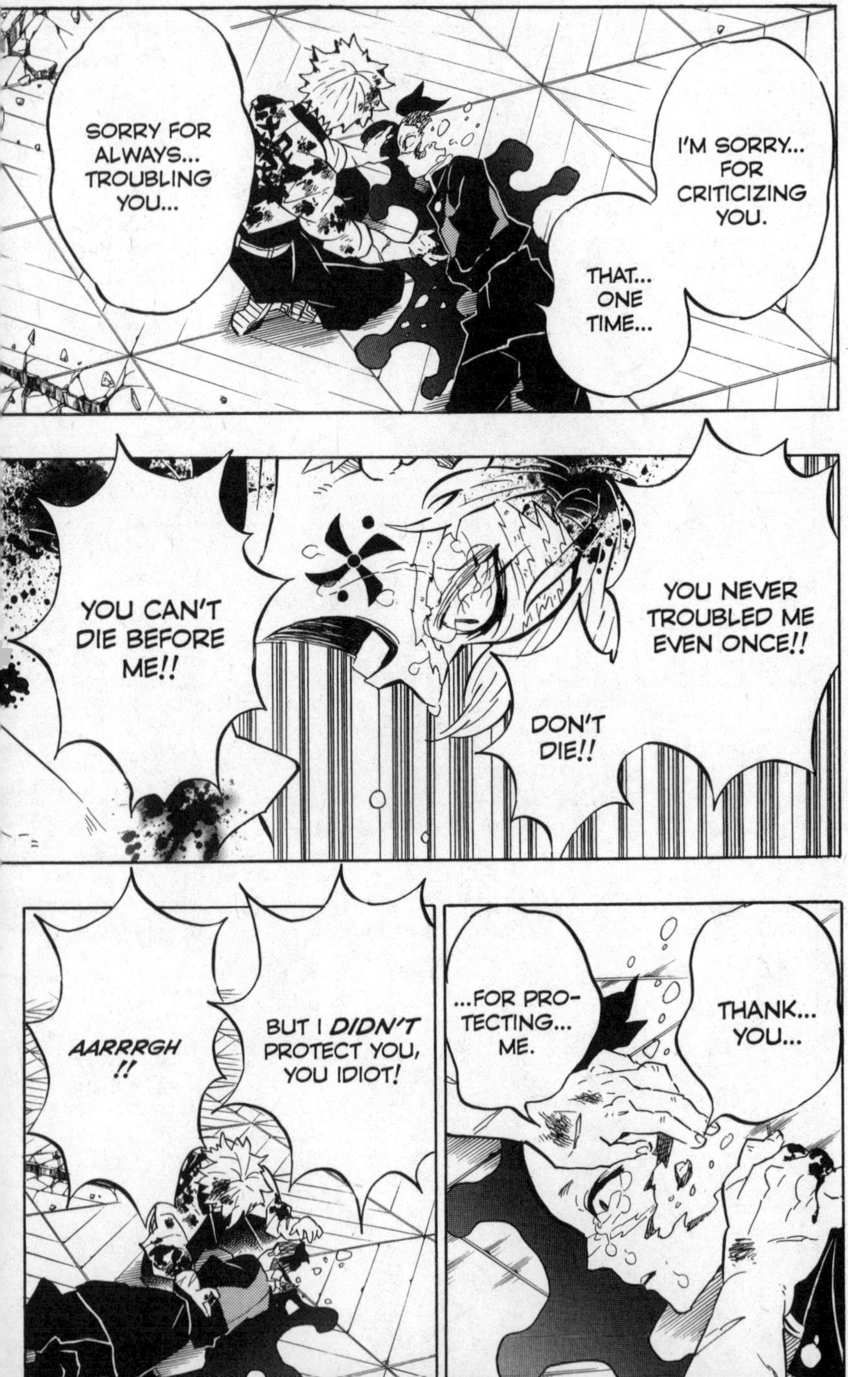
I'M SORRY... FOR CRITICIZING YOU.
THAT... ONE TIME...
SORRY FOR ALWAYS... TROUBLING YOU...
YOU NEVER TROUBLED ME EVEN ONCE!!
DON'T DIE!!
YOU CAN'T DIE BEFORE ME!!
THANK... YOU...
...FOR PRO-TECTING... ME.
BUT I DIDN'T PROTECT YOU, YOU IDIOT!
AARRRGH!!

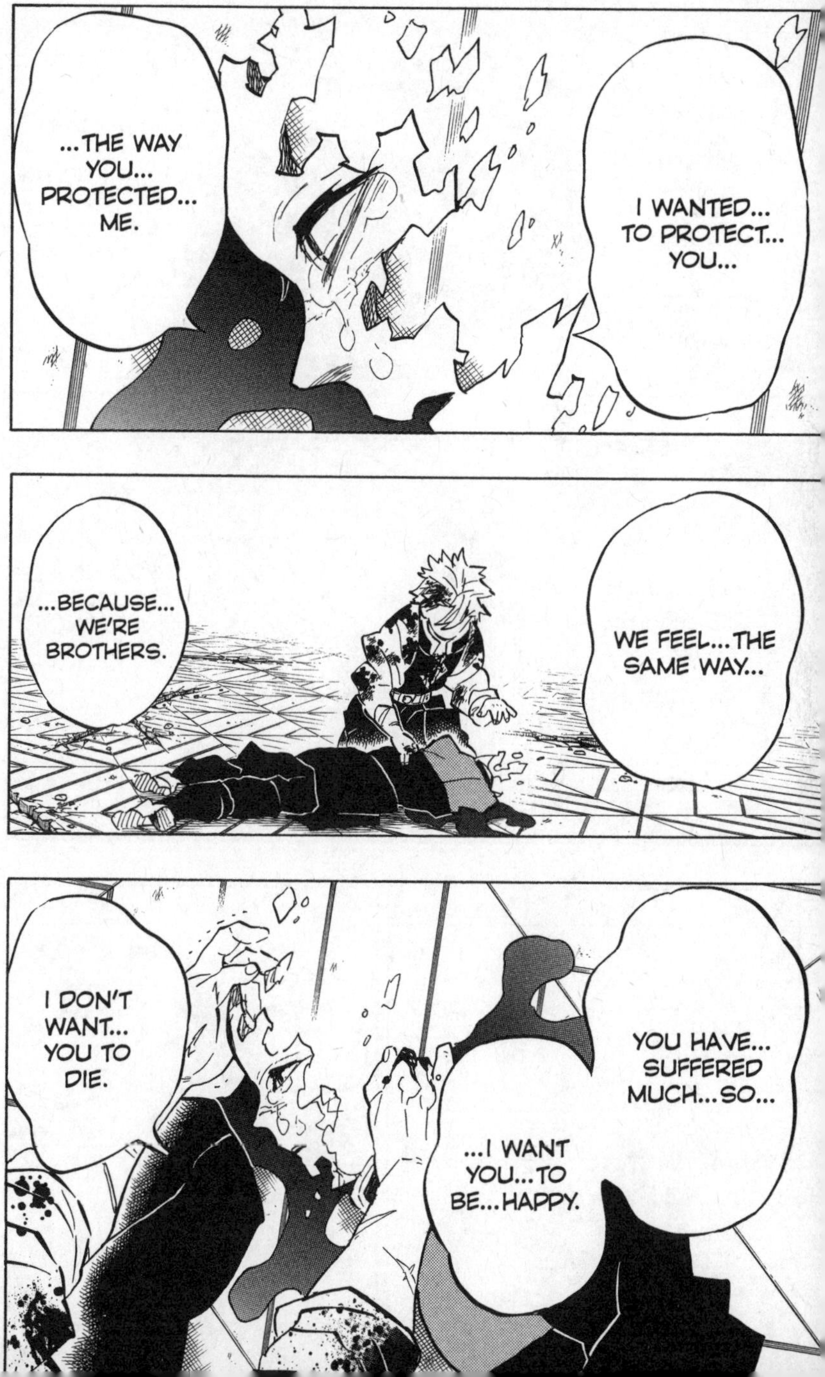
I WANTED... TO PROTECT... YOU...
...THE WAY YOU... PROTECTED... ME.
WE FEEL...THE SAME WAY...
...BECAUSE... WE'RE BROTHERS.
YOU HAVE... SUFFERED MUCH...SO...
...I WANT YOU...TO BE...HAPPY.
I DON'T WANT... YOU TO DIE.

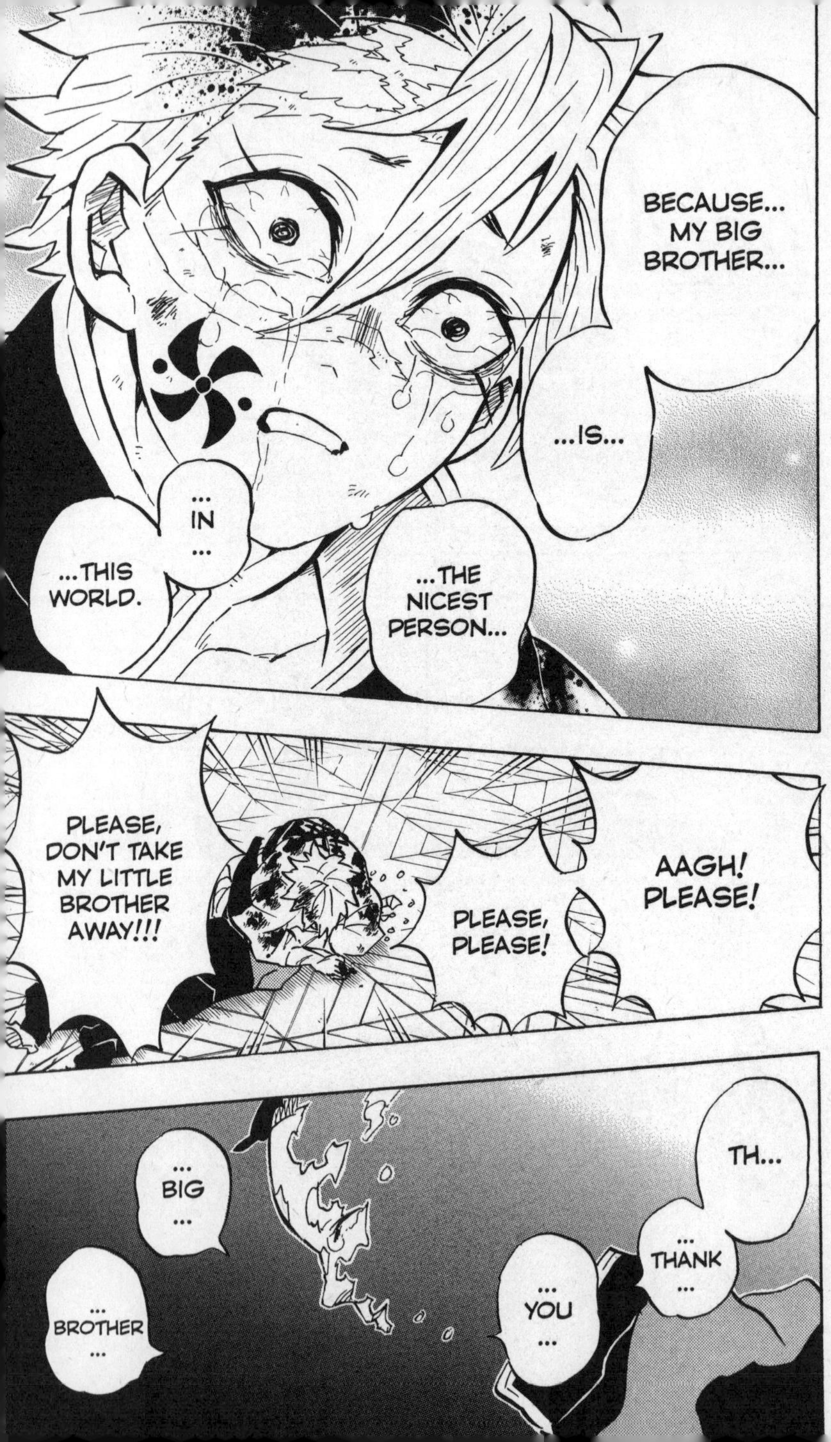
BECAUSE... MY BIG BROTHER...
...IS...
...THE NICEST PERSON...
... IN ...
...THIS WORLD.
AAGH! PLEASE!
PLEASE, PLEASE!
PLEASE, DON'T TAKE MY LITTLE BROTHER AWAY!!!
TH...
... THANK ...
... YOU ...
... BIG ...
... BROTHER ...

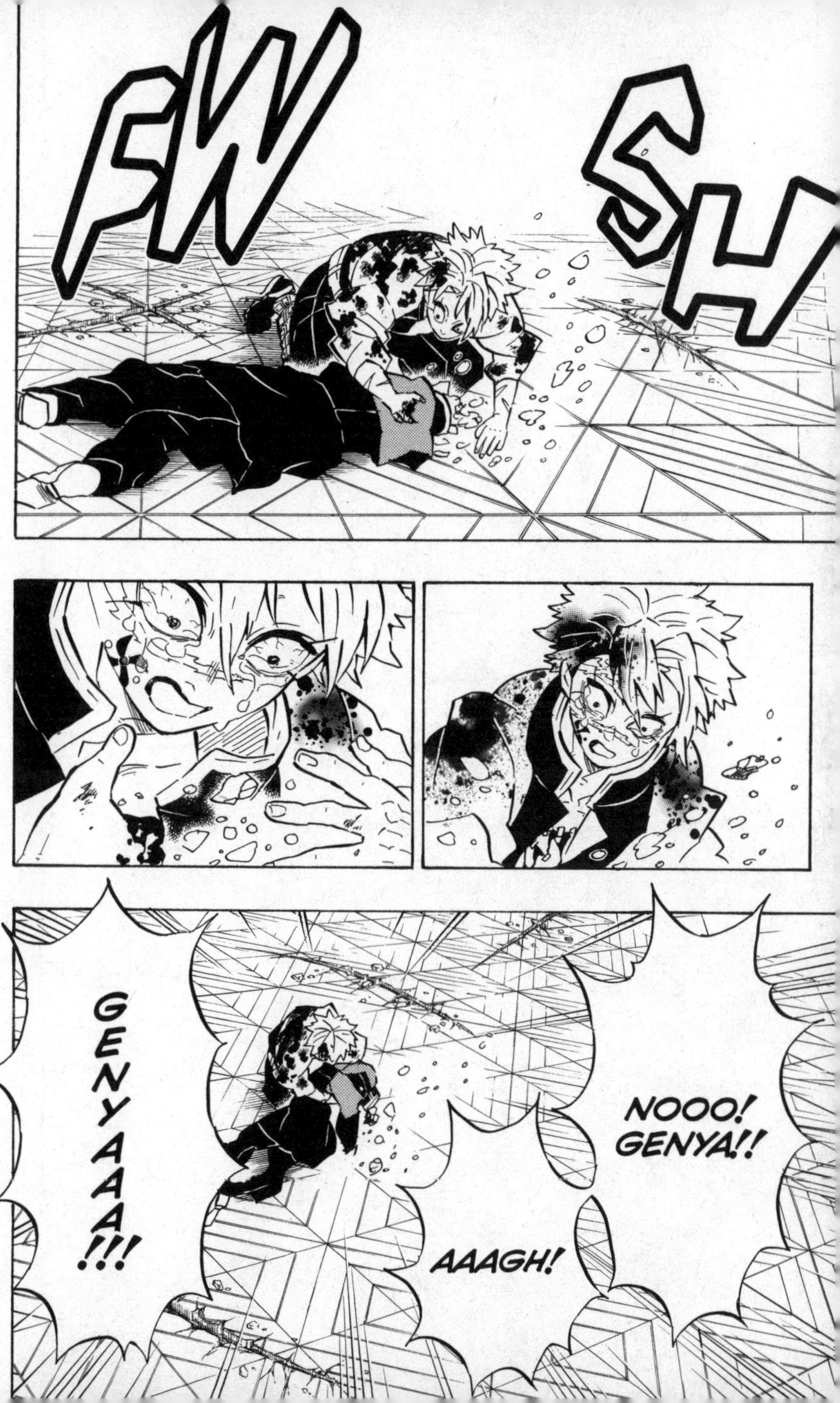
FW
SH
NOOO! GENYA!!
GENYAAAA!!!
AAAGH!

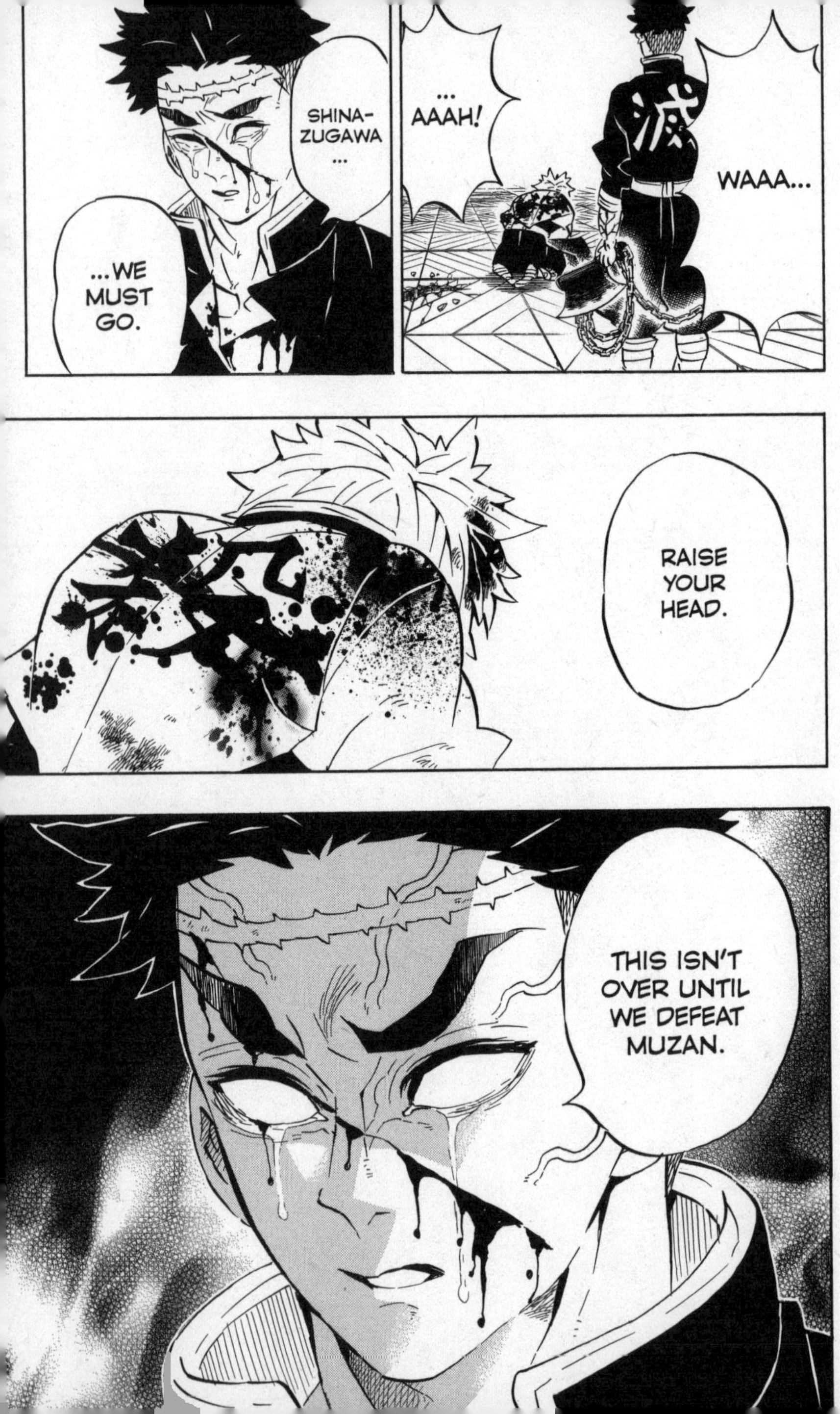
WAAA...
... AAAH!
SHINA-ZUGAWA ...
...WE MUST GO.
RAISE YOUR HEAD.
THIS ISN'T OVER UNTIL WE DEFEAT MUZAN.

CHAPTER 180: RECOVERY

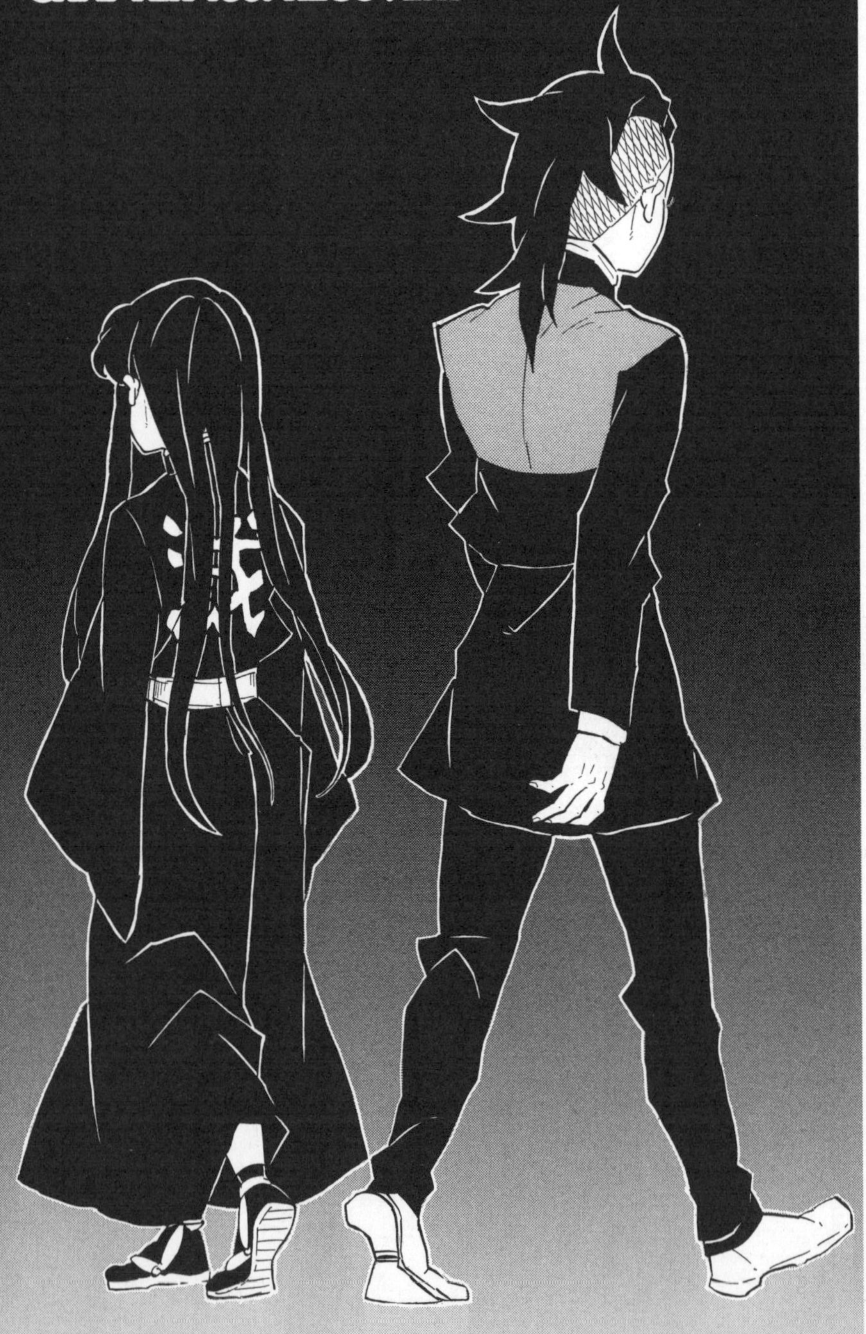

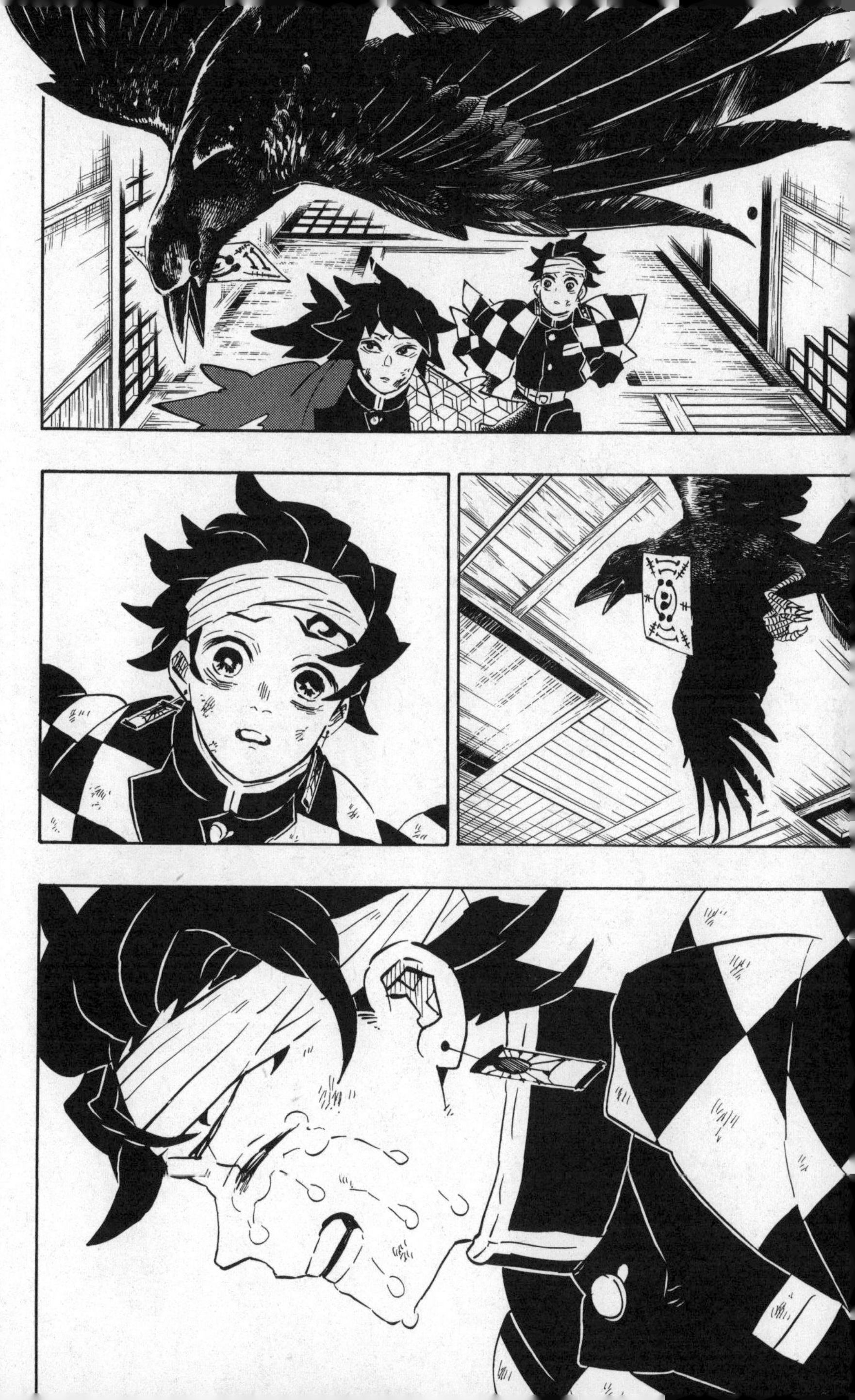

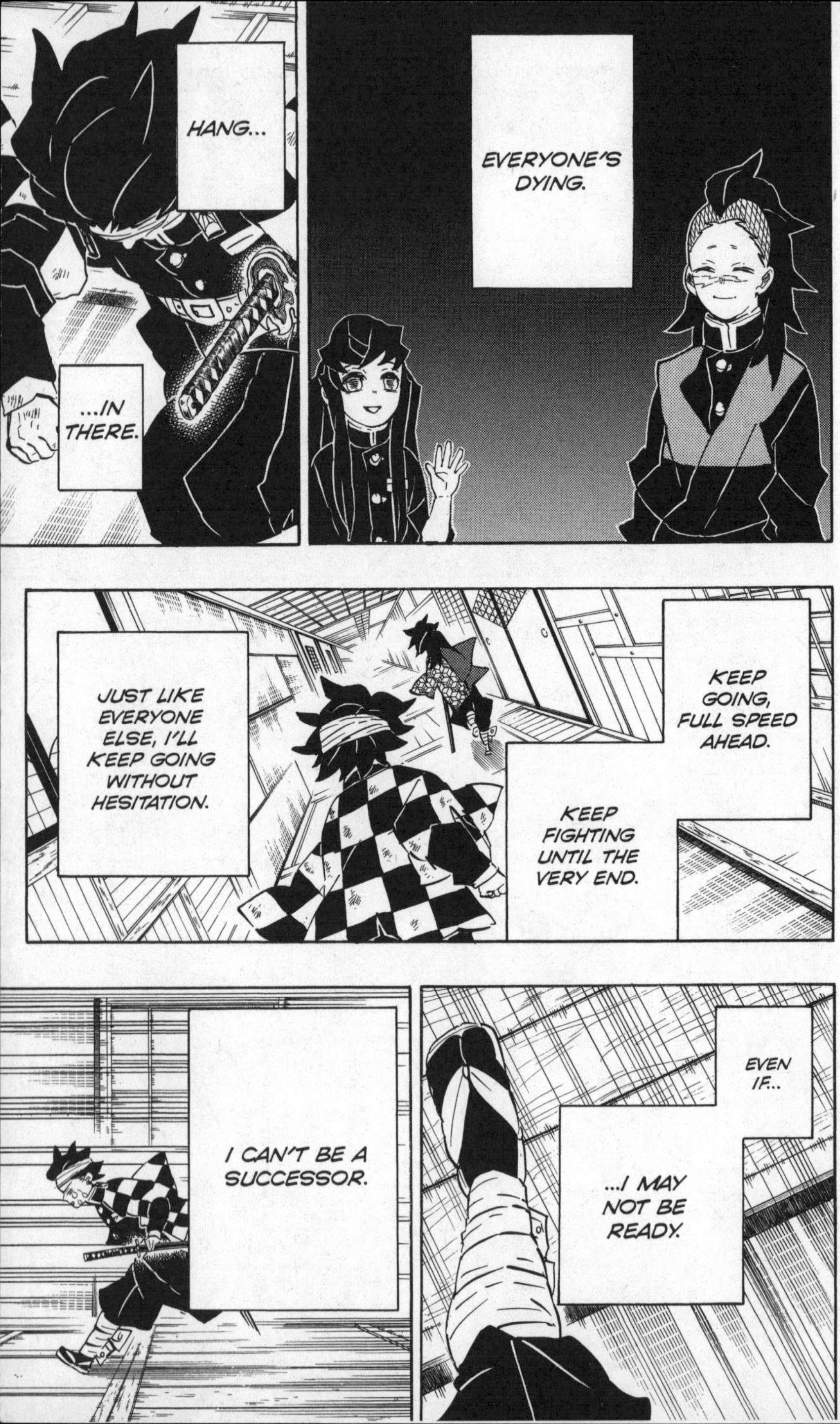
EVERYONE'S DYING.
HANG...
...IN THERE.
KEEP GOING, FULL SPEED AHEAD.
KEEP FIGHTING UNTIL THE VERY END.
JUST LIKE EVERYONE ELSE, I'LL KEEP GOING WITHOUT HESITATION.
EVEN IF...
...I MAY NOT BE READY.
I CAN'T BE A SUCCESSOR.

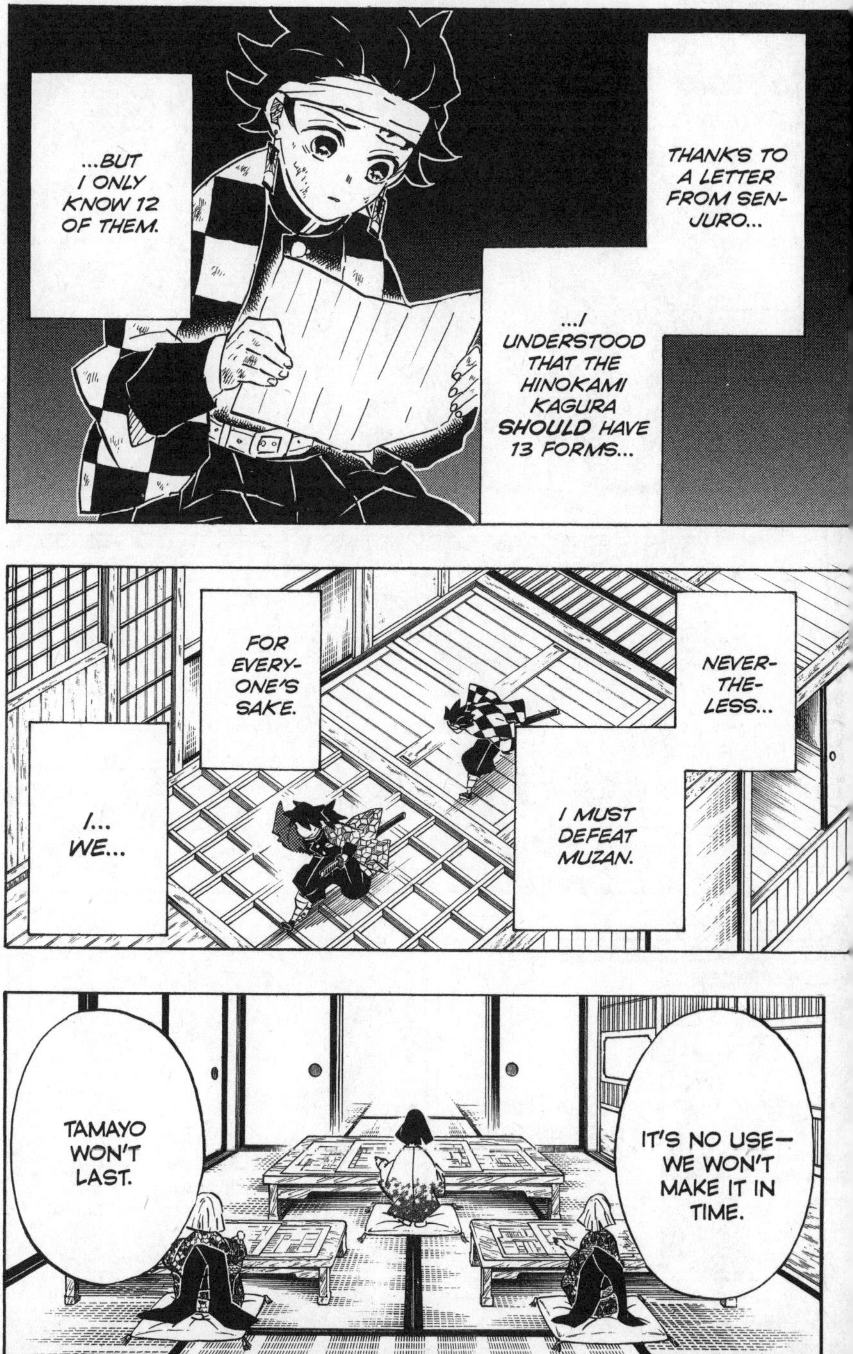
THANK'S TO A LETTER FROM SEN-JURO...
...I UNDERSTOOD THAT THE HINOKAMI KAGURA SHOULD HAVE 13 FORMS...
...BUT I ONLY KNOW 12 OF THEM.
NEVER-THE-LESS...
I MUST DEFEAT MUZAN.
FOR EVERY-ONE'S SAKE.
I... WE...
IT'S NO USE— WE WON'T MAKE IT IN TIME.
TAMAYO WON'T LAST.

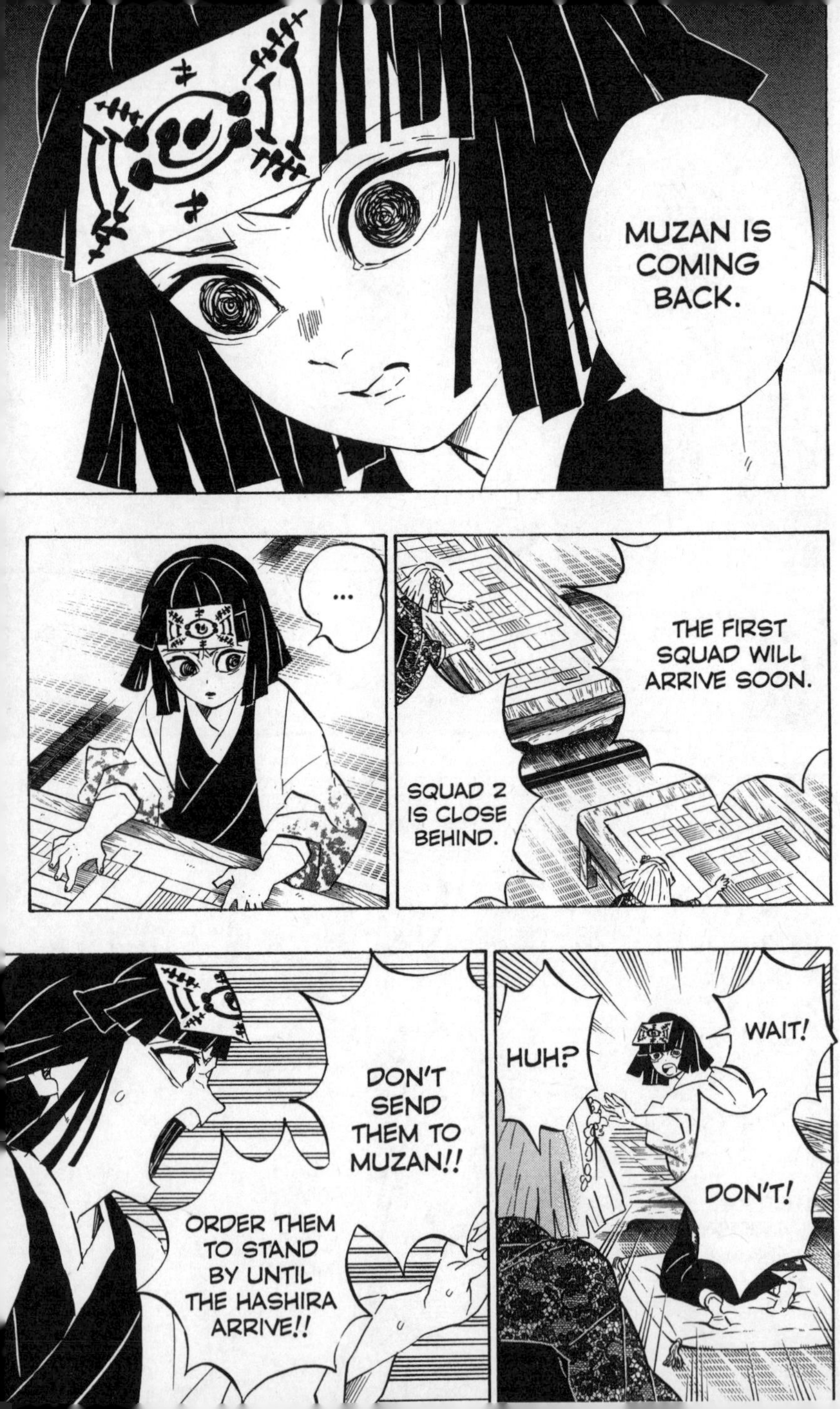
MUZAN IS COMING BACK.
THE FIRST SQUAD WILL ARRIVE SOON.
SQUAD 2 IS CLOSE BEHIND.
...
WAIT!
HUH?
DON'T!
DON'T SEND THEM TO MUZAN!!
ORDER THEM TO STAND BY UNTIL THE HASHIRA ARRIVE!!

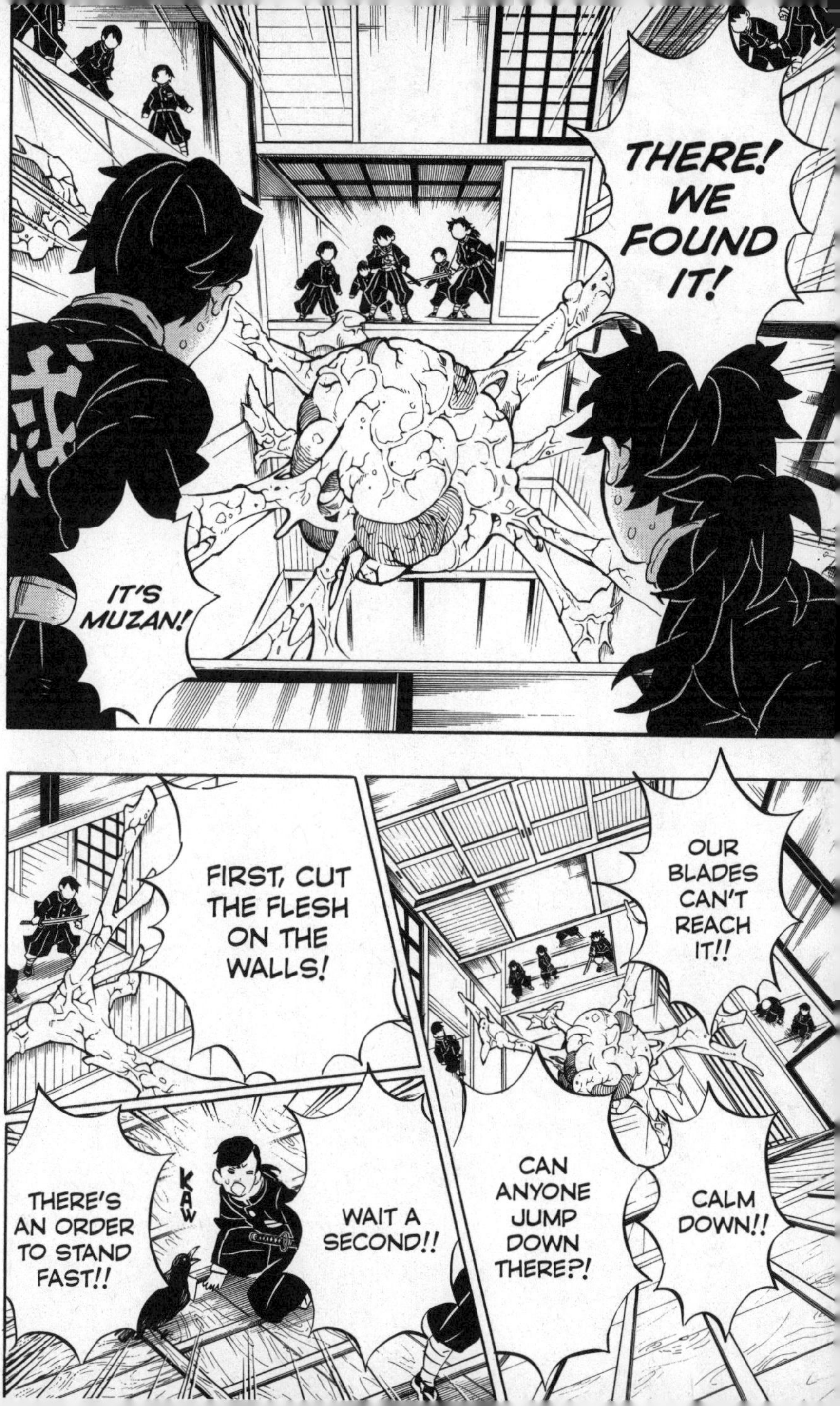
THERE! WE FOUND IT!
IT'S MUZAN!
OUR BLADES CAN'T REACH IT!!
FIRST, CUT THE FLESH ON THE WALLS!
CALM DOWN!!
CAN ANYONE JUMP DOWN THERE?!
WAIT A SECOND!!
KAW
THERE'S AN ORDER TO STAND FAST!!

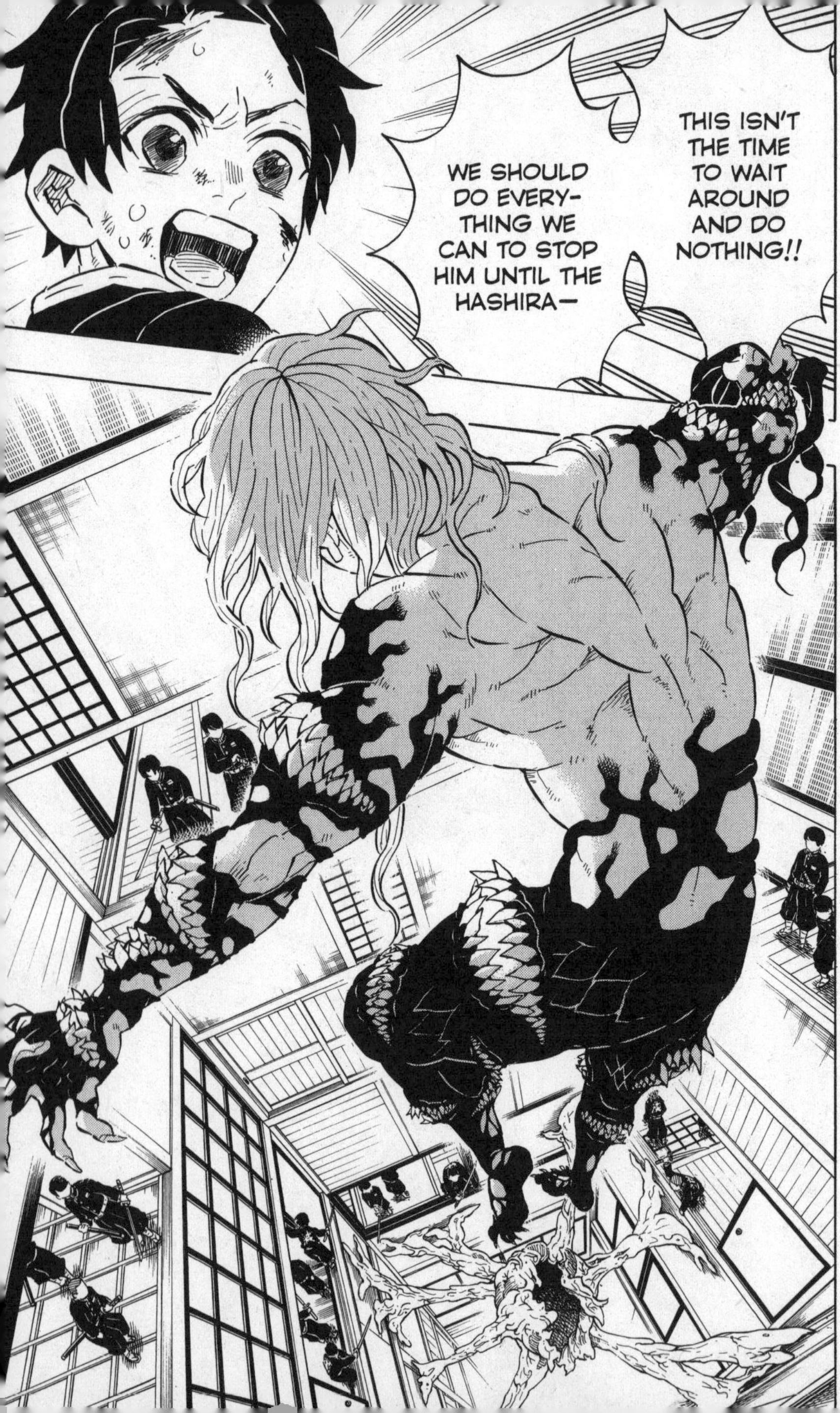
THIS ISN'T THE TIME TO WAIT AROUND AND DO NOTHING!!
WE SHOULD DO EVERY-THING WE CAN TO STOP HIM UNTIL THE HASHIRA—

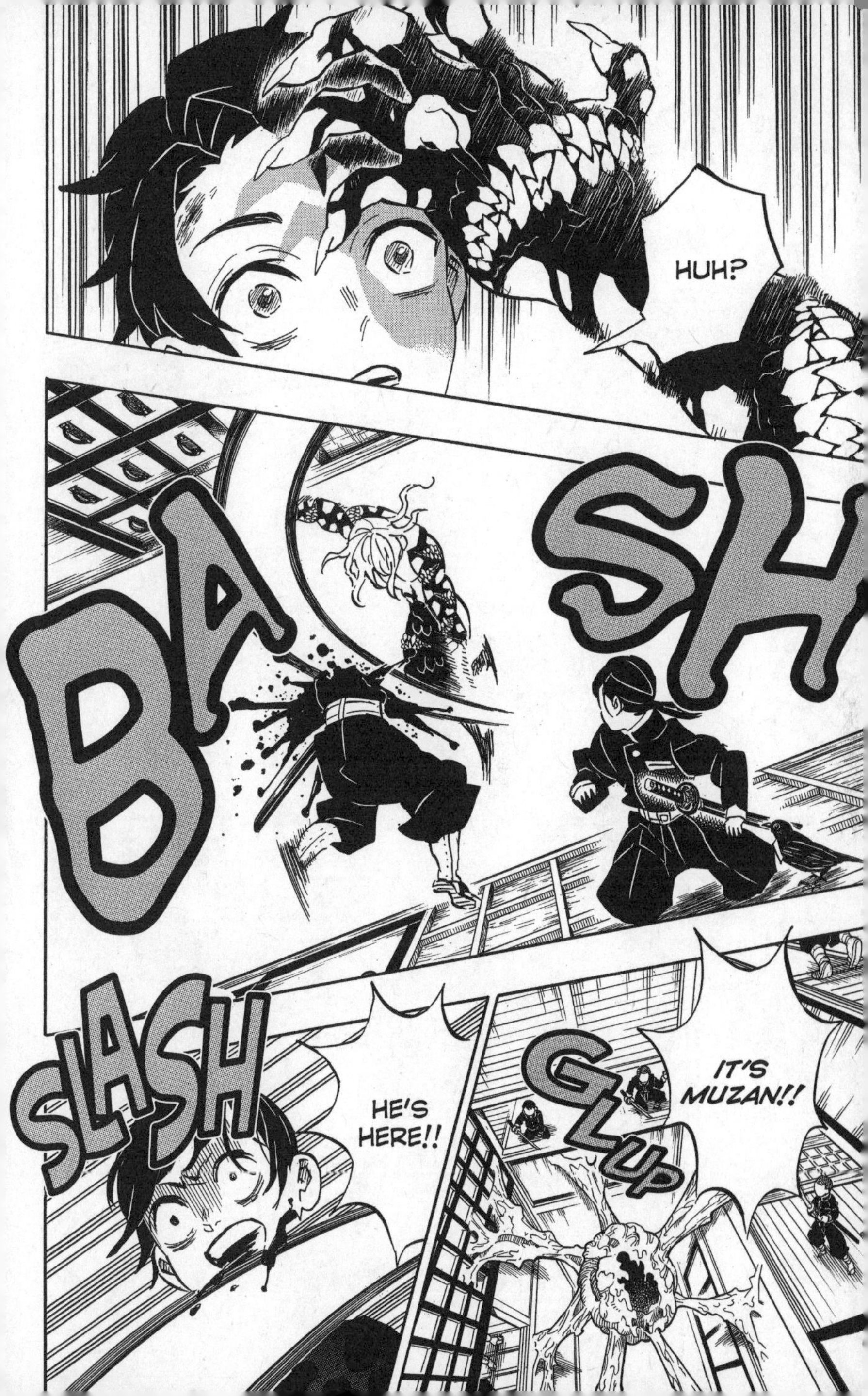
HUH?
BASH
IT'S MUZAN!!
GLUP
HE'S HERE!!
SLASH

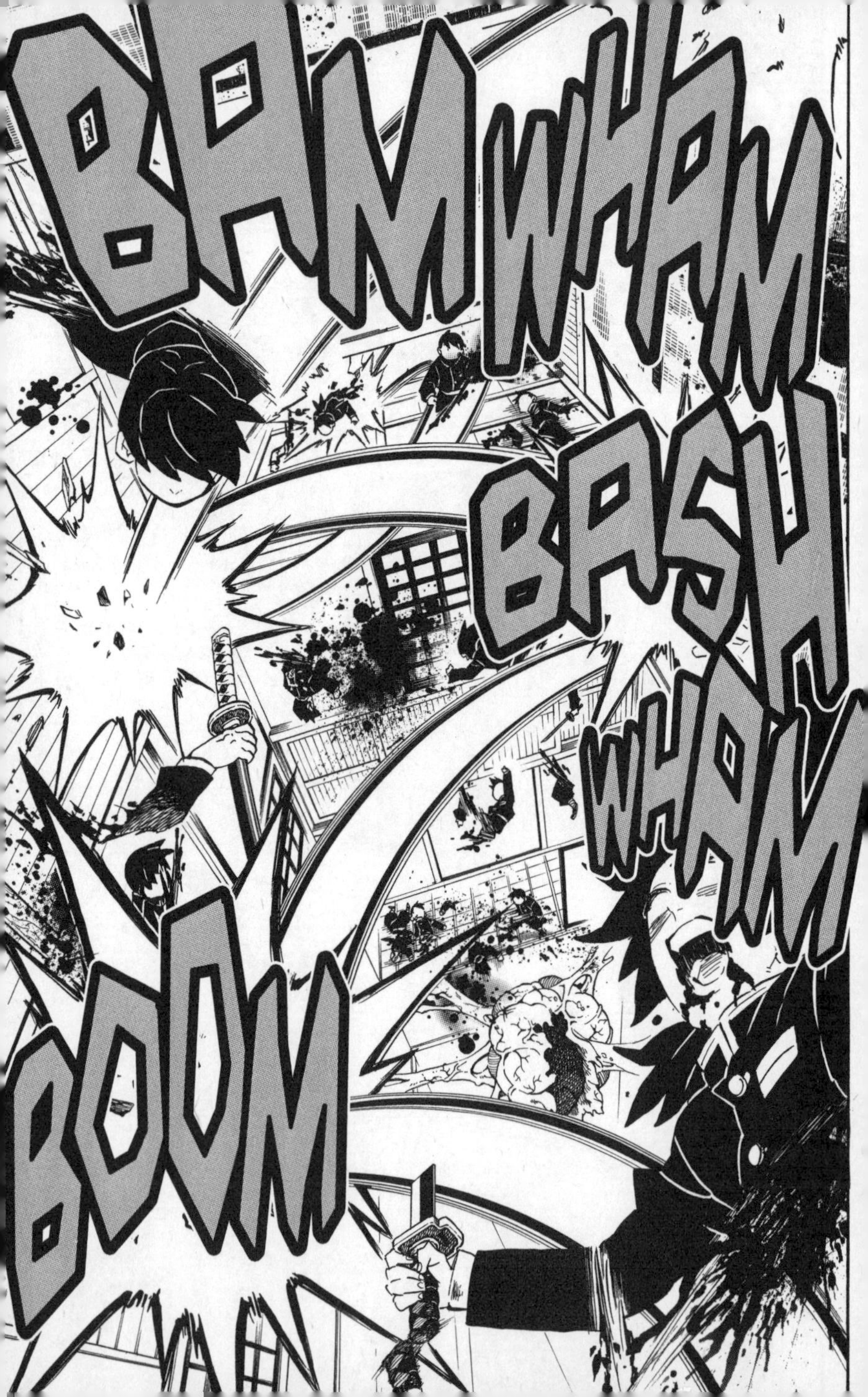
WHAM
BAM
BASH
WHAM
BOOM

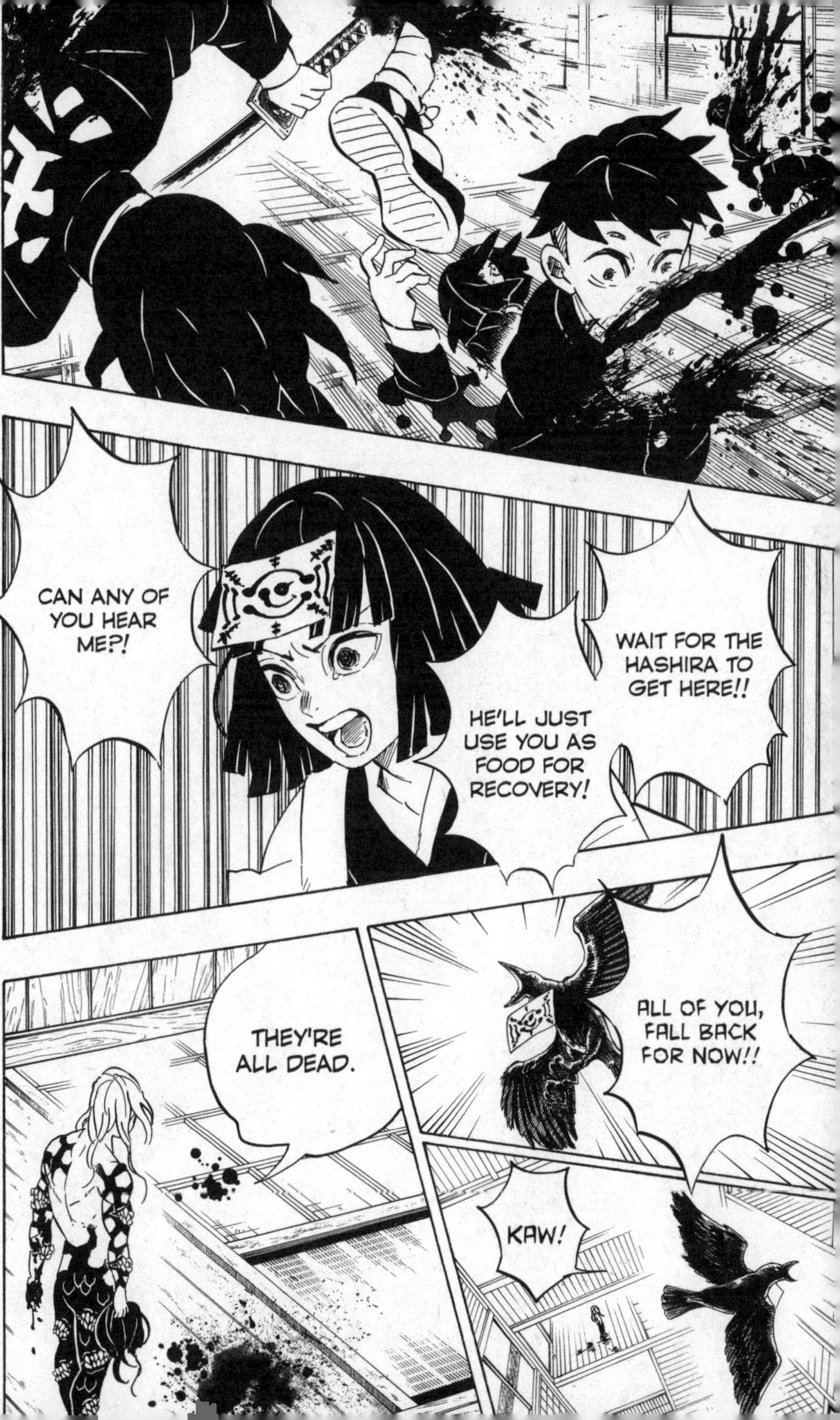
WAIT FOR THE HASHIRA TO GET HERE!!
HE'LL JUST USE YOU AS FOOD FOR RECOVERY!
CAN ANY OF YOU HEAR ME?!
ALL OF YOU, FALL BACK FOR NOW!!
KAW!
THEY'RE ALL DEAD.

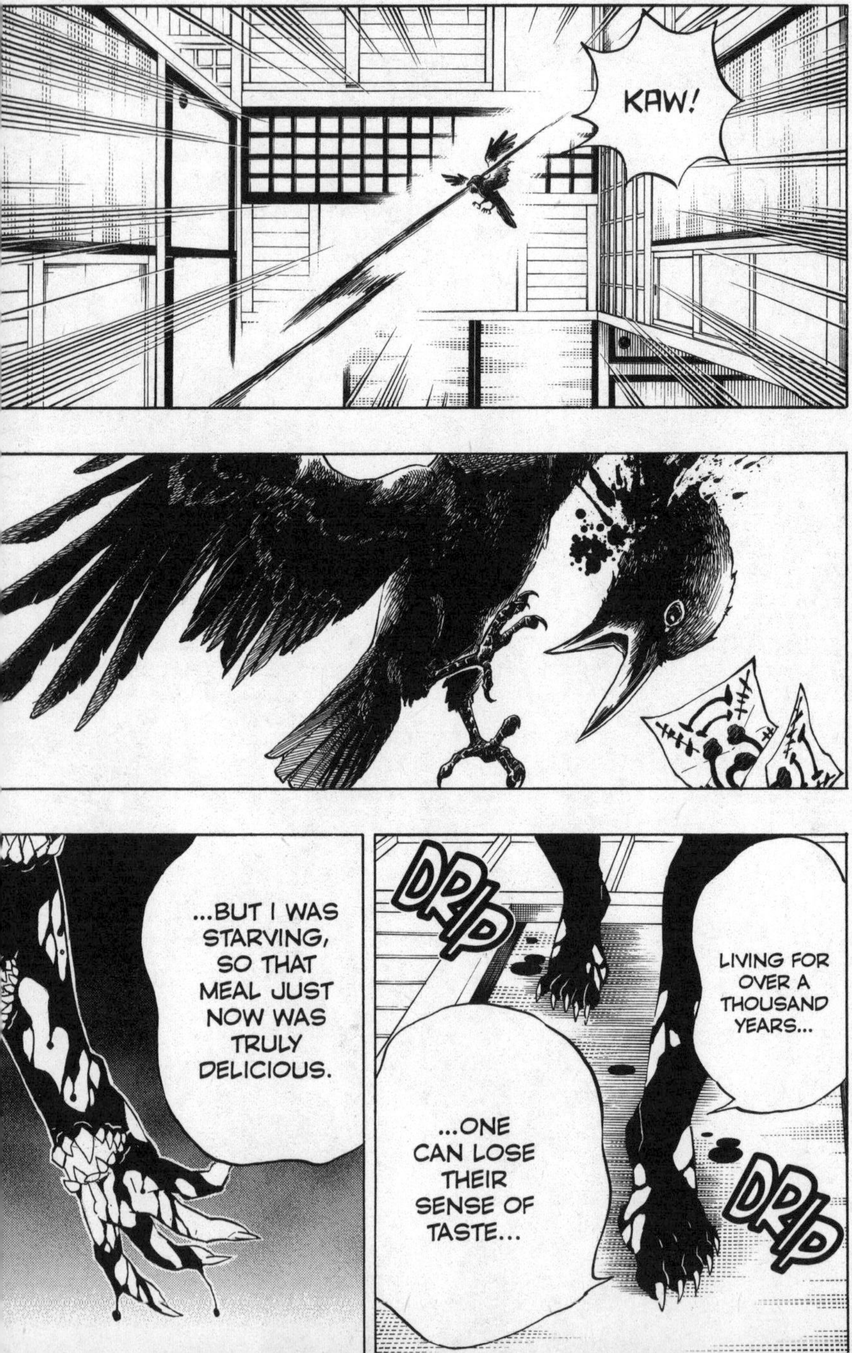
KAW!
DRIP
LIVING FOR OVER A THOUSAND YEARS...
...ONE CAN LOSE THEIR SENSE OF TASTE...
DRIP
...BUT I WAS STARVING, SO THAT MEAL JUST NOW WAS TRULY DELICIOUS.

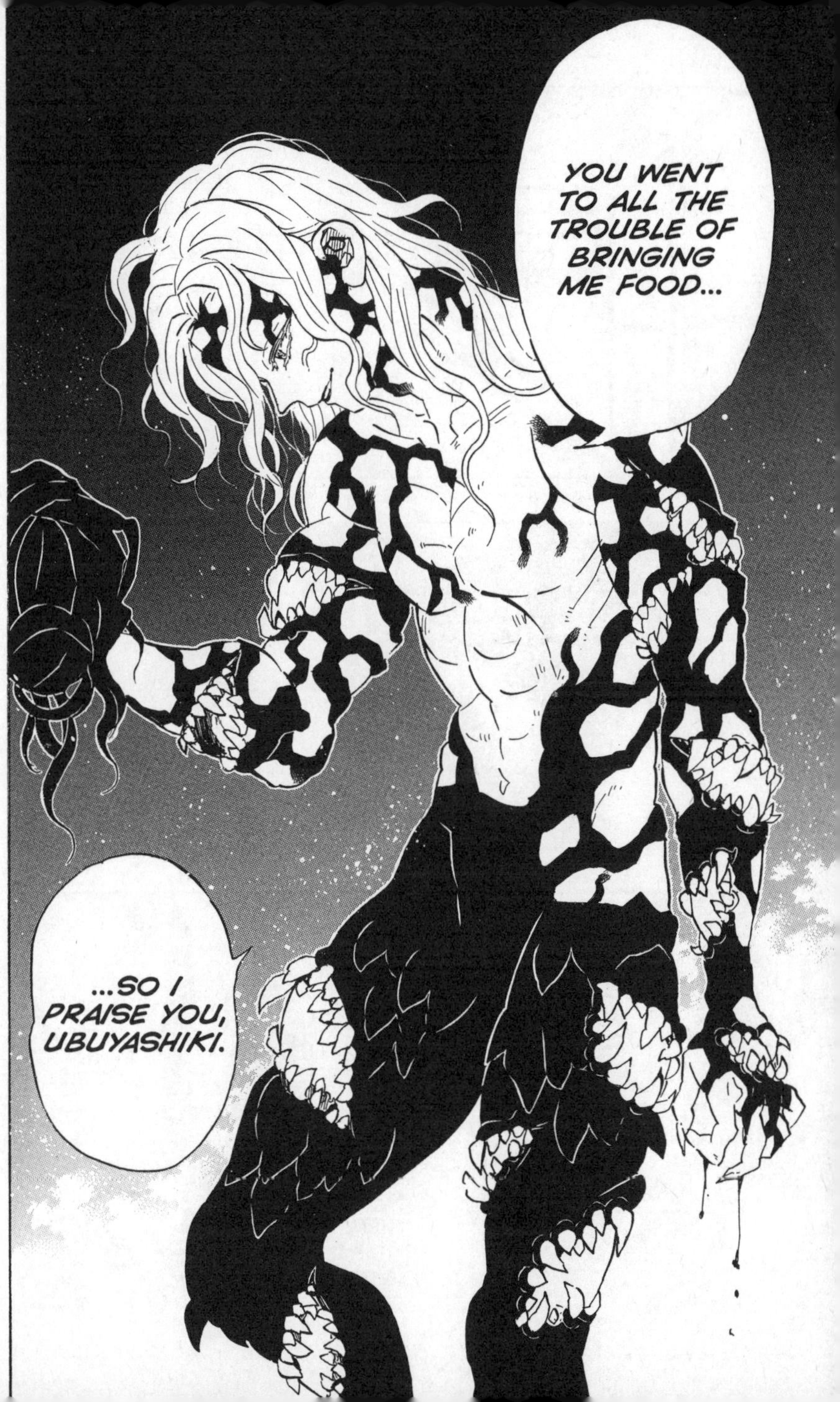
YOU WENT TO ALL THE TROUBLE OF BRINGING ME FOOD...
...SO I PRAISE YOU, UBUYASHIKI.

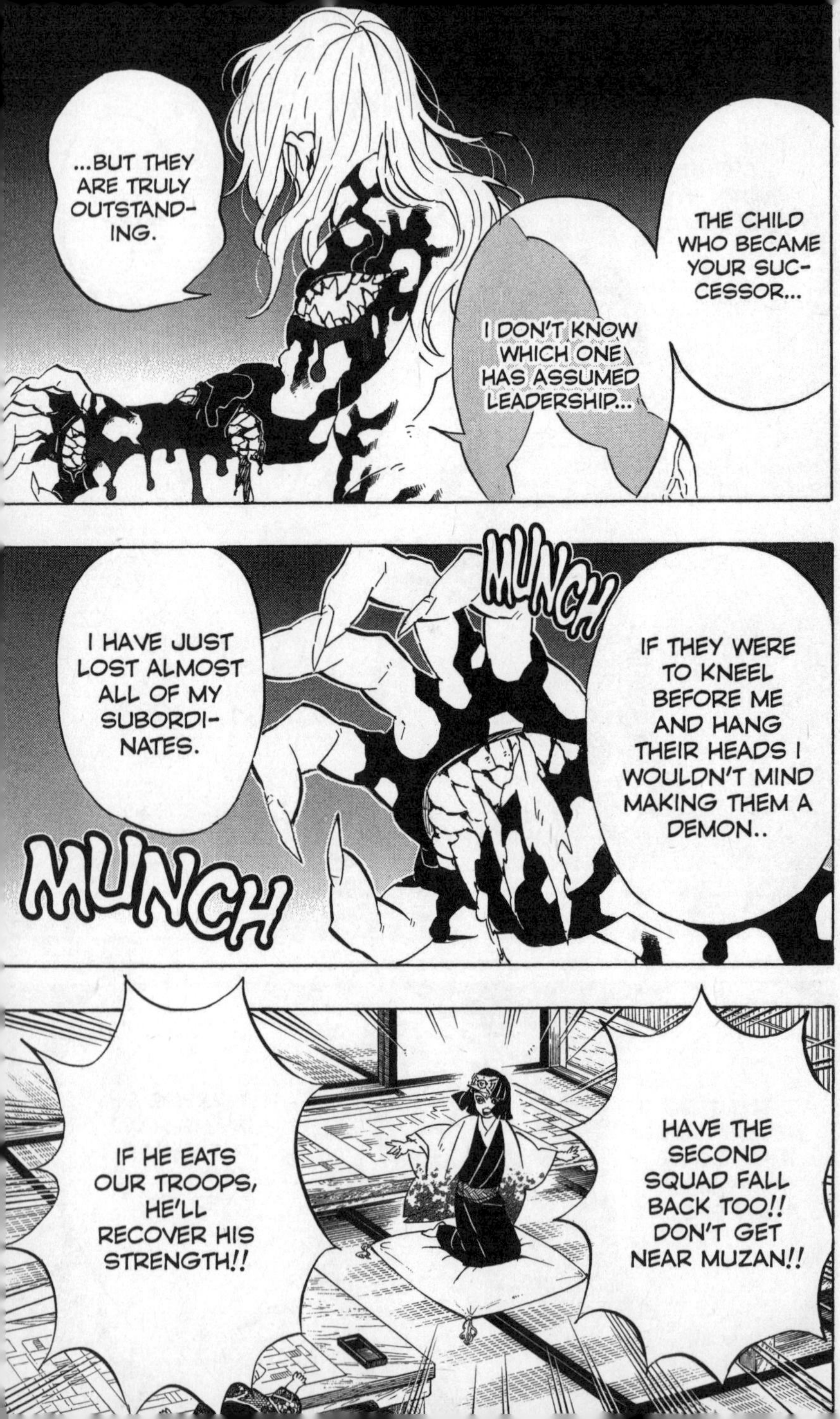
THE CHILD WHO BECAME YOUR SUC-CESSOR...
I DON'T KNOW WHICH ONE HAS ASSUMED LEADERSHIP...
...BUT THEY ARE TRULY OUTSTAND-ING.
MUNCH
IF THEY WERE TO KNEEL BEFORE ME AND HANG THEIR HEADS I WOULDN'T MIND MAKING THEM A DEMON..
I HAVE JUST LOST ALMOST ALL OF MY SUBORDI-NATES.
MUNCH
HAVE THE SECOND SQUAD FALL BACK TOO!! DON'T GET NEAR MUZAN!!
IF HE EATS OUR TROOPS, HE'LL RECOVER HIS STRENGTH!!

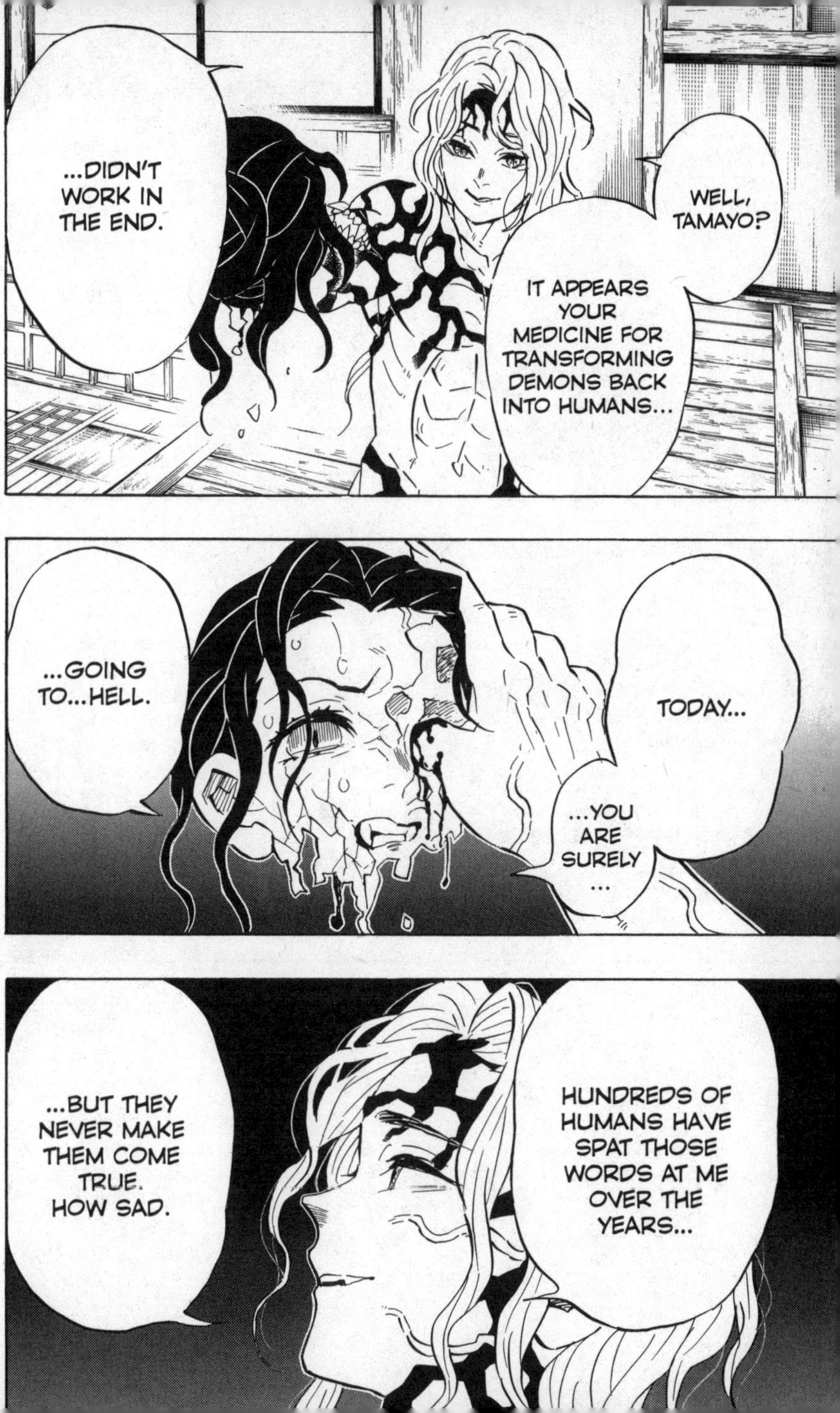
WELL, TAMAYO?
IT APPEARS YOUR MEDICINE FOR TRANSFORMING DEMONS BACK INTO HUMANS...
...DIDN'T WORK IN THE END.
TODAY...
...YOU ARE SURELY ...
...GOING TO...HELL.
HUNDREDS OF HUMANS HAVE SPAT THOSE WORDS AT ME OVER THE YEARS...
...BUT THEY NEVER MAKE THEM COME TRUE. HOW SAD.

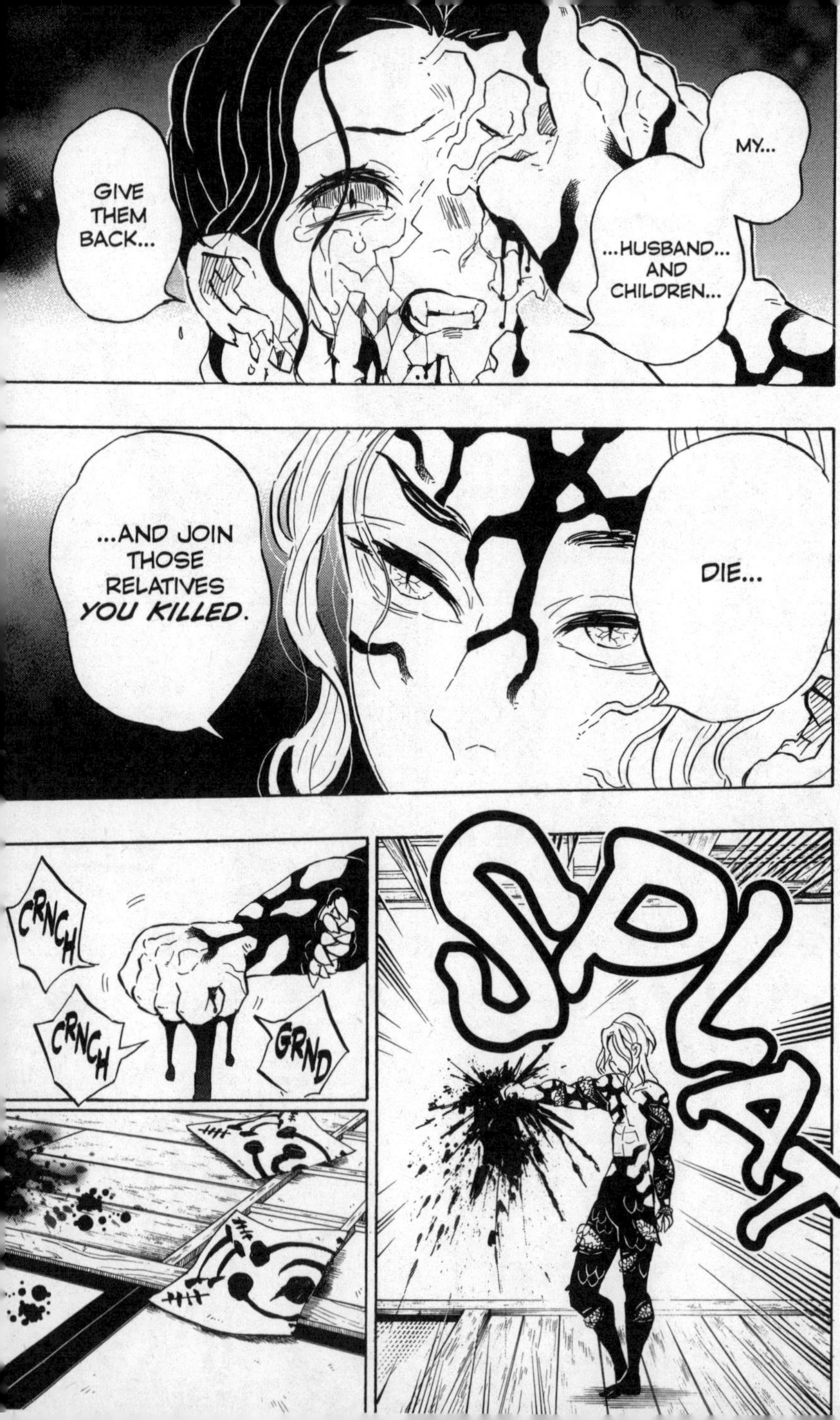
MY...
...HUSBAND... AND CHILDREN...
GIVE THEM BACK...
DIE...
...AND JOIN THOSE RELATIVES *YOU KILLED*.
SPLAT
CRNCH
CRNCH
GRND

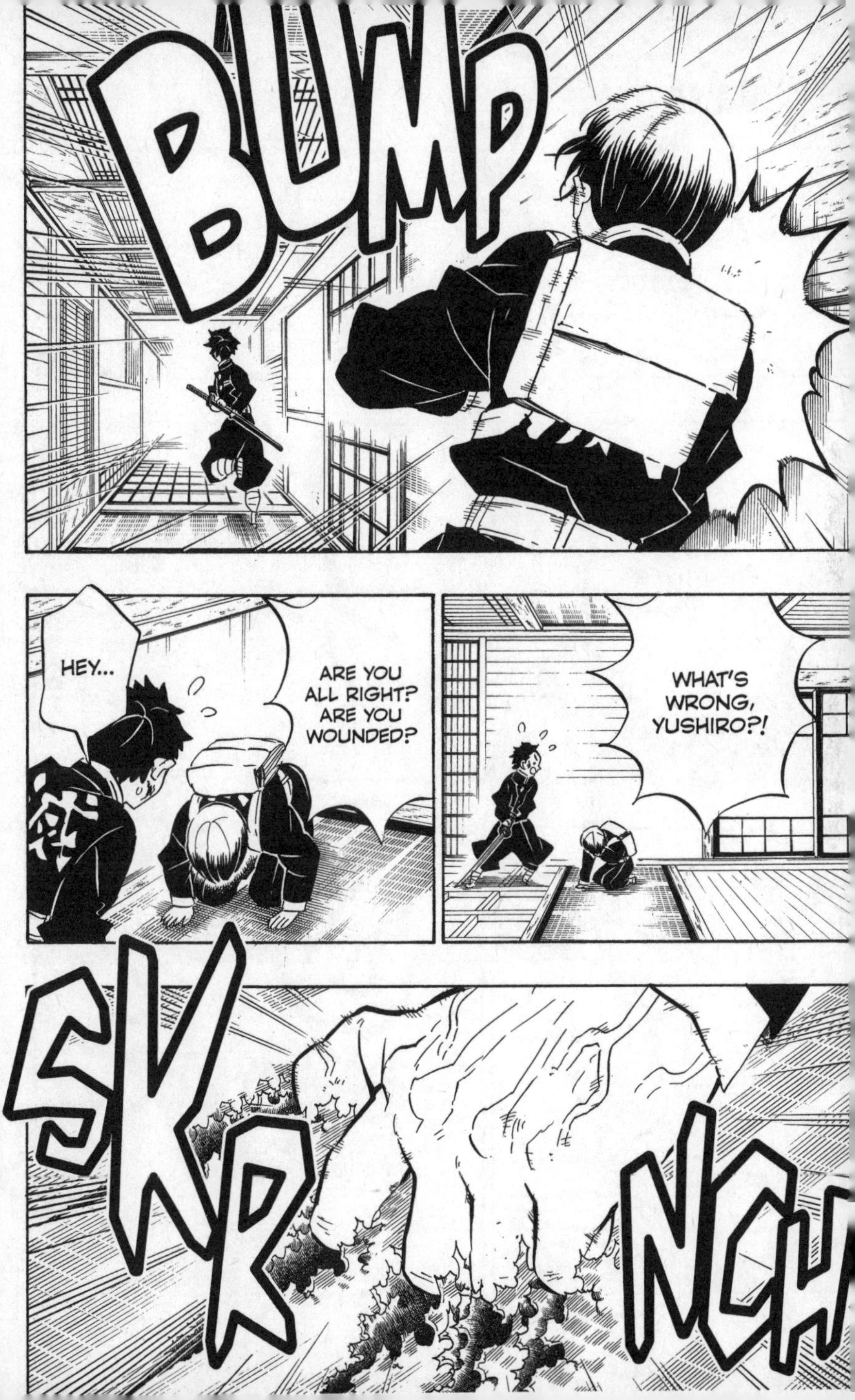
BUMP
WHAT'S WRONG, YUSHIRO?!
ARE YOU ALL RIGHT? ARE YOU WOUNDED?
HEY...
SKRNCH

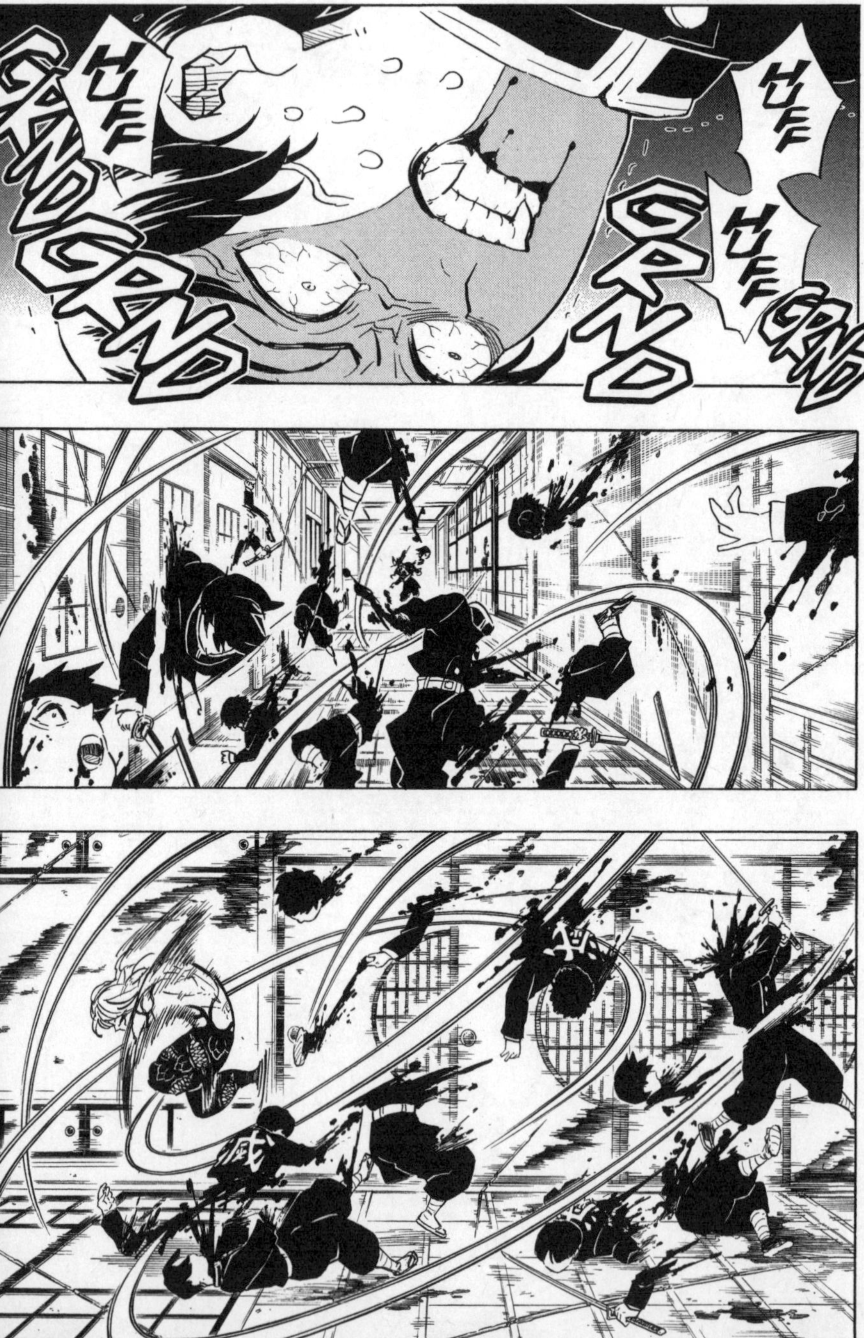
HUFF
HUFF
GRND
GRND
HUFF
GRND GRND

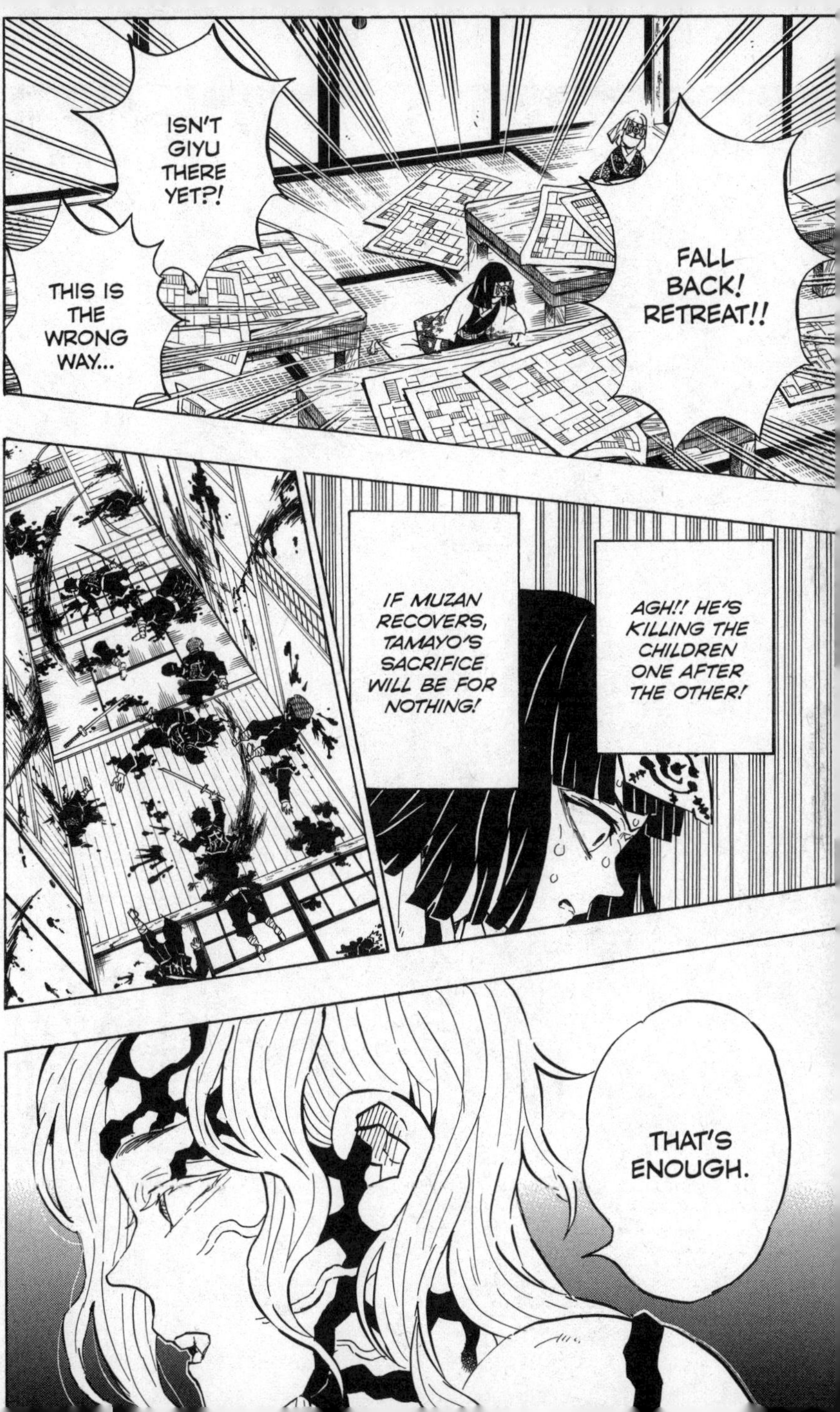
FALL BACK! RETREAT!!
ISN'T GIYU THERE YET?!
THIS IS THE WRONG WAY...
AGH!! HE'S KILLING THE CHILDREN ONE AFTER THE OTHER!
IF MUZAN RECOVERS, TAMAYO'S SACRIFICE WILL BE FOR NOTHING!
THAT'S ENOUGH.

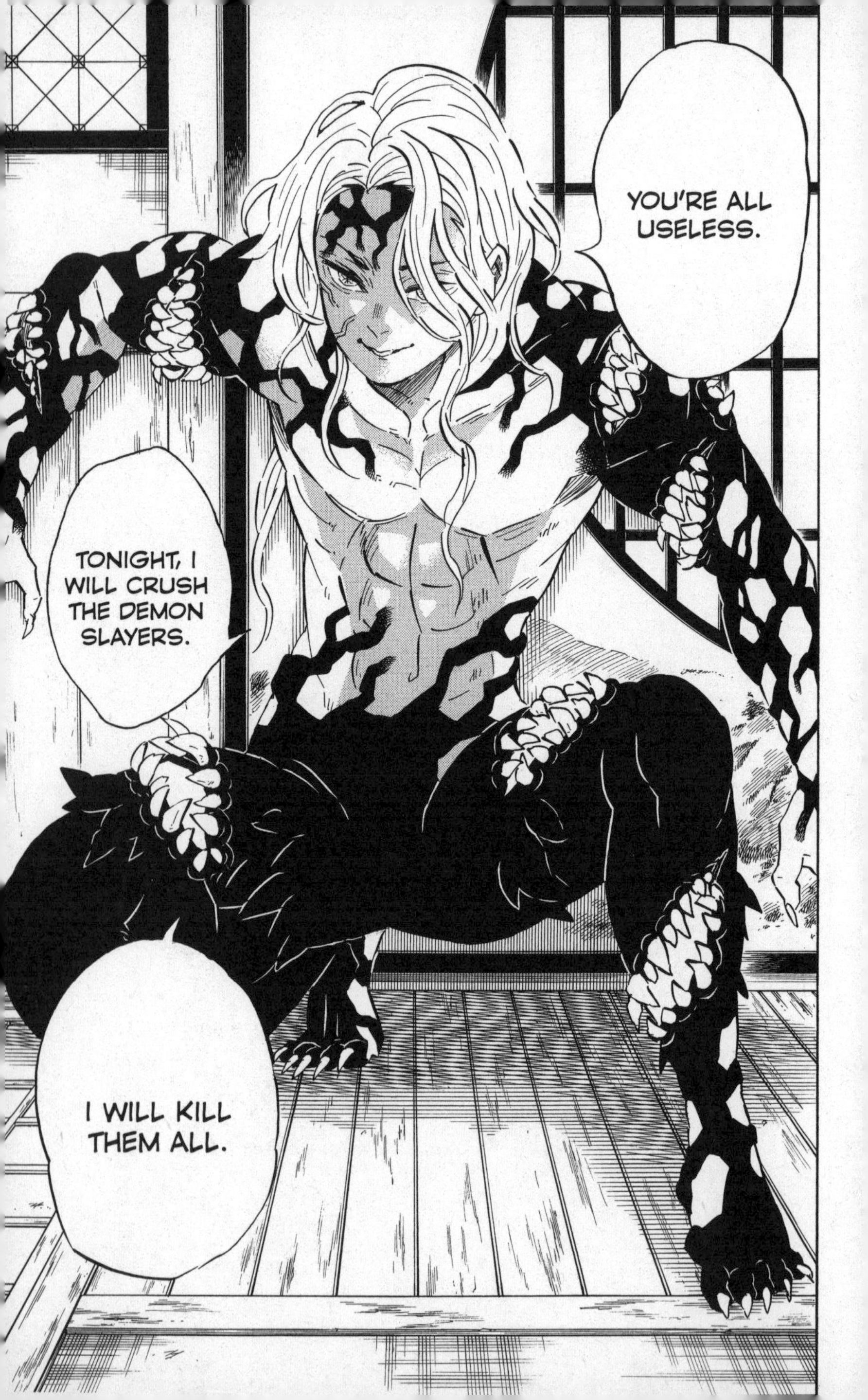
YOU'RE ALL USELESS.
TONIGHT, I WILL CRUSH THE DEMON SLAYERS.
I WILL KILL THEM ALL.

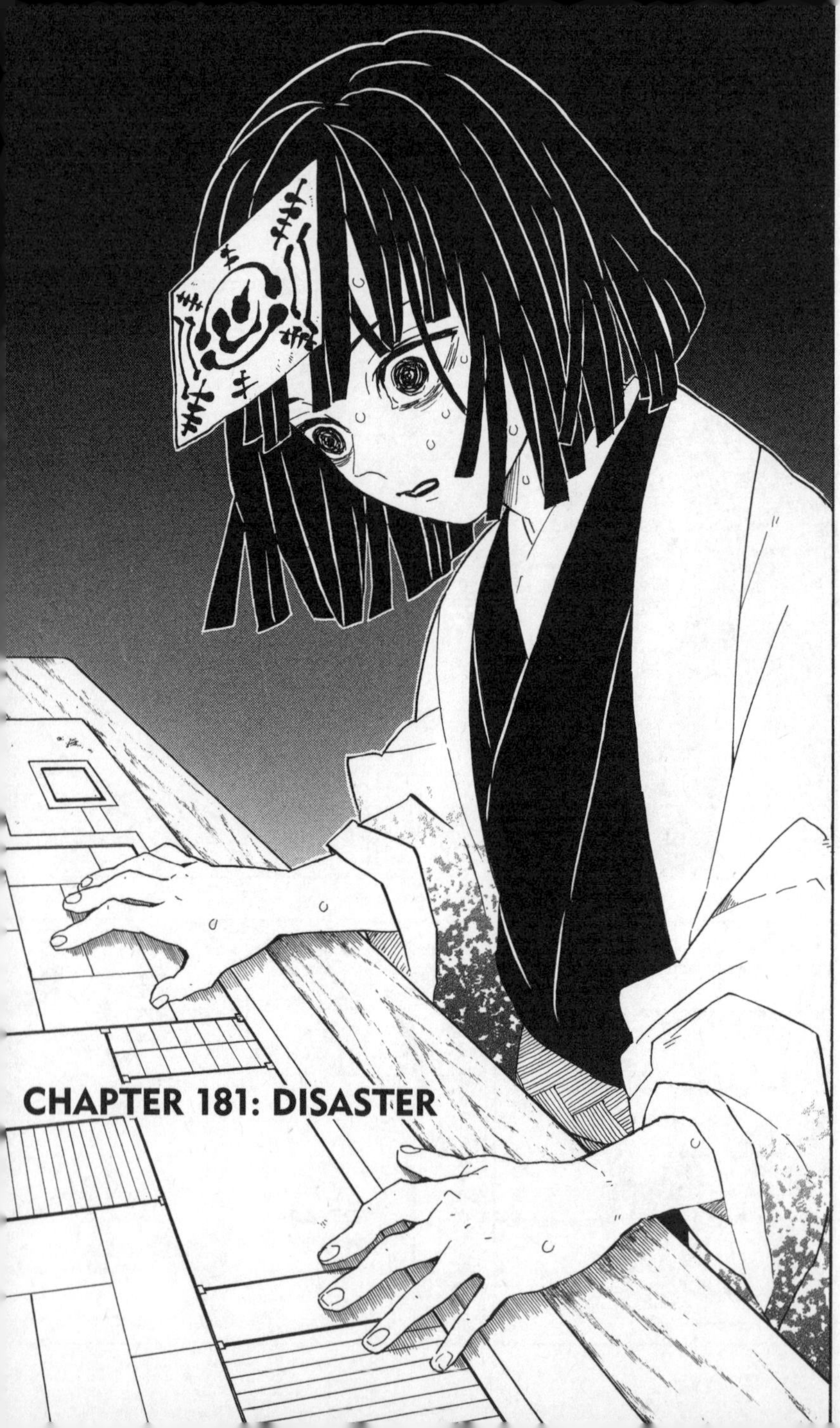
CHAPTER 181: DISASTER

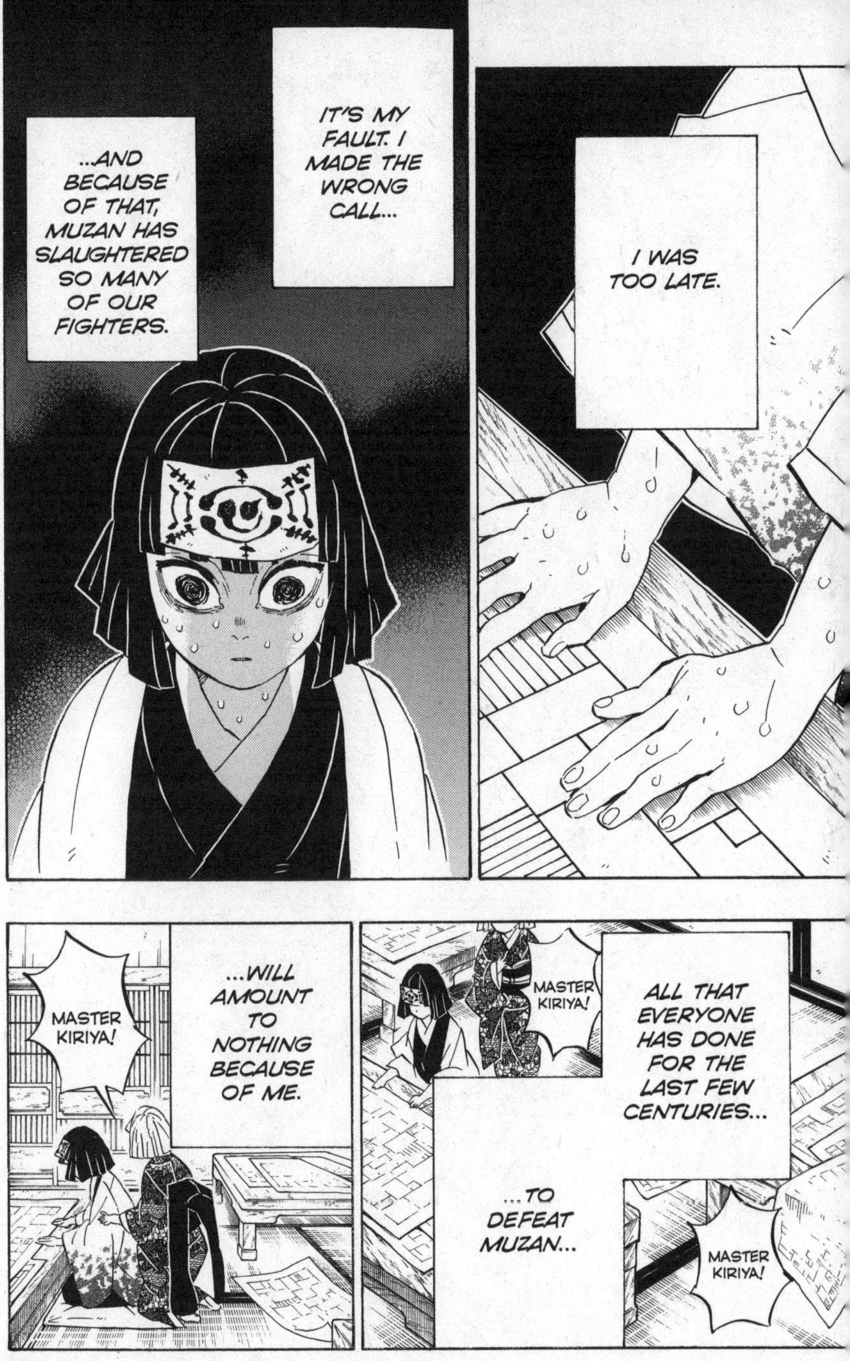
I WAS TOO LATE.
IT'S MY FAULT. I MADE THE WRONG CALL...
...AND BECAUSE OF THAT, MUZAN HAS SLAUGHTERED SO MANY OF OUR FIGHTERS.
ALL THAT EVERYONE HAS DONE FOR THE LAST FEW CENTURIES...
MASTER KIRIYA!
...TO DEFEAT MUZAN...
MASTER KIRIYA!
...WILL AMOUNT TO NOTHING BECAUSE OF ME.
MASTER KIRIYA!

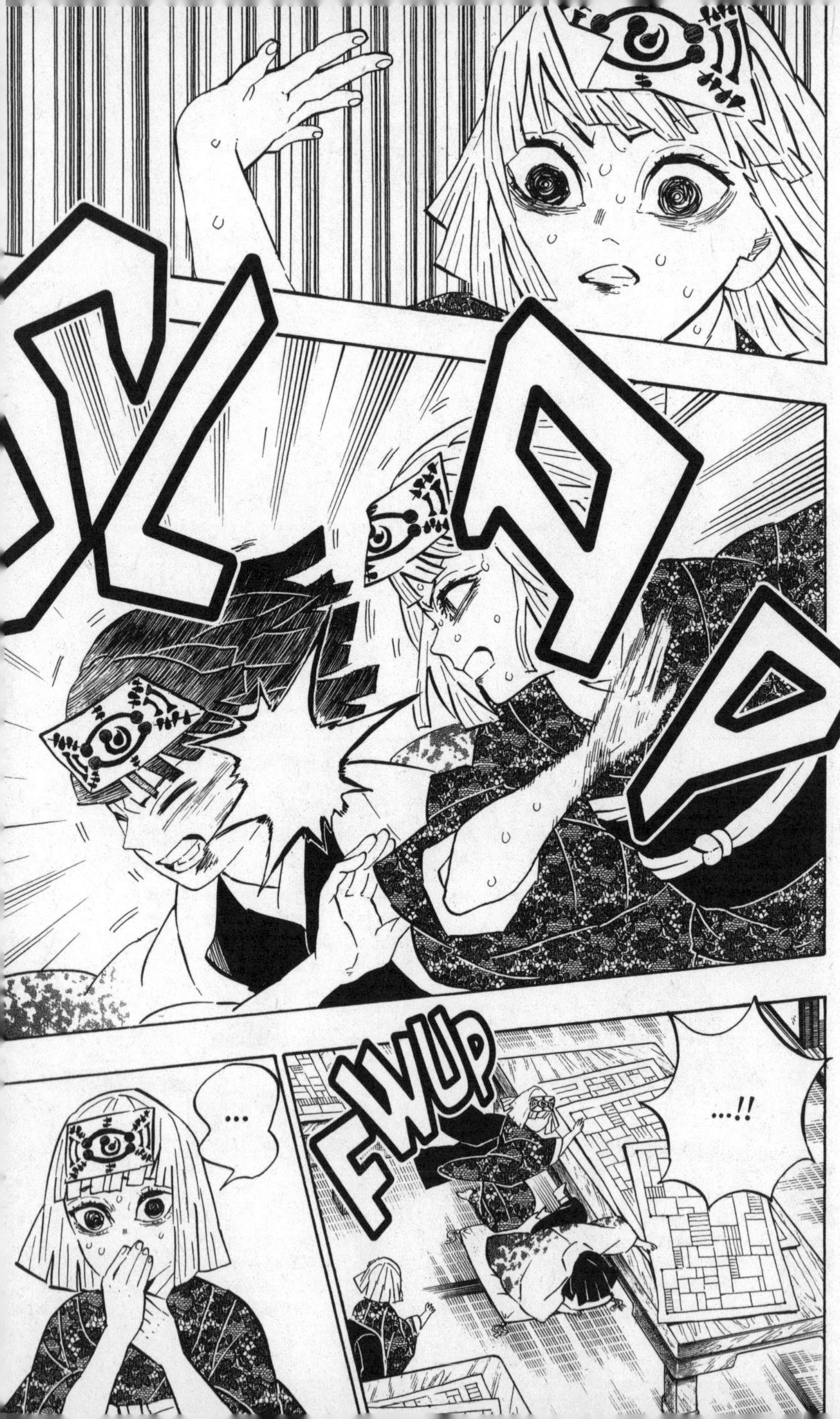
SLAP
...!!
FWUP
...

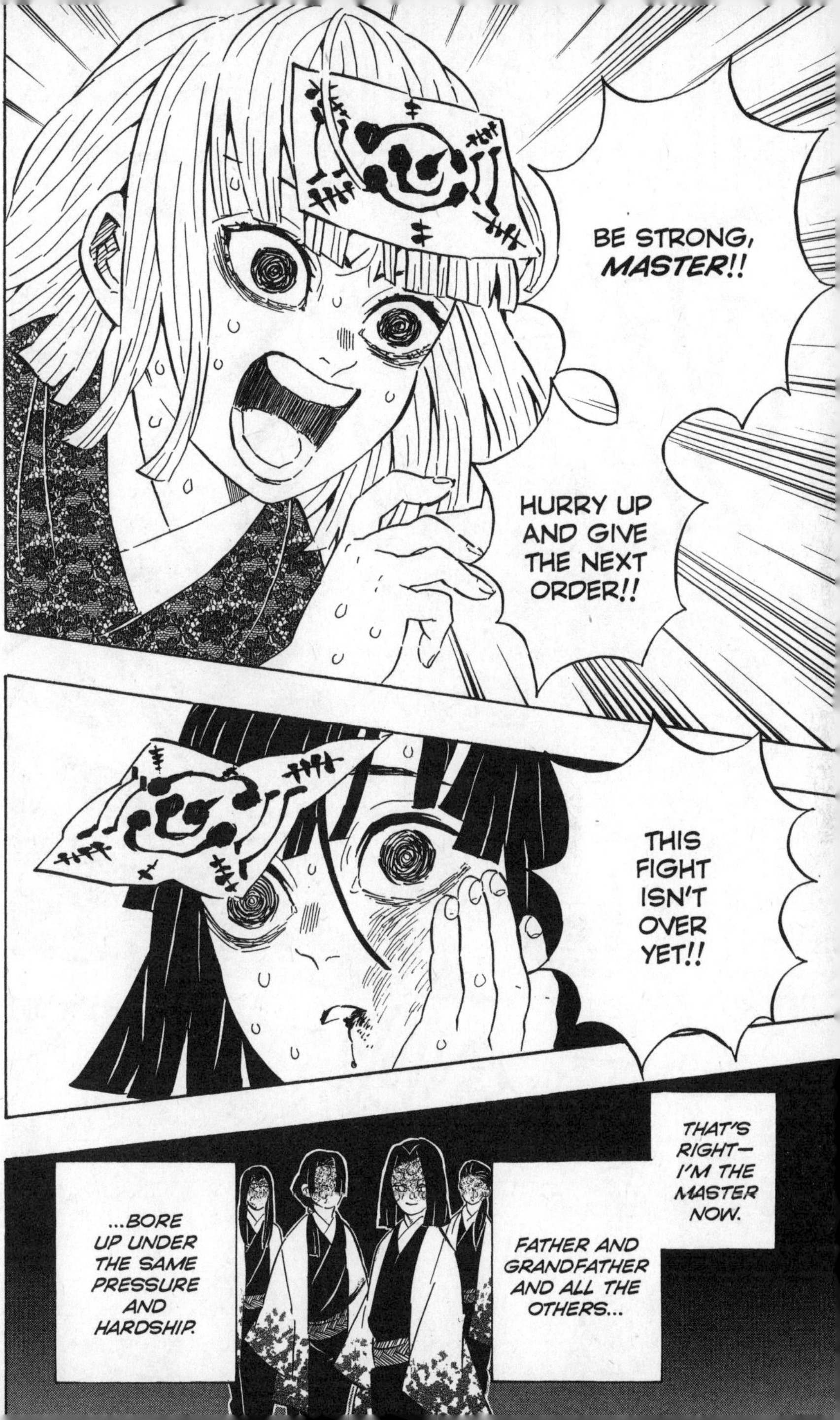
BE STRONG, MASTER!!
HURRY UP AND GIVE THE NEXT ORDER!!
THIS FIGHT ISN'T OVER YET!!
THAT'S RIGHT— I'M THE MASTER NOW.
FATHER AND GRANDFATHER AND ALL THE OTHERS...
...BORE UP UNDER THE SAME PRESSURE AND HARDSHIP.

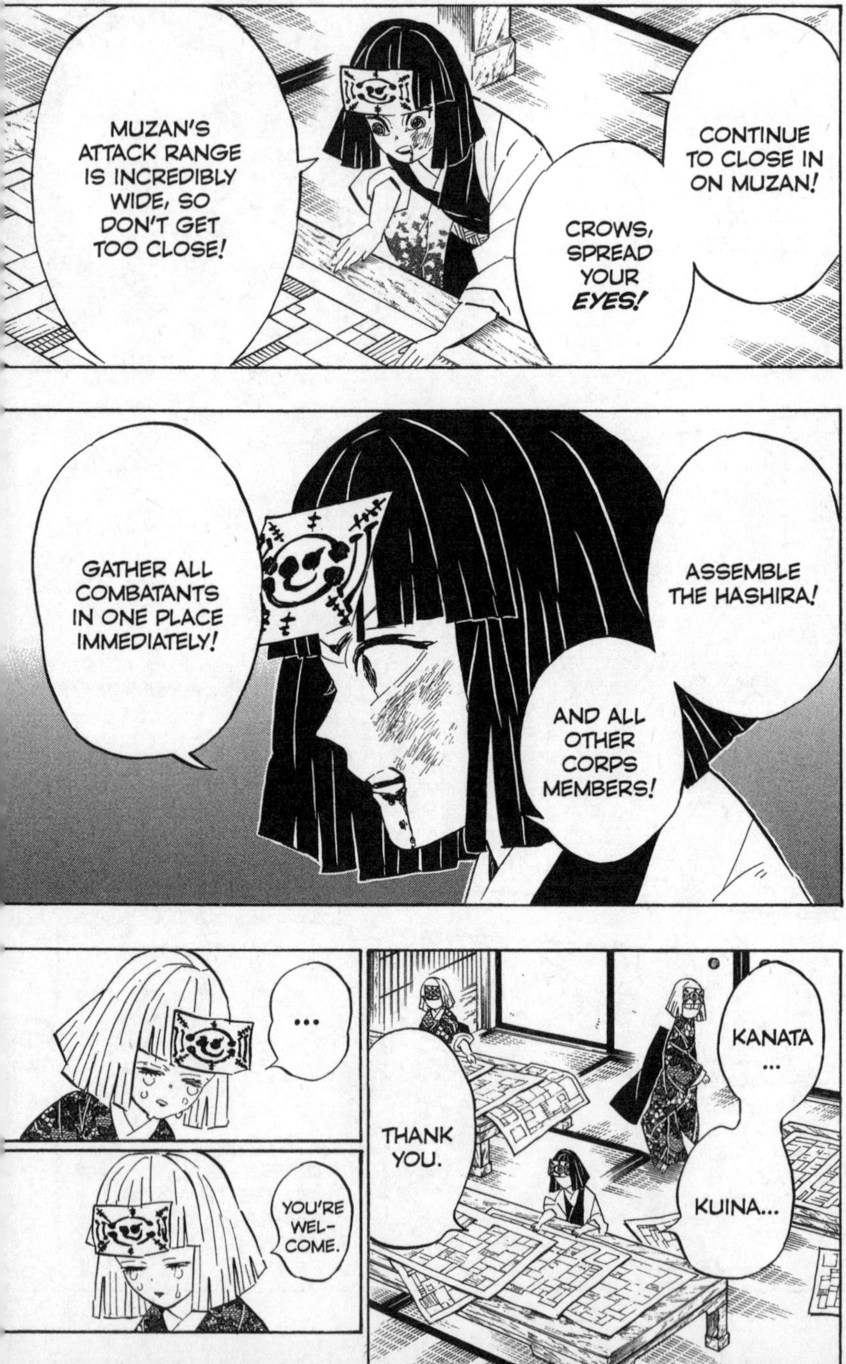
CONTINUE TO CLOSE IN ON MUZAN!
CROWS, SPREAD YOUR *EYES!*
MUZAN'S ATTACK RANGE IS INCREDIBLY WIDE, SO DON'T GET TOO CLOSE!
ASSEMBLE THE HASHIRA!
AND ALL OTHER CORPS MEMBERS!
GATHER ALL COMBATANTS IN ONE PLACE IMMEDIATELY!
KANATA...
KUINA...
THANK YOU.
...
YOU'RE WEL-COME.

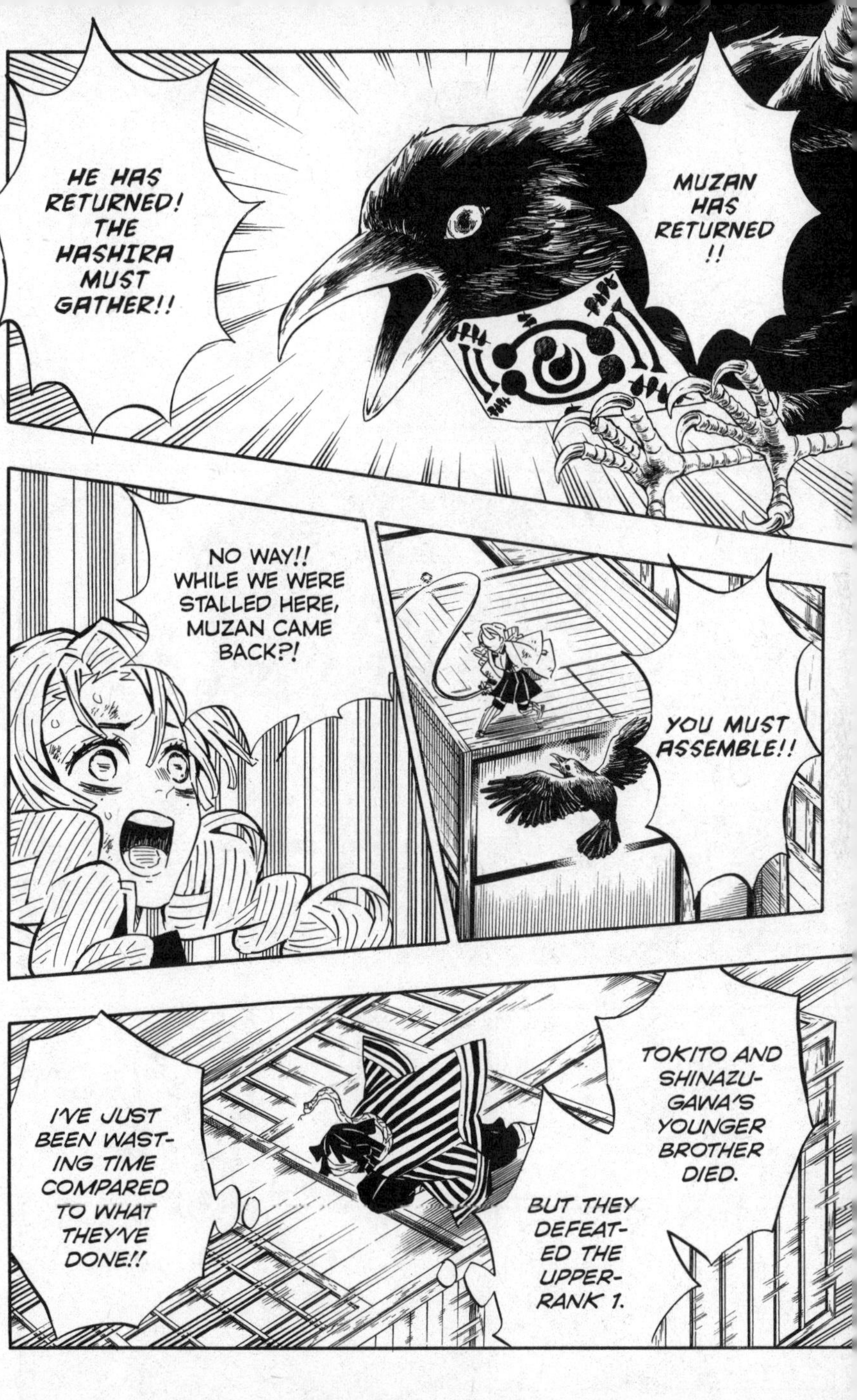
MUZAN HAS RETURNED!!
HE HAS RETURNED! THE HASHIRA MUST GATHER!!
YOU MUST ASSEMBLE!!
NO WAY!! WHILE WE WERE STALLED HERE, MUZAN CAME BACK?!
TOKITO AND SHINAZU-GAWA'S YOUNGER BROTHER DIED.
BUT THEY DEFEAT-ED THE UPPER-RANK 1.
I'VE JUST BEEN WAST-ING TIME COMPARED TO WHAT THEY'VE DONE!!

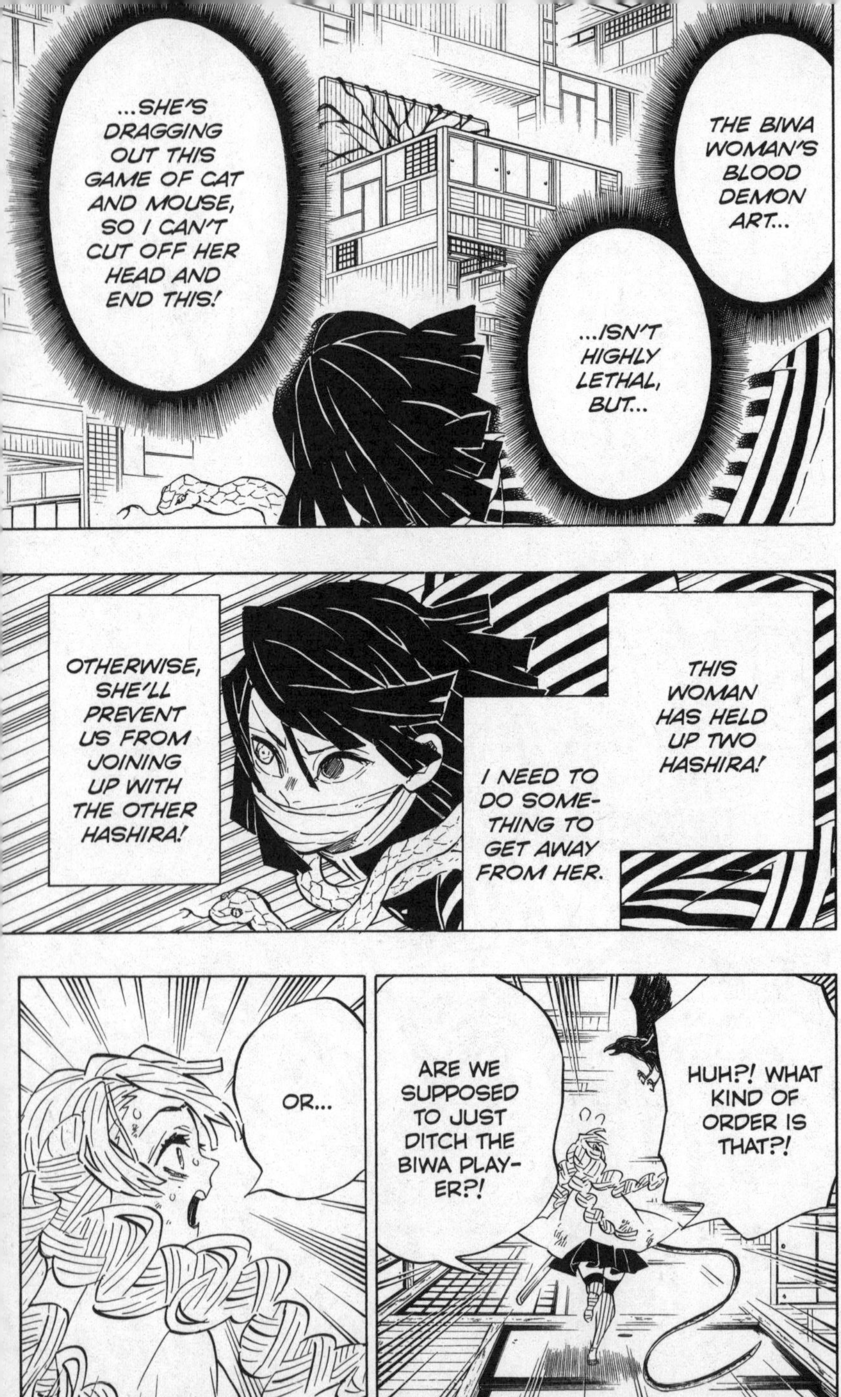
THE BIWA WOMAN'S BLOOD DEMON ART...
...ISN'T HIGHLY LETHAL, BUT...
...SHE'S DRAGGING OUT THIS GAME OF CAT AND MOUSE, SO I CAN'T CUT OFF HER HEAD AND END THIS!
THIS WOMAN HAS HELD UP TWO HASHIRA!
I NEED TO DO SOME-THING TO GET AWAY FROM HER.
OTHERWISE, SHE'LL PREVENT US FROM JOINING UP WITH THE OTHER HASHIRA!
HUH?! WHAT KIND OF ORDER IS THAT?!
ARE WE SUPPOSED TO JUST DITCH THE BIWA PLAY-ER?!
OR...

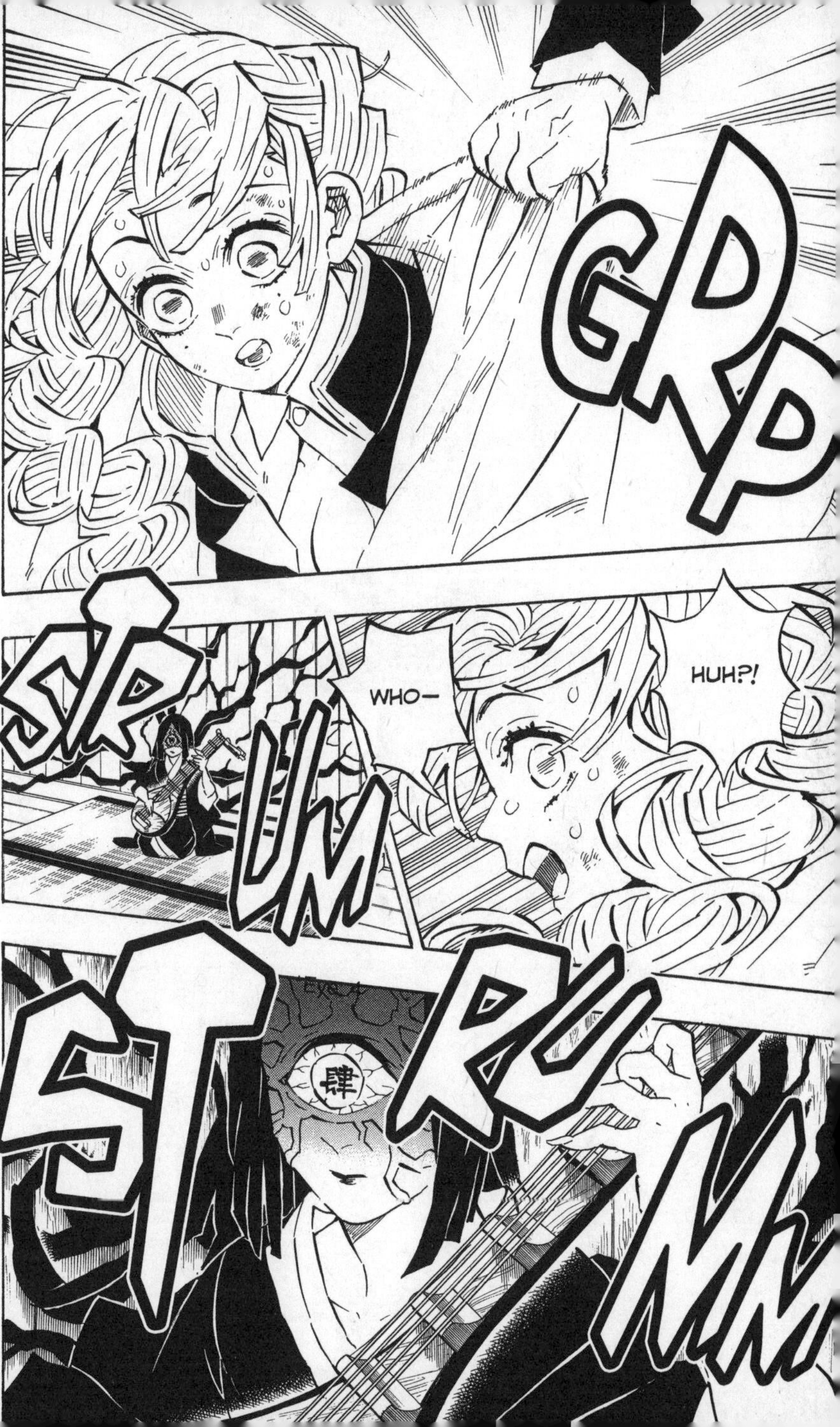
GRIP
HUH?!
WHO—
STRUM
STRUM

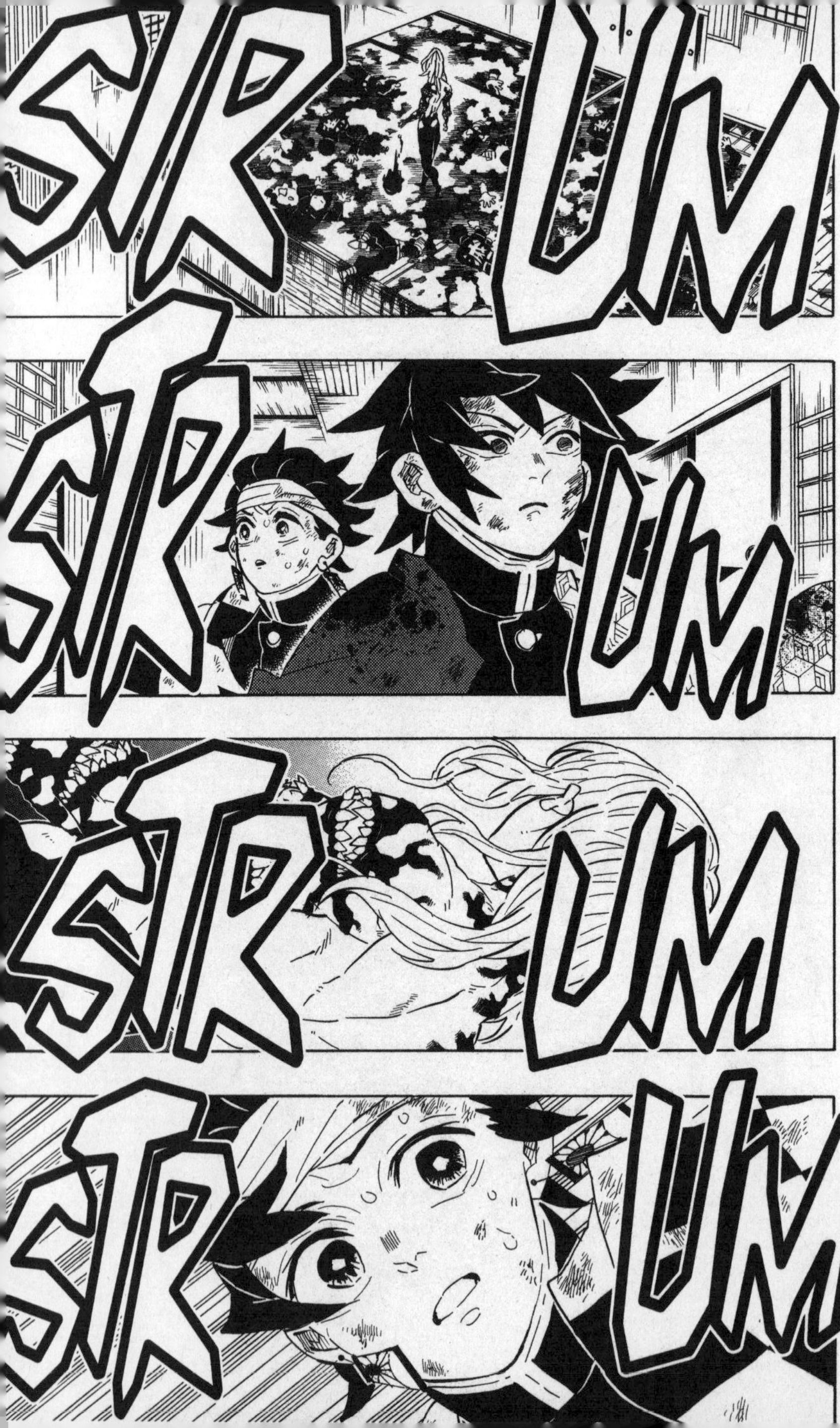
STRUM
STRUM
STRUM
STRUM

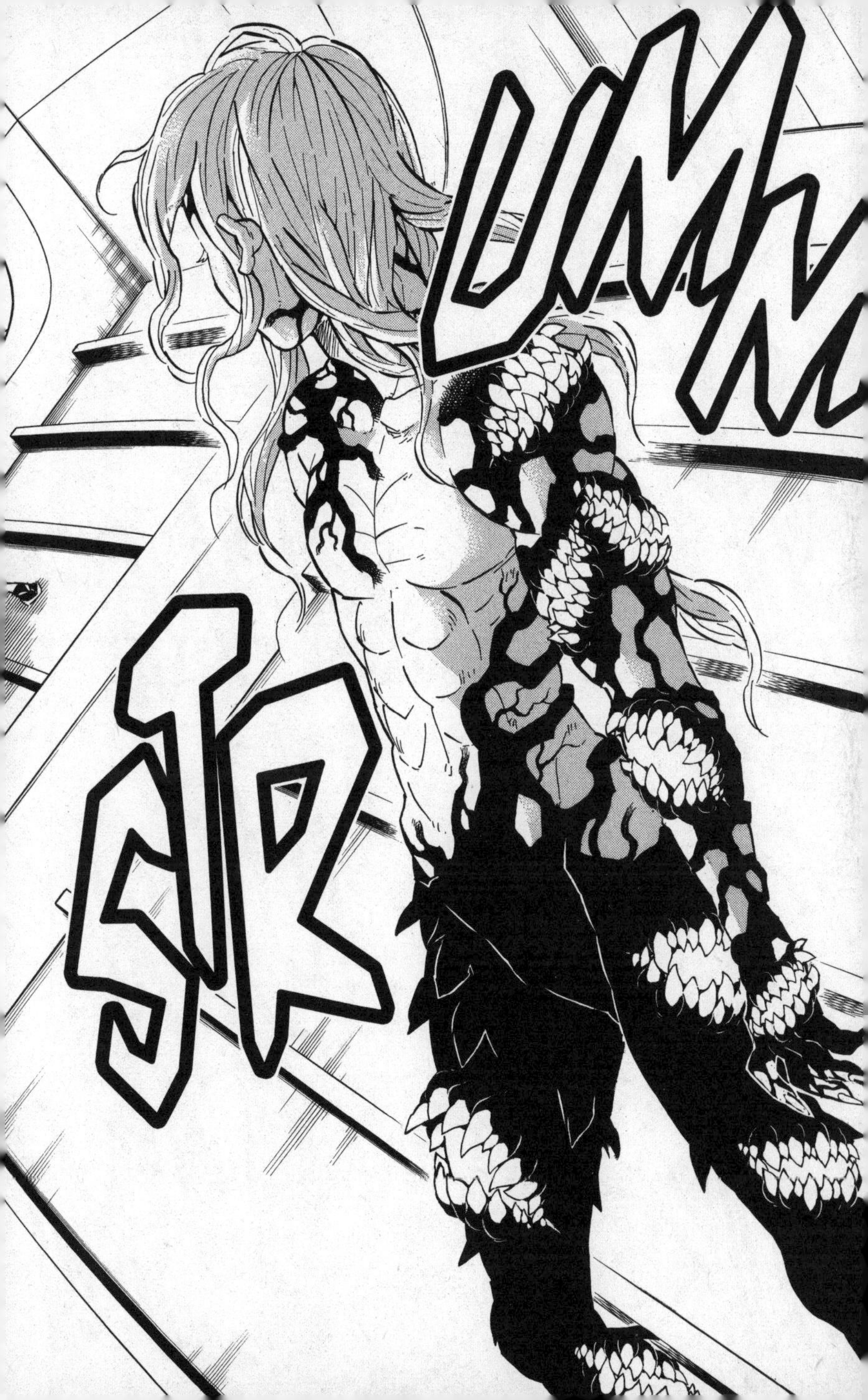

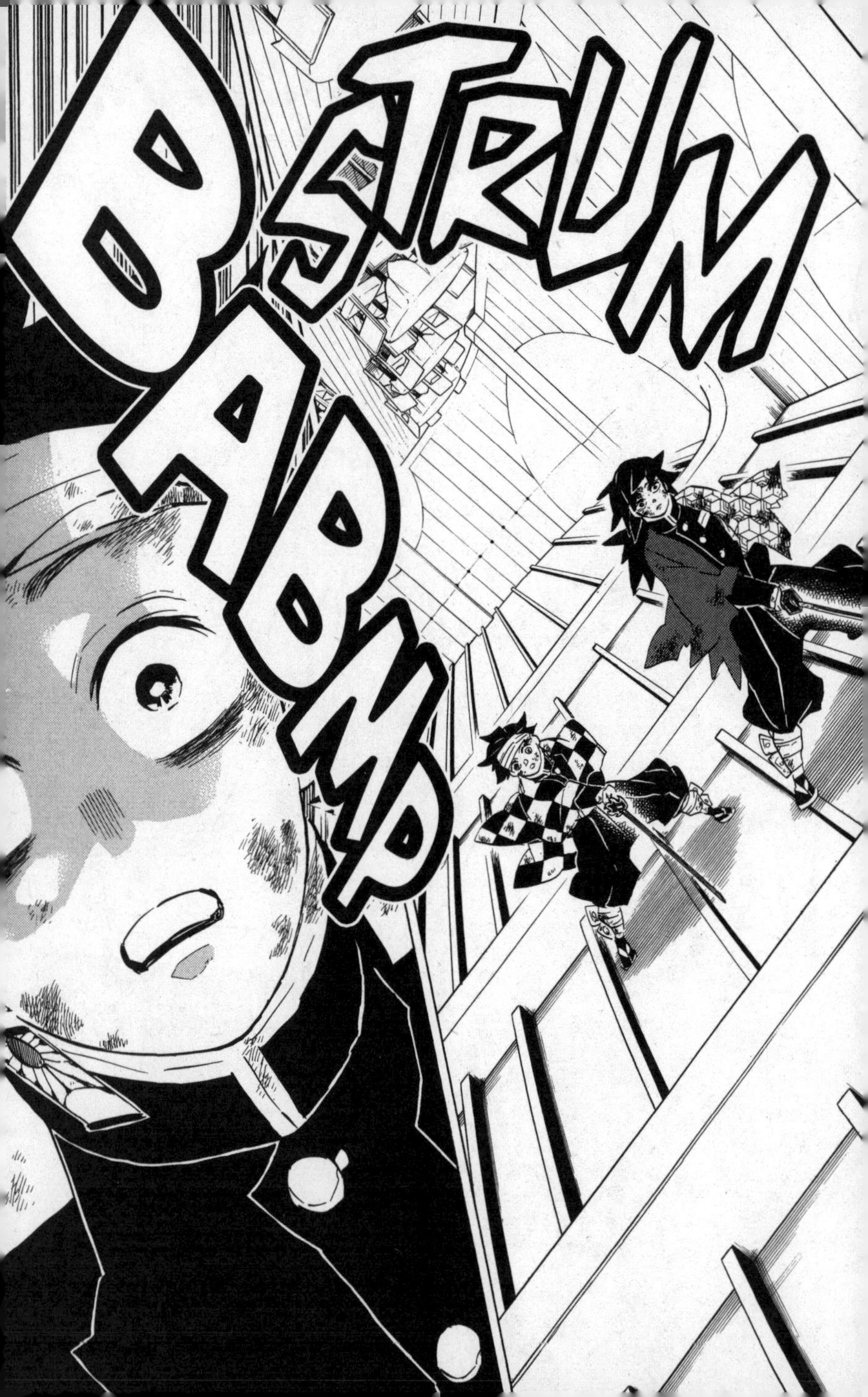
BA-DUMP
BA-DUMP

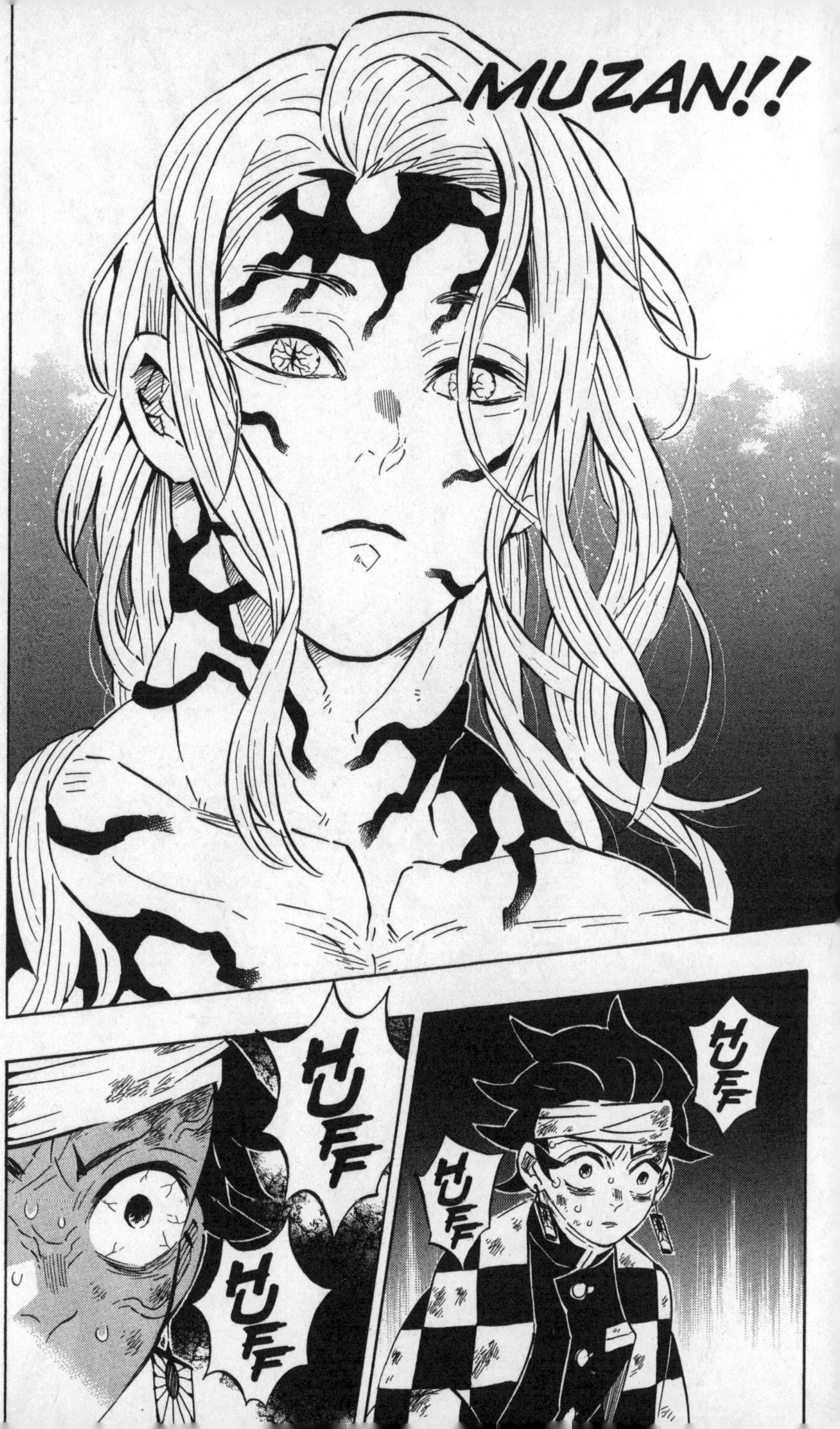
MUZAN!!
HUFF
HUFF
HUFF
HUFF

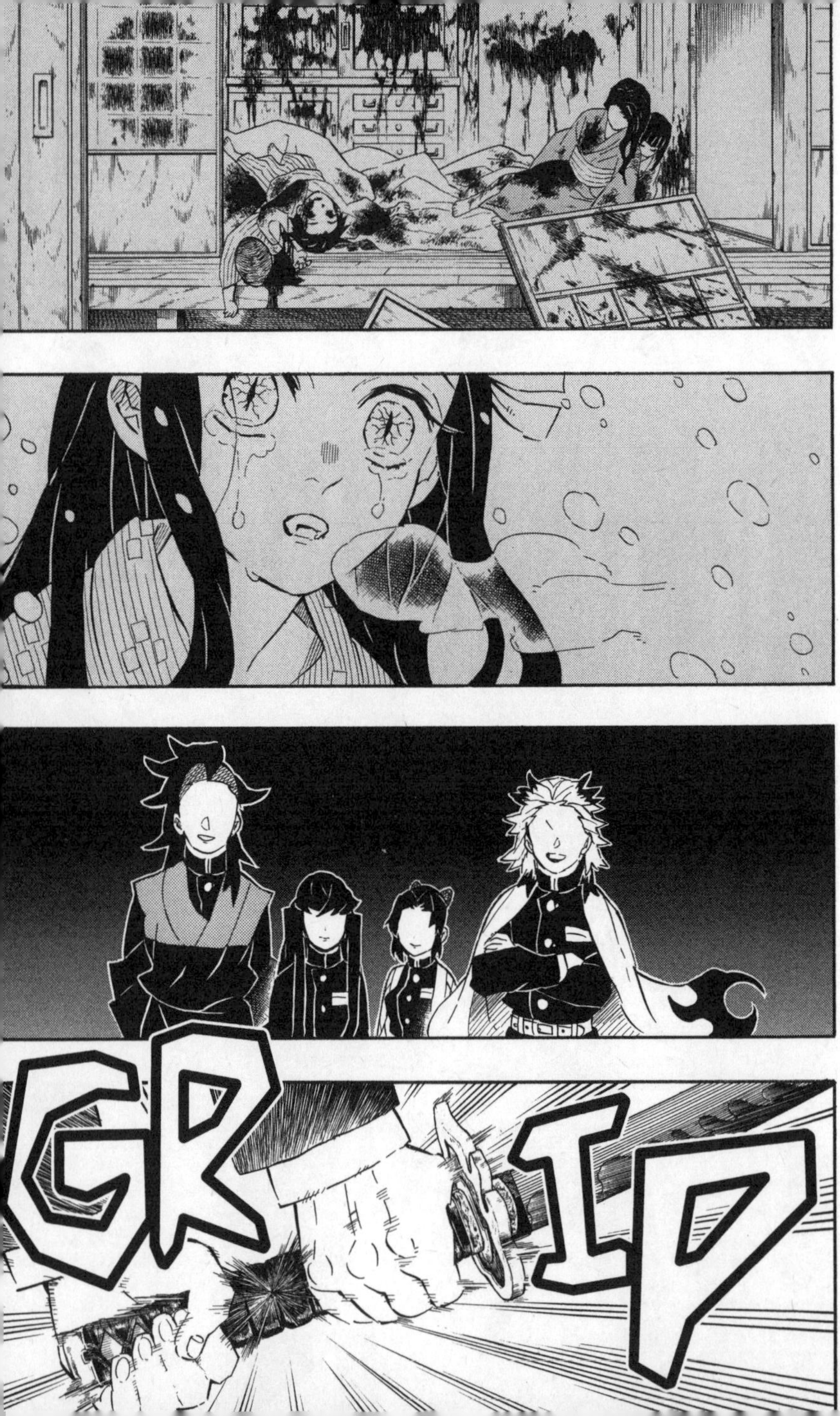
GRIP

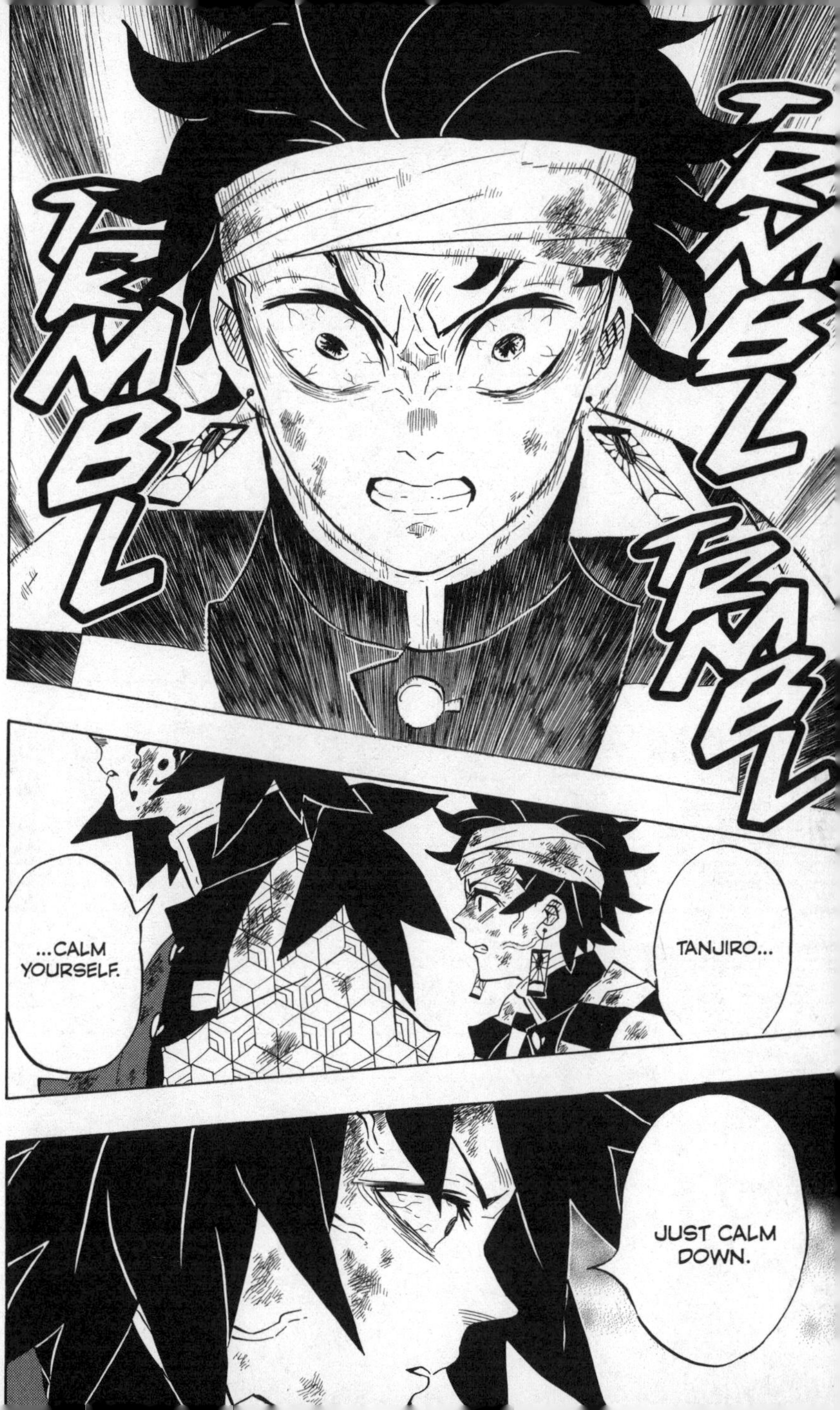
TREMBL
TREMBL
TREMBL
TANJIRO...
...CALM YOURSELF.
JUST CALM DOWN.

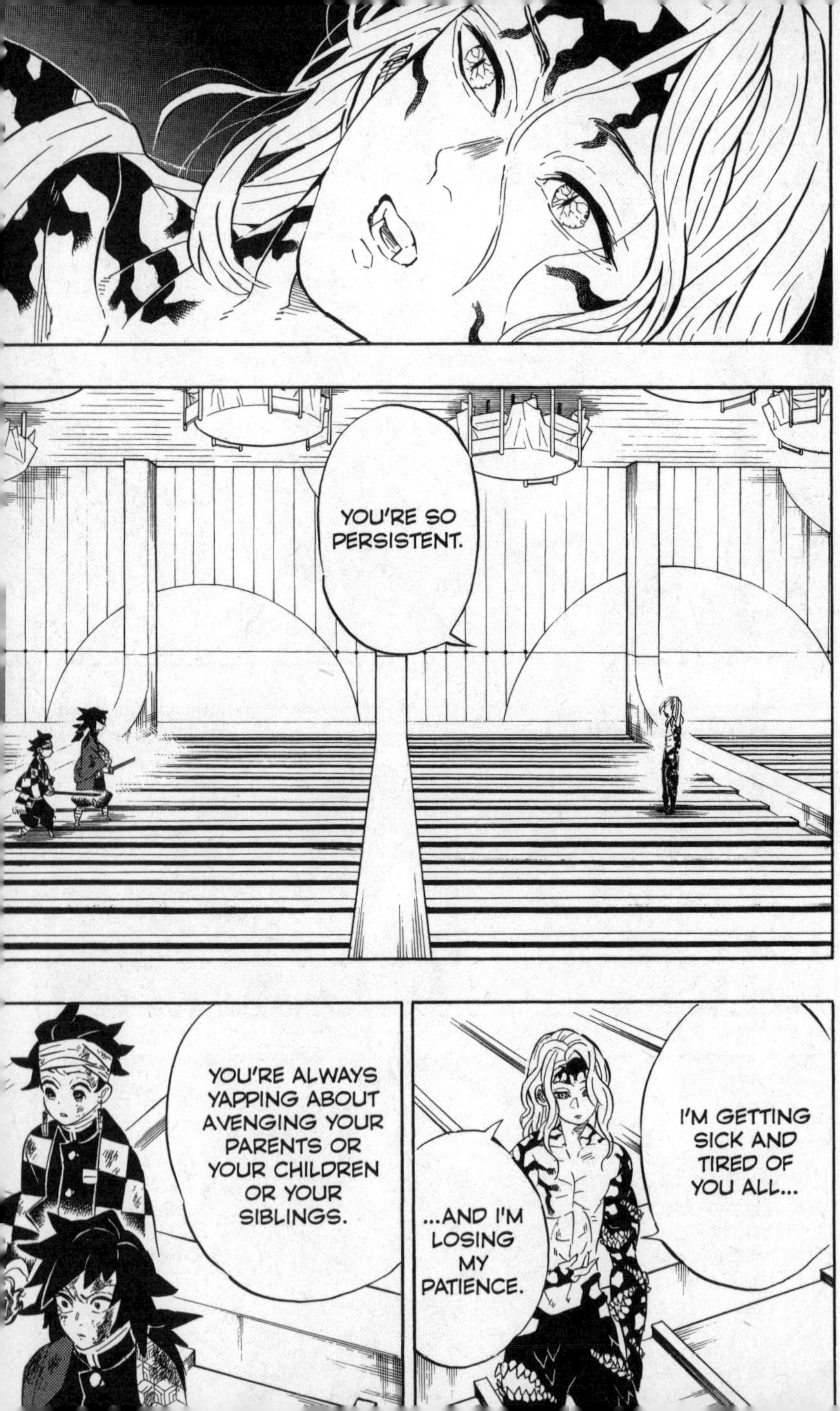
YOU'RE SO PERSISTENT.
I'M GETTING SICK AND TIRED OF YOU ALL...
...AND I'M LOSING MY PATIENCE.
YOU'RE ALWAYS YAPPING ABOUT AVENGING YOUR PARENTS OR YOUR CHILDREN OR YOUR SIBLINGS.

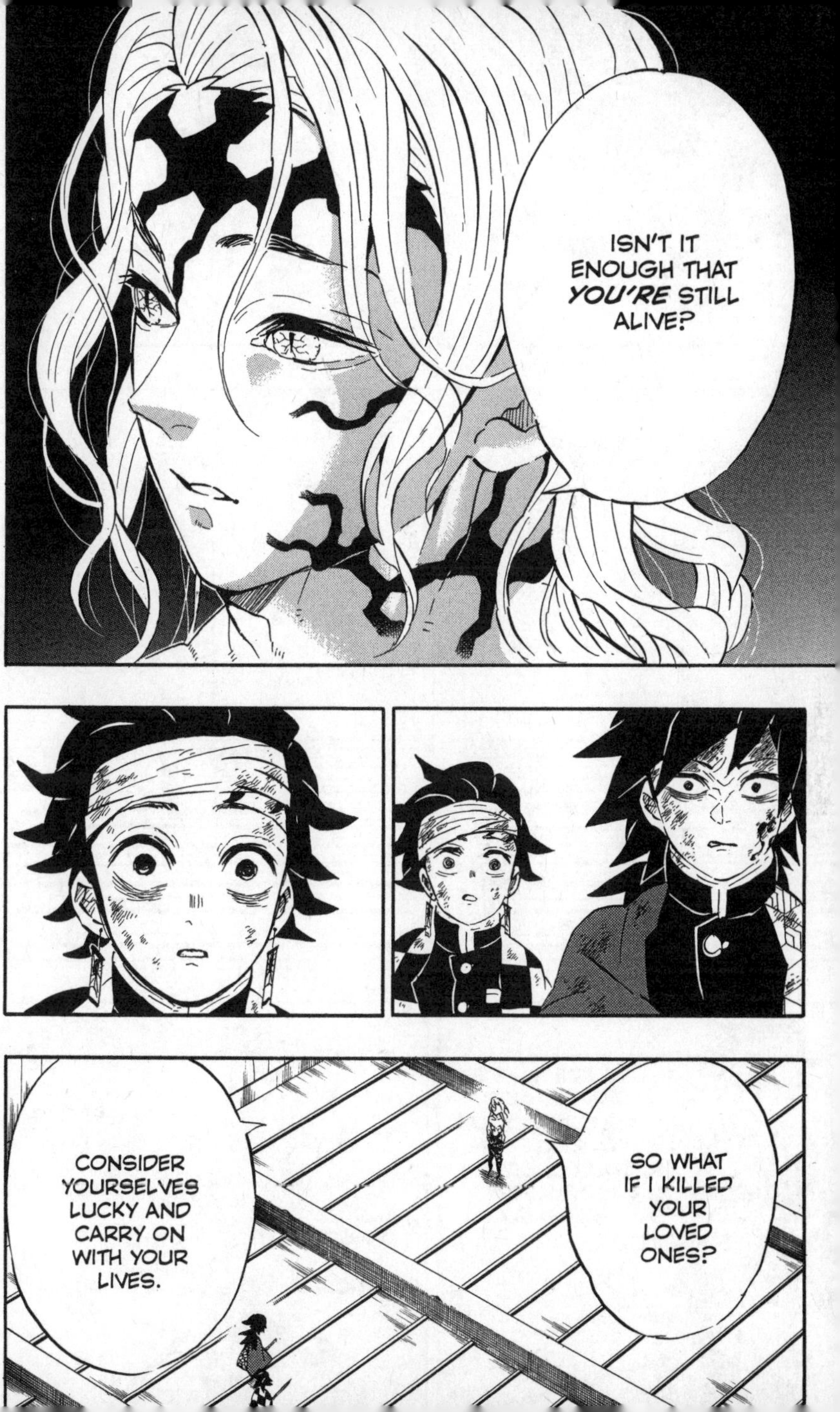
ISN'T IT ENOUGH THAT *YOU'RE* STILL ALIVE?
SO WHAT IF I KILLED YOUR LOVED ONES?
CONSIDER YOURSELVES LUCKY AND CARRY ON WITH YOUR LIVES.

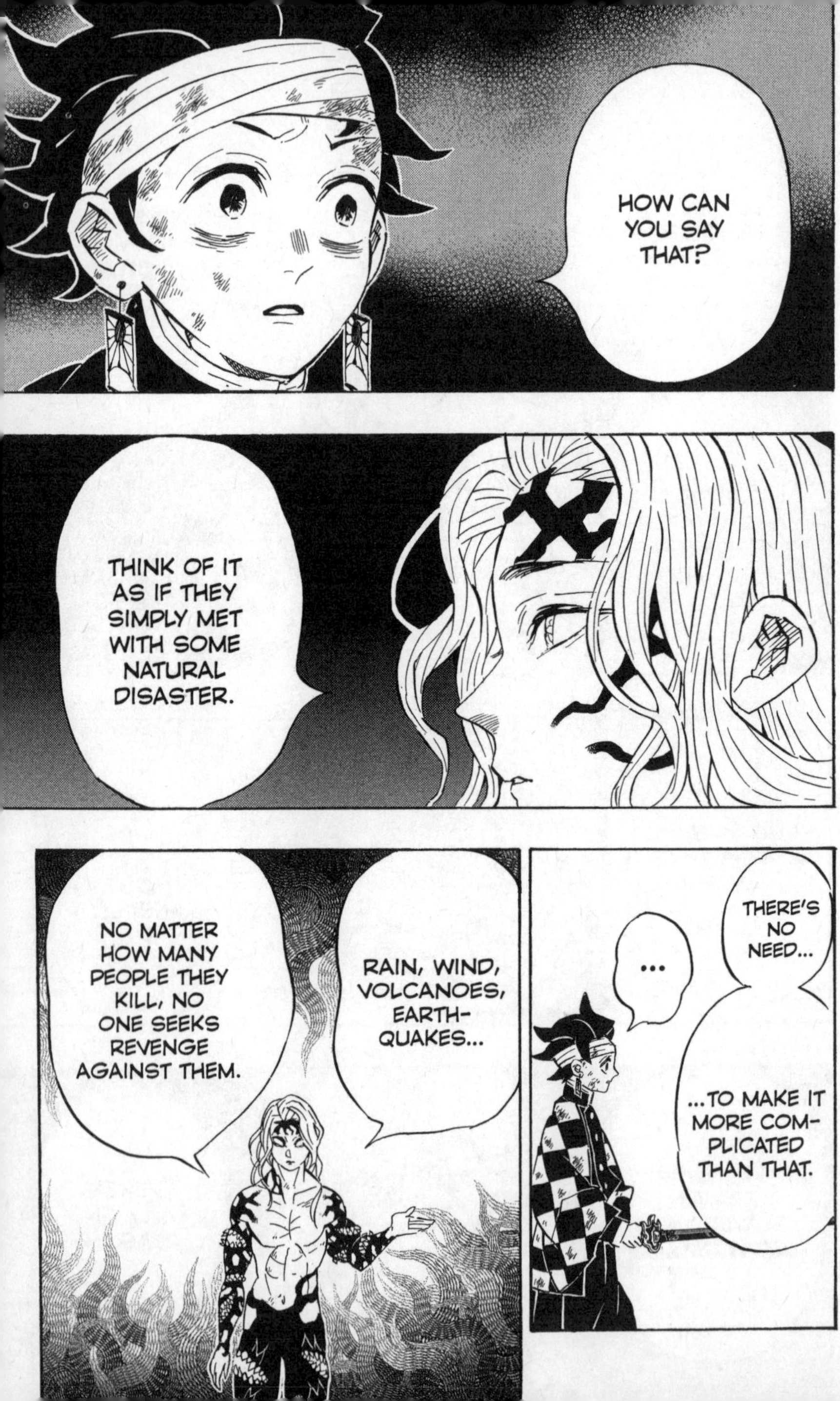
HOW CAN YOU SAY THAT?
THINK OF IT AS IF THEY SIMPLY MET WITH SOME NATURAL DISASTER.
THERE'S NO NEED...
...
...TO MAKE IT MORE COM-PLICATED THAN THAT.
RAIN, WIND, VOLCANOES, EARTH-QUAKES...
NO MATTER HOW MANY PEOPLE THEY KILL, NO ONE SEEKS REVENGE AGAINST THEM.

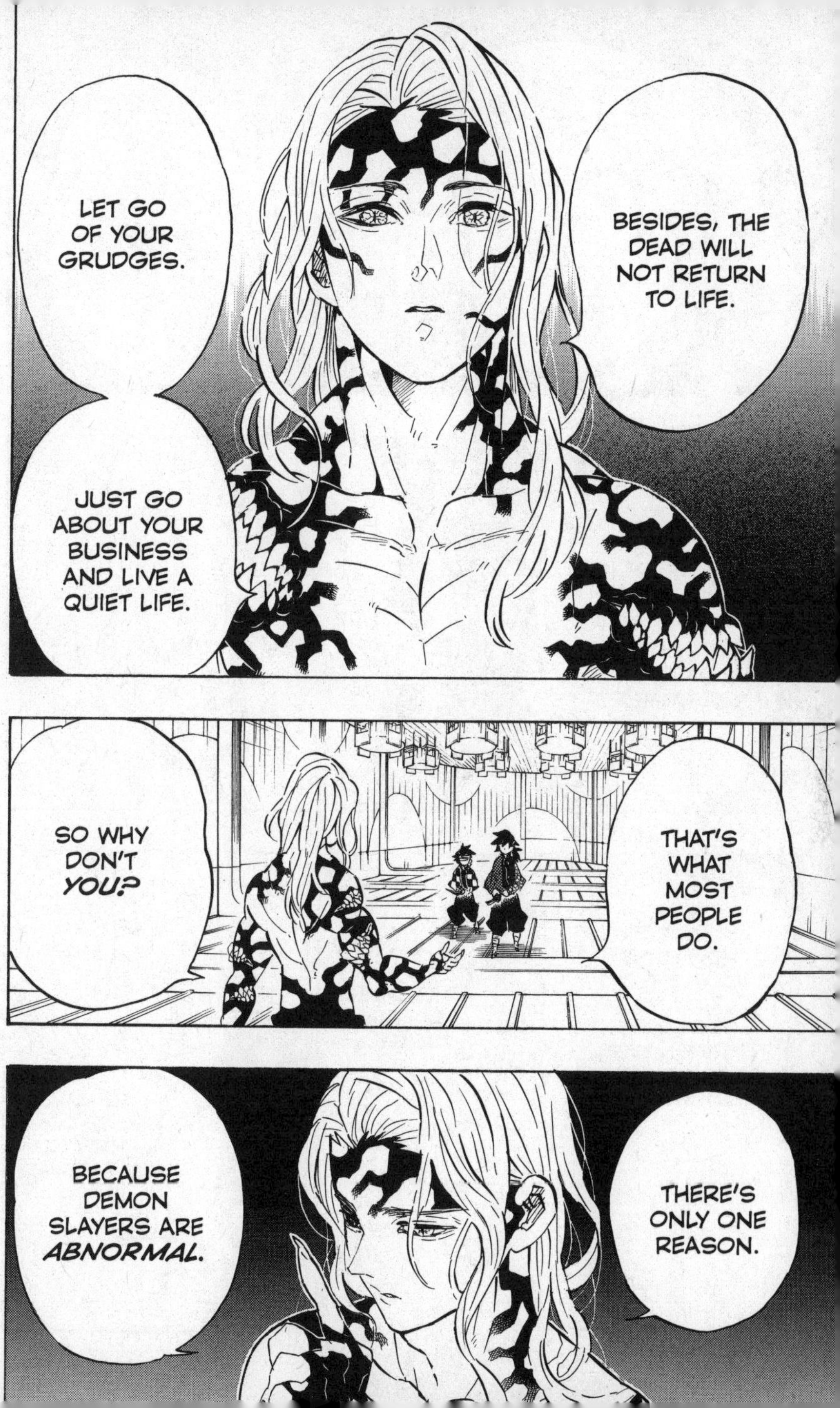
BESIDES, THE DEAD WILL NOT RETURN TO LIFE.
LET GO OF YOUR GRUDGES.
JUST GO ABOUT YOUR BUSINESS AND LIVE A QUIET LIFE.
THAT'S WHAT MOST PEOPLE DO.
SO WHY DON'T *YOU?*
THERE'S ONLY ONE REASON.
BECAUSE DEMON SLAYERS ARE *ABNORMAL.*

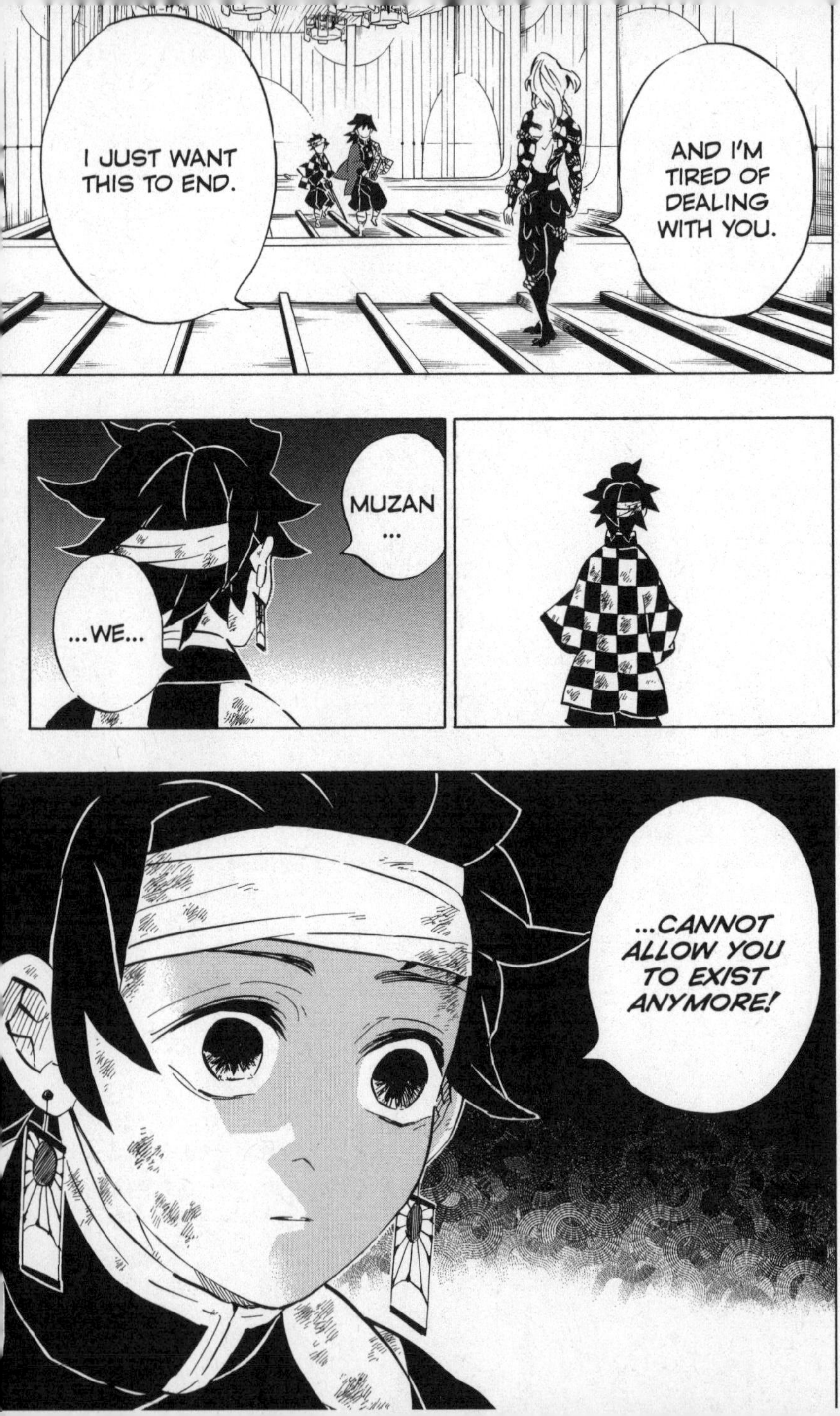
AND I'M TIRED OF DEALING WITH YOU.
I JUST WANT THIS TO END.
MUZAN ...
...WE...
...CANNOT ALLOW YOU TO EXIST ANYMORE!

Physical Skills

Not so good
↴

Good
↴

The Slapper

Kanata

Timid, fainted when a
spider crawled across
her hand, good at
playing the koto.

Kuina

Bold, doesn't mind
insects, can touch
them with her bare
hands.

CHAPTER 182: RAGE

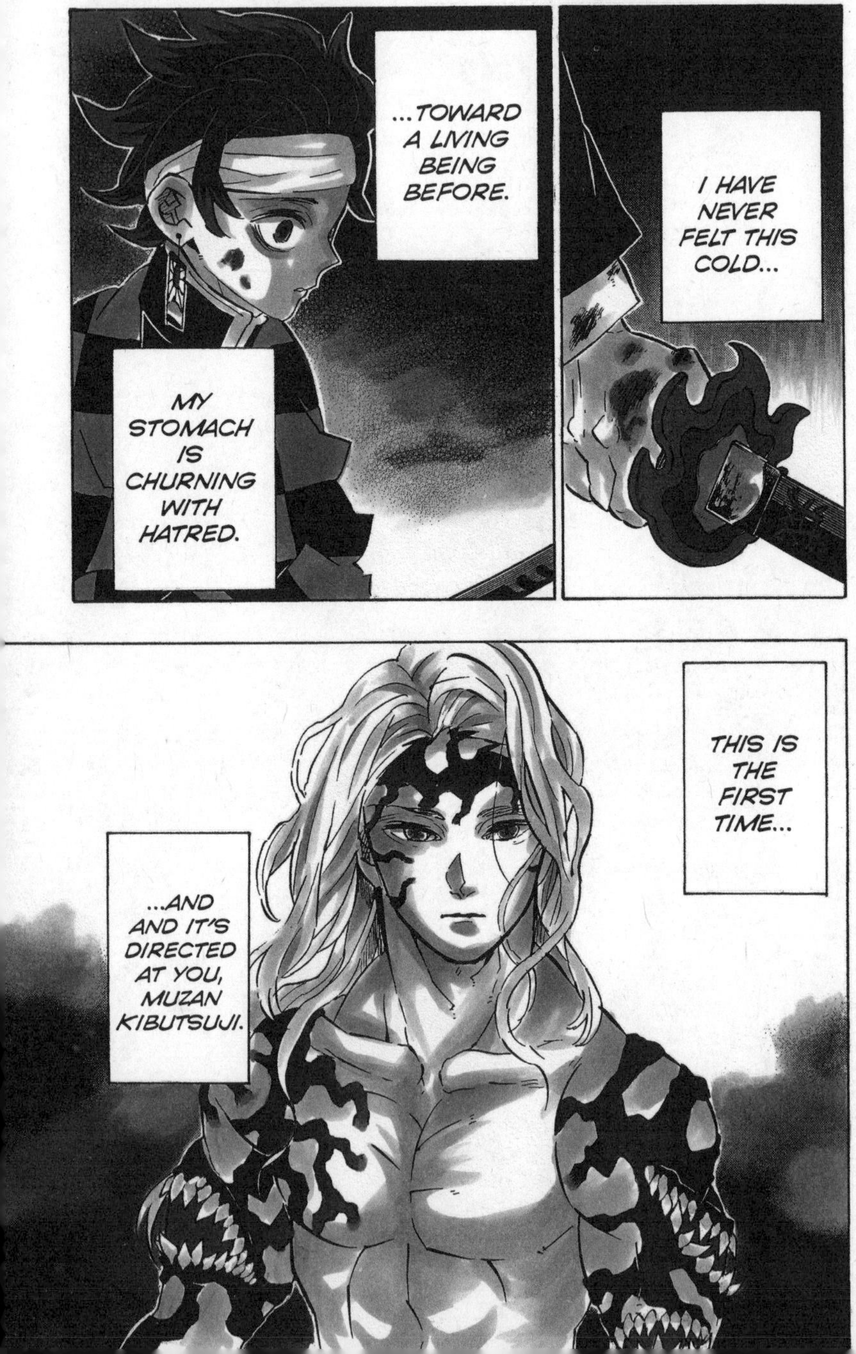
I HAVE NEVER FELT THIS COLD...
...TOWARD A LIVING BEING BEFORE.
MY STOMACH IS CHURNING WITH HATRED.
THIS IS THE FIRST TIME...
...AND AND IT'S DIRECTED AT YOU, MUZAN KIBUTSUJI.

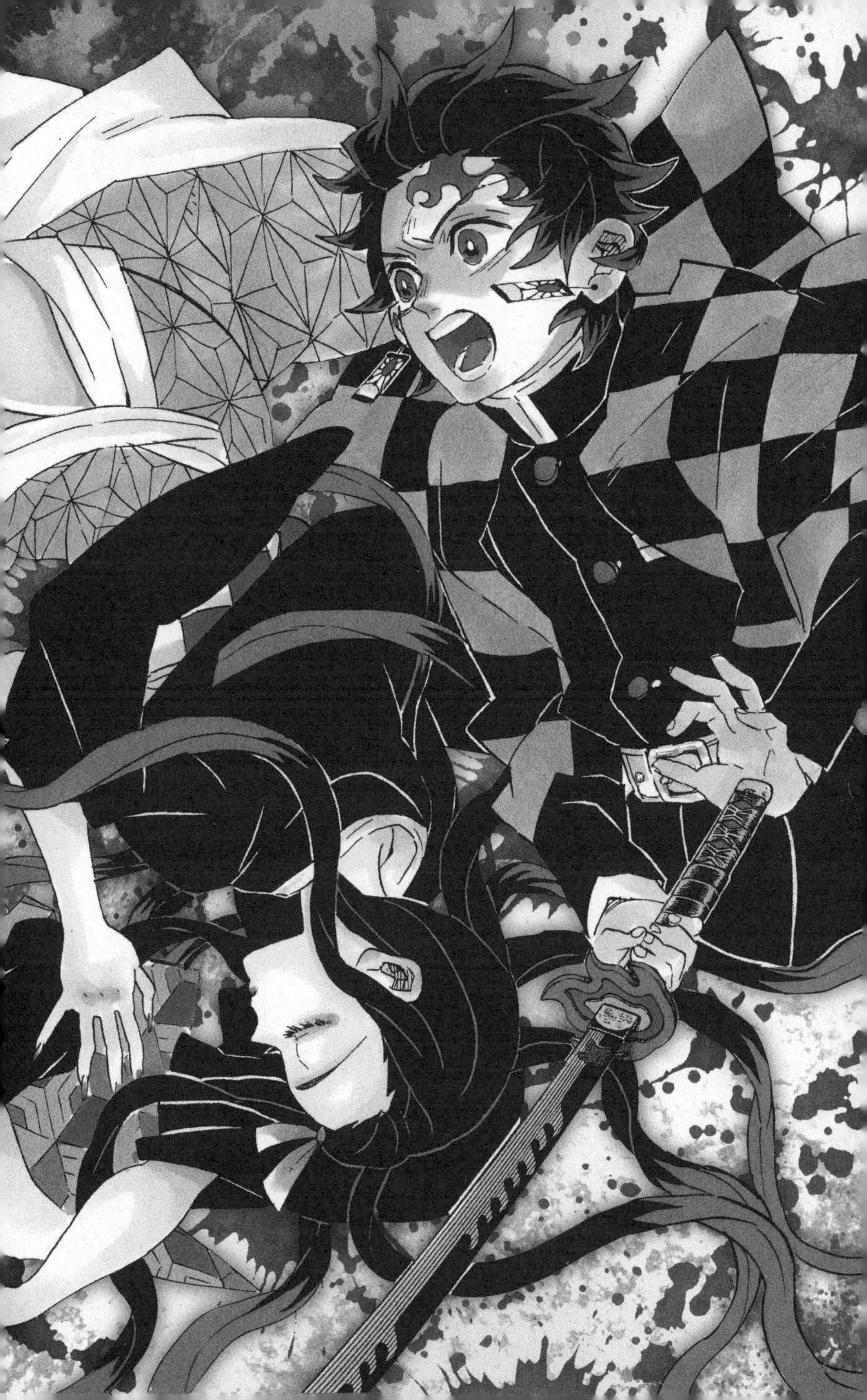

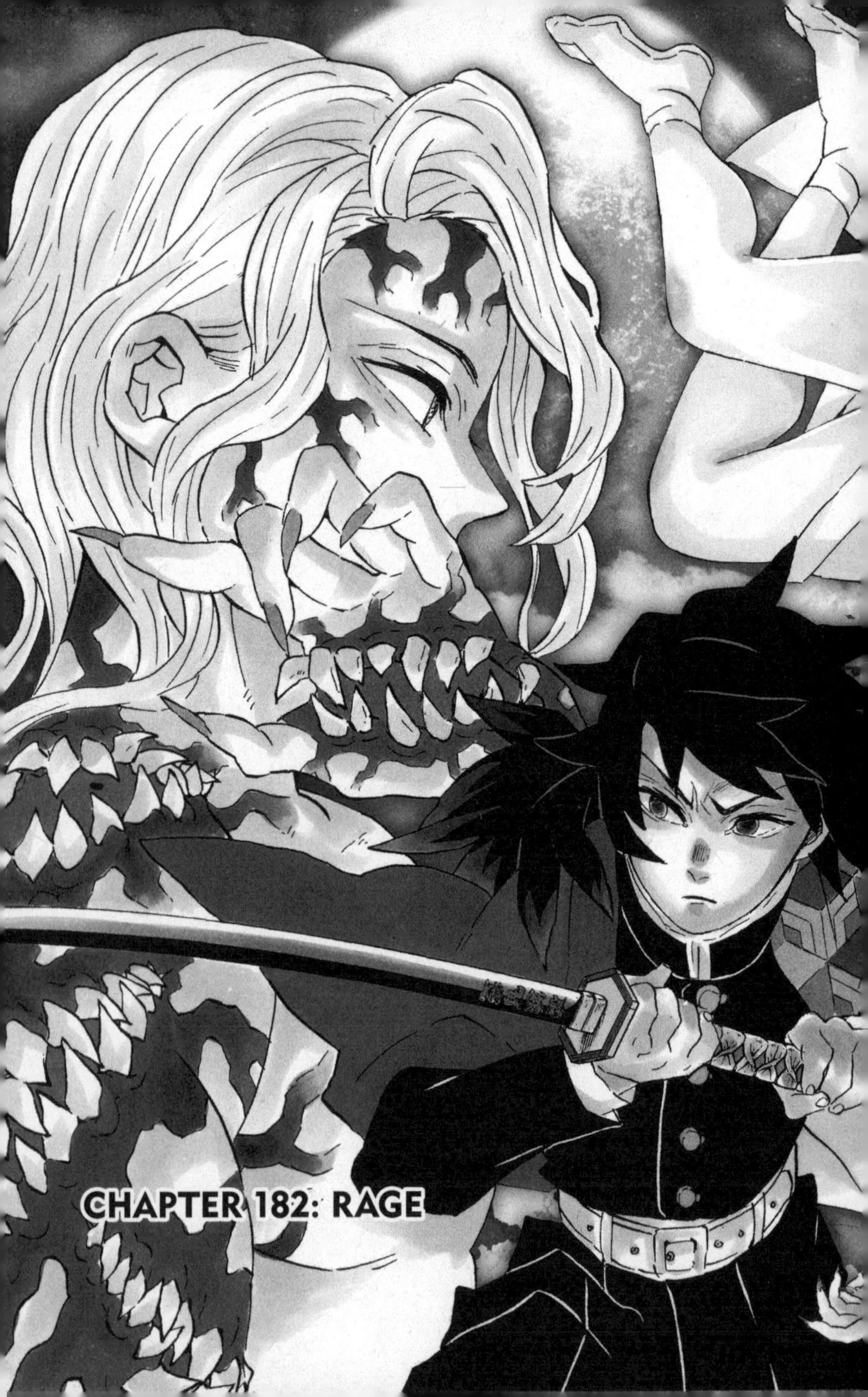
CHAPTER 182: RAGE

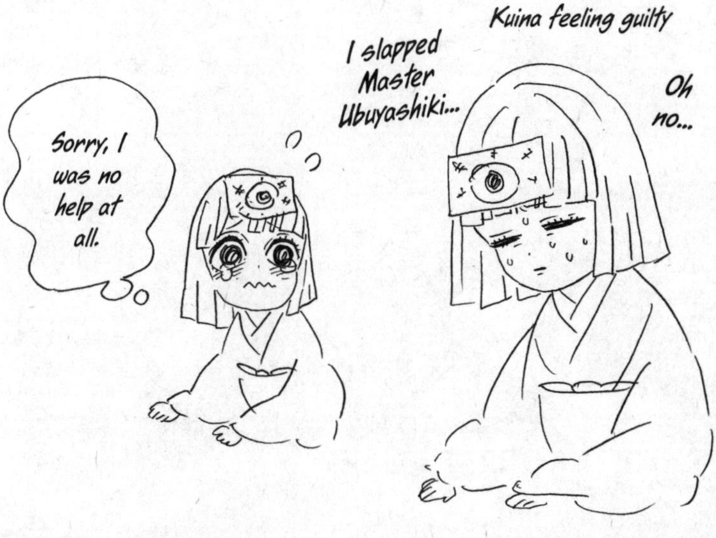
Kuina feeling guilty
Oh no...
I slapped Master Ubuyashiki...
Sorry, I was no help at all.

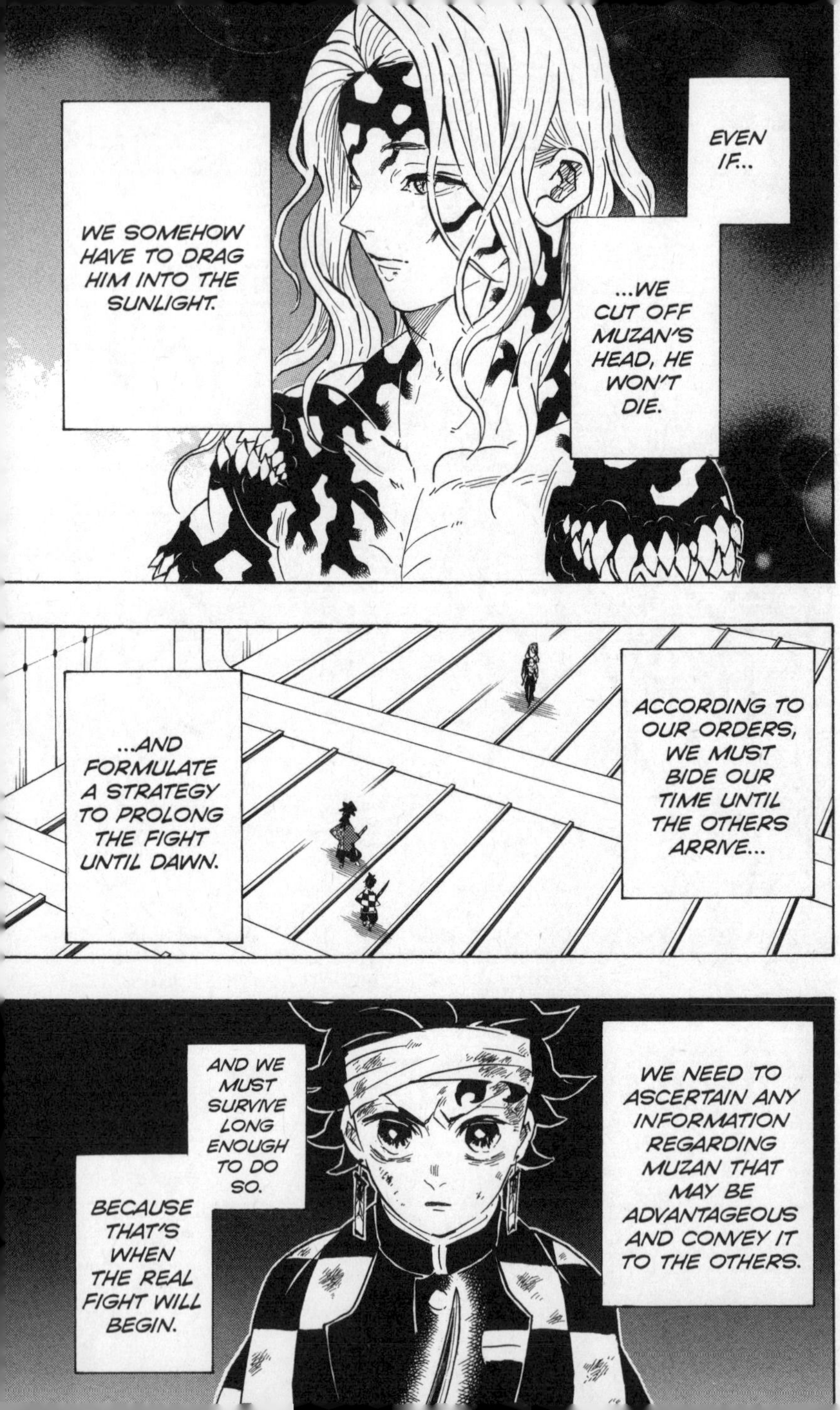
EVEN IF...
...WE CUT OFF MUZAN'S HEAD, HE WON'T DIE.
WE SOMEHOW HAVE TO DRAG HIM INTO THE SUNLIGHT.
ACCORDING TO OUR ORDERS, WE MUST BIDE OUR TIME UNTIL THE OTHERS ARRIVE...
...AND FORMULATE A STRATEGY TO PROLONG THE FIGHT UNTIL DAWN.
WE NEED TO ASCERTAIN ANY INFORMATION REGARDING MUZAN THAT MAY BE ADVANTAGEOUS AND CONVEY IT TO THE OTHERS.
AND WE MUST SURVIVE LONG ENOUGH TO DO SO.
BECAUSE THAT'S WHEN THE REAL FIGHT WILL BEGIN.

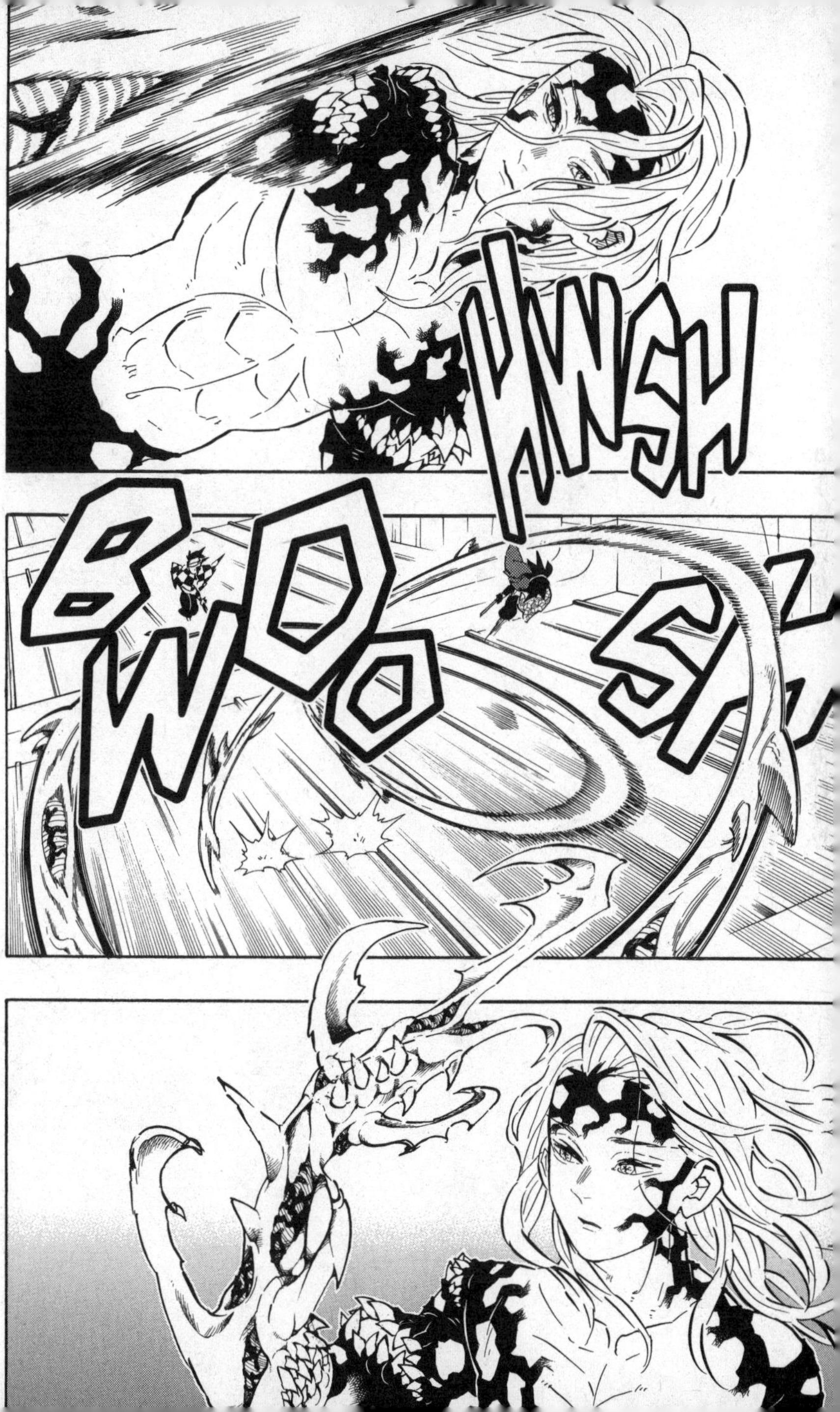
WHSH
SH
BWOOSH

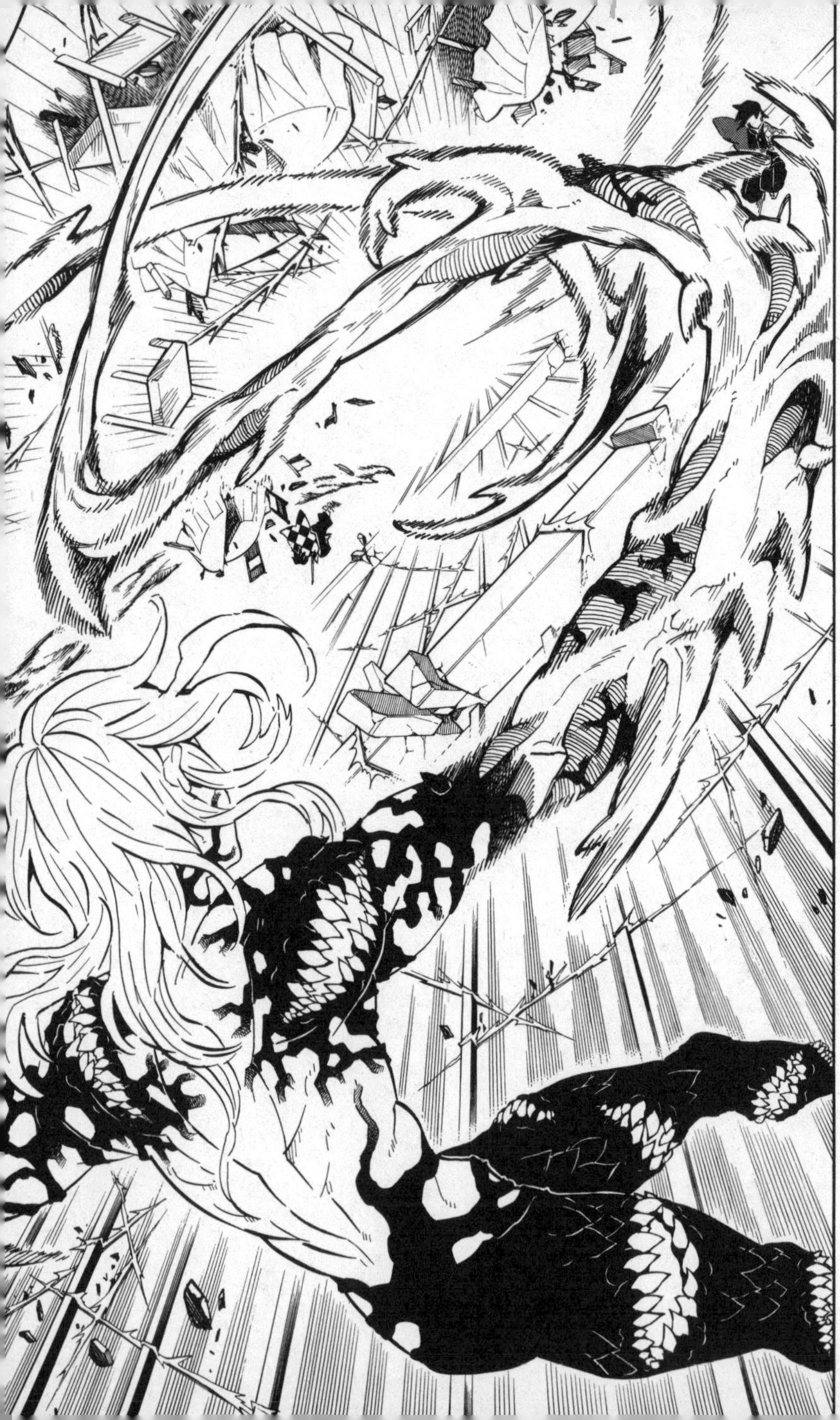

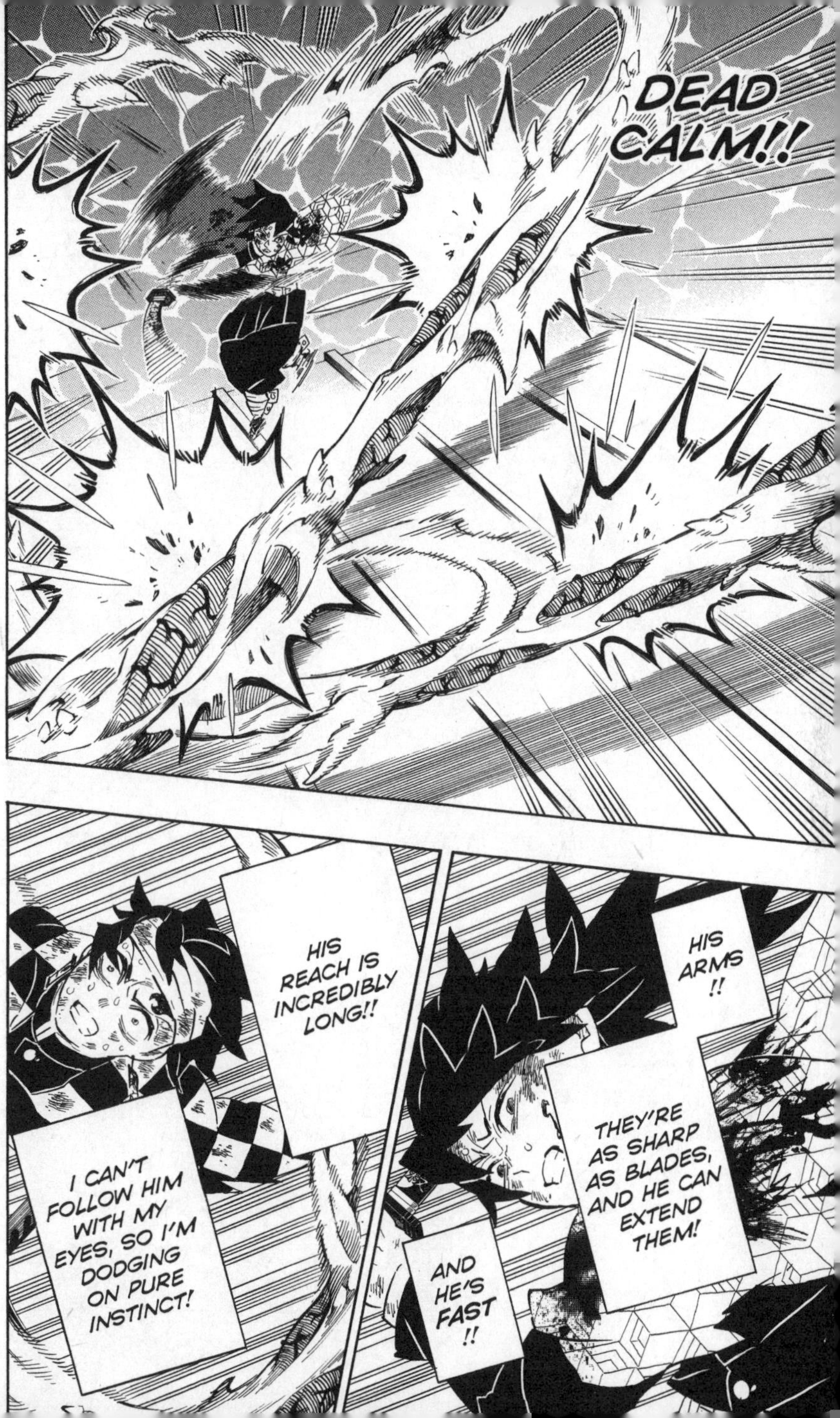
DEAD CALM!!
HIS ARMS!!
THEY'RE AS SHARP AS BLADES, AND HE CAN EXTEND THEM!
AND HE'S FAST!!
HIS REACH IS INCREDIBLY LONG!!
I CAN'T FOLLOW HIM WITH MY EYES, SO I'M DODGING ON PURE INSTINCT!

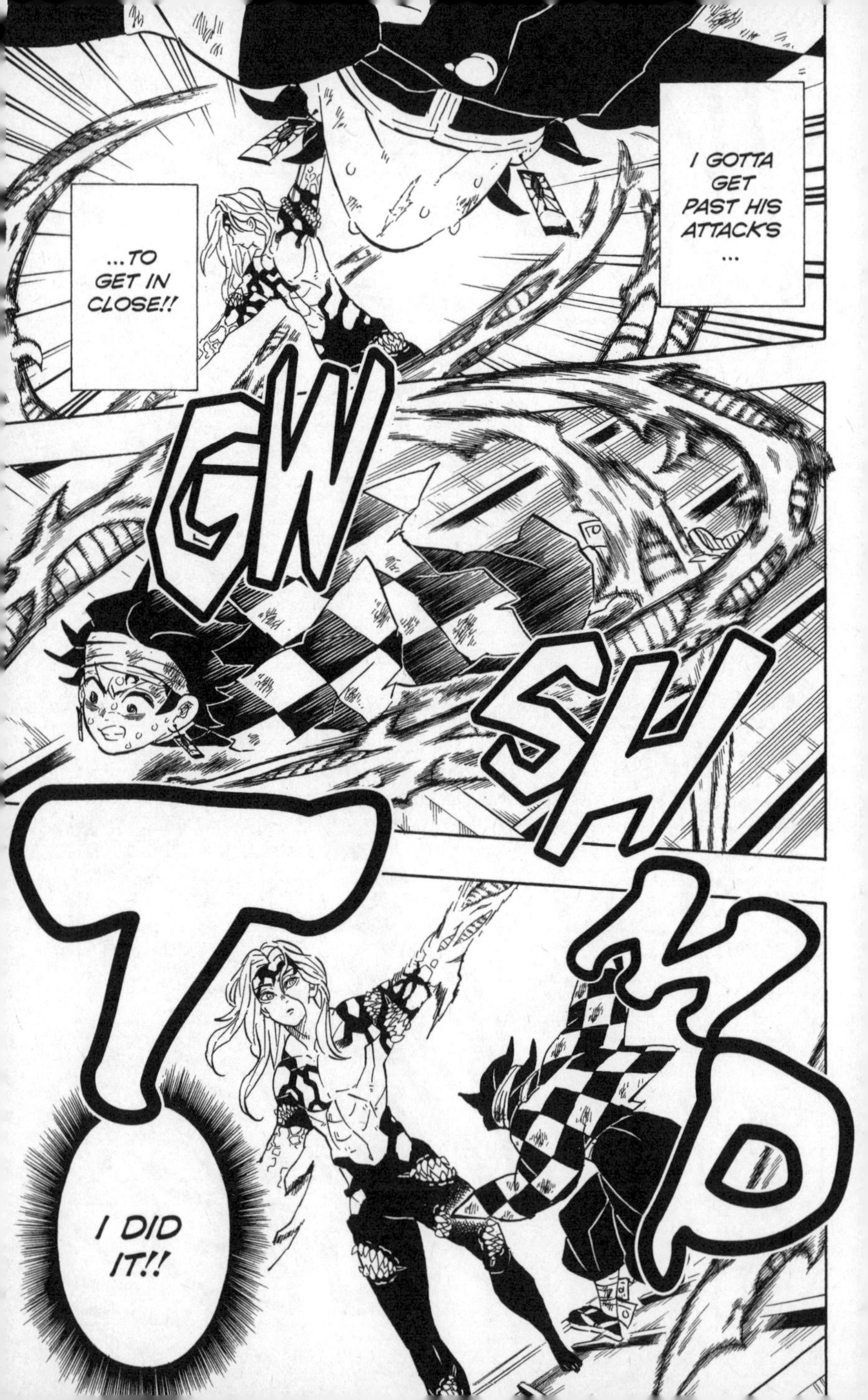
I GOTTA GET PAST HIS ATTACKS ...
...TO GET IN CLOSE!!
CWSH
TMP
I DID IT!!

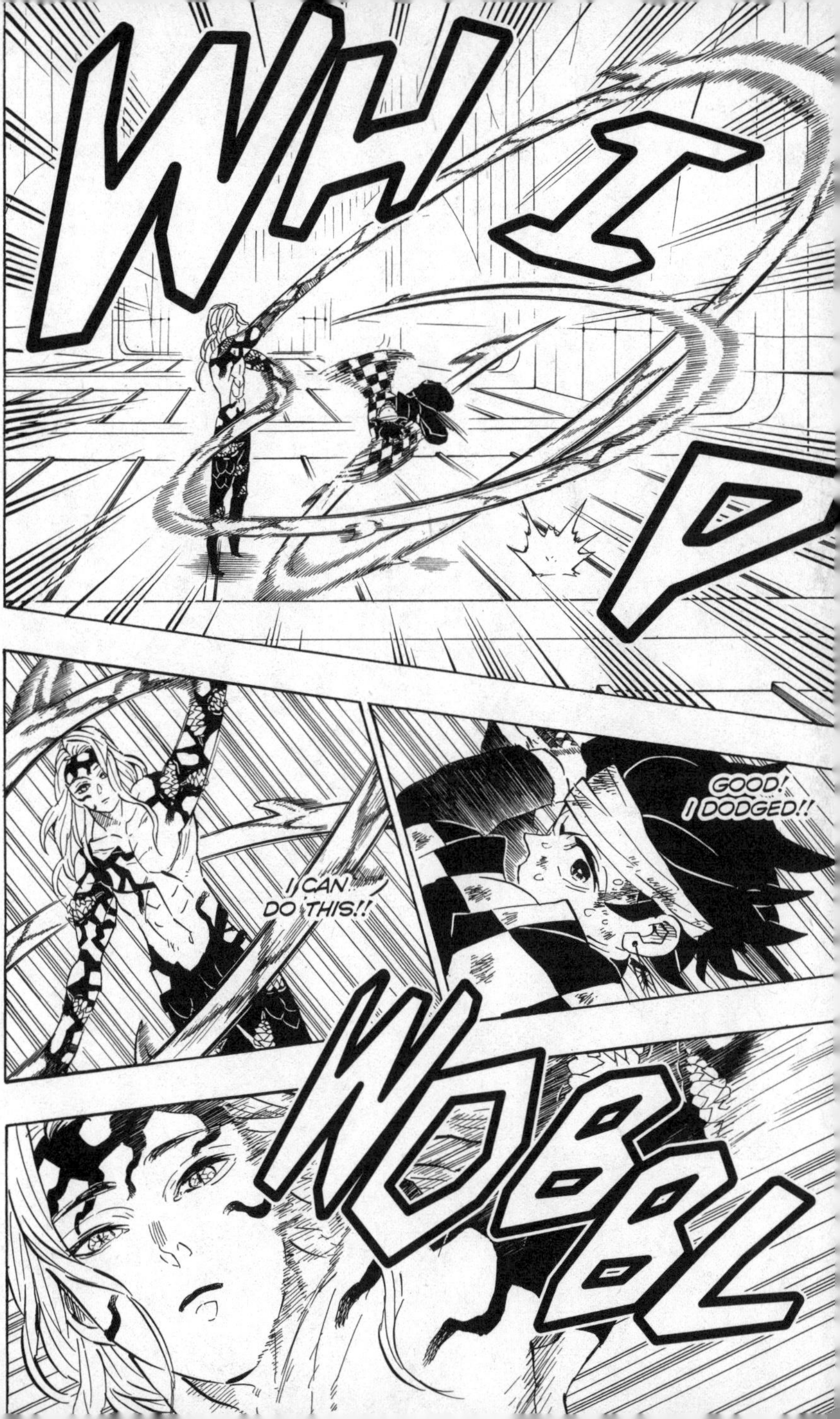
WHIP
GOOD! I DODGED!!
I CAN DO THIS!!
WOBBL

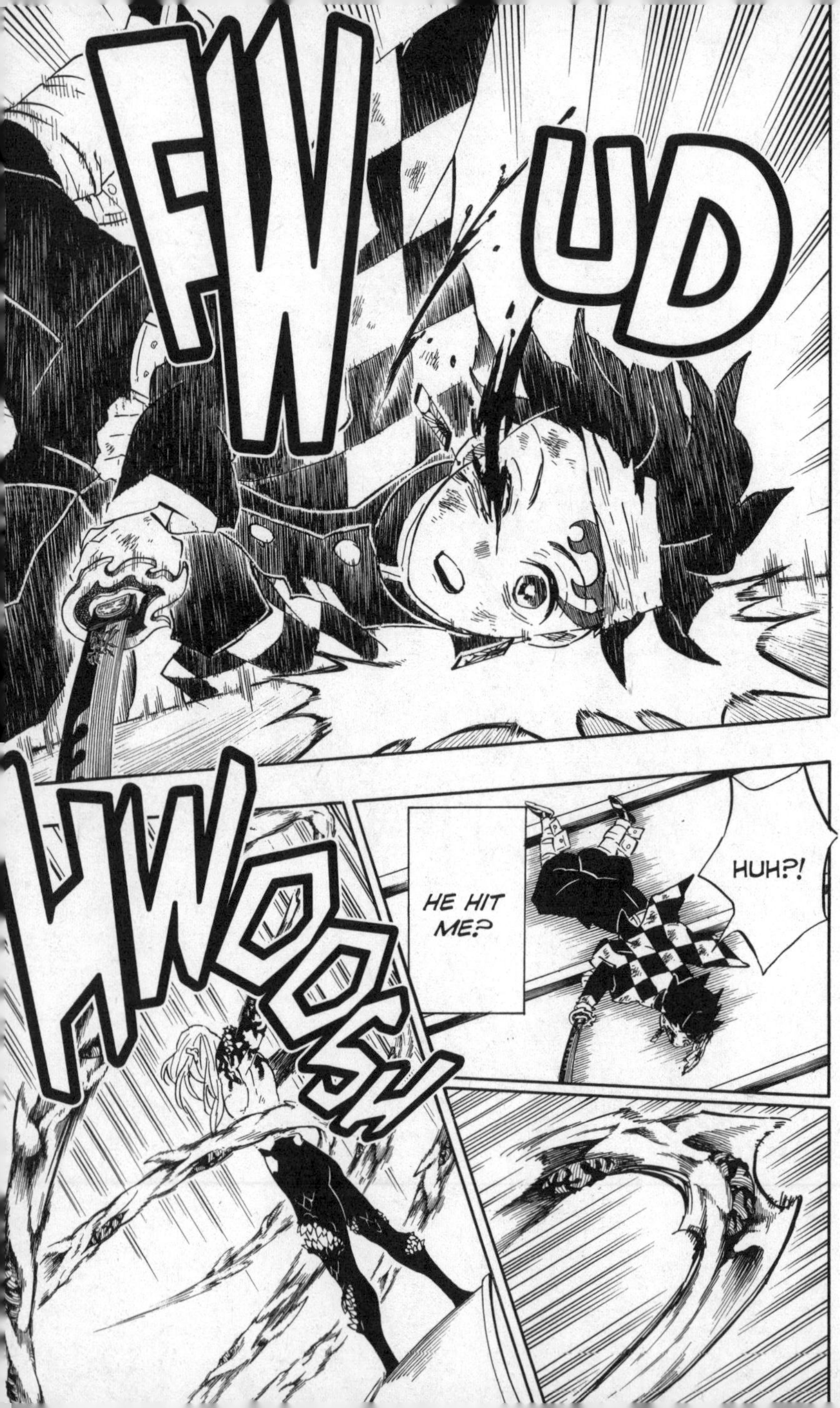
FWUD
HUH?!
HE HIT ME?
WHOOSH

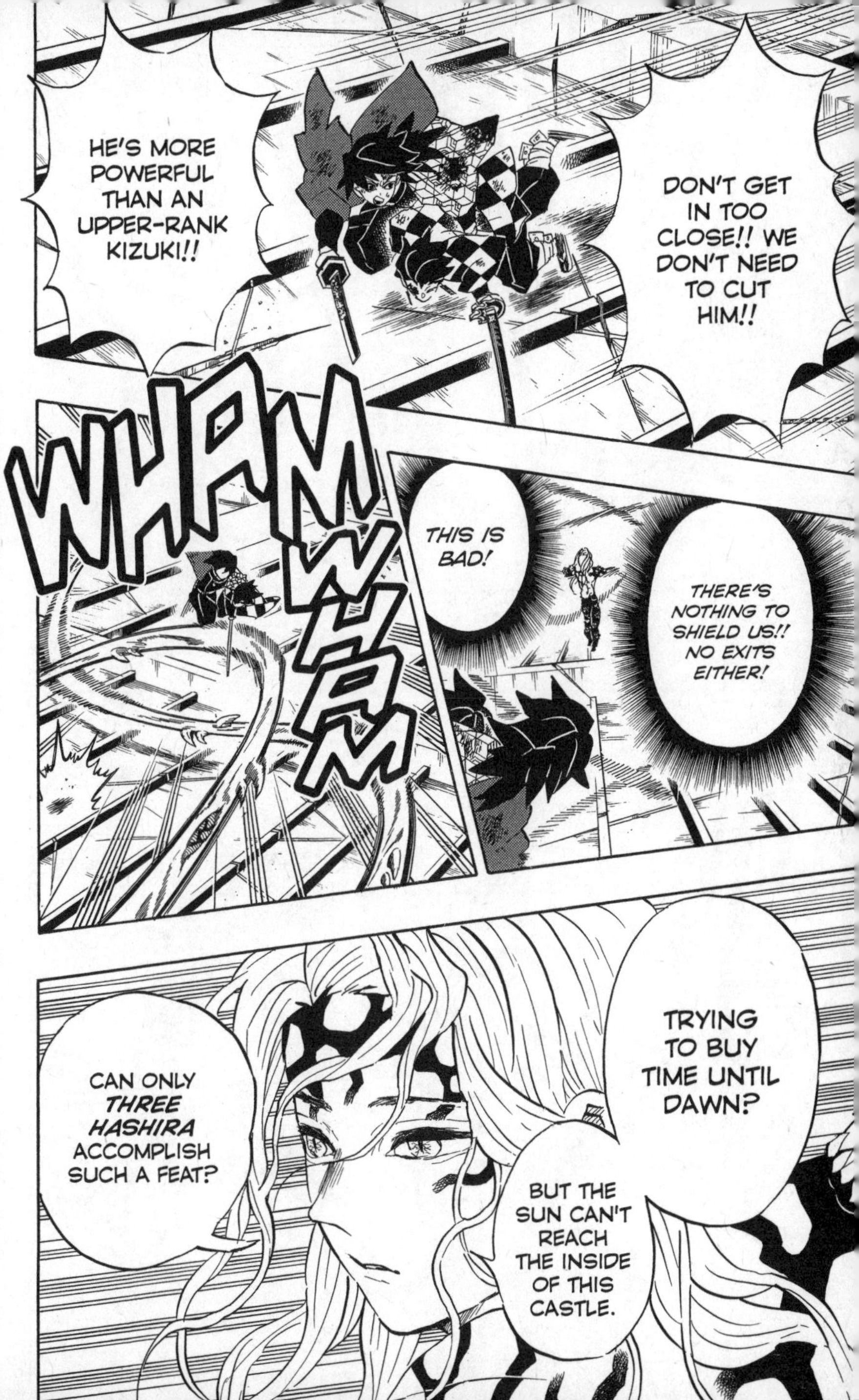
DON'T GET IN TOO CLOSE!! WE DON'T NEED TO CUT HIM!!
HE'S MORE POWERFUL THAN AN UPPER-RANK KIZUKI!!
THIS IS BAD!
THERE'S NOTHING TO SHIELD US!! NO EXITS EITHER!
WHAM
WHAM
TRYING TO BUY TIME UNTIL DAWN?
BUT THE SUN CAN'T REACH THE INSIDE OF THIS CASTLE.
CAN ONLY *THREE HASHIRA* ACCOMPLISH SUCH A FEAT?

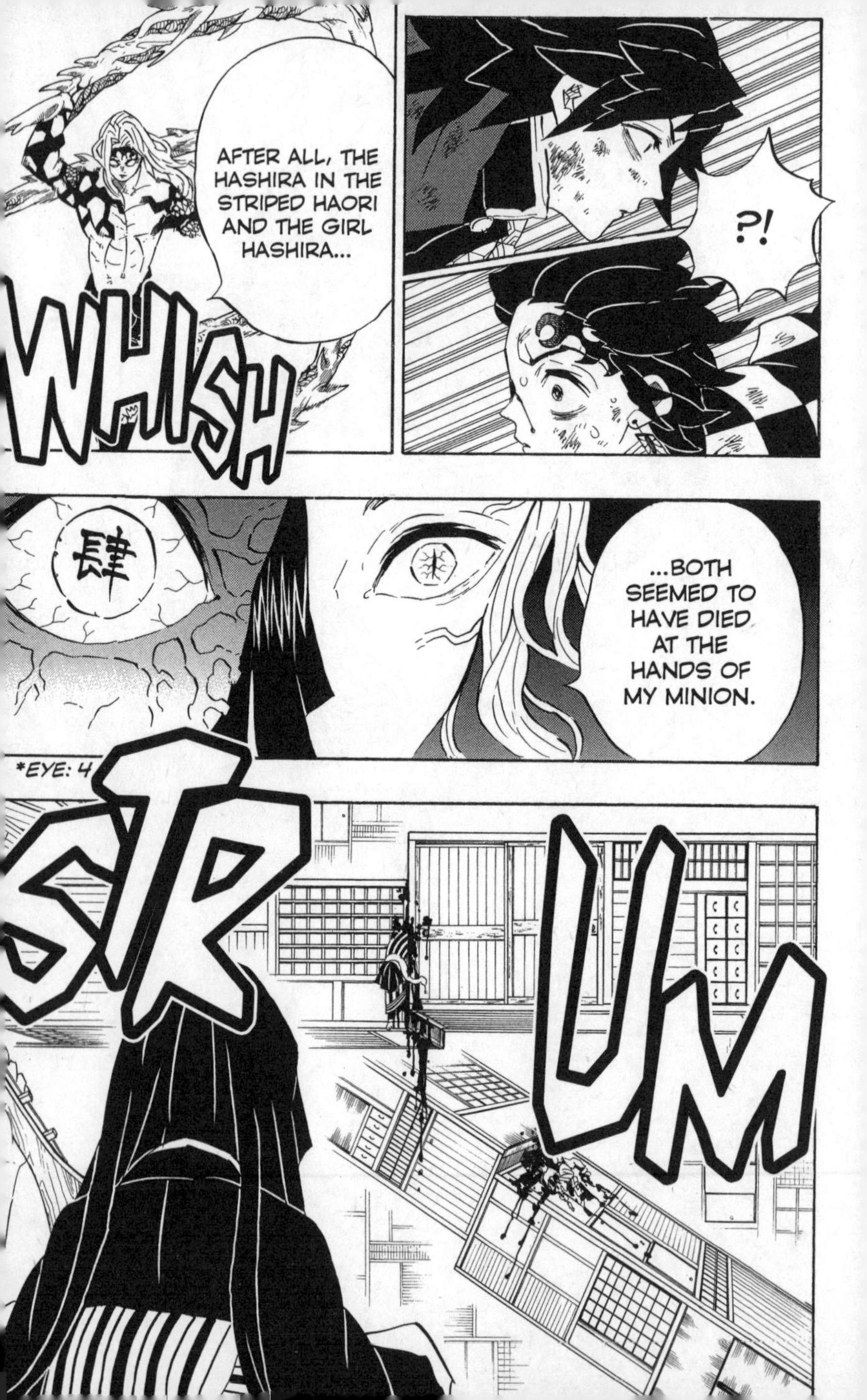
?!
AFTER ALL, THE HASHIRA IN THE STRIPED HAORI AND THE GIRL HASHIRA...
WHISH
...BOTH SEEMED TO HAVE DIED AT THE HANDS OF MY MINION.
肆
*EYE: 4

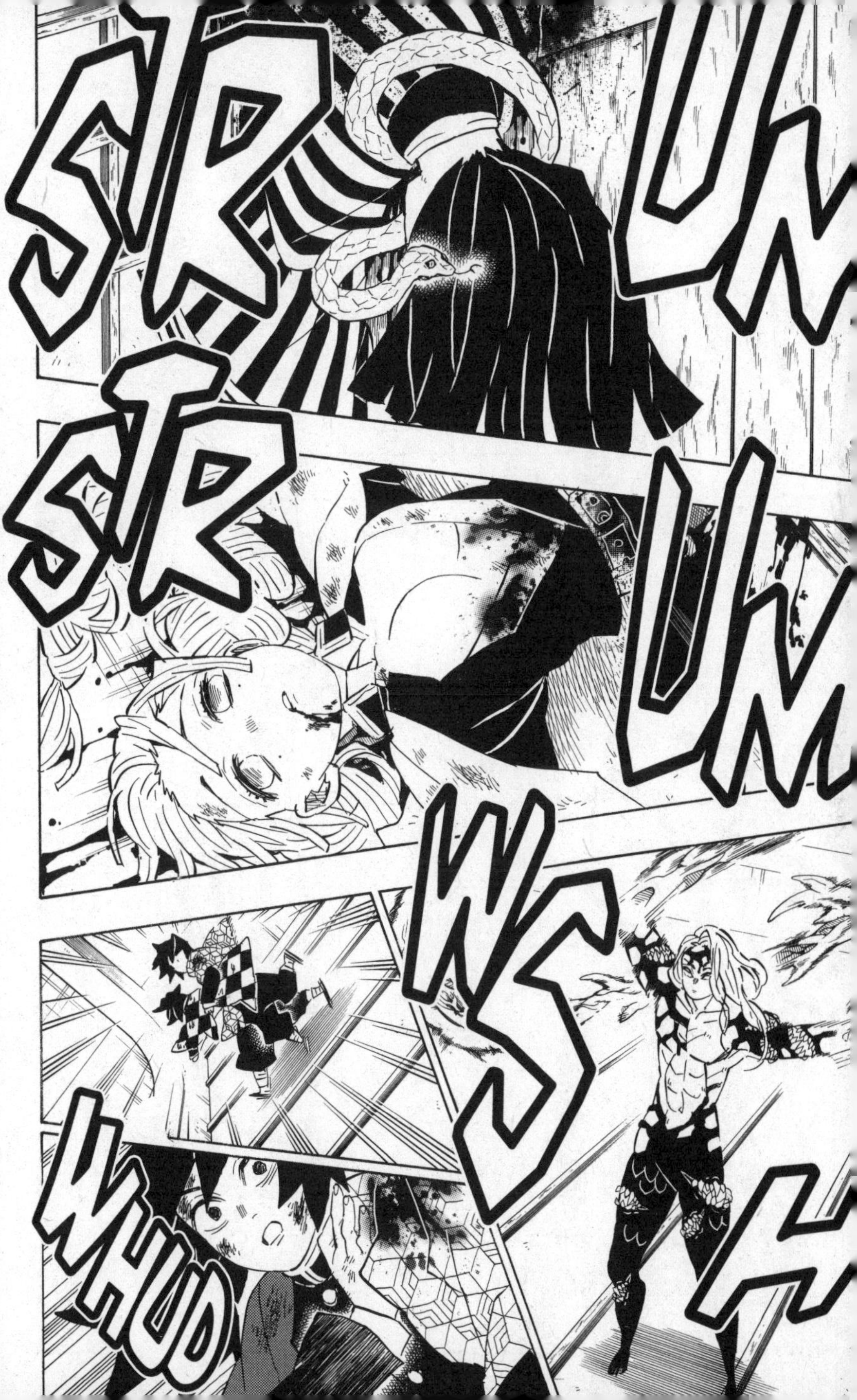

SP
UN
SP
UN
WS
H
WHUD

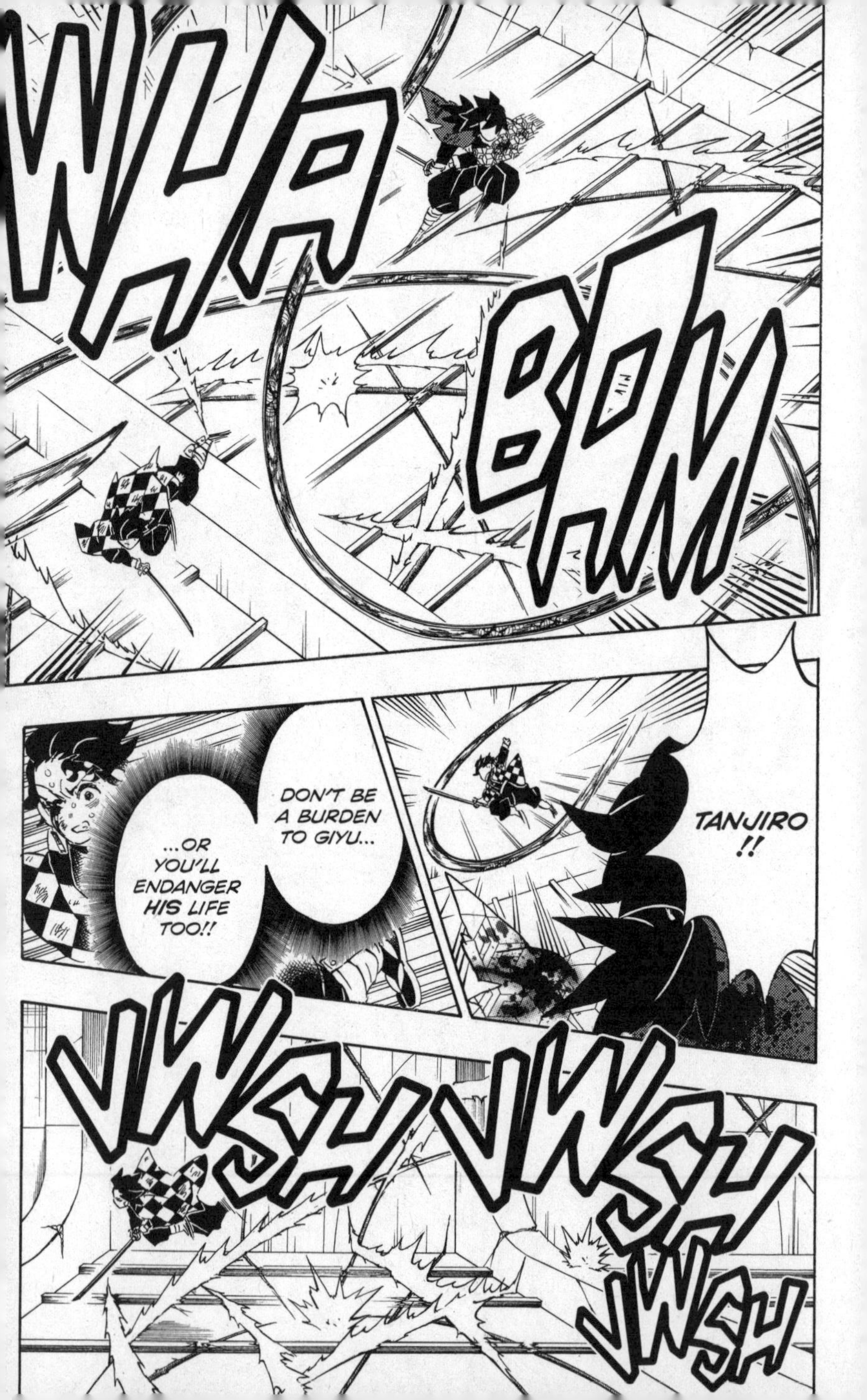
WHA
BAM
TANJIRO!!
DON'T BE A BURDEN TO GIYU...
...OR YOU'LL ENDANGER HIS LIFE TOO!!
VWSH
VWSH
VWSH

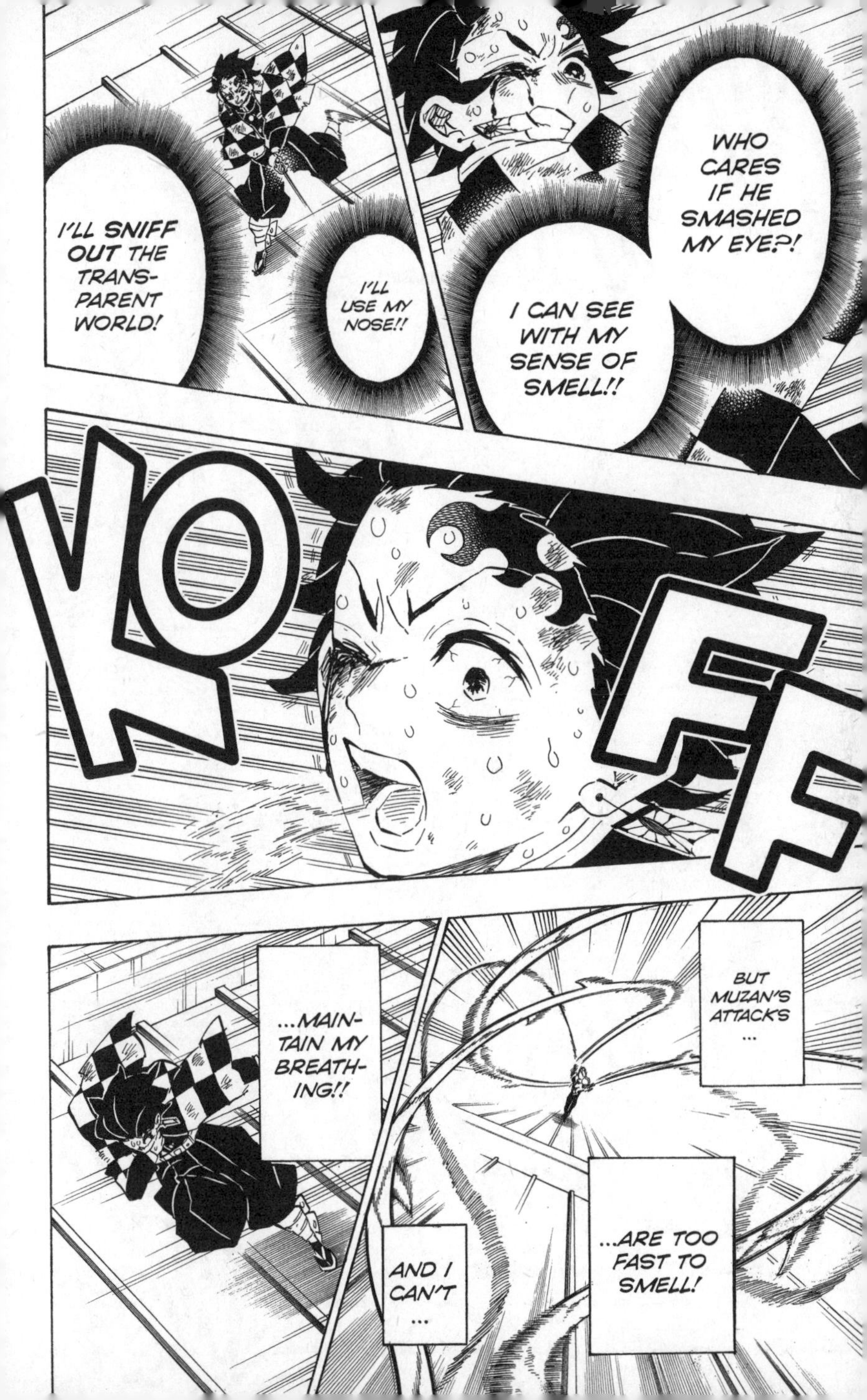
WHO CARES IF HE SMASHED MY EYE?!
I CAN SEE WITH MY SENSE OF SMELL!!
I'LL USE MY NOSE!!
I'LL SNIFF OUT THE TRANSPARENT WORLD!
VOFF
BUT MUZAN'S ATTACKS ...
...ARE TOO FAST TO SMELL!
AND I CAN'T ...
...MAINTAIN MY BREATHING!!

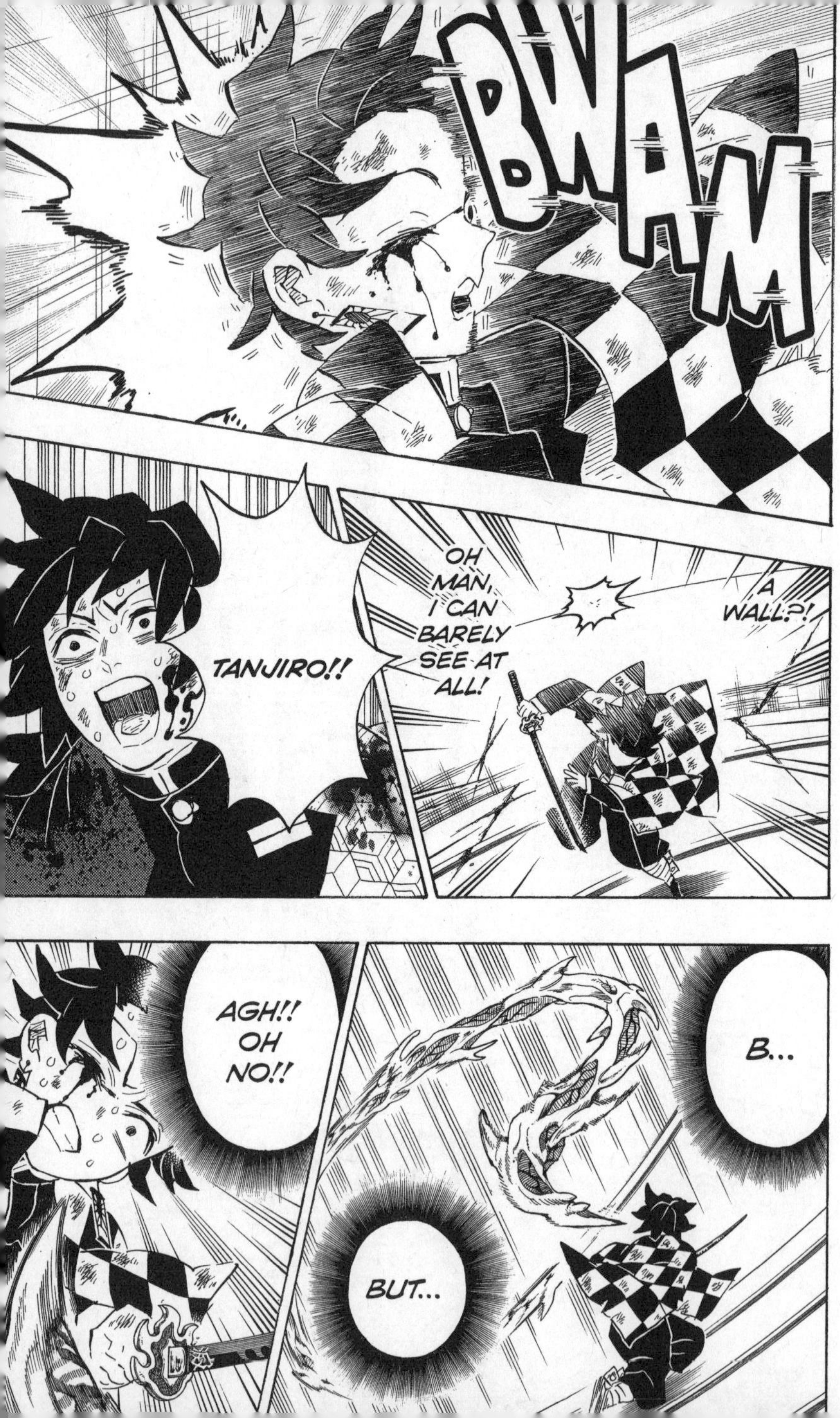
BWAM
A WALL?!
OH MAN, I CAN BARELY SEE AT ALL!
TANJIRO!!
B...
BUT...
AGH!! OH NO!!

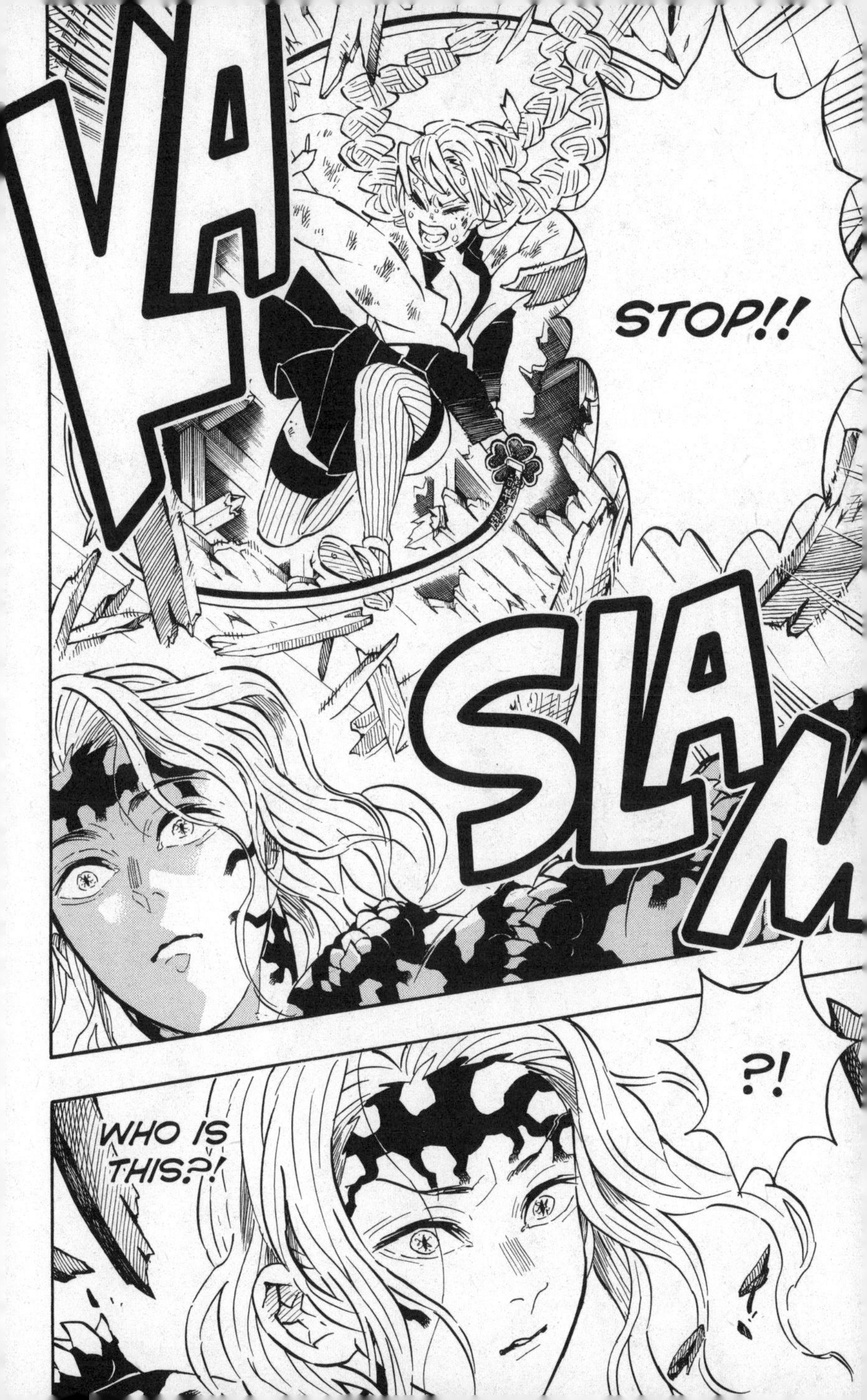
STOP!!
VA
SLA
?!
WHO IS THIS?!

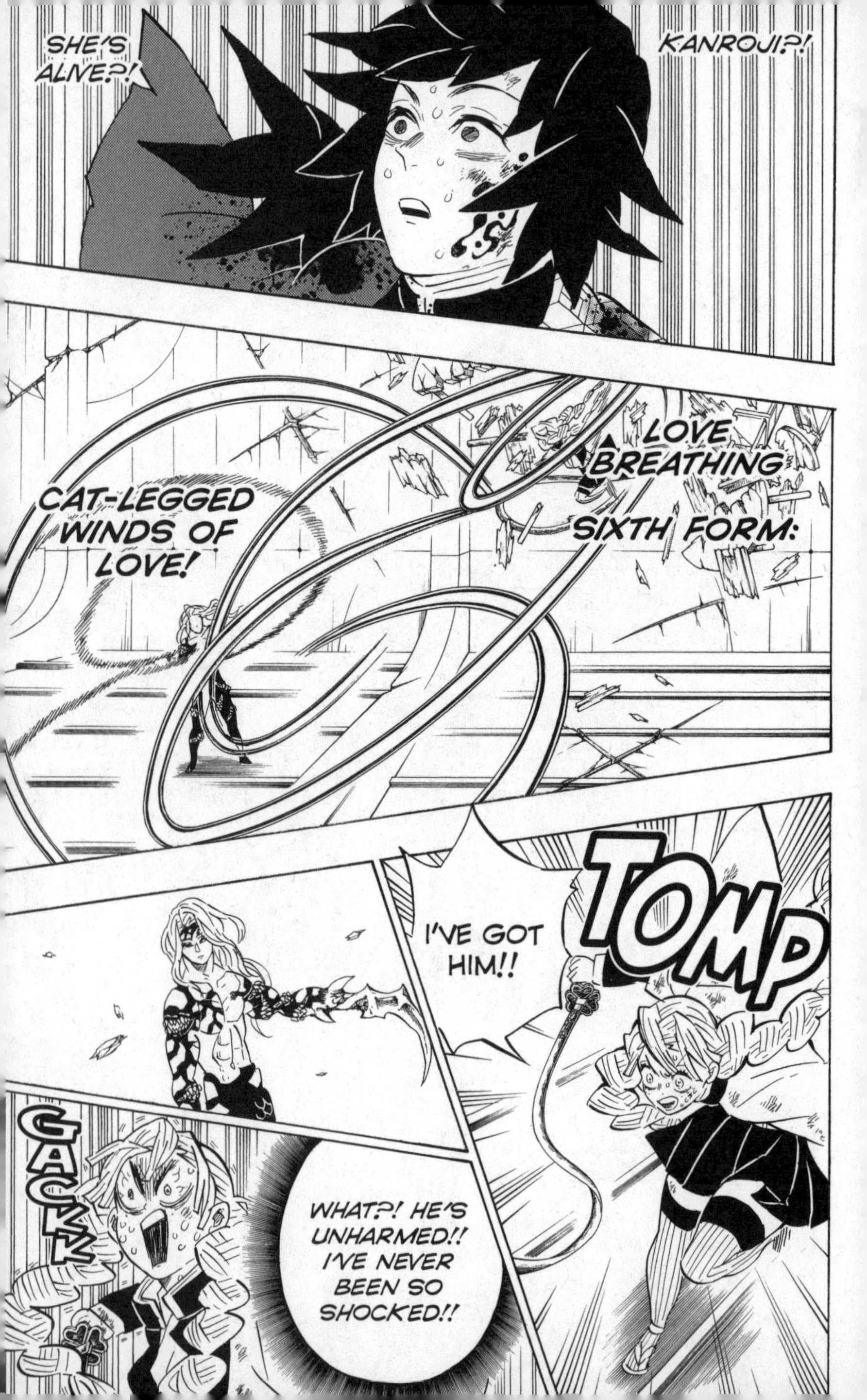
KANROJI?!
SHE'S ALIVE?!
LOVE BREATHING
SIXTH FORM:
CAT-LEGGED WINDS OF LOVE!
TOMP
I'VE GOT HIM!!
GACK
WHAT?! HE'S UNHARMED!! I'VE NEVER BEEN SO SHOCKED!!

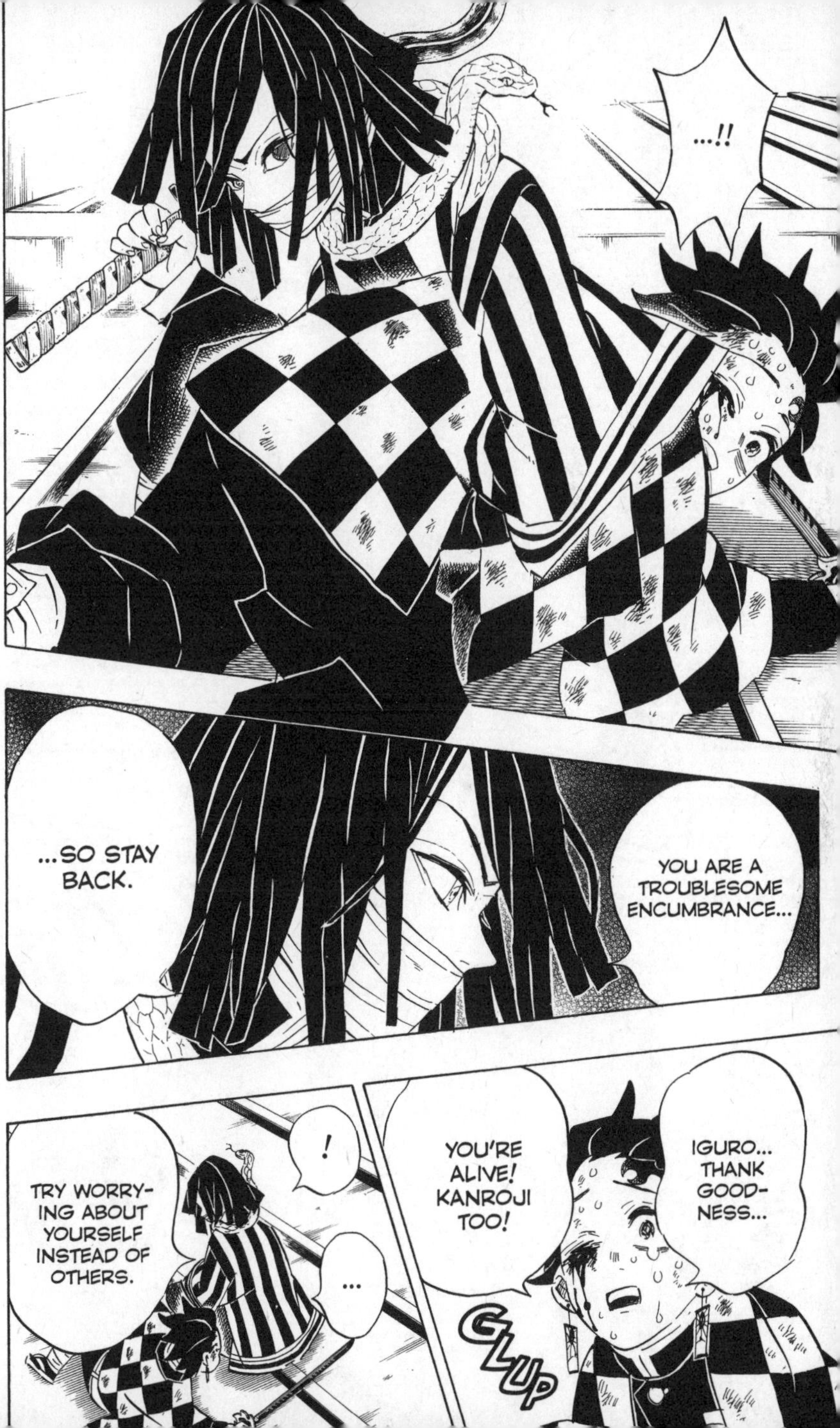
...!!
YOU ARE A TROUBLESOME ENCUMBRANCE...
...SO STAY BACK.
IGURO... THANK GOODNESS...
YOU'RE ALIVE! KANROJI TOO!
GLUP
!
TRY WORRYING ABOUT YOURSELF INSTEAD OF OTHERS.
...

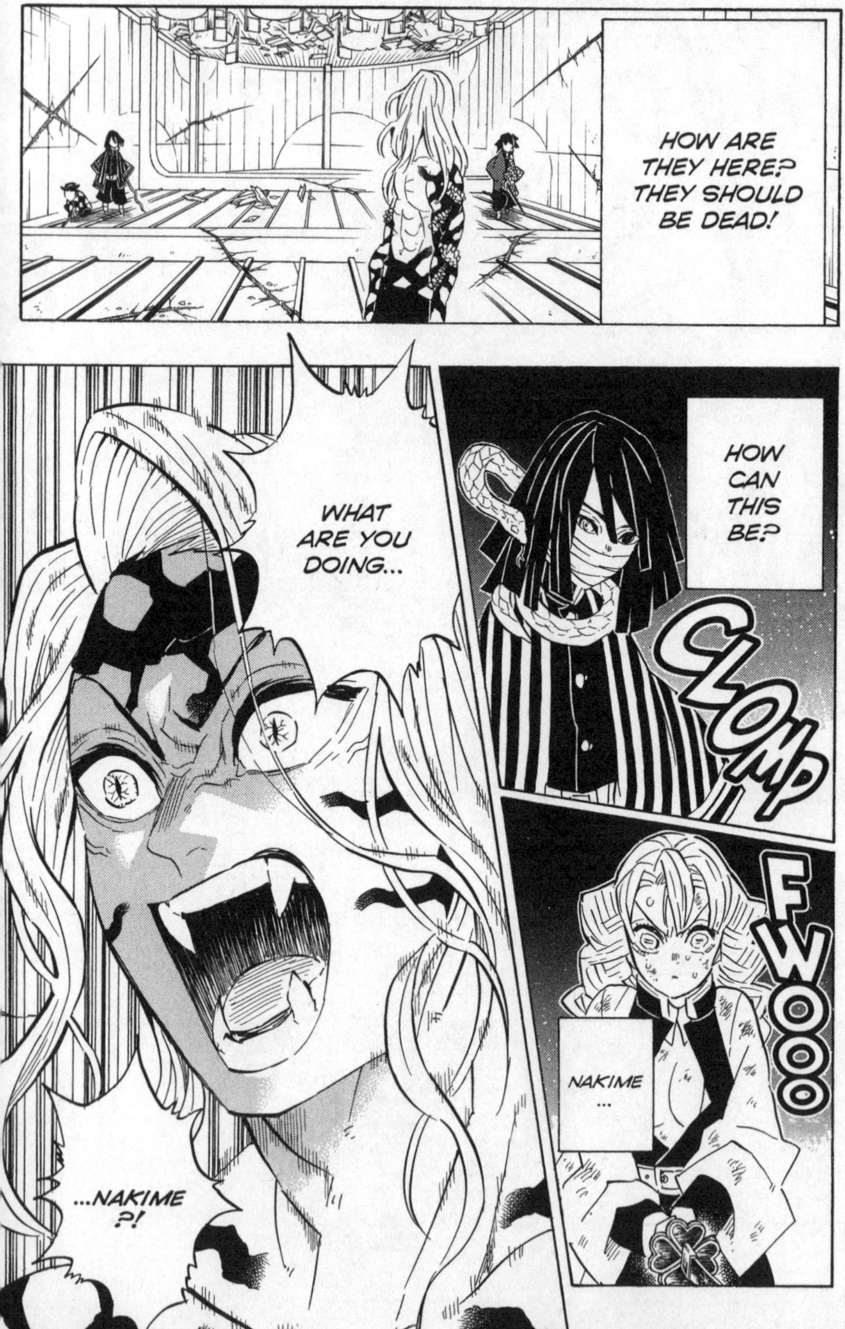
HOW ARE THEY HERE? THEY SHOULD BE DEAD!
HOW CAN THIS BE?
CLOMP
FWOOO
NAKIME ...
WHAT ARE YOU DOING...
...NAKIME ?!

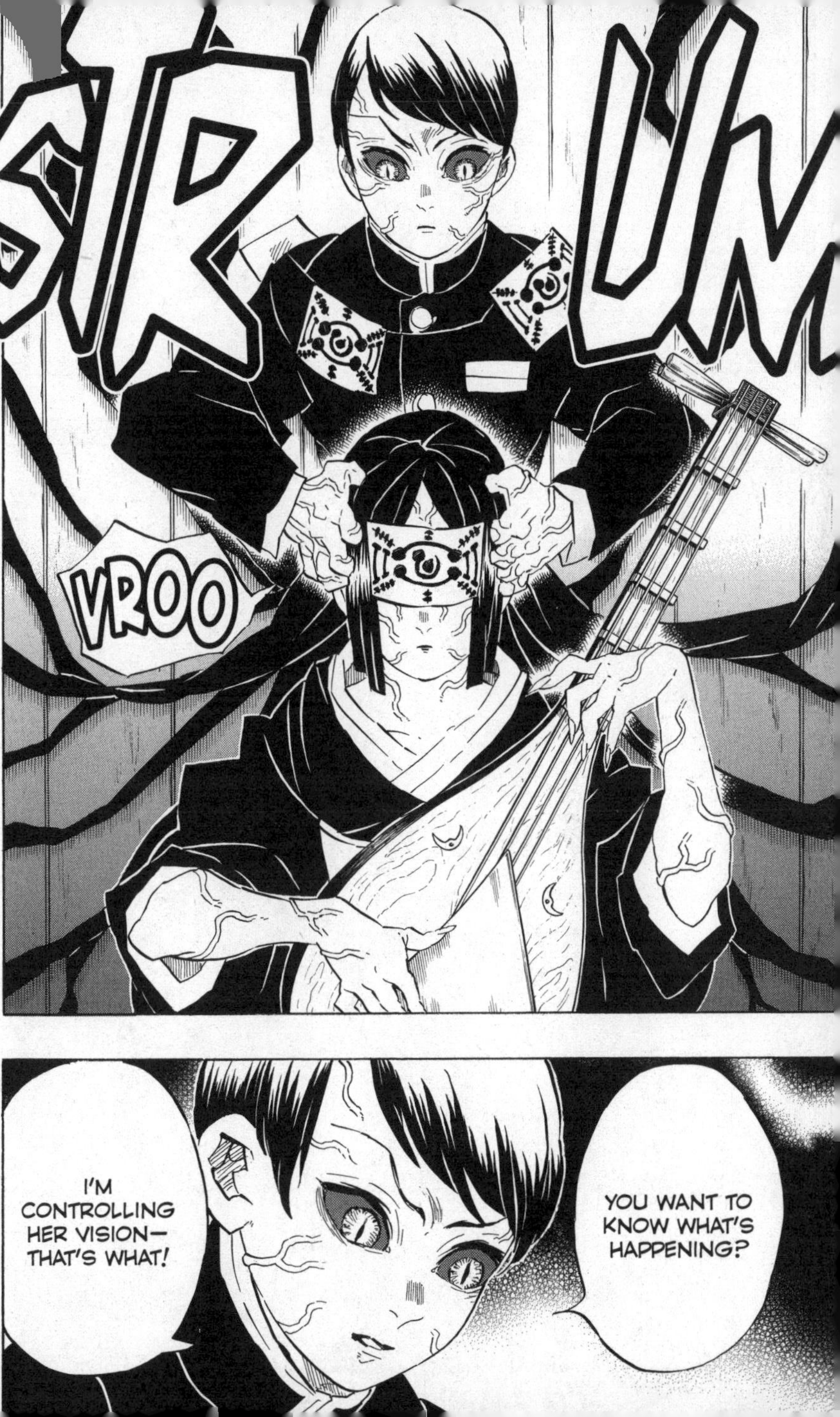
VROO
YOU WANT TO KNOW WHAT'S HAPPENING?
I'M CONTROLLING HER VISION— THAT'S WHAT!

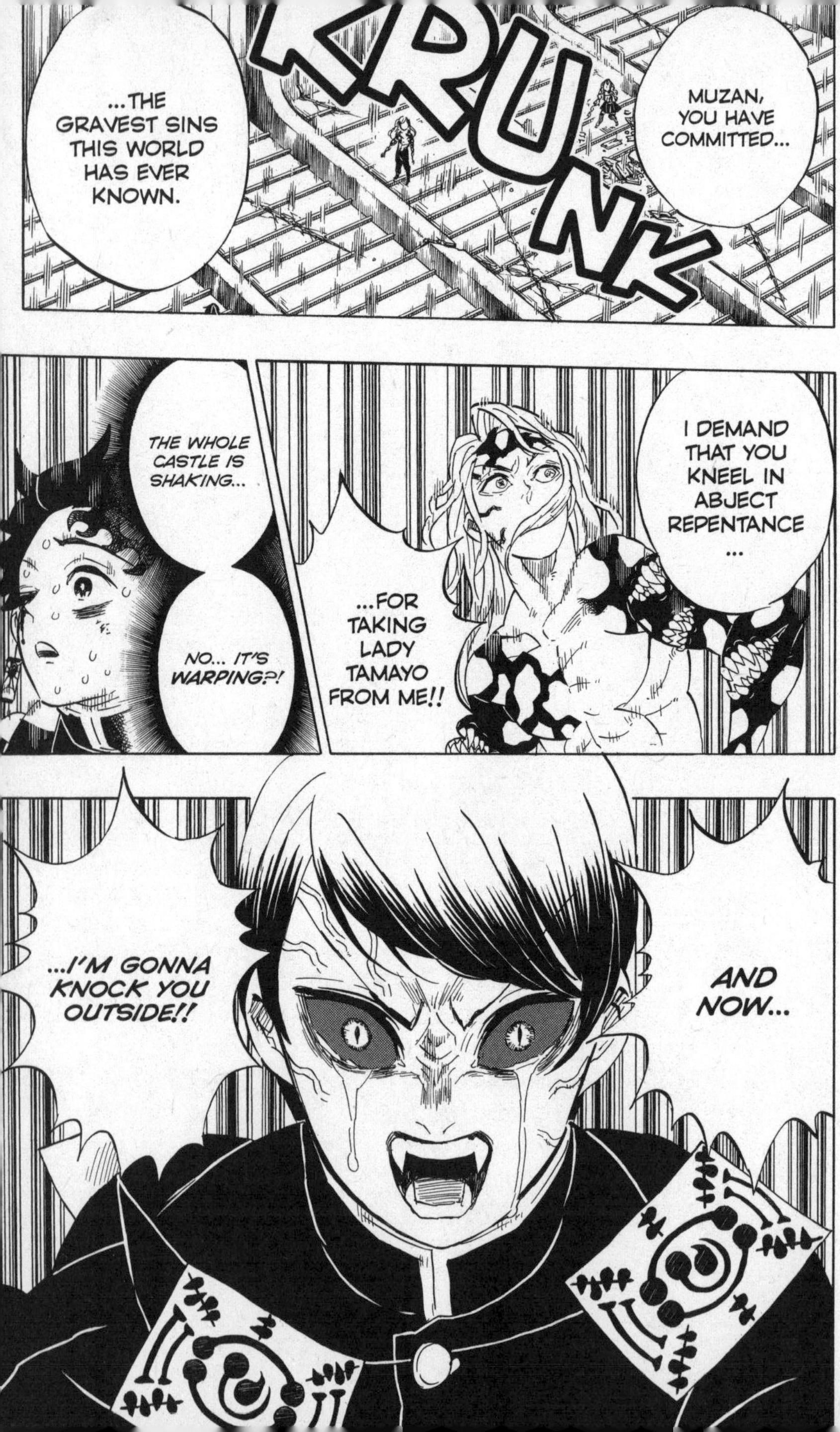
MUZAN, YOU HAVE COMMITTED...
KRUNK
...THE GRAVEST SINS THIS WORLD HAS EVER KNOWN.
I DEMAND THAT YOU KNEEL IN ABJECT REPENTANCE ...
...FOR TAKING LADY TAMAYO FROM ME!!
THE WHOLE CASTLE IS SHAKING...
NO... IT'S WARPING?!
AND NOW...
...I'M GONNA KNOCK YOU OUTSIDE!!

Demon Slayer Corps uniform tailor
Masao Maeda

Q.

Are Kanao's culottes getting shorter and shorter?

A.

No! Of course not! Why do you say that? They just look that way because you have a dirty mind! Are you crazy?! I can't believe you! And I'm talking fast? That's your imagination. You really are annoying. I'm not angry. But I'm leaving now. Why are you calling for Shinazugawa?! No, don't!!

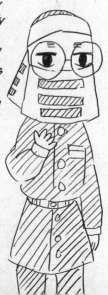

CHAPTER 183: A CLASH OF WILLS

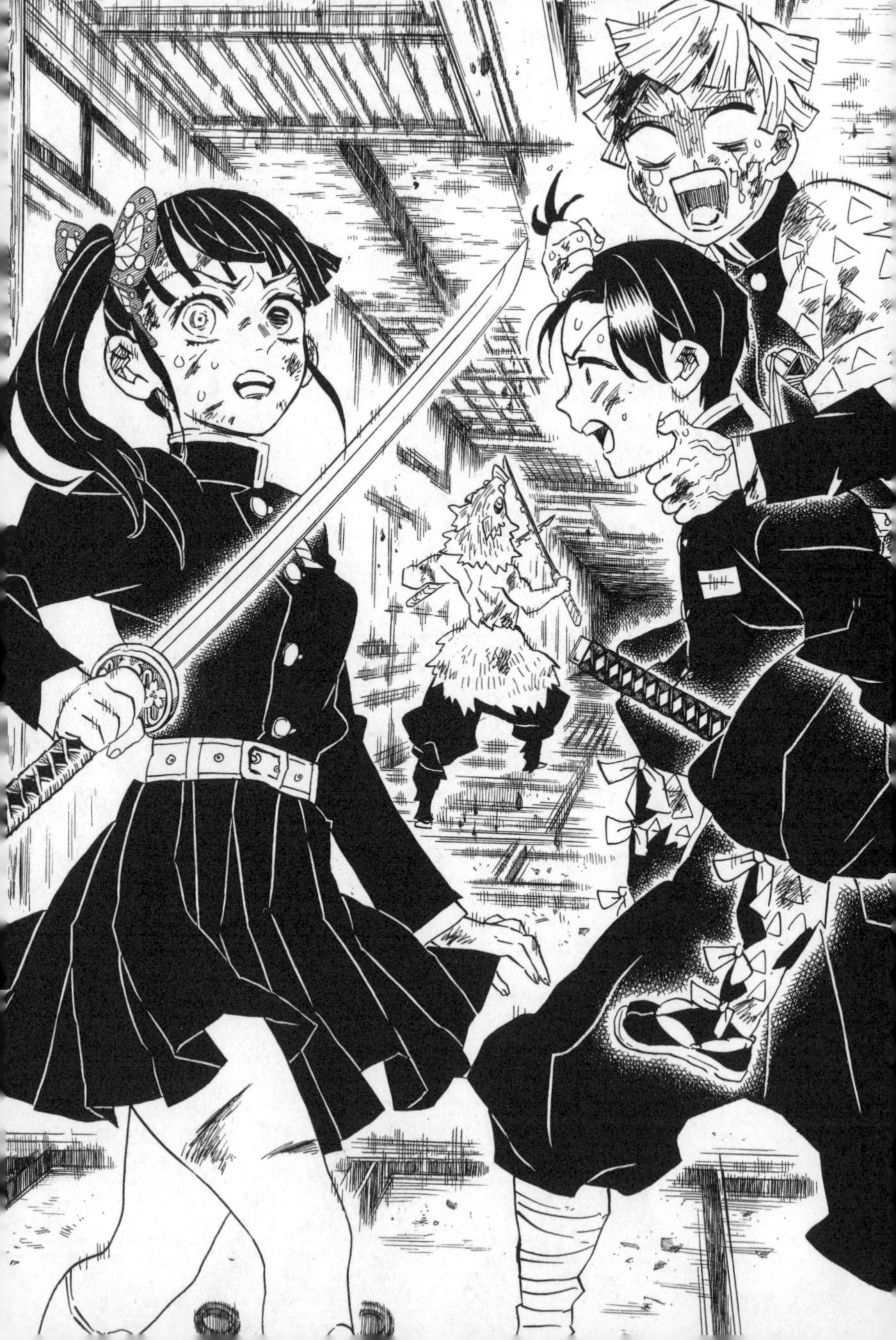

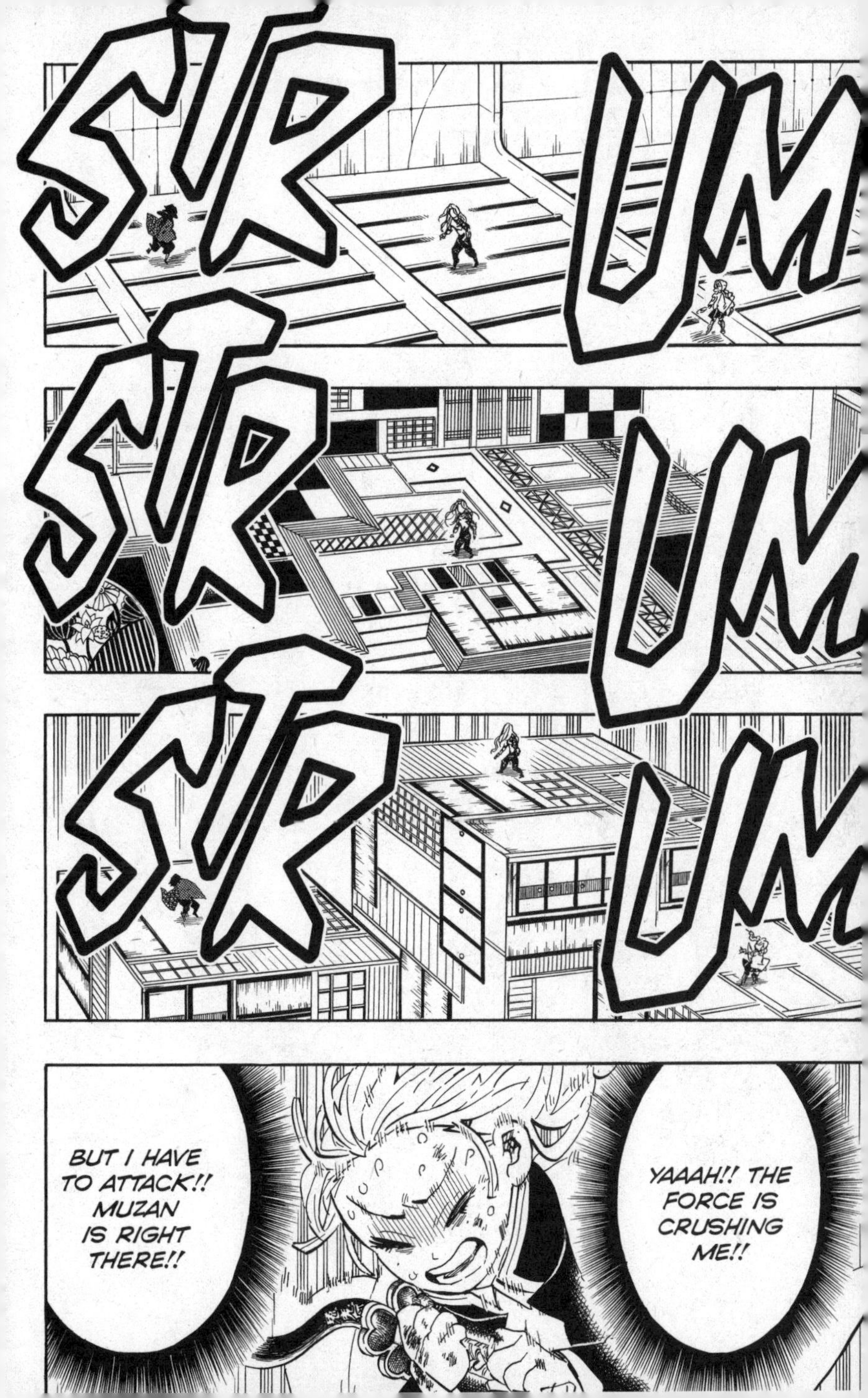
YAAAH!! THE FORCE IS CRUSHING ME!!
BUT I HAVE TO ATTACK!! MUZAN IS RIGHT THERE!!

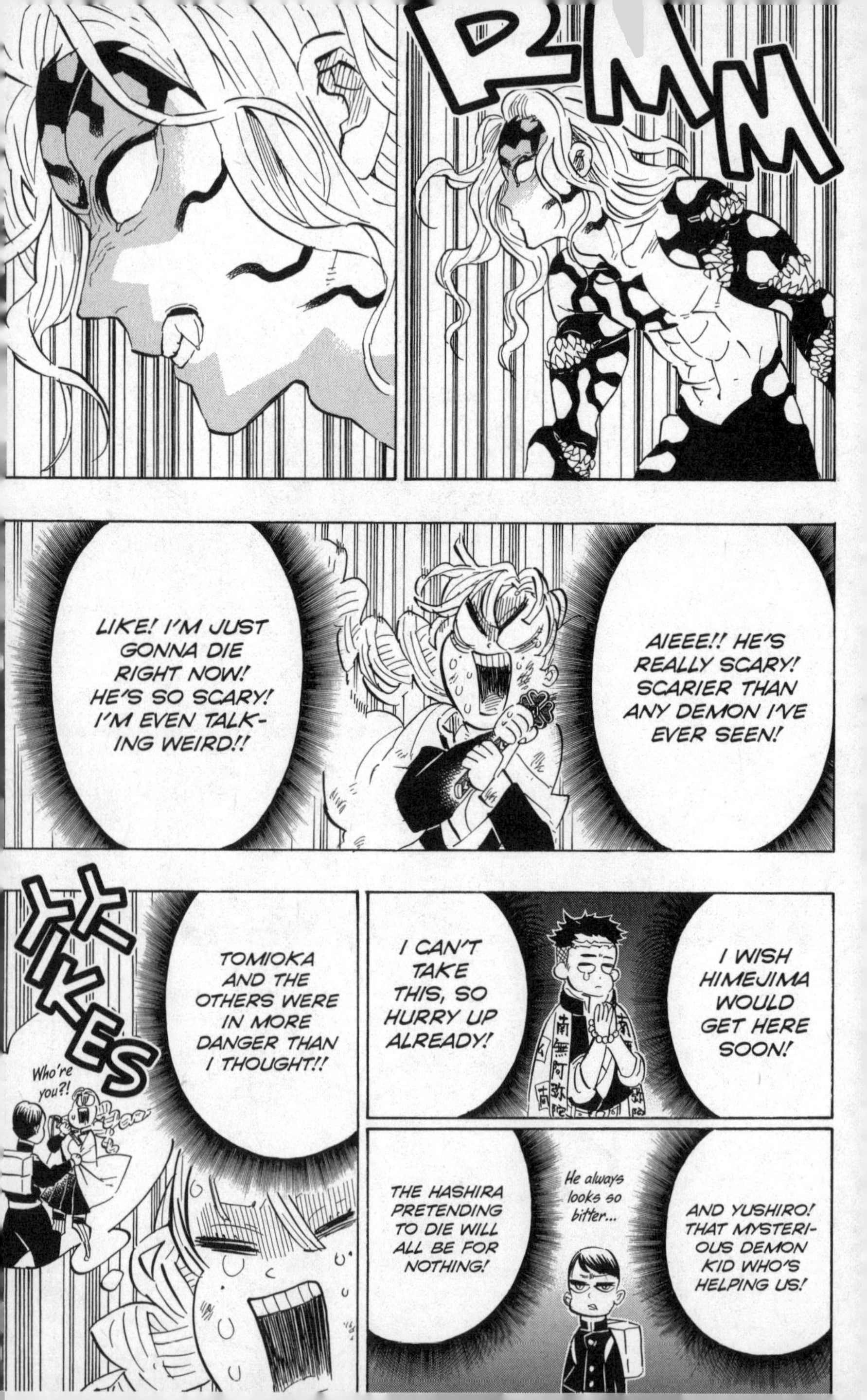
RMM
AIEEE!! HE'S REALLY SCARY! SCARIER THAN ANY DEMON I'VE EVER SEEN!
LIKE! I'M JUST GONNA DIE RIGHT NOW! HE'S SO SCARY! I'M EVEN TALKING WEIRD!!
I WISH HIMEJIMA WOULD GET HERE SOON!
I CAN'T TAKE THIS, SO HURRY UP ALREADY!
AND YUSHIRO! THAT MYSTERIOUS DEMON KID WHO'S HELPING US!
He always looks so bitter...
THE HASHIRA PRETENDING TO DIE WILL ALL BE FOR NOTHING!
TOMIOKA AND THE OTHERS WERE IN MORE DANGER THAN I THOUGHT!!
Y-YIKES
Who're you?!

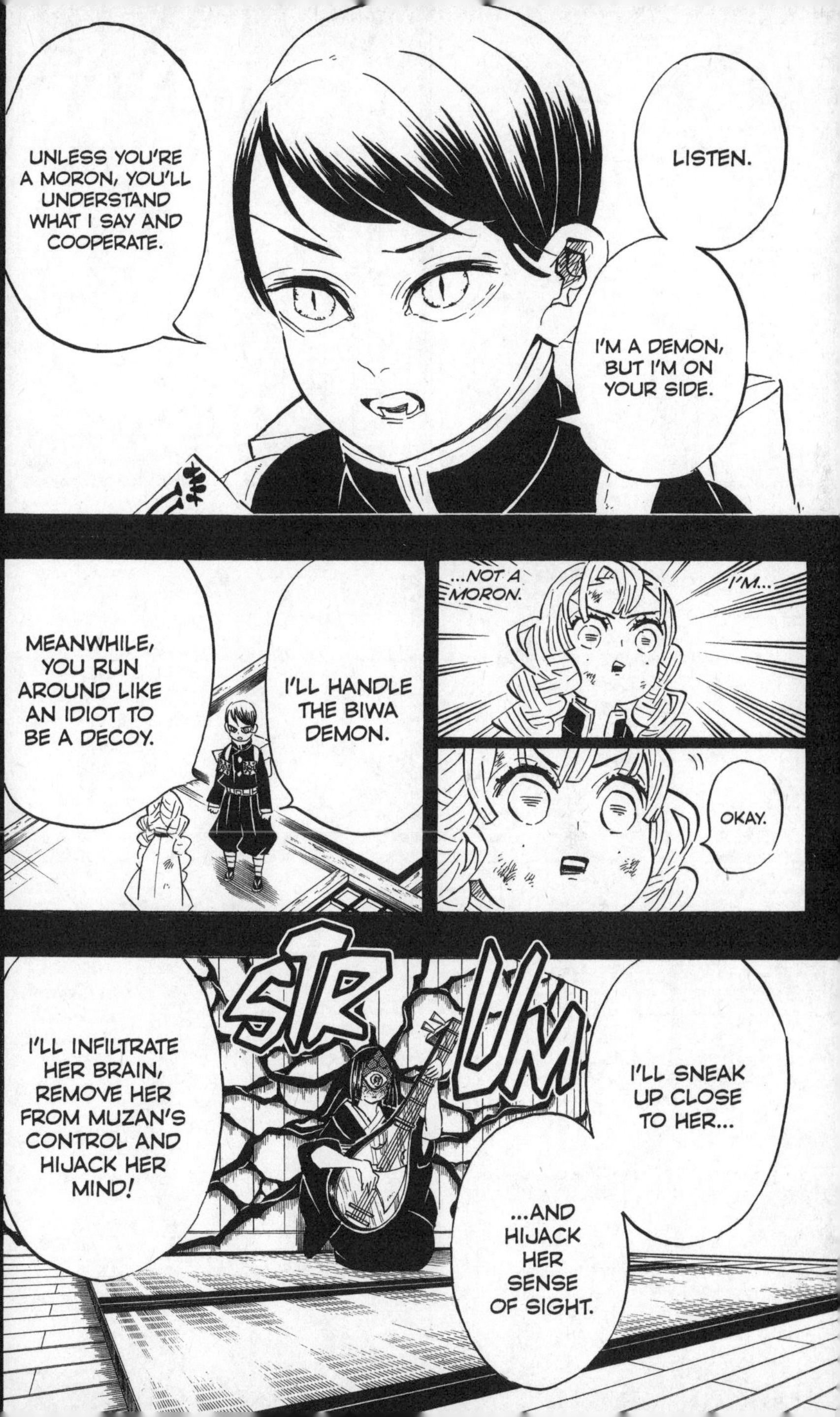
LISTEN.
I'M A DEMON, BUT I'M ON YOUR SIDE.
UNLESS YOU'RE A MORON, YOU'LL UNDERSTAND WHAT I SAY AND COOPERATE.
I'M...
...NOT A MORON.
OKAY.
I'LL HANDLE THE BIWA DEMON.
MEANWHILE, YOU RUN AROUND LIKE AN IDIOT TO BE A DECOY.
STRUM
I'LL SNEAK UP CLOSE TO HER...
...AND HIJACK HER SENSE OF SIGHT.
I'LL INFILTRATE HER BRAIN, REMOVE HER FROM MUZAN'S CONTROL AND HIJACK HER MIND!

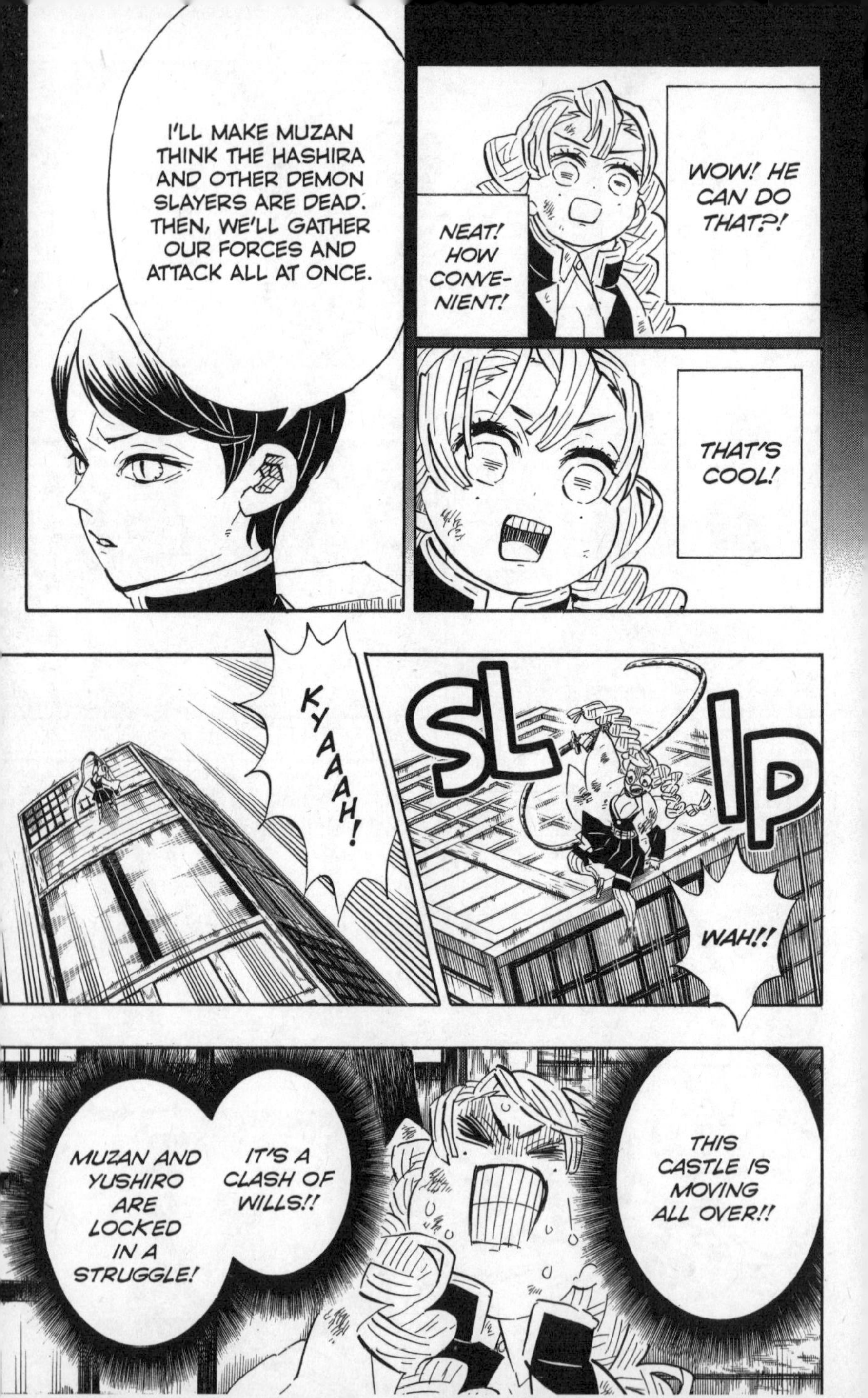
WOW! HE CAN DO THAT?!
NEAT! HOW CONVENIENT!
THAT'S COOL!
I'LL MAKE MUZAN THINK THE HASHIRA AND OTHER DEMON SLAYERS ARE DEAD. THEN, WE'LL GATHER OUR FORCES AND ATTACK ALL AT ONCE.
SLIP
WAH!!
KYAAAAH!
THIS CASTLE IS MOVING ALL OVER!!
IT'S A CLASH OF WILLS!!
MUZAN AND YUSHIRO ARE LOCKED IN A STRUGGLE!

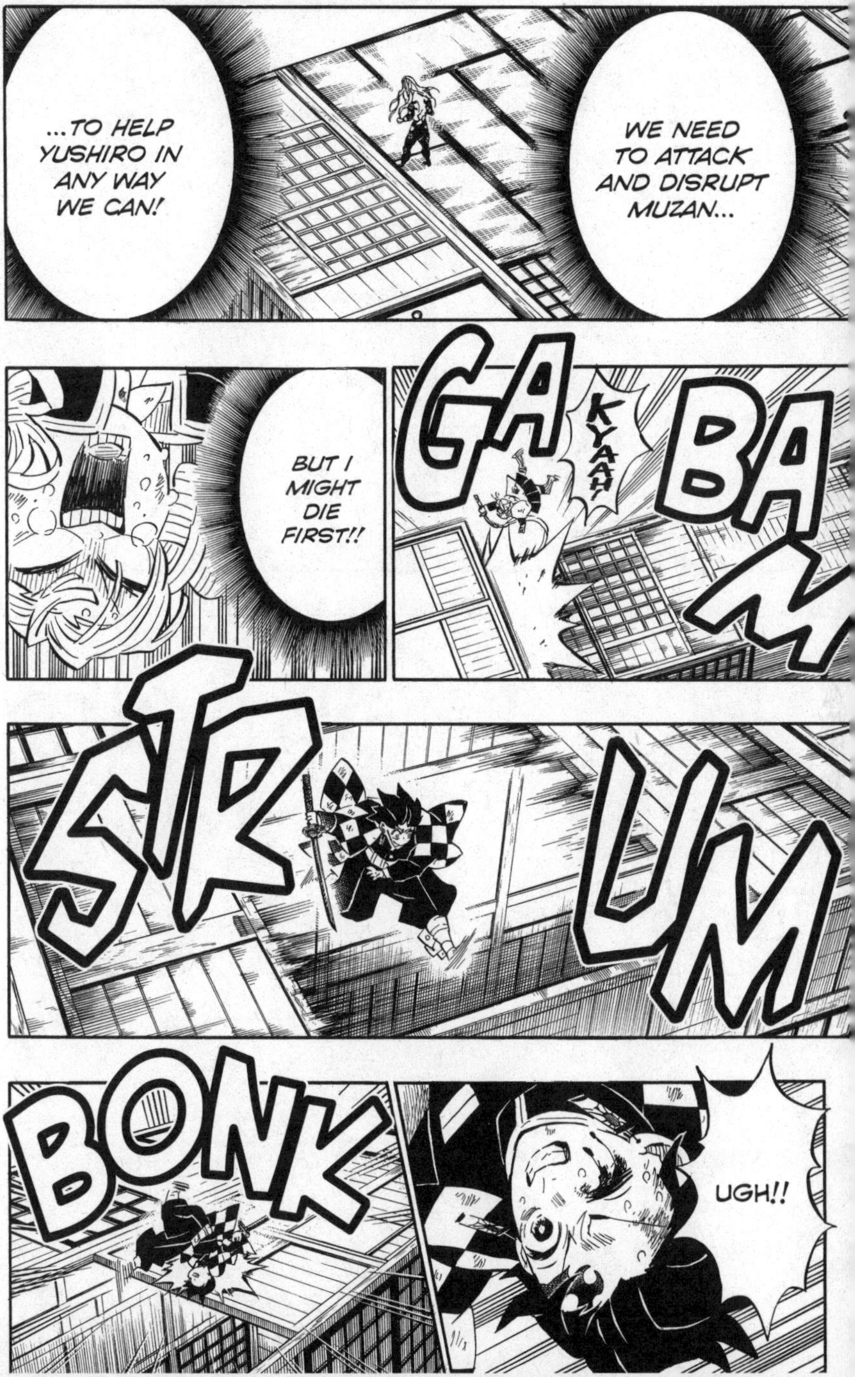
WE NEED TO ATTACK AND DISRUPT MUZAN...
...TO HELP YUSHIRO IN ANY WAY WE CAN!
GABAM
KYAAH!
BUT I MIGHT DIE FIRST!!
STRUM
UGH!!
BONK

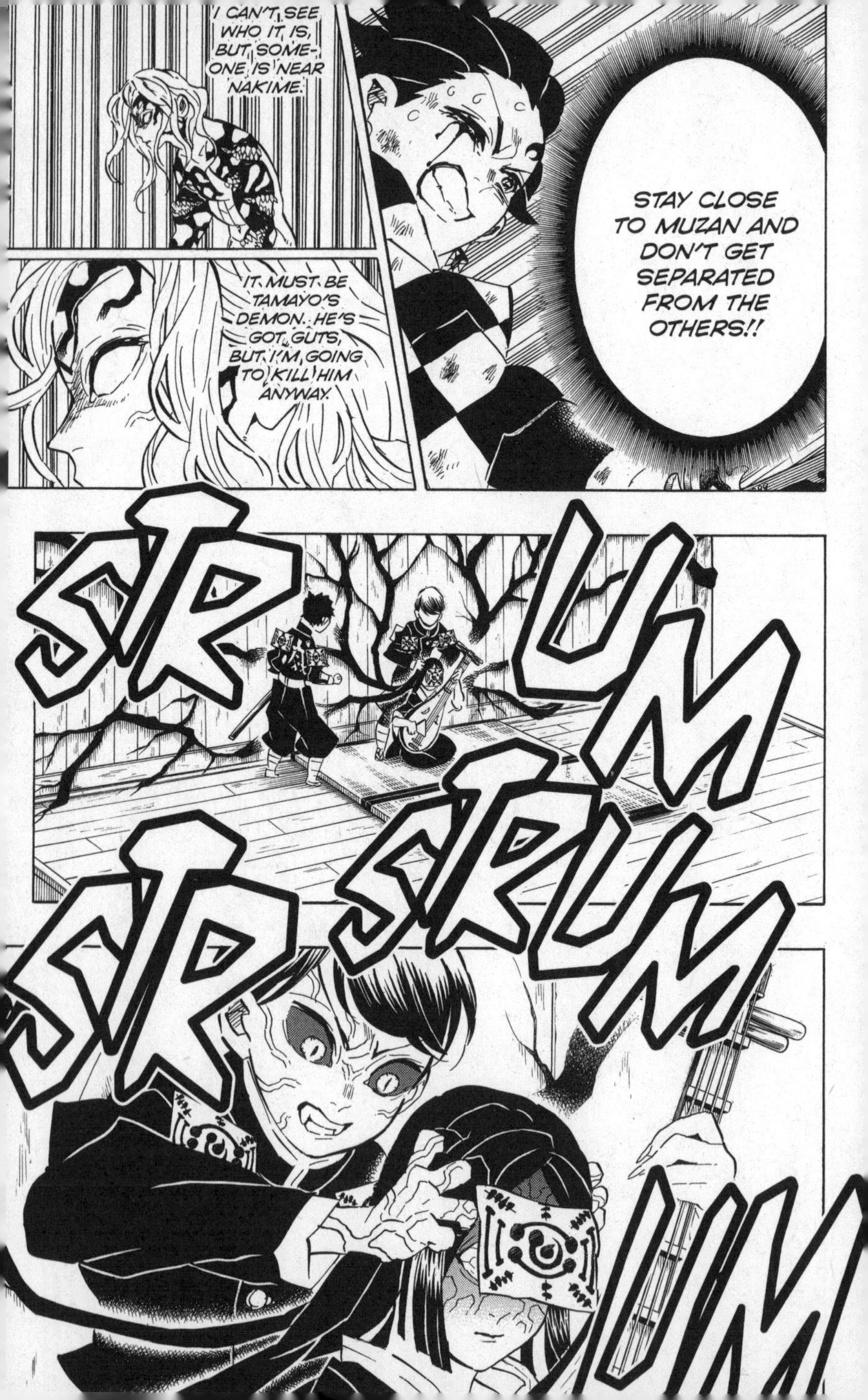
STAY CLOSE TO MUZAN AND DON'T GET SEPARATED FROM THE OTHERS!!
I CAN'T SEE WHO IT IS, BUT SOMEONE IS NEAR NAKIME.
IT MUST BE TAMAYO'S DEMON. HE'S GOT GUTS, BUT I'M GOING TO KILL HIM ANYWAY.
STRUM
STRUM
STRUM

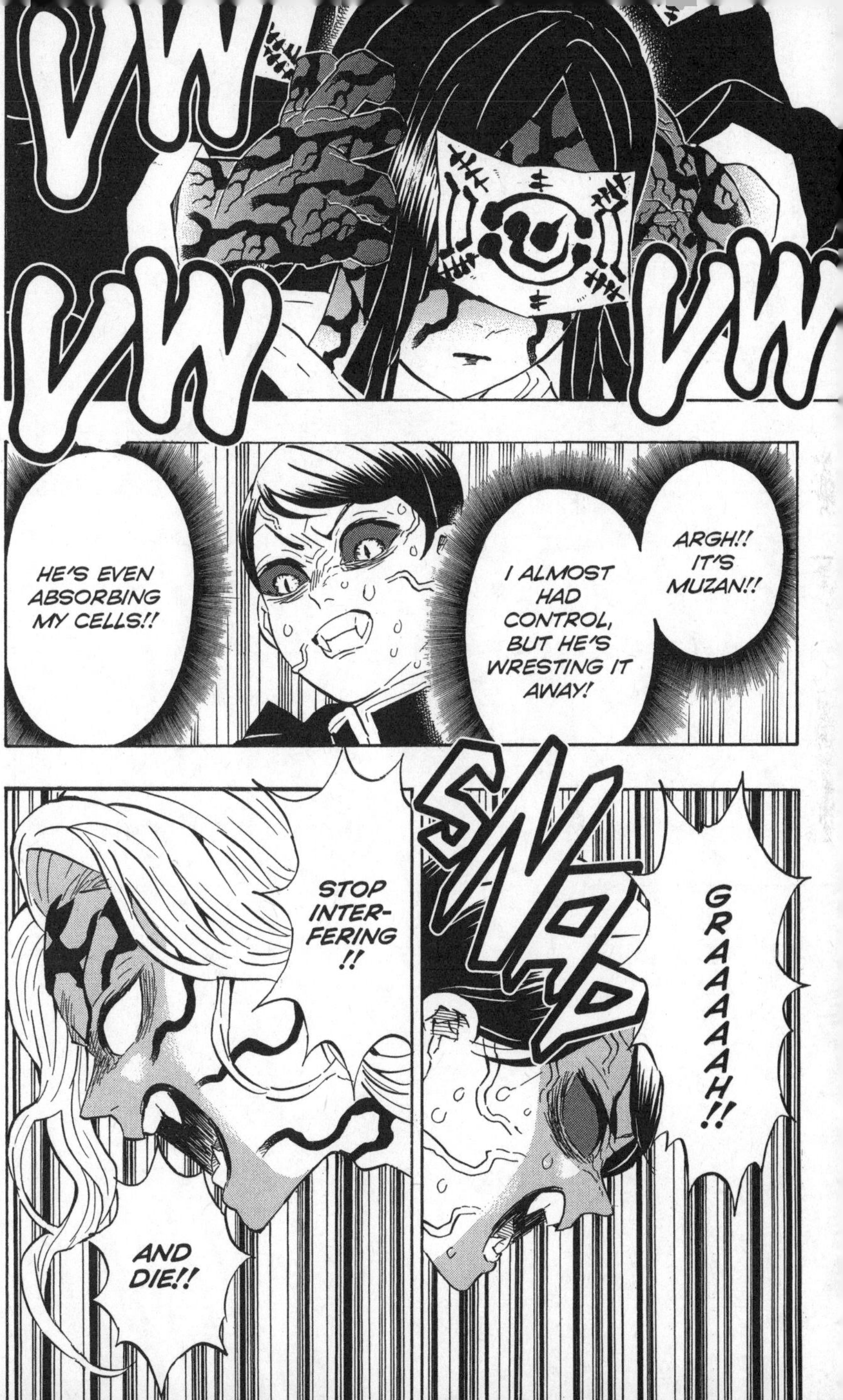
VW
VW
VW
ARGH!! IT'S MUZAN!!
I ALMOST HAD CONTROL, BUT HE'S WRESTING IT AWAY!
HE'S EVEN ABSORBING MY CELLS!!
GRAAAAAH!!
SNAP
STOP INTER-FERING!!
AND DIE!!

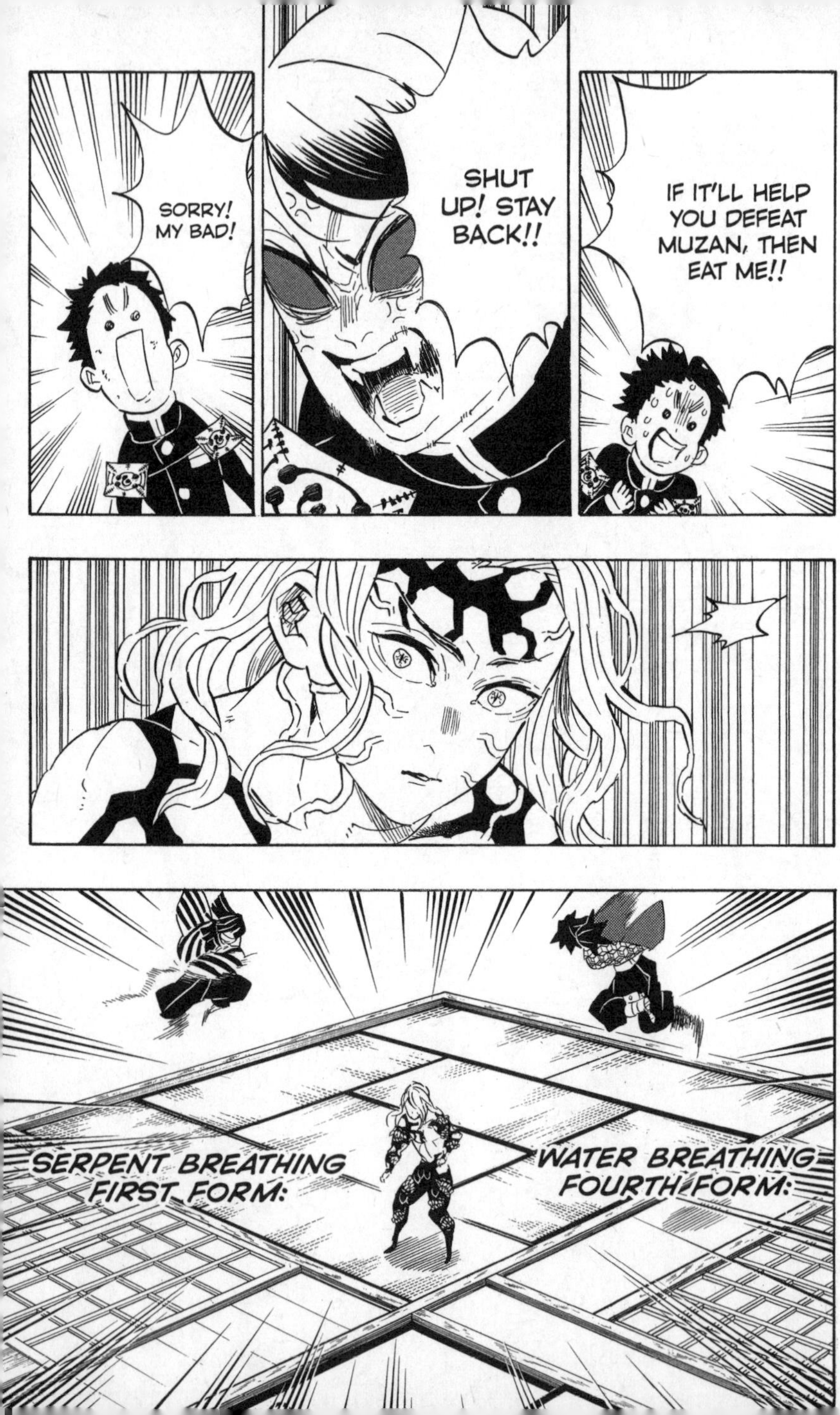
IF IT'LL HELP YOU DEFEAT MUZAN, THEN EAT ME!!
SHUT UP! STAY BACK!!
SORRY! MY BAD!
WATER BREATHING FOURTH FORM:
SERPENT BREATHING FIRST FORM:

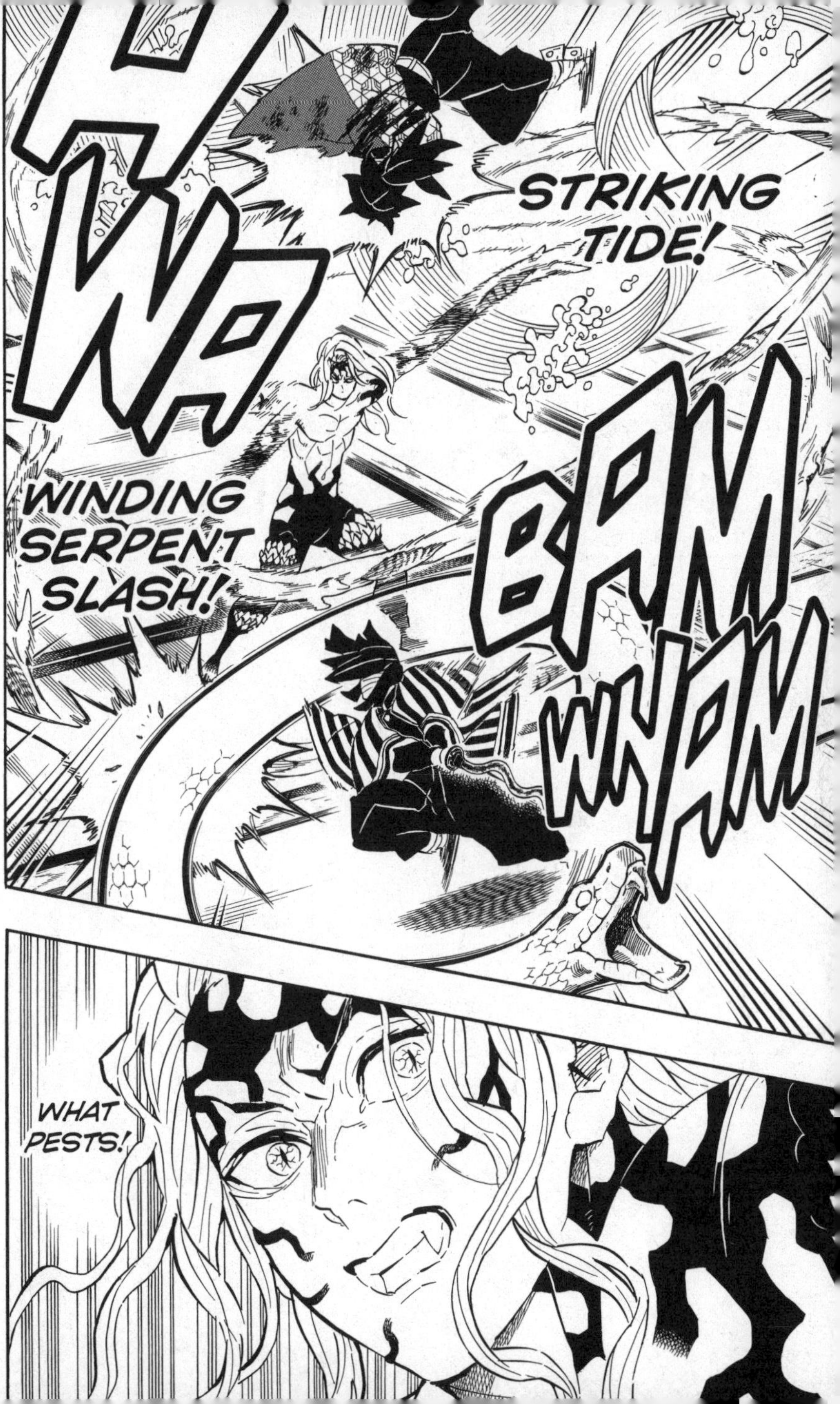
STRIKING TIDE!
BAM
WHAM
WINDING SERPENT SLASH!
WA
WHAT PESTS!

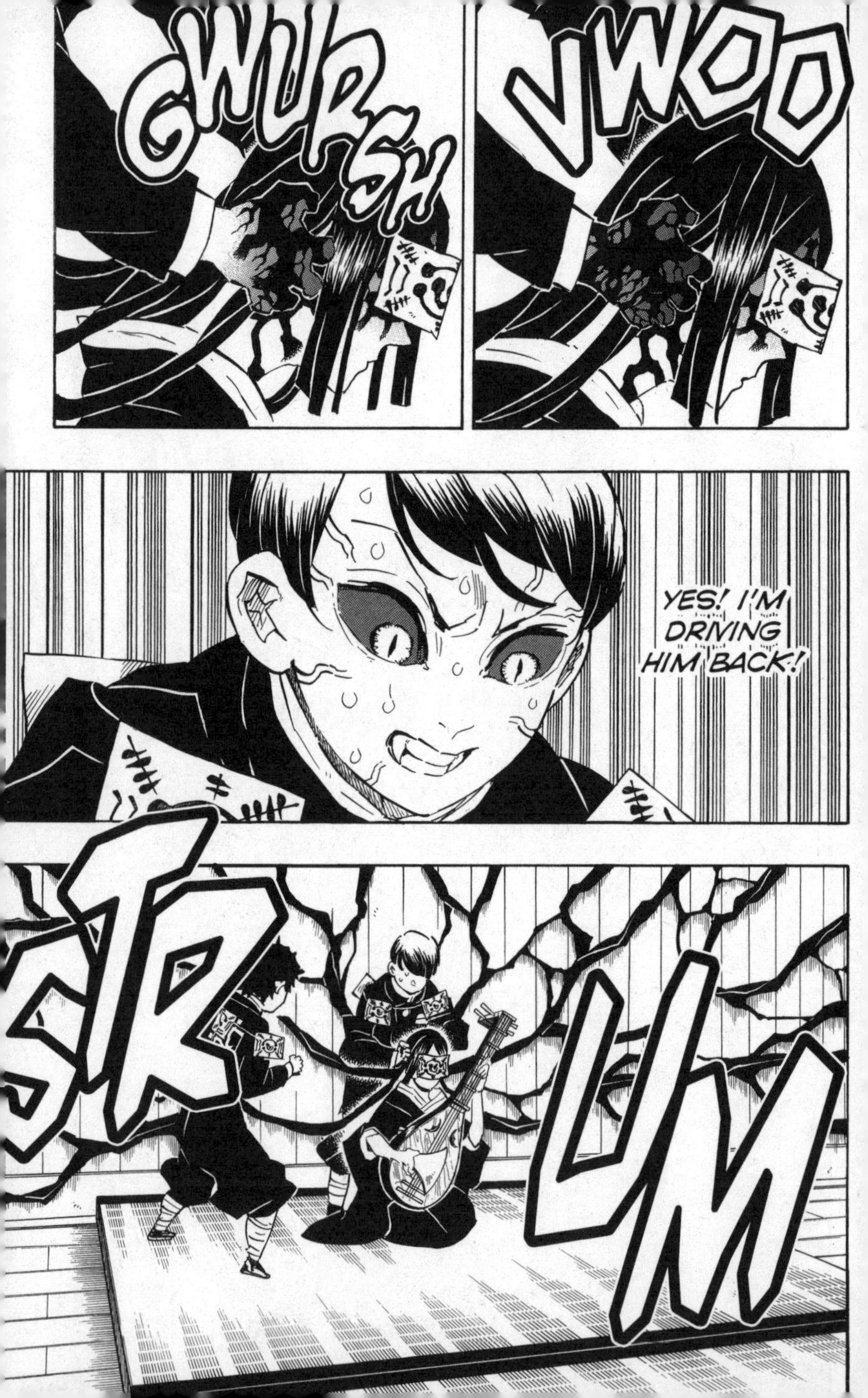
VWOO
GWURSH
YES! I'M DRIVING HIM BACK!
STRUM

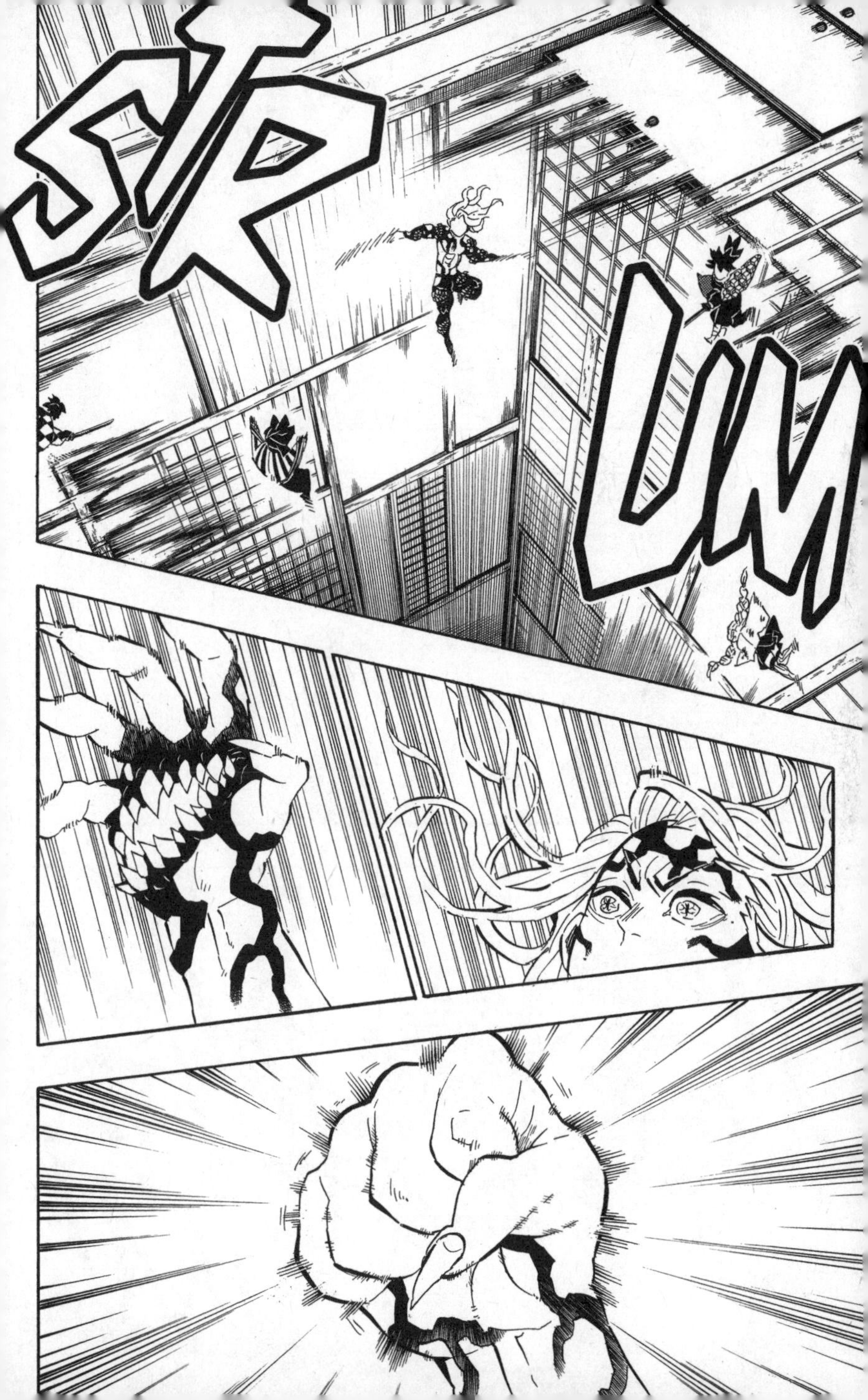

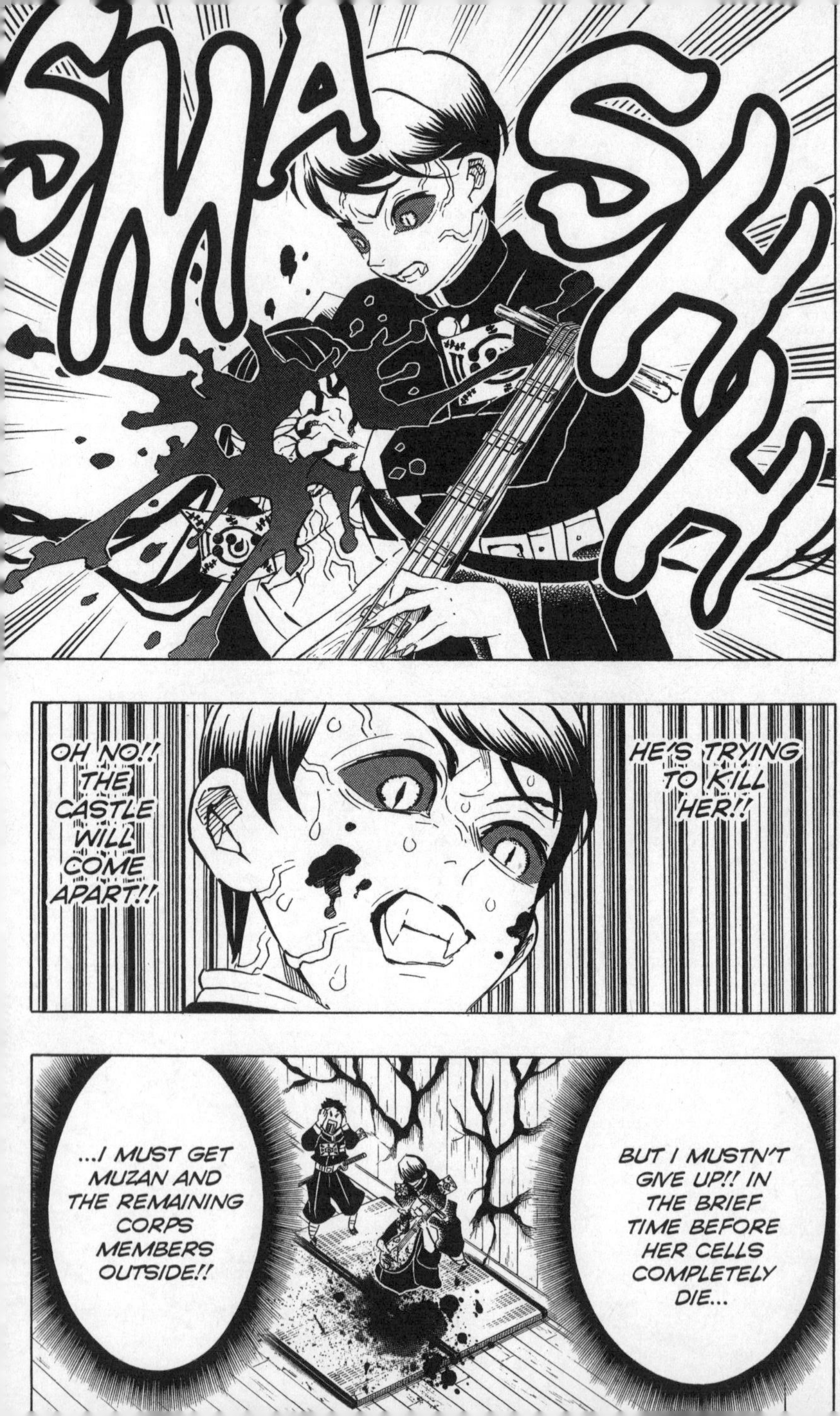
SMASH
HE'S TRYING TO KILL HER!!
OH NO!! THE CASTLE WILL COME APART!!
BUT I MUSTN'T GIVE UP!! IN THE BRIEF TIME BEFORE HER CELLS COMPLETELY DIE...
...I MUST GET MUZAN AND THE REMAINING CORPS MEMBERS OUTSIDE!!

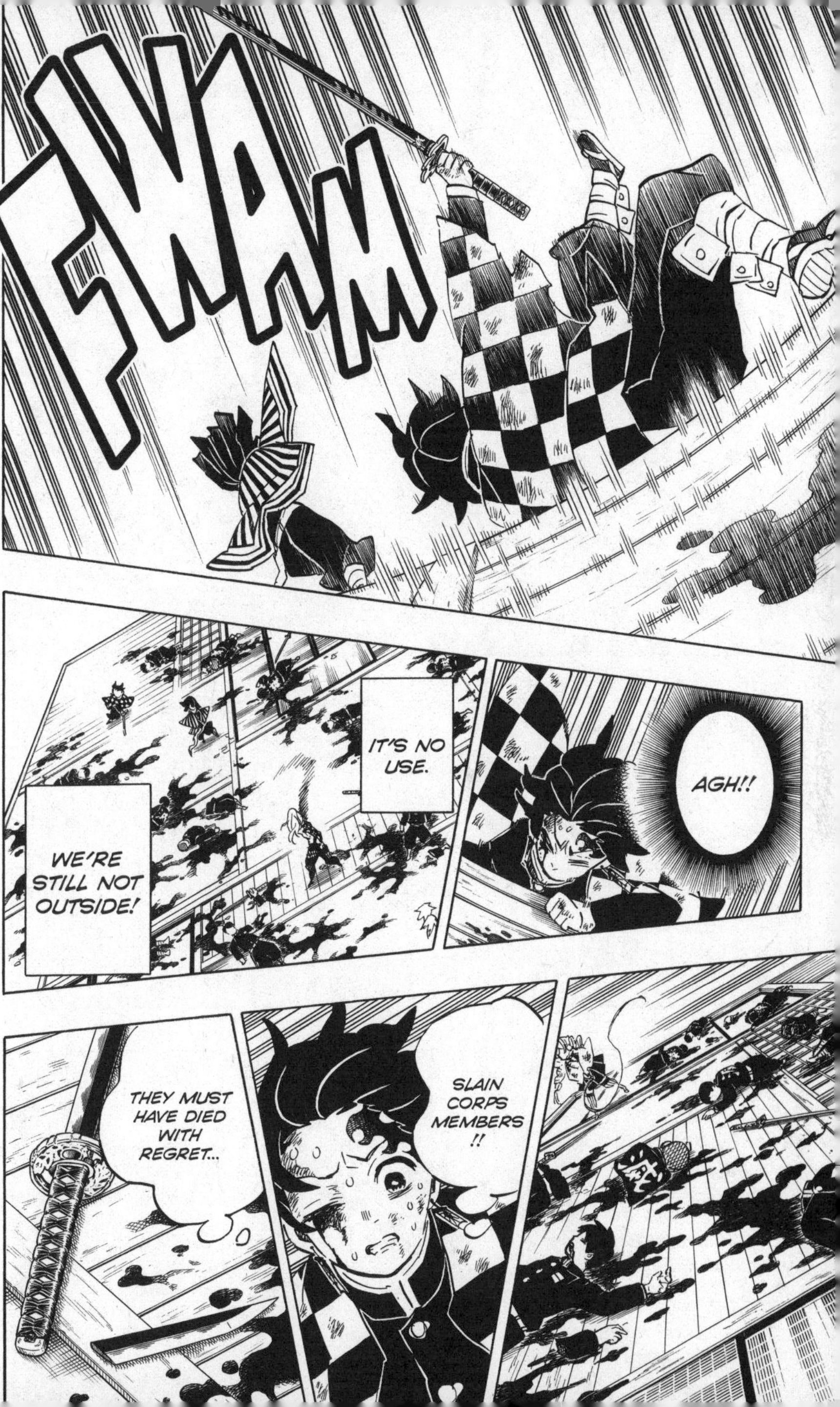
FWAM
AGH!!
IT'S NO USE.
WE'RE STILL NOT OUTSIDE!
SLAIN CORPS MEMBERS !!
THEY MUST HAVE DIED WITH REGRET...

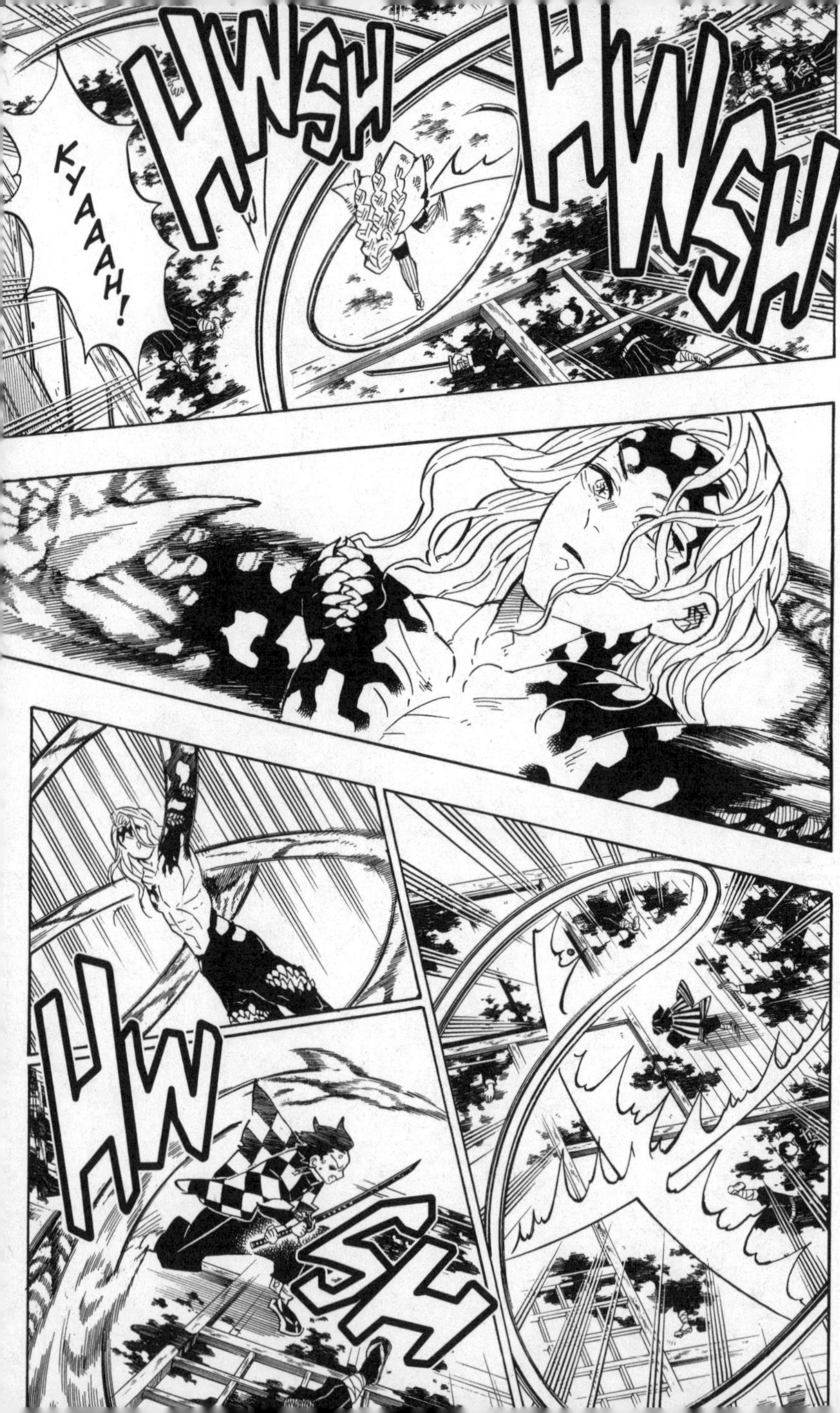
HWSH
HWSH
KYAAAAH!
HWSH

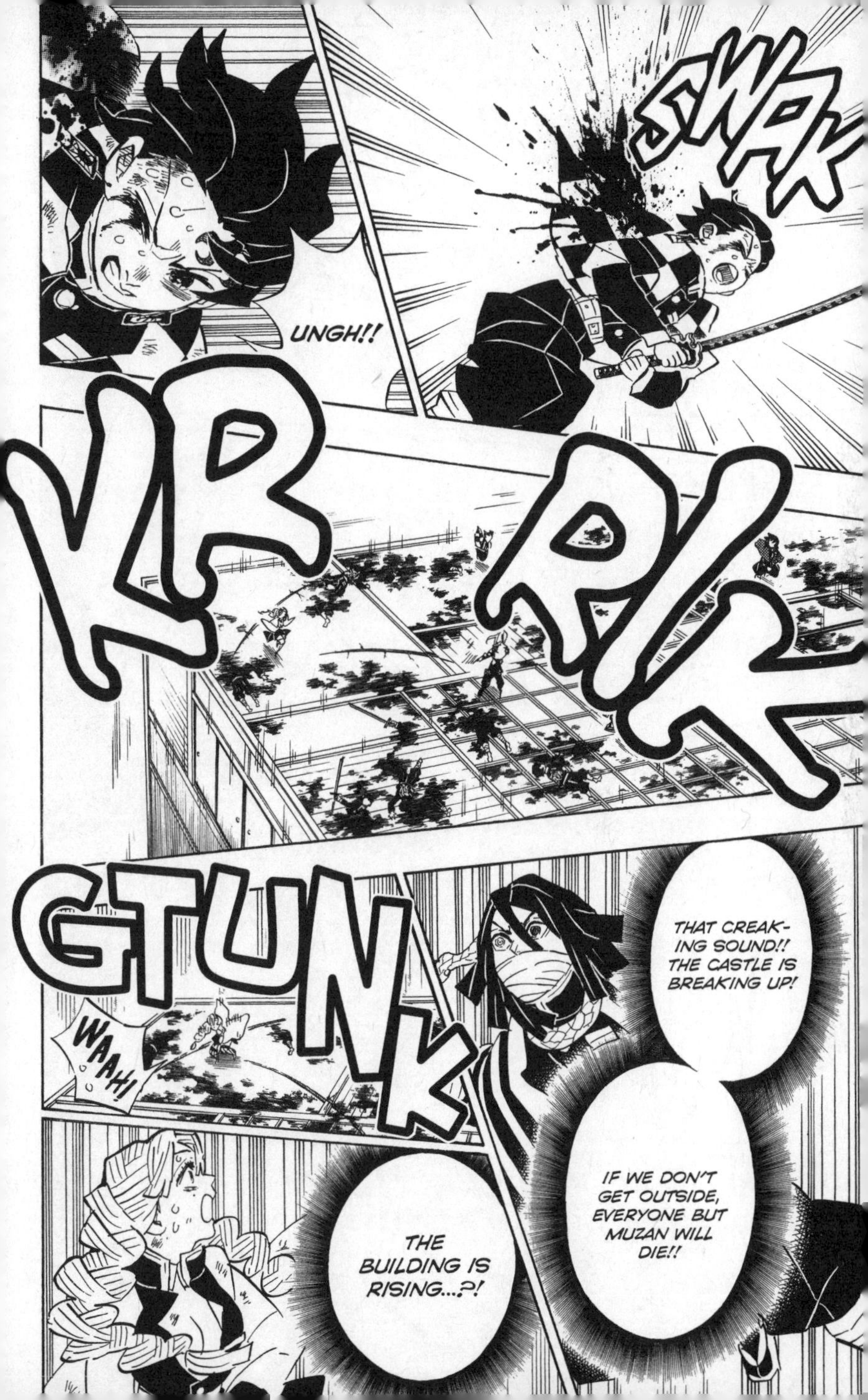
SWAK
UNGH!!
VRRK
THAT CREAK-ING SOUND!! THE CASTLE IS BREAKING UP!
IF WE DON'T GET OUTSIDE, EVERYONE BUT MUZAN WILL DIE!!
GTUNK
WAAH!
THE BUILDING IS RISING...?!

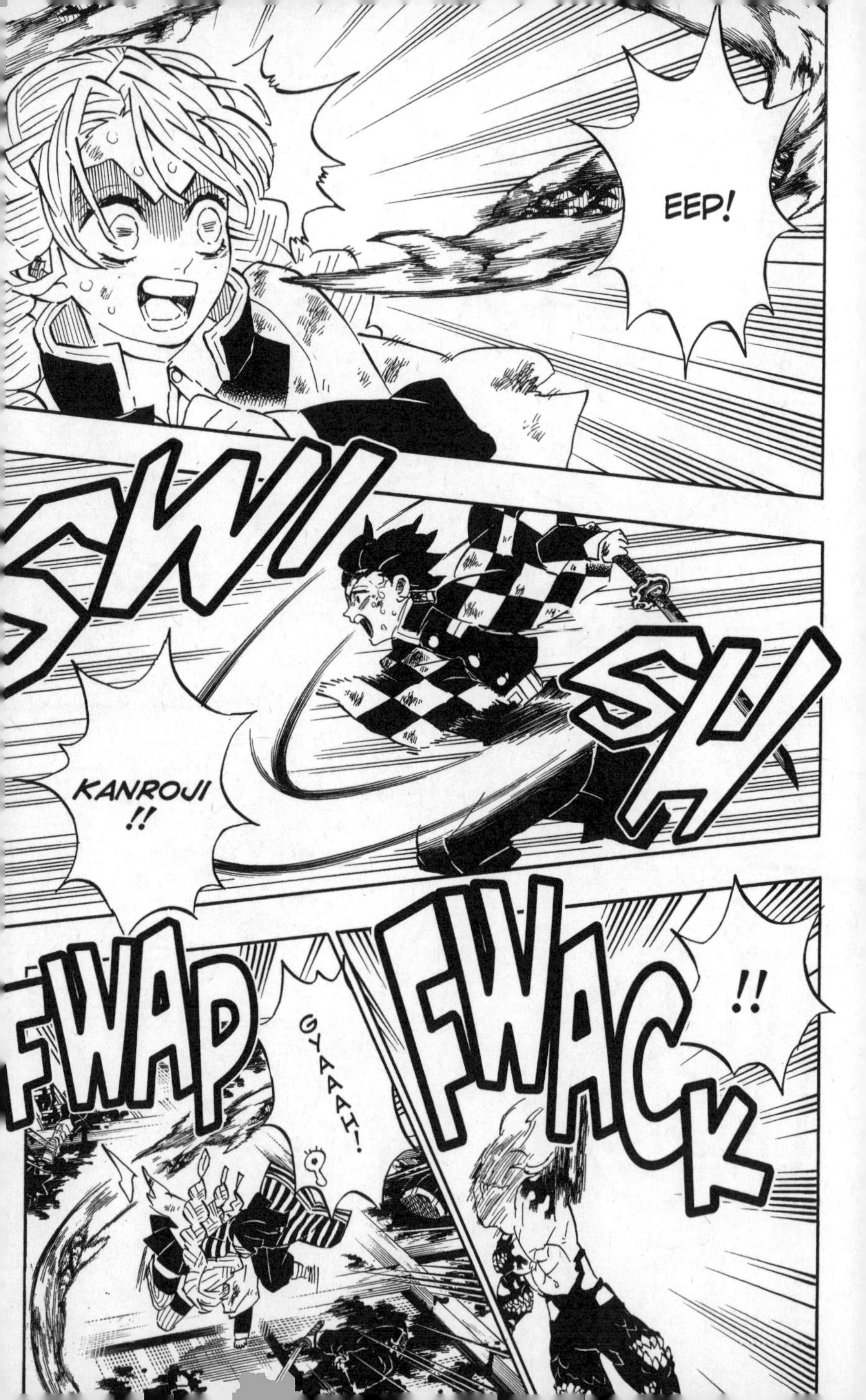

EEP!
SWISH
KANROJI !!
FWACK !!
FWAP
GYAAAH!

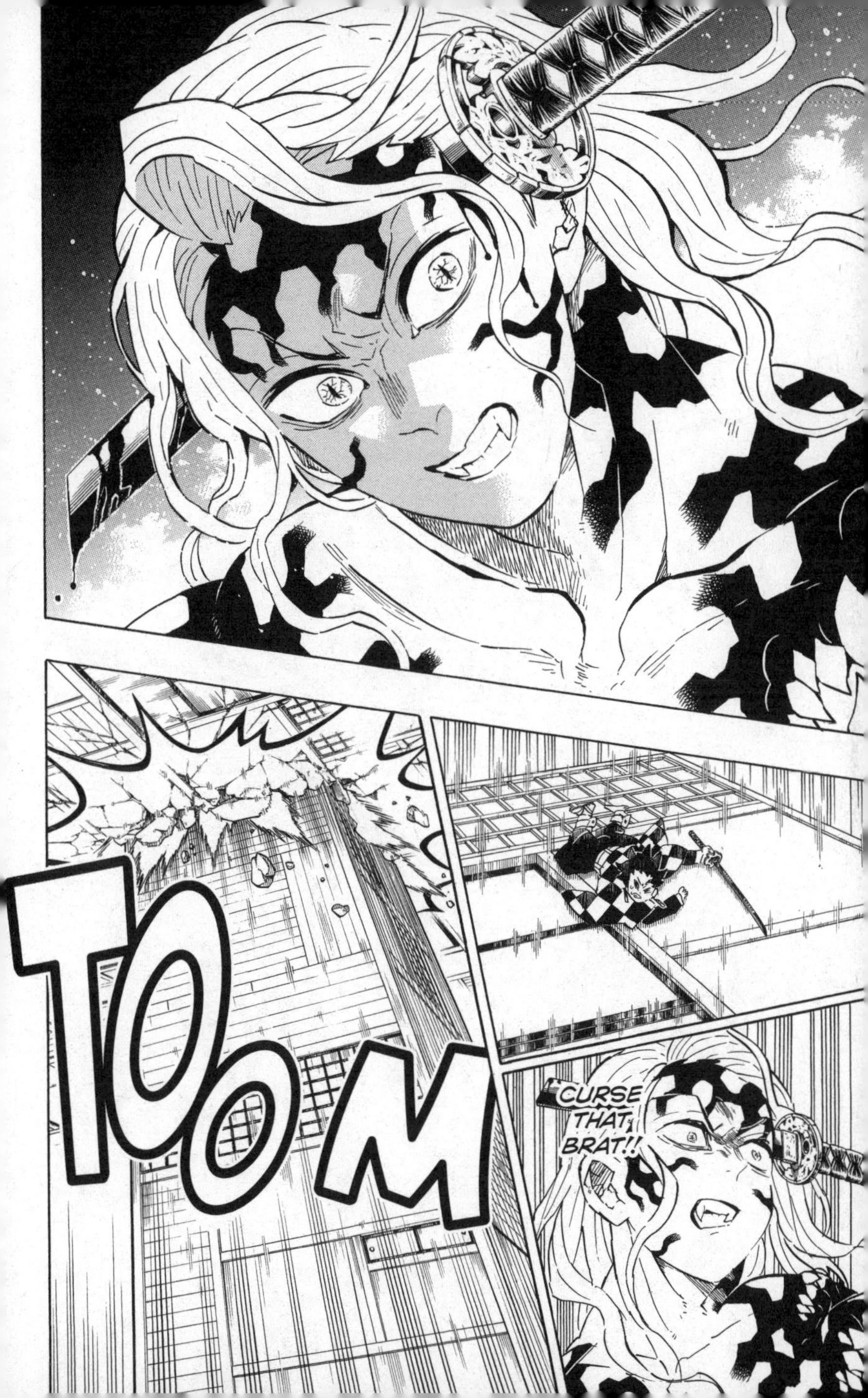
TOOOM
CURSE THAT BRAT!!

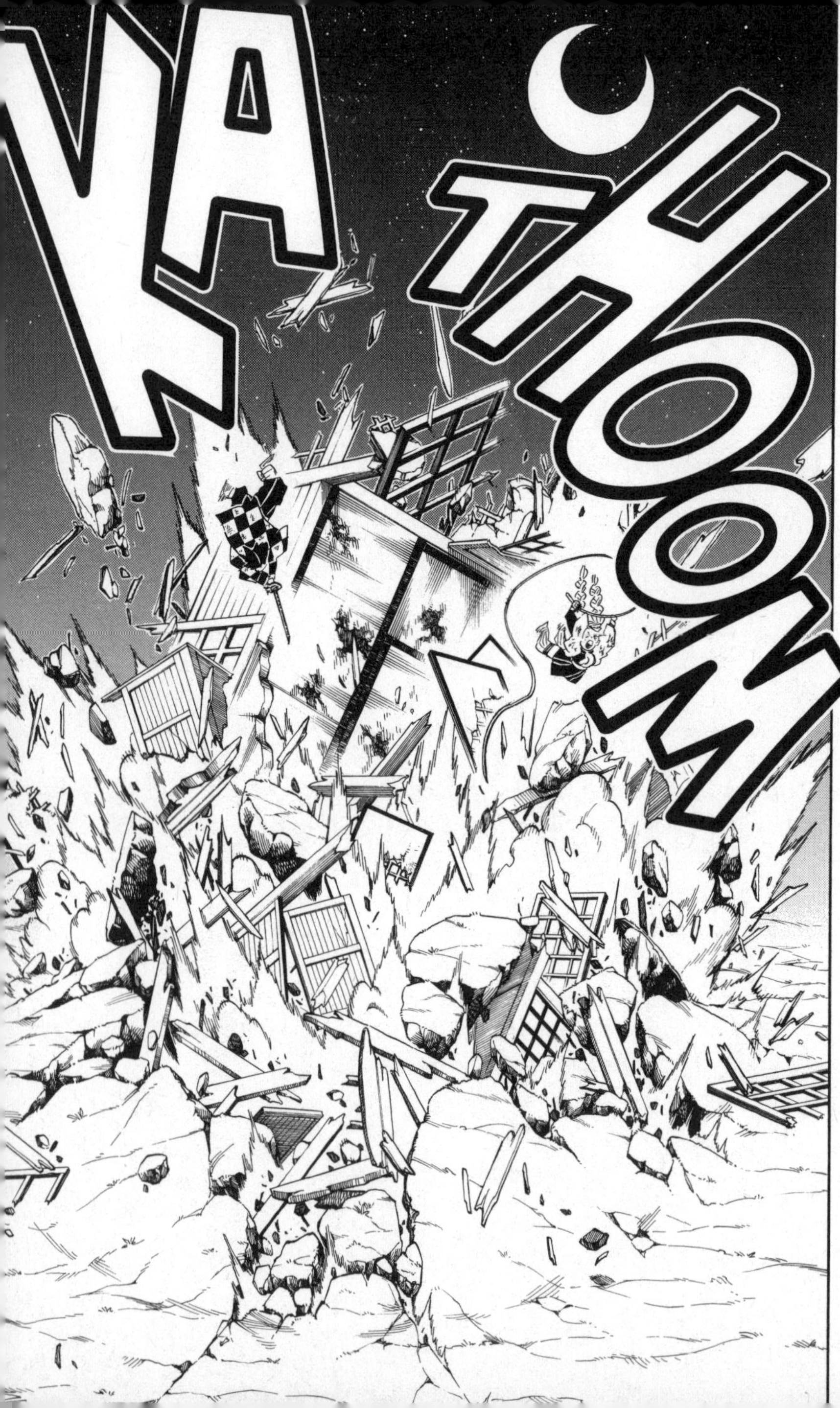
VA THOOM

Takeuchi thinks he enraged Yushiro by speaking to him and that's why Yushiro crushed Nakime's head.

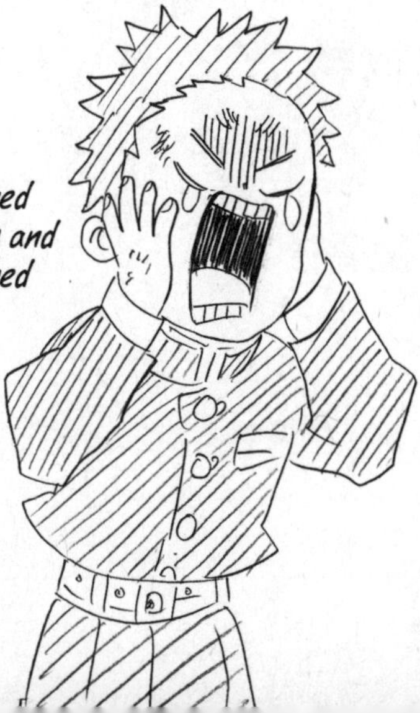

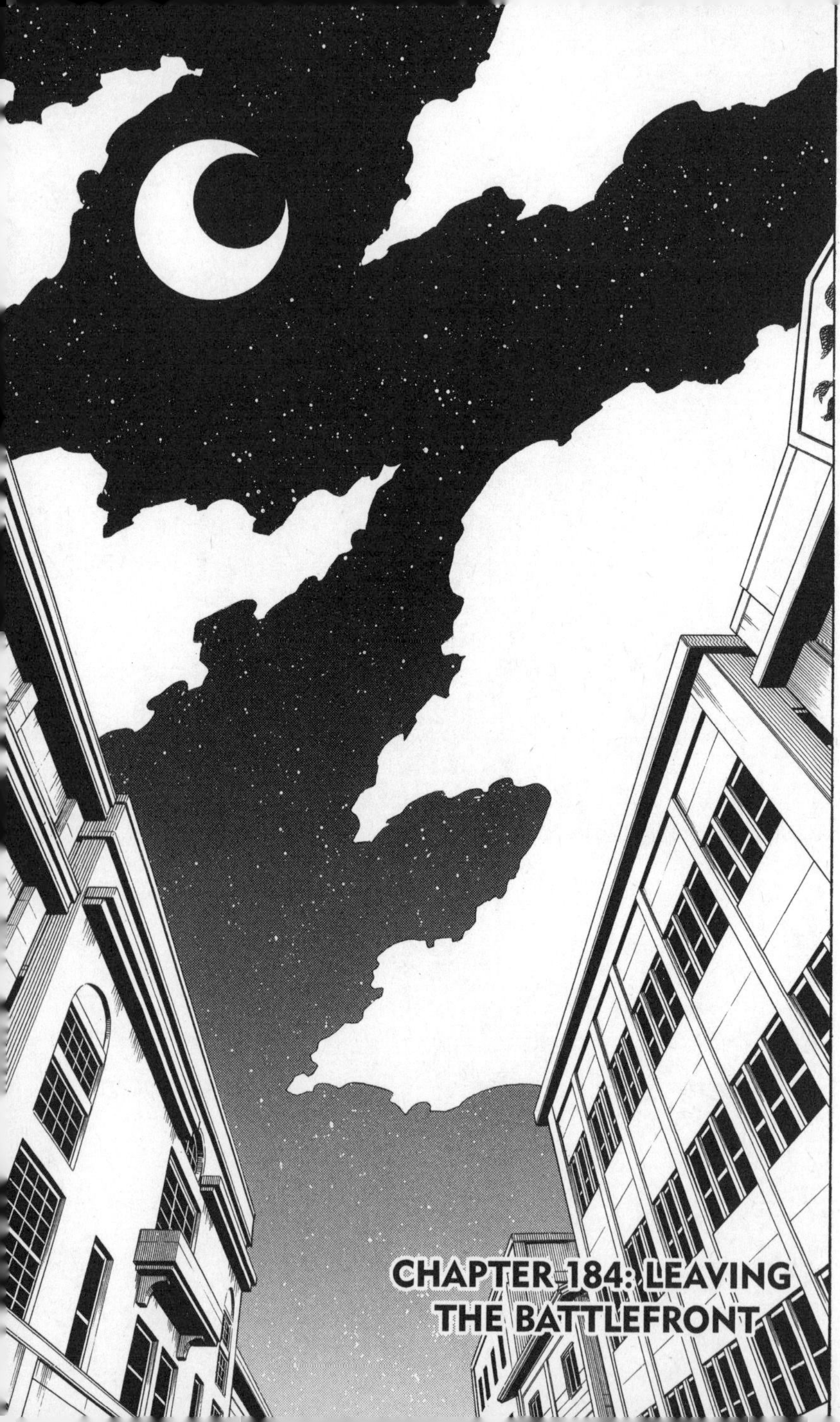
CHAPTER 184: LEAVING THE BATTLEFRONT

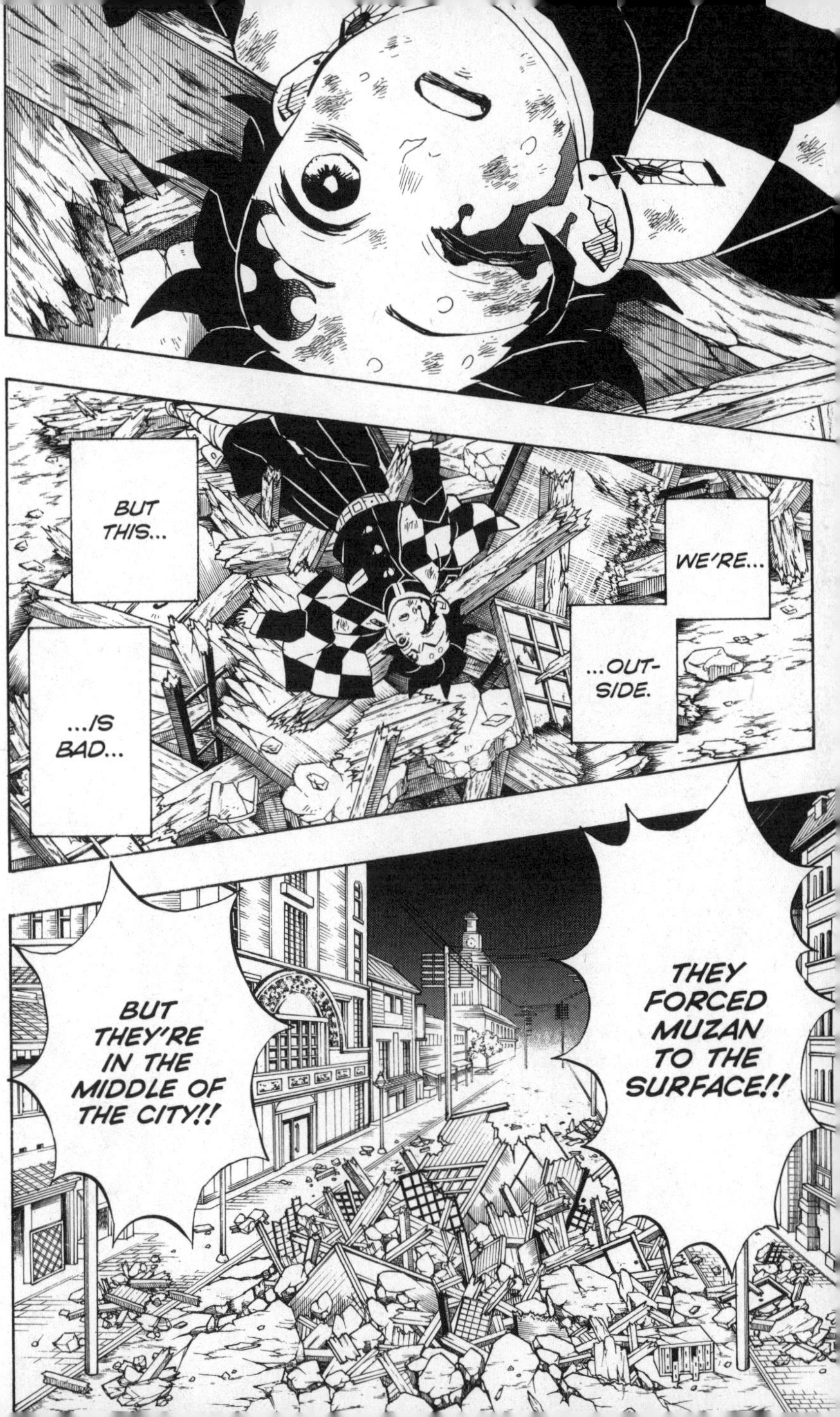
WE'RE...
...OUT-SIDE.
BUT THIS...
...IS BAD...
THEY FORCED MUZAN TO THE SURFACE!!
BUT THEY'RE IN THE MIDDLE OF THE CITY!!

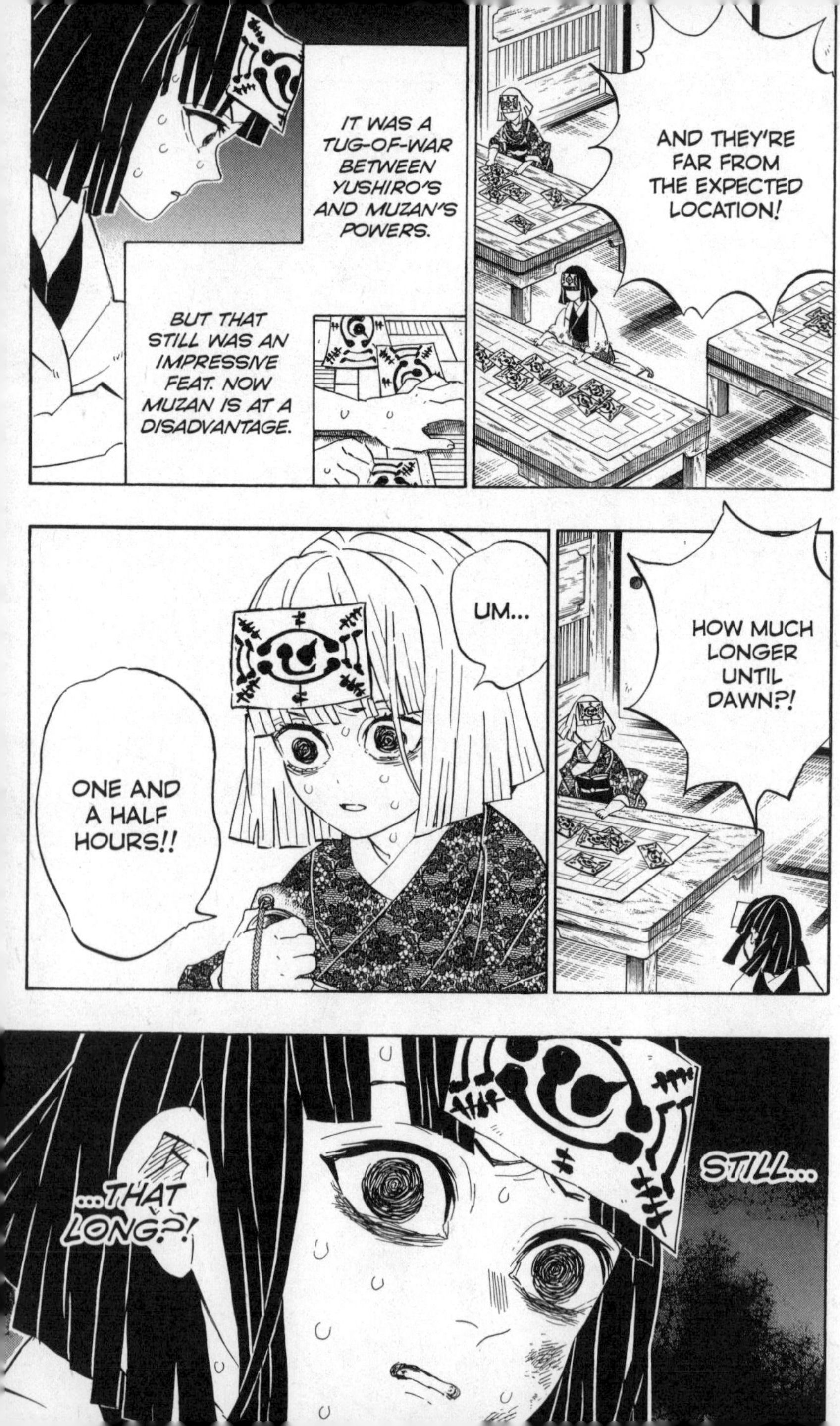
AND THEY'RE FAR FROM THE EXPECTED LOCATION!
IT WAS A TUG-OF-WAR BETWEEN YUSHIRO'S AND MUZAN'S POWERS.
BUT THAT STILL WAS AN IMPRESSIVE FEAT. NOW MUZAN IS AT A DISADVANTAGE.
HOW MUCH LONGER UNTIL DAWN?!
UM...
ONE AND A HALF HOURS!!
STILL...
...THAT LONG?!

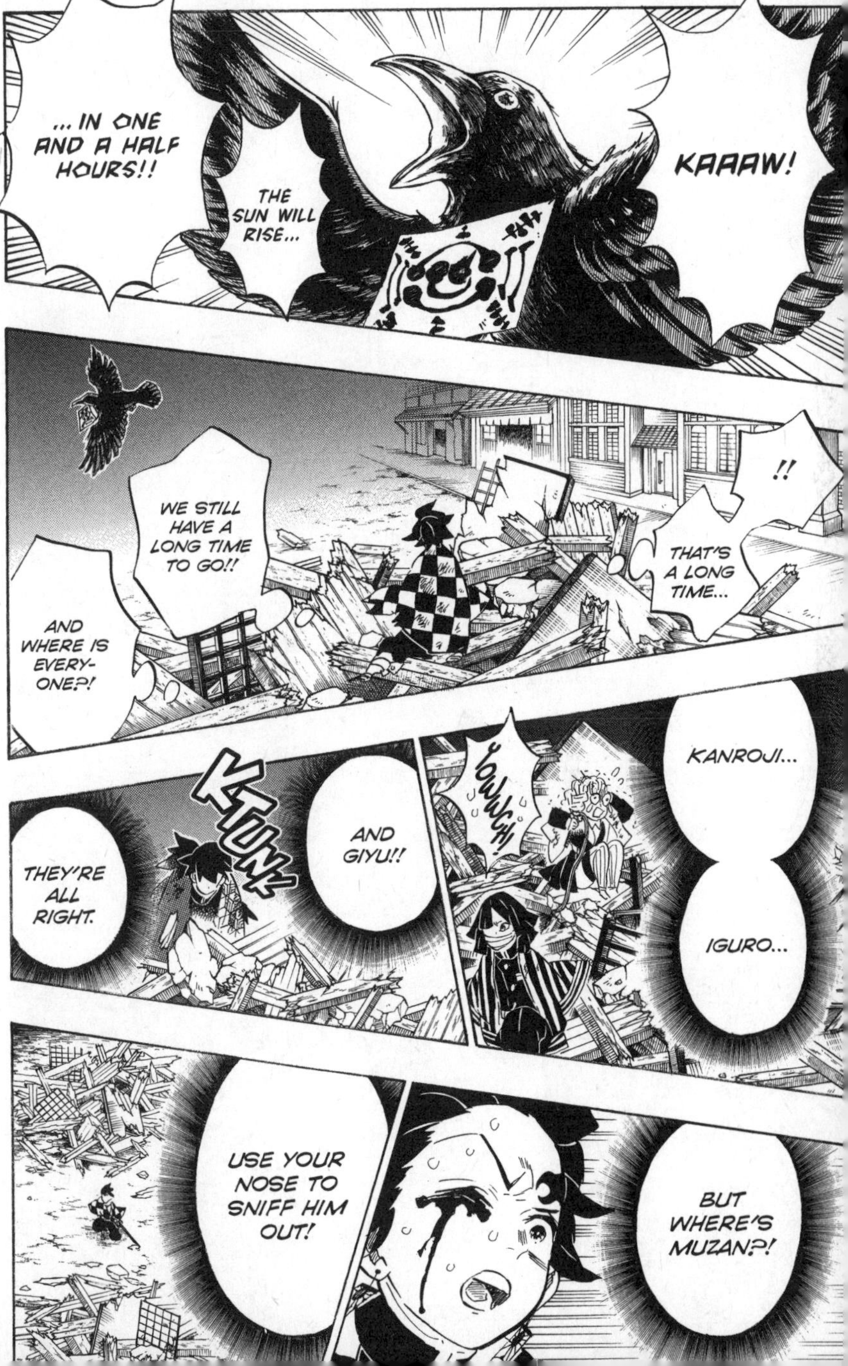
KAAAW!
THE SUN WILL RISE...
...IN ONE AND A HALF HOURS!!
!!
THAT'S A LONG TIME...
WE STILL HAVE A LONG TIME TO GO!!
AND WHERE IS EVERYONE?!
KANROJI...
IGURO...
OWWCH!
AND GIYU!!
KTUNK
THEY'RE ALL RIGHT.
BUT WHERE'S MUZAN?!
USE YOUR NOSE TO SNIFF HIM OUT!

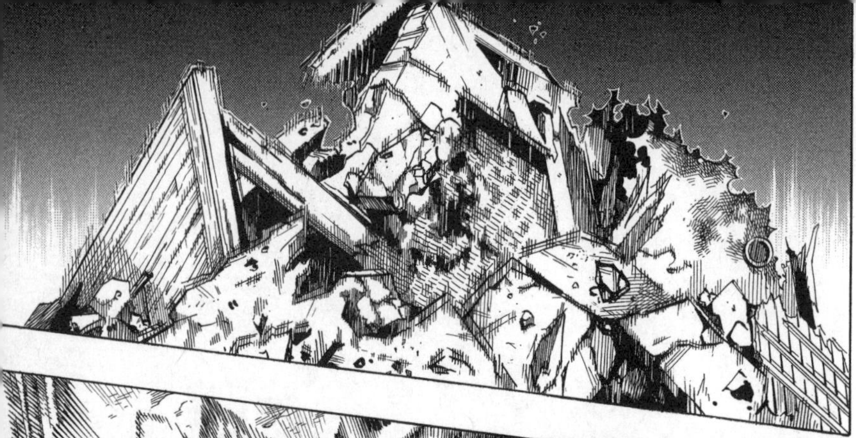
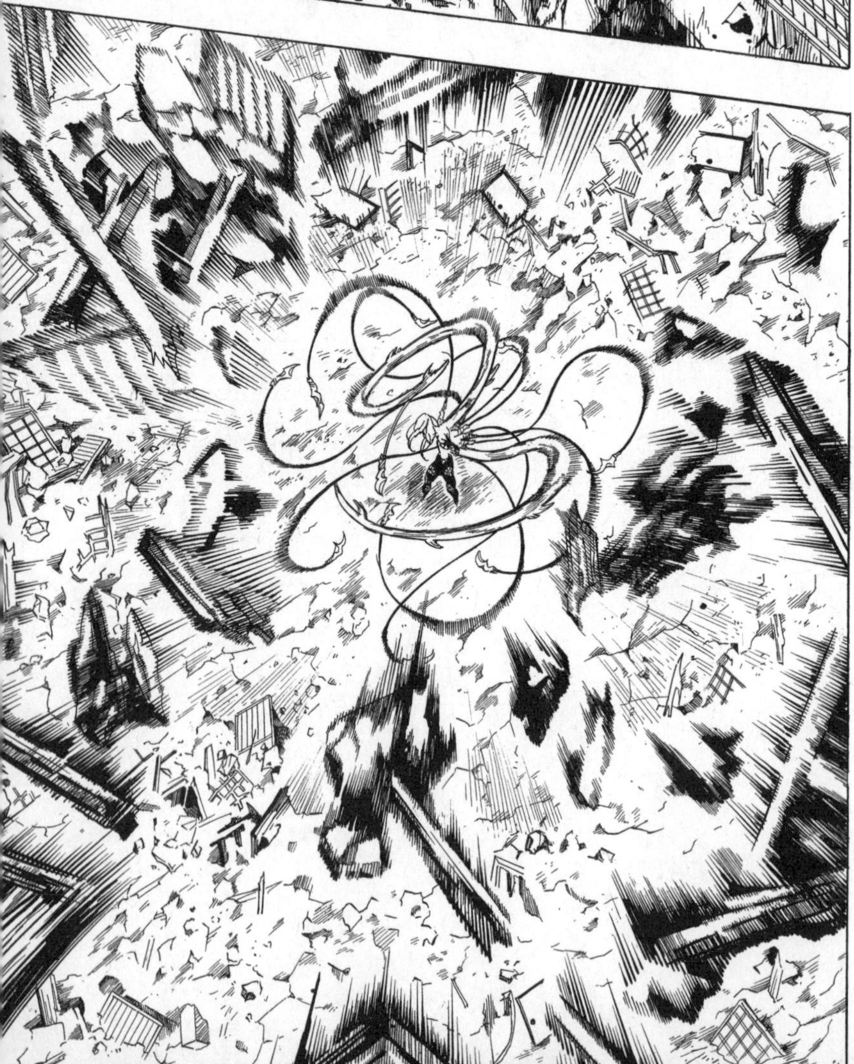

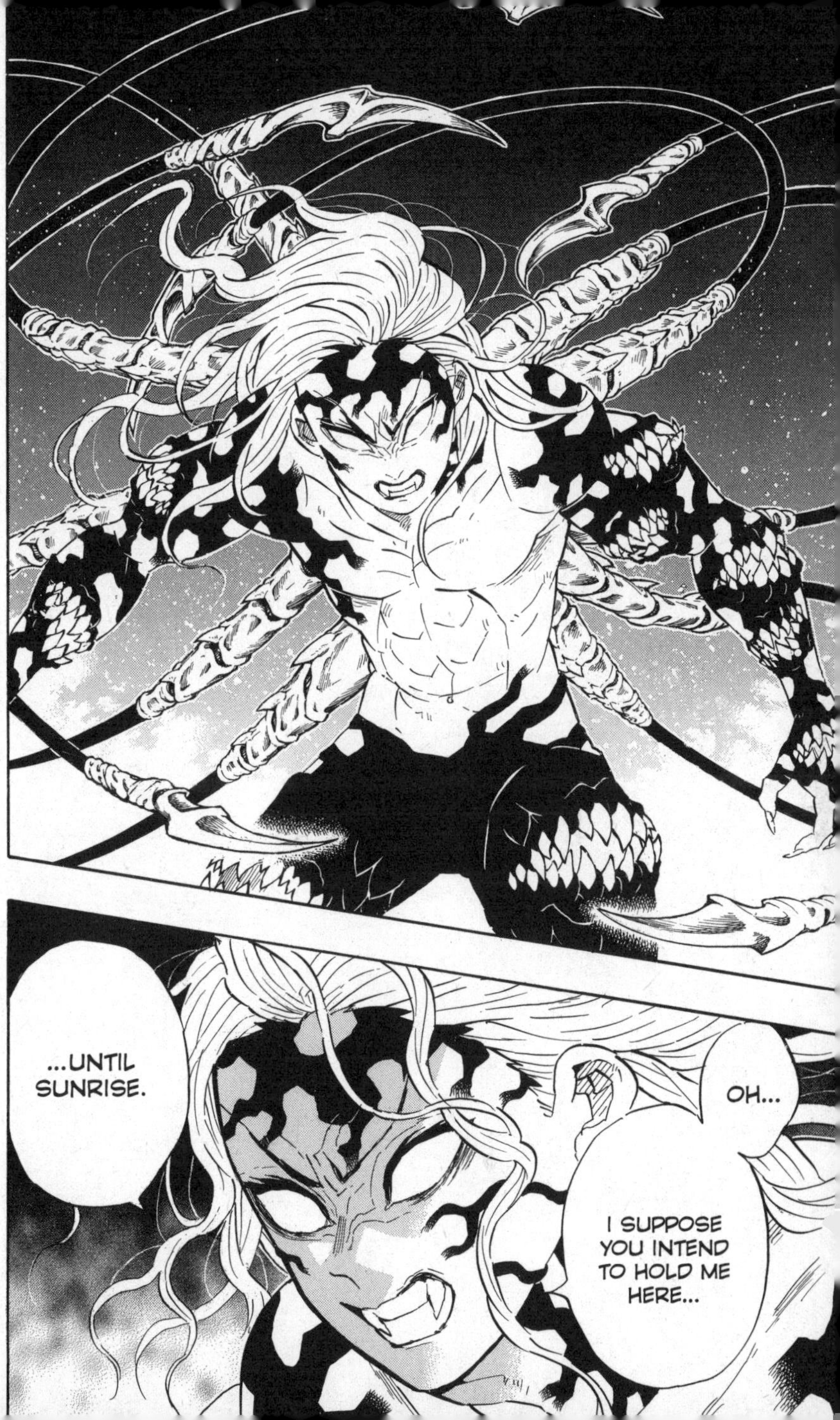
OH...
I SUPPOSE YOU INTEND TO HOLD ME HERE...
...UNTIL SUNRISE.

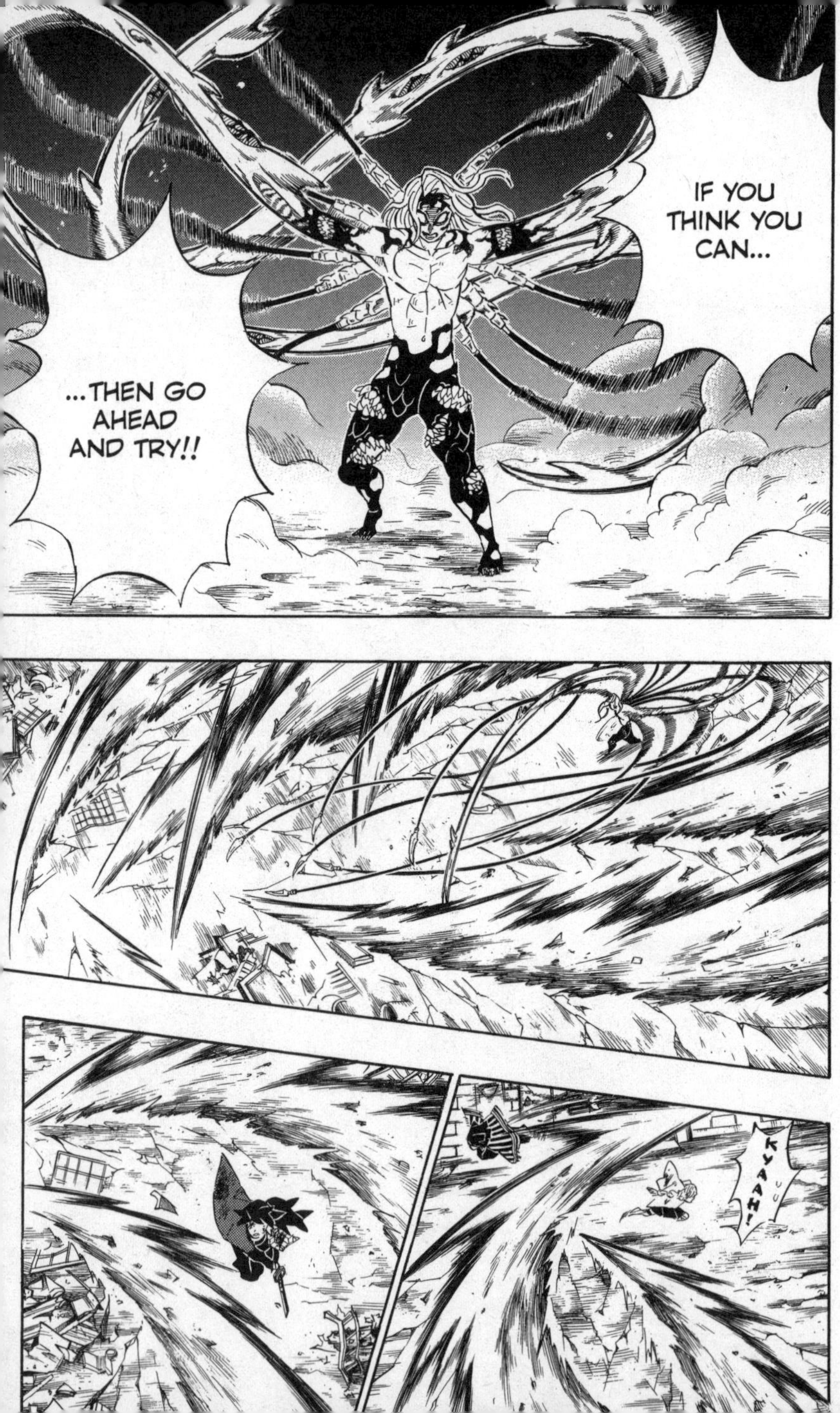
IF YOU THINK YOU CAN...
...THEN GO AHEAD AND TRY!!
KYAAAH!

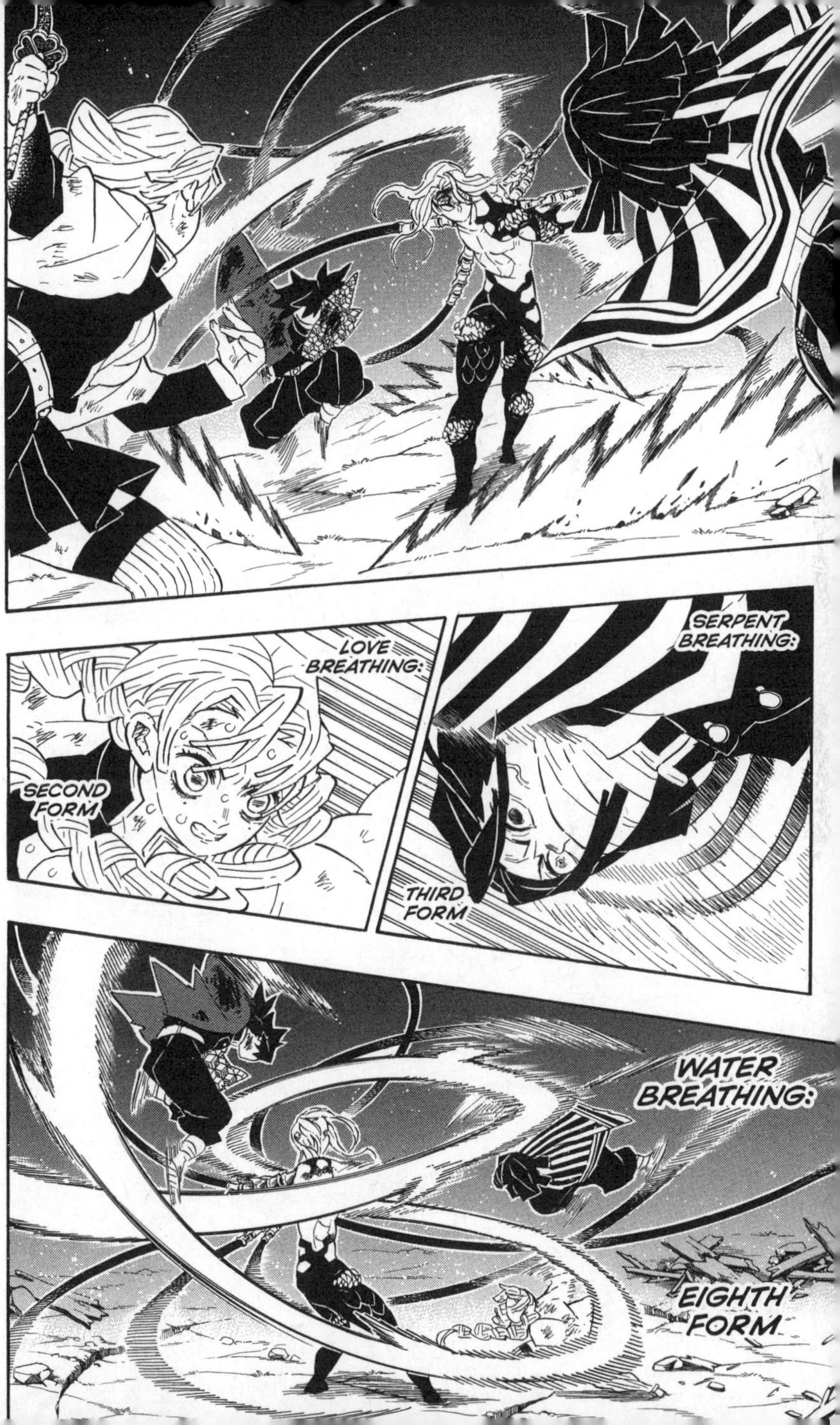
SERPENT BREATHING:
THIRD FORM
LOVE BREATHING:
SECOND FORM
WATER BREATHING:
EIGHTH FORM

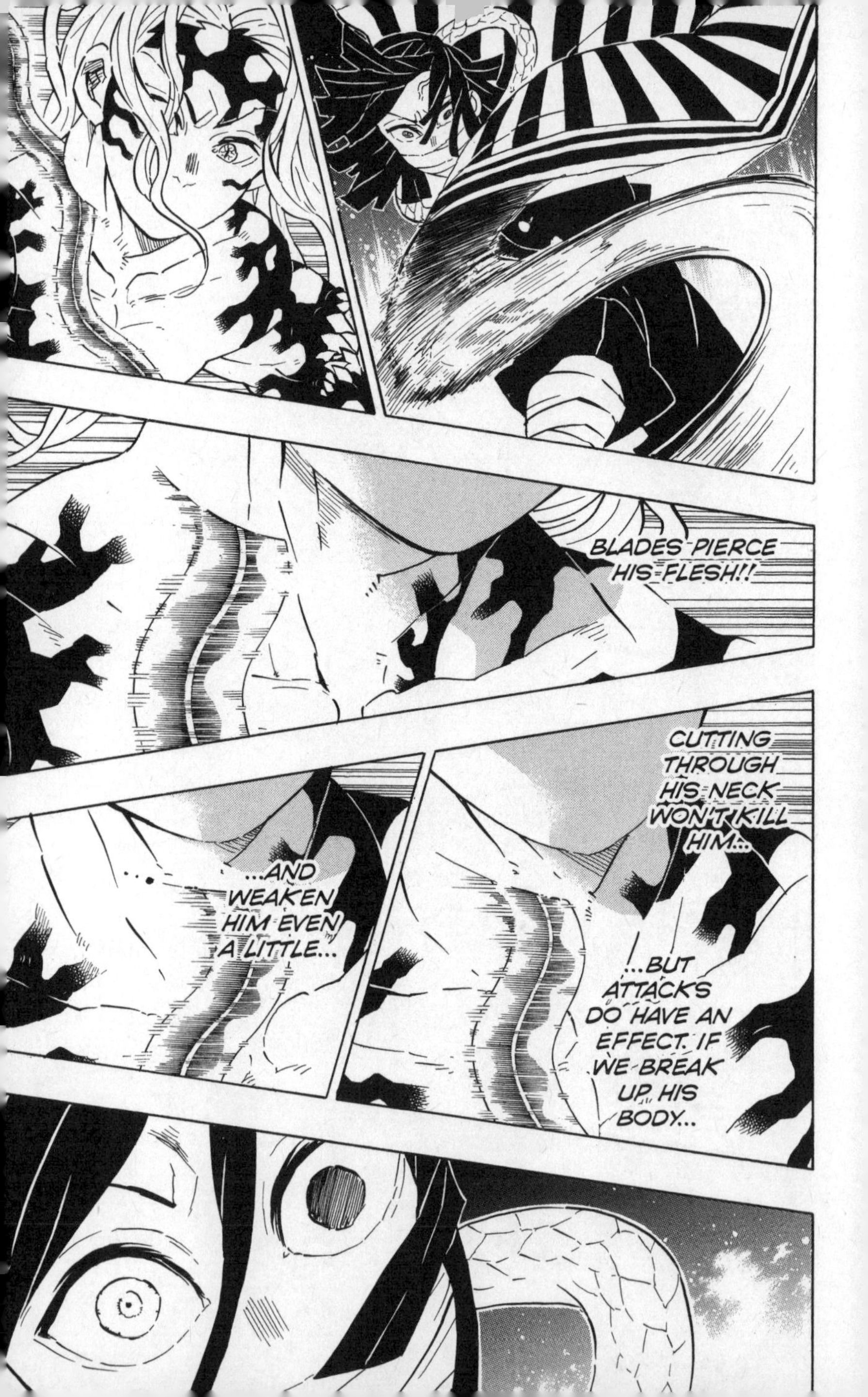
BLADES PIERCE HIS FLESH!!
CUTTING THROUGH HIS NECK WON'T KILL HIM...
...BUT ATTACKS DO HAVE AN EFFECT IF WE BREAK UP HIS BODY...
...AND WEAKEN HIM EVEN A LITTLE...

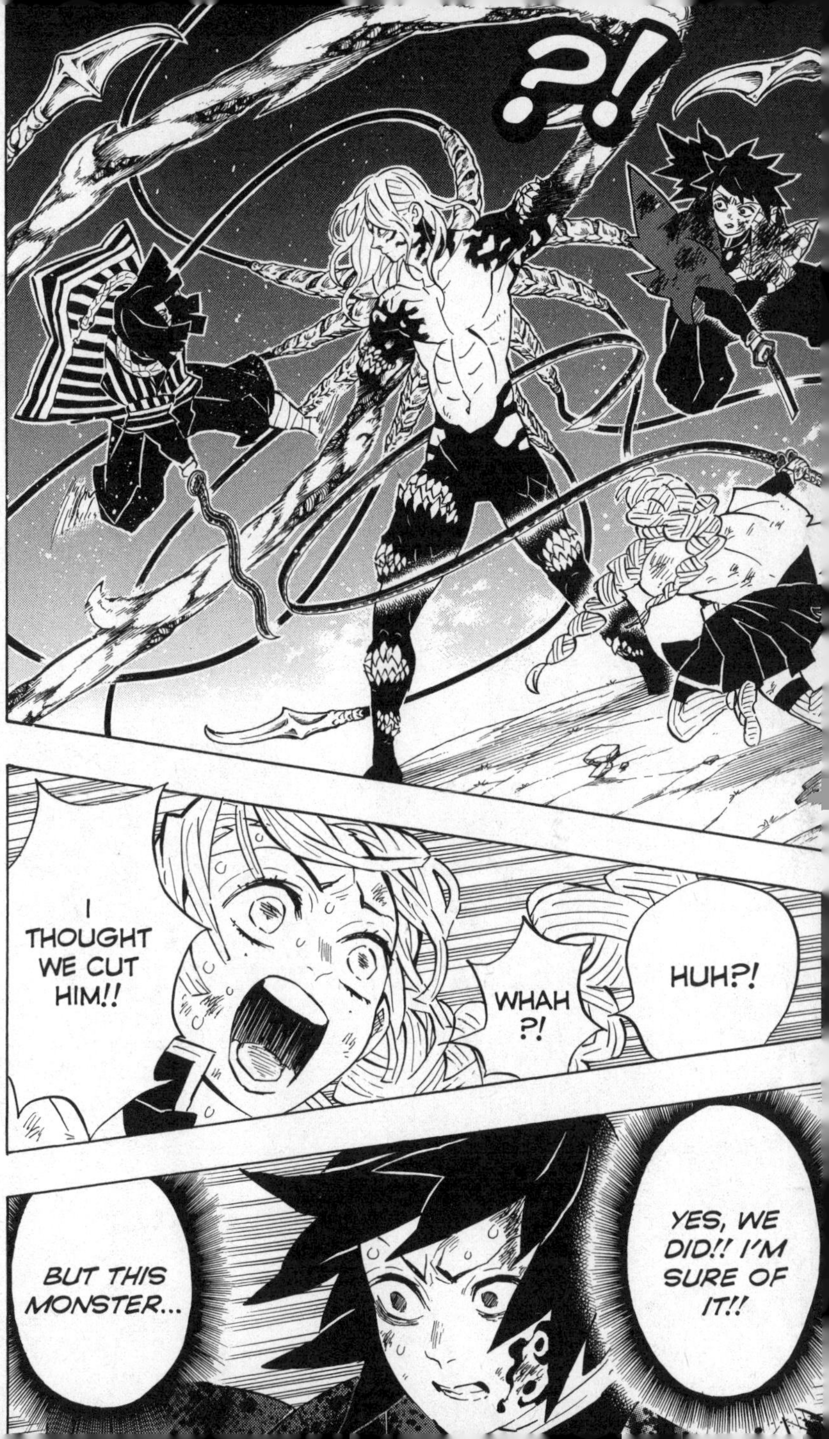
?!
HUH?!
WHAH ?!
I THOUGHT WE CUT HIM!!
YES, WE DID!! I'M SURE OF IT!!
BUT THIS MONSTER...

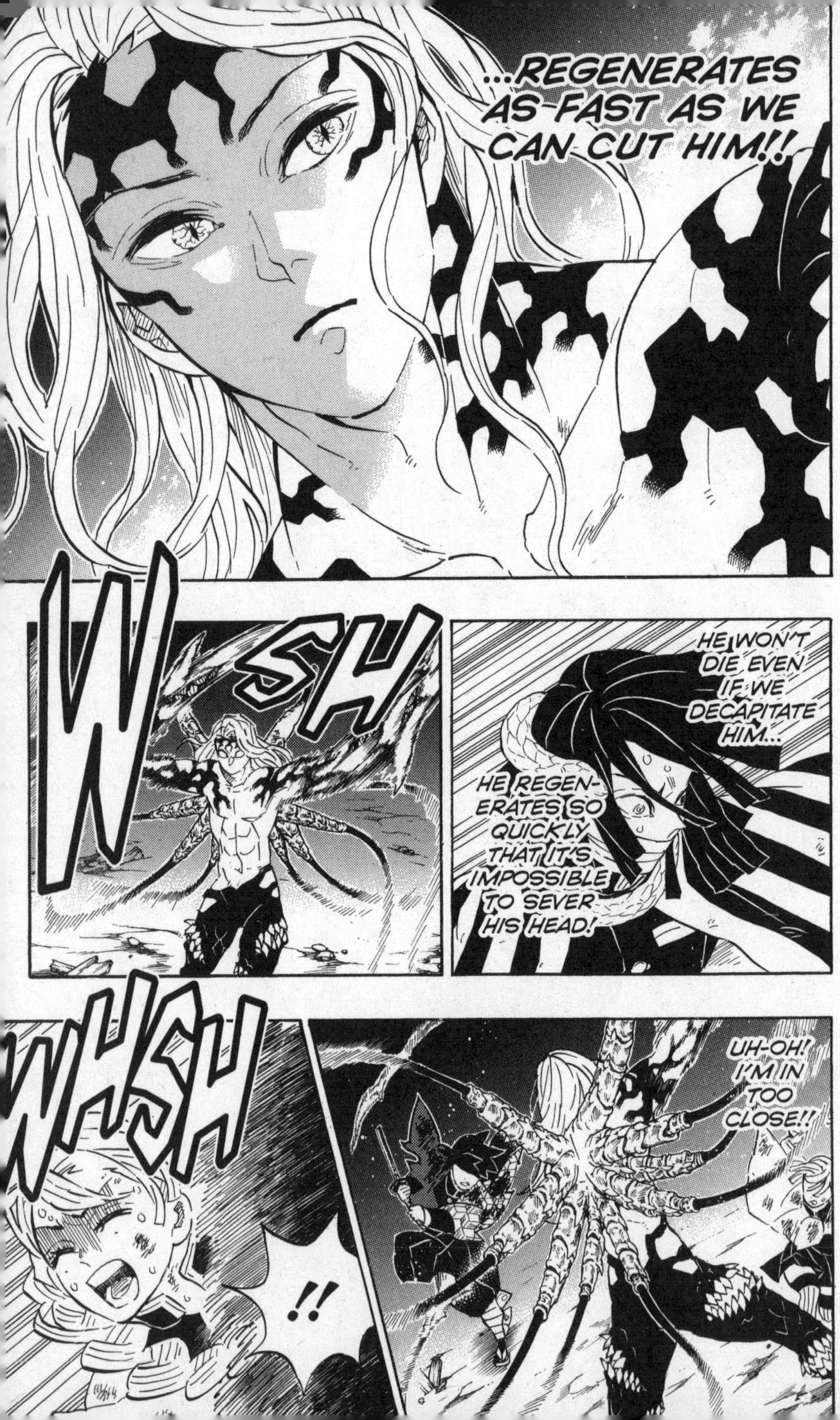
...REGENERATES AS FAST AS WE CAN CUT HIM!!
HE WON'T DIE EVEN IF WE DECAPITATE HIM...
HE REGEN-ERATES SO QUICKLY THAT IT'S IMPOSSIBLE TO SEVER HIS HEAD!
WSH
UH-OH! I'M IN TOO CLOSE!!
WHSH
!!

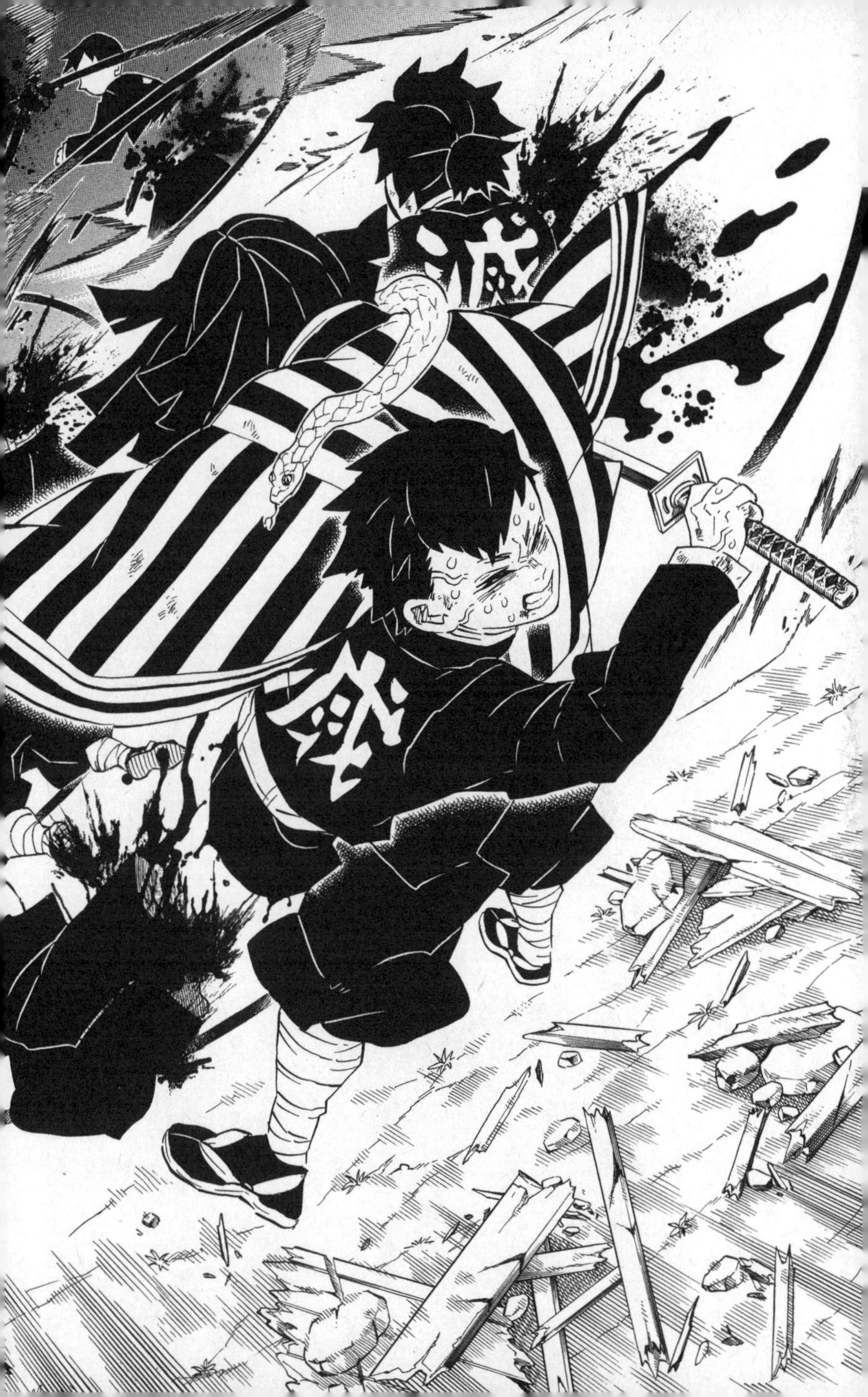

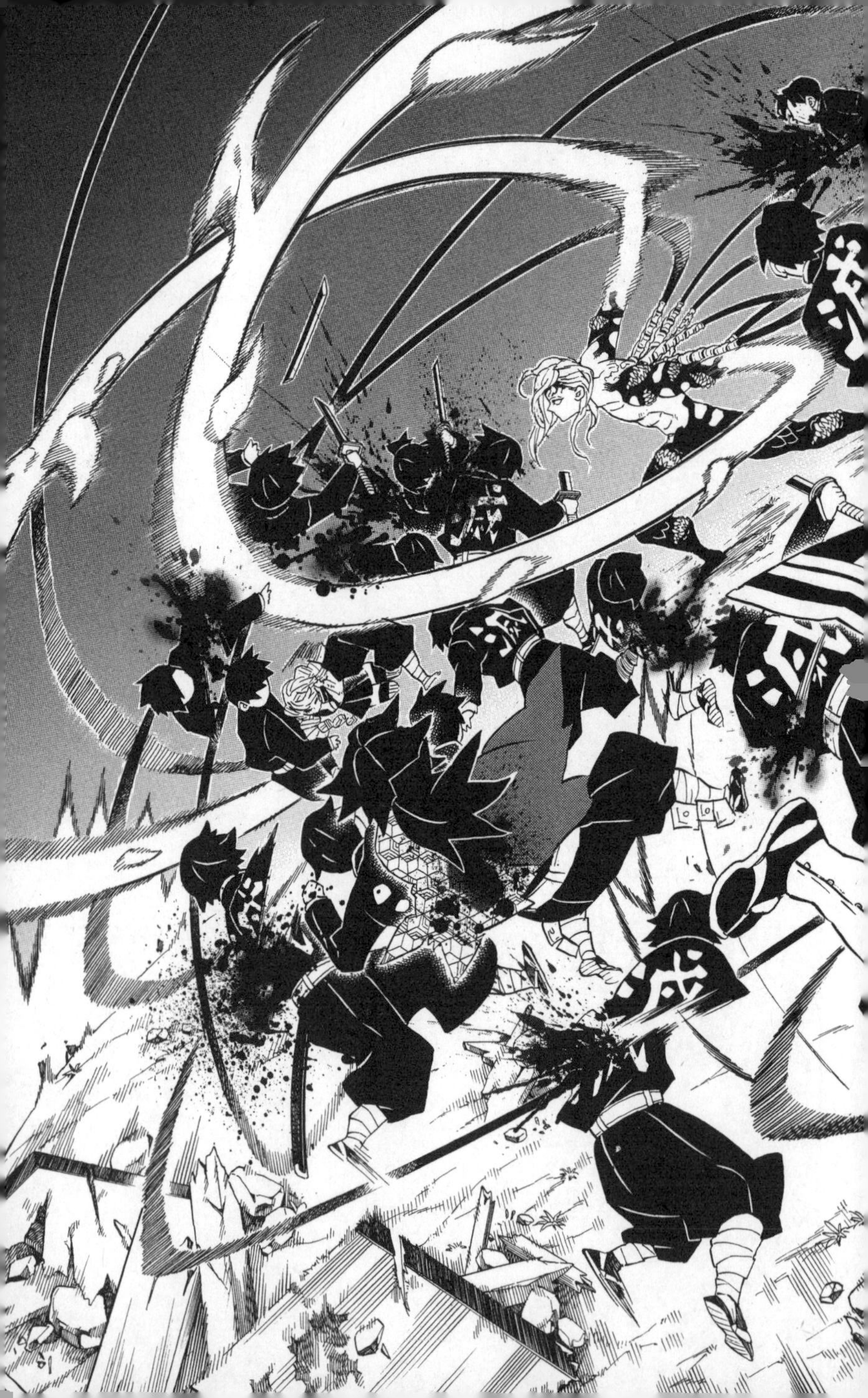

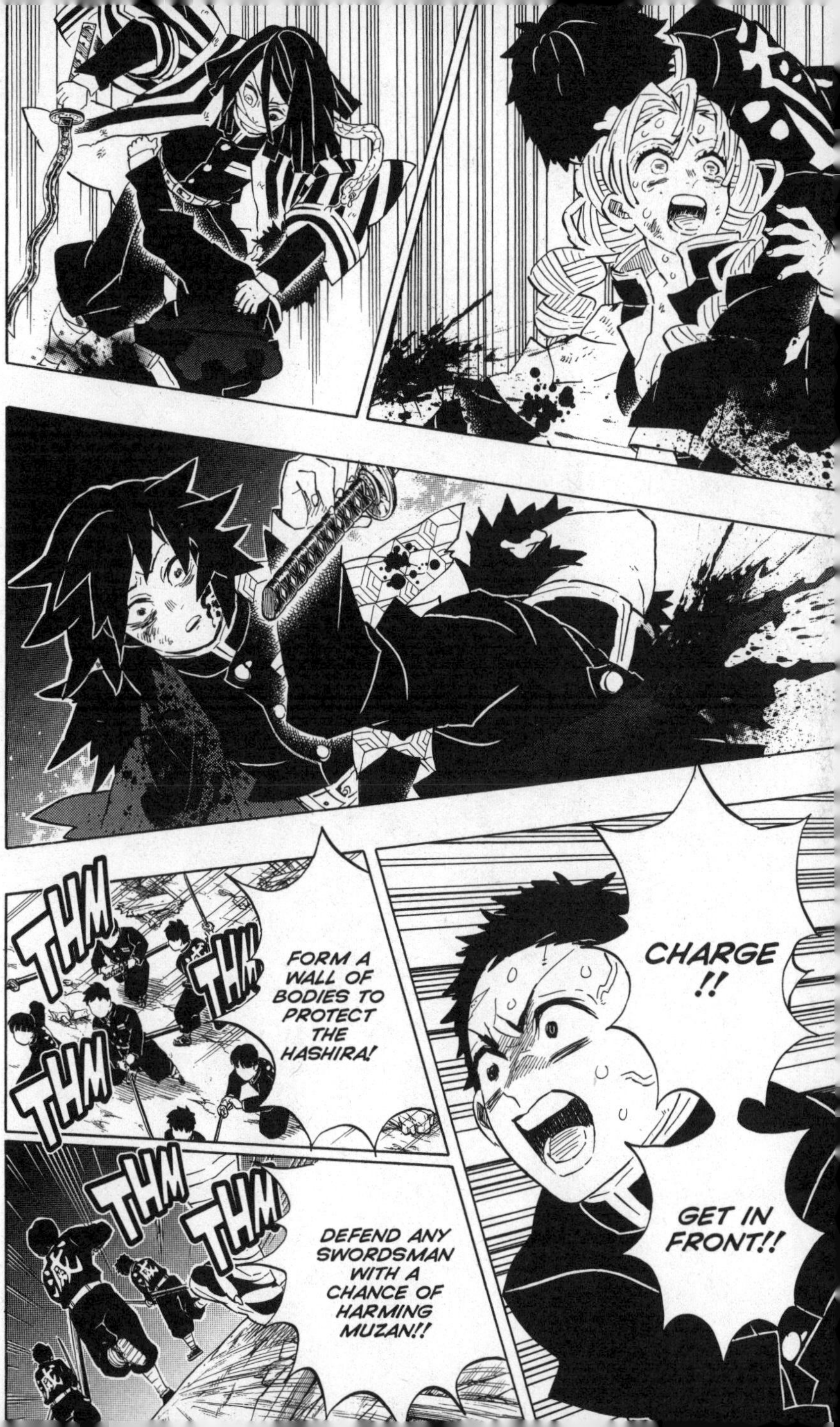
CHARGE!!
GET IN FRONT!!
FORM A WALL OF BODIES TO PROTECT THE HASHIRA!
THM
THK
THM
DEFEND ANY SWORDSMAN WITH A CHANCE OF HARMING MUZAN!!
THM
THM
THM

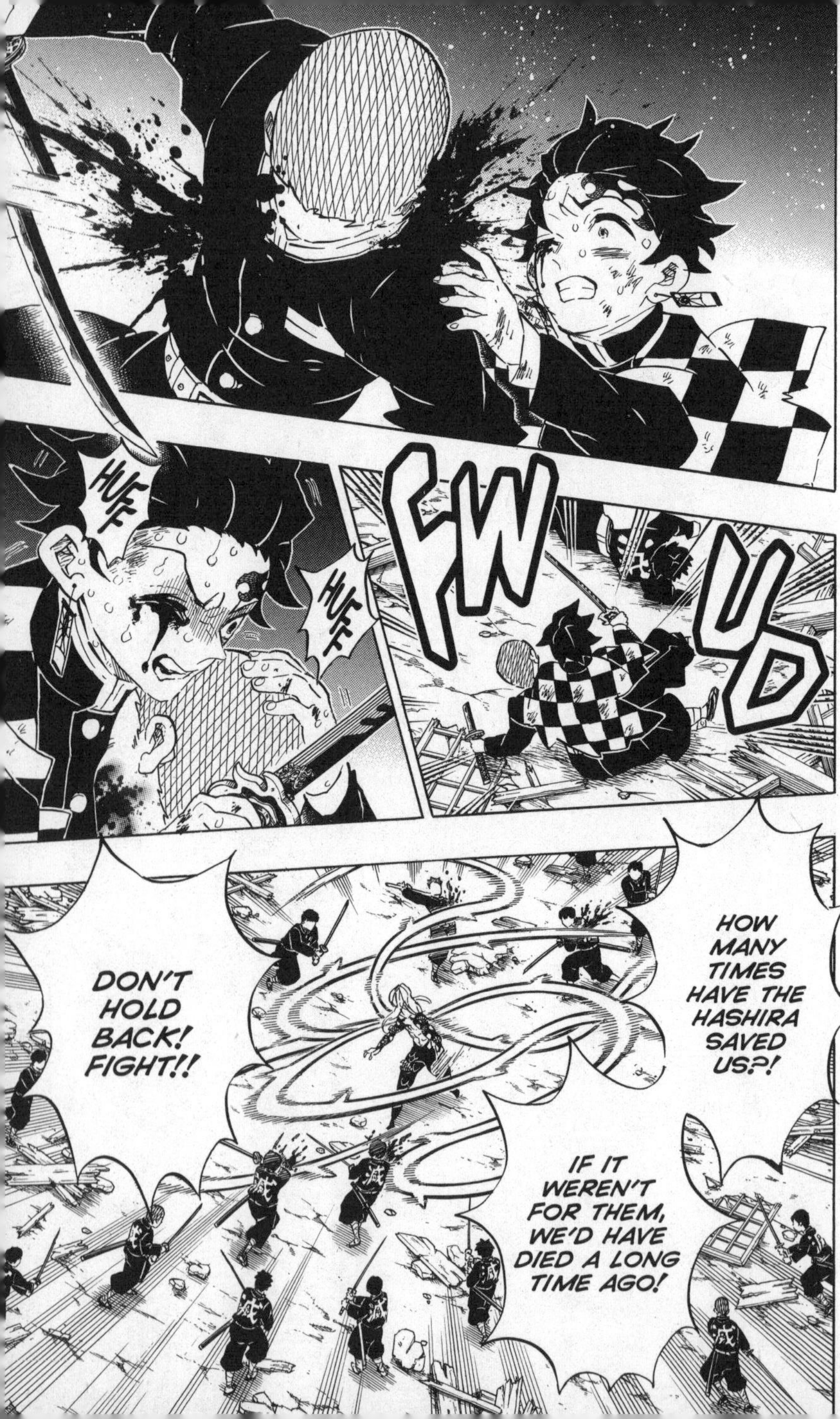
FWUD
HUFF
HUFF
HOW MANY TIMES HAVE THE HASHIRA SAVED US?!
IF IT WEREN'T FOR THEM, WE'D HAVE DIED A LONG TIME AGO!
DON'T HOLD BACK! FIGHT!!

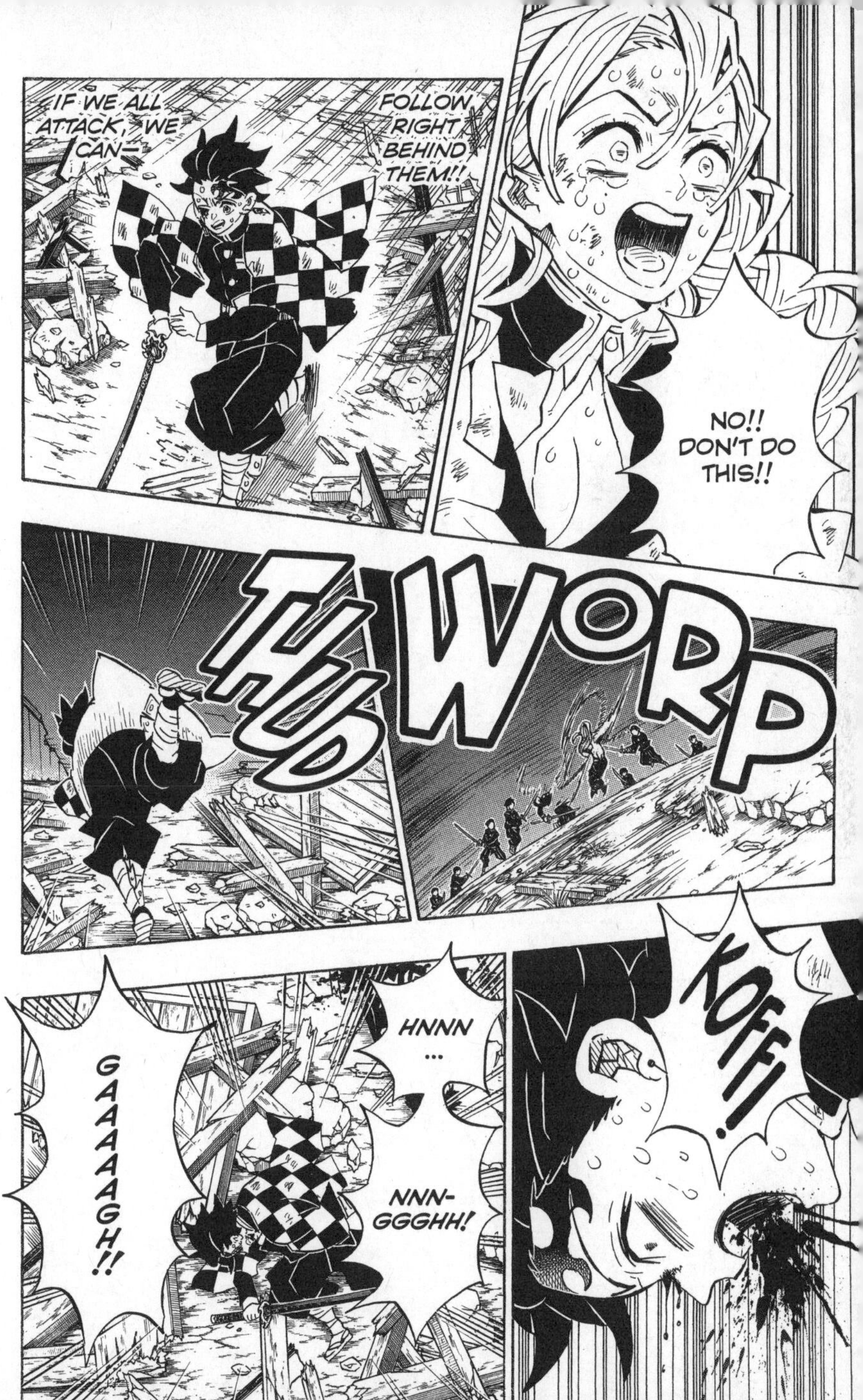
NO!! DON'T DO THIS!!
FOLLOW RIGHT BEHIND THEM!!
IF WE ALL ATTACK, WE CAN—
THWORP
THUD
KOFF!!
HNNN...
NNN-GGGHH!
GAAAAAAGH!!

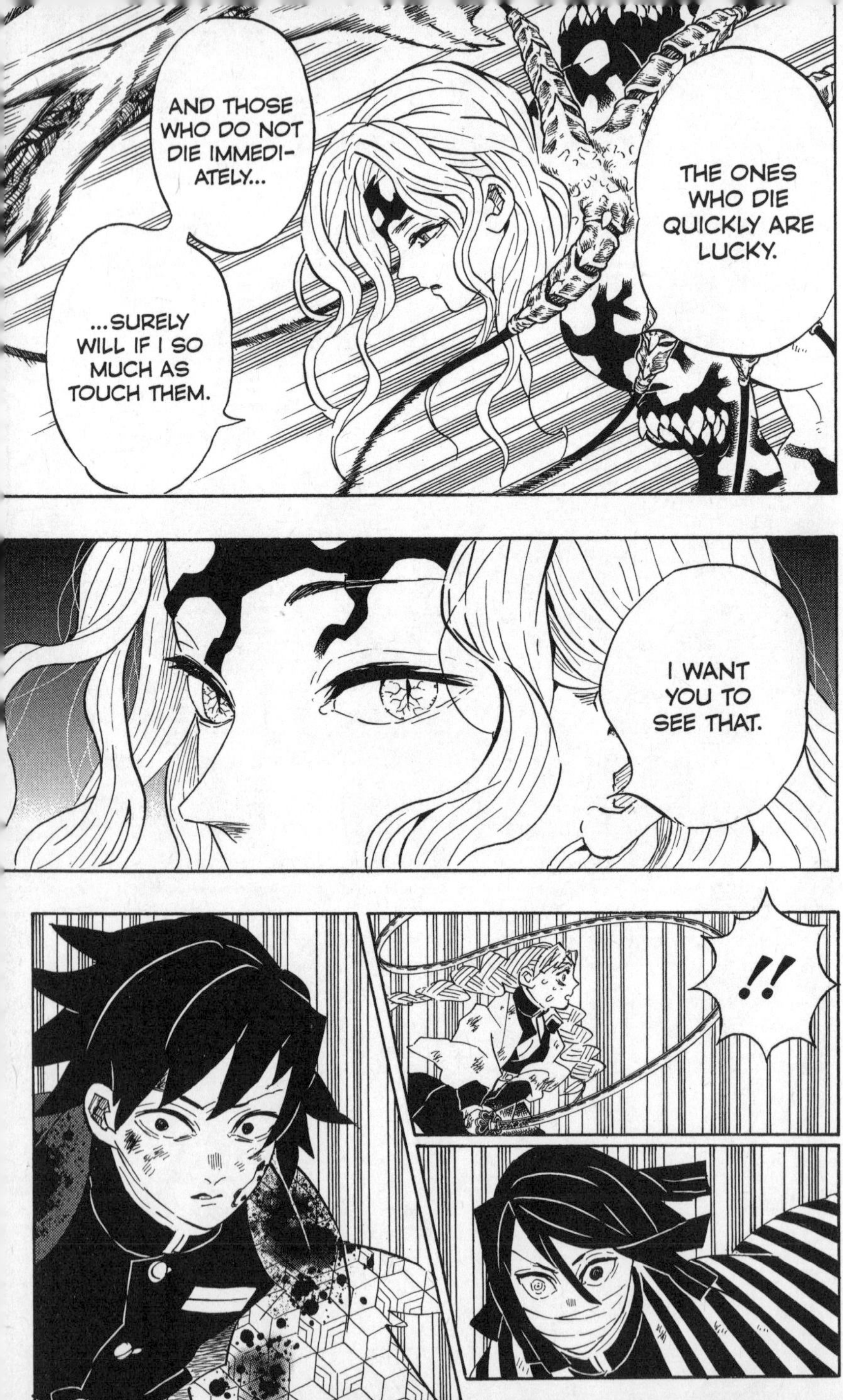
THE ONES WHO DIE QUICKLY ARE LUCKY.
AND THOSE WHO DO NOT DIE IMMEDI-ATELY...
...SURELY WILL IF I SO MUCH AS TOUCH THEM.
I WANT YOU TO SEE THAT.
!!

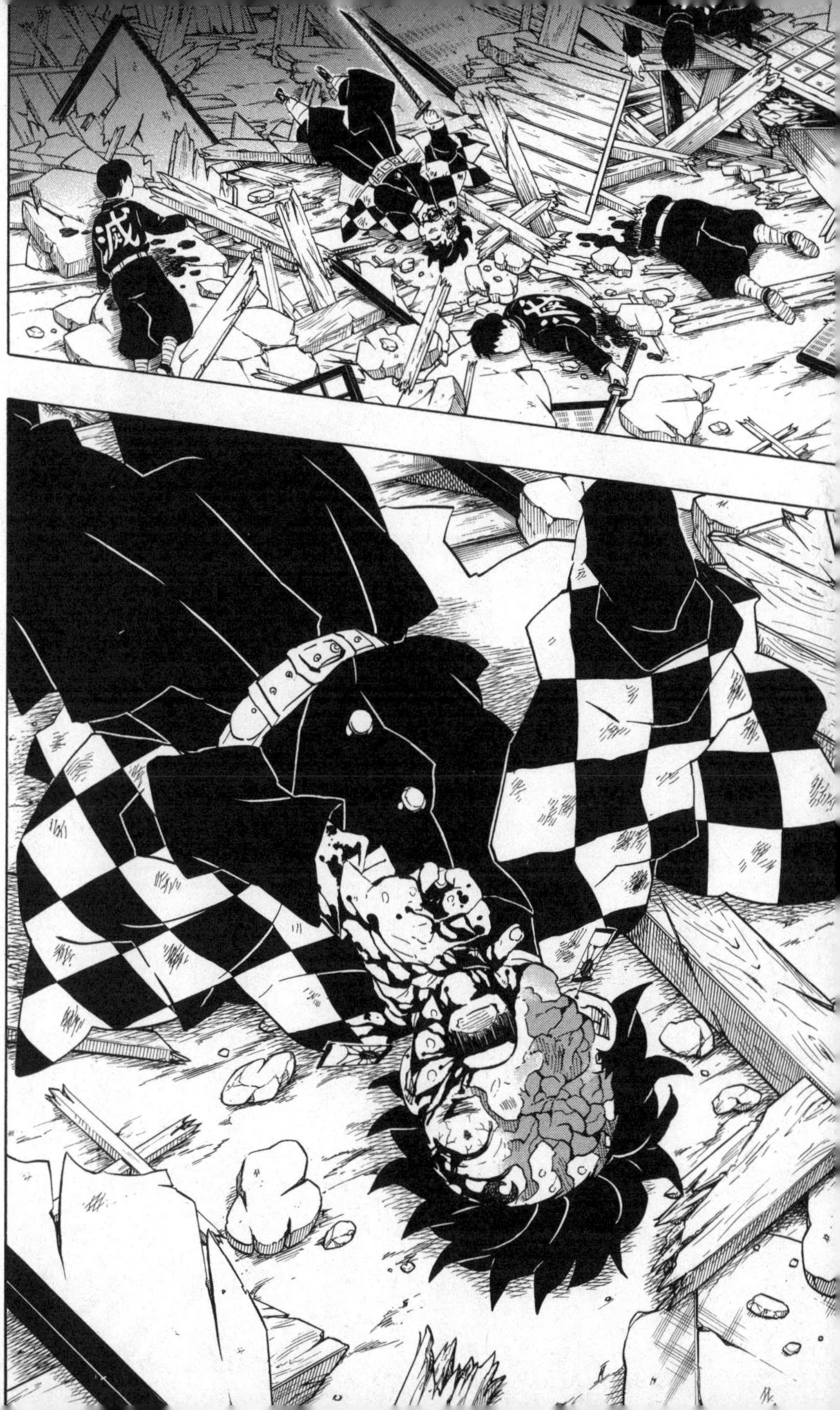
滅

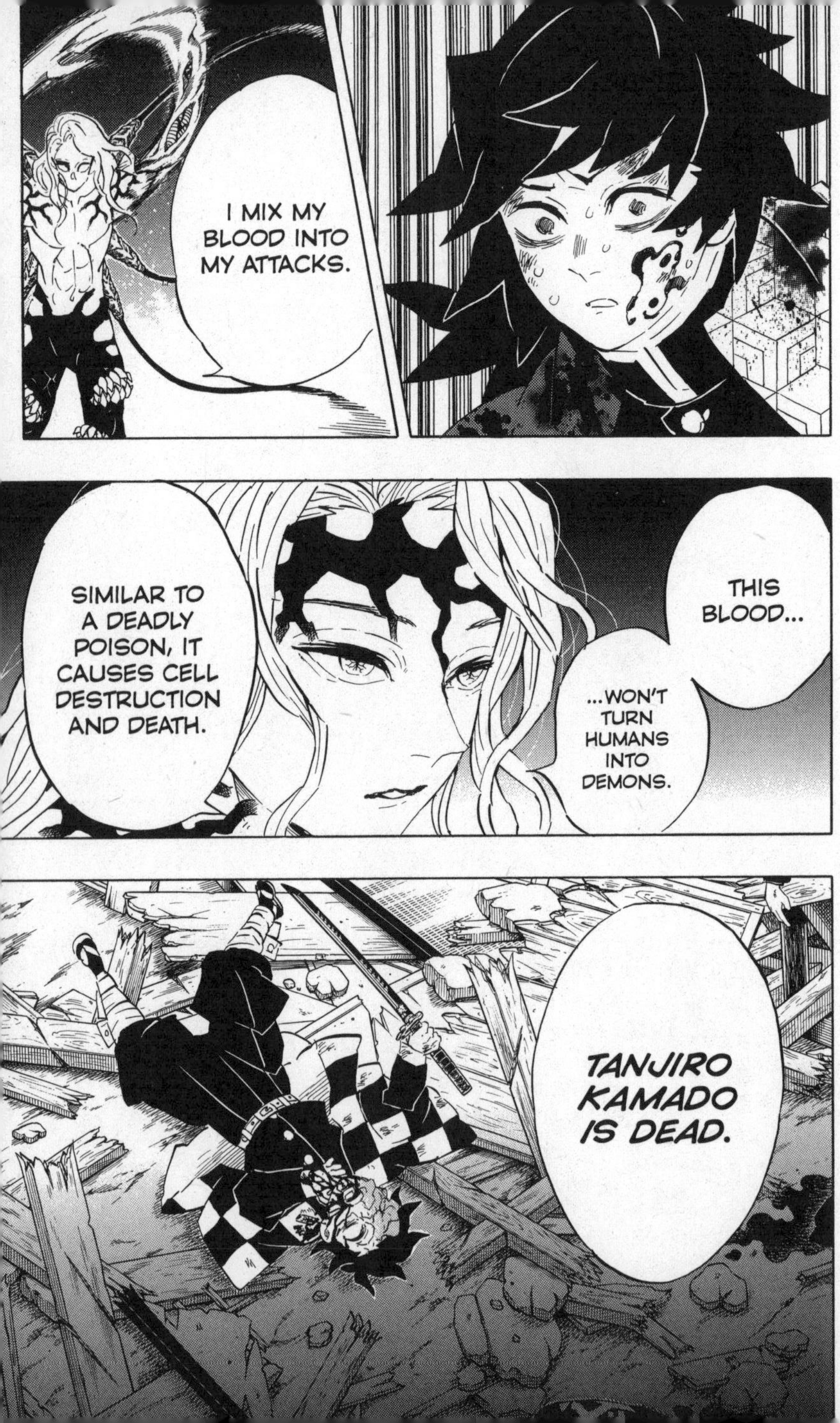
I MIX MY BLOOD INTO MY ATTACKS.
THIS BLOOD...
...WON'T TURN HUMANS INTO DEMONS.
SIMILAR TO A DEADLY POISON, IT CAUSES CELL DESTRUCTION AND DEATH.
TANJIRO KAMADO IS DEAD.

During the final battle, the crows are receiving orders in writing. Kuina and Kanata jot down in shorthand what Master Ubuyashiki says and show it to the crows. Shorthand is a kind of simple code. It's interesting, so watch a video about it sometime when you have a moment. It's fun!

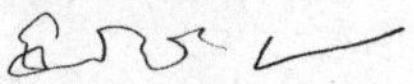

← It's like this. Cool, huh?

Crows that can talk and read! Amazing!

A crow puffed up with pride.

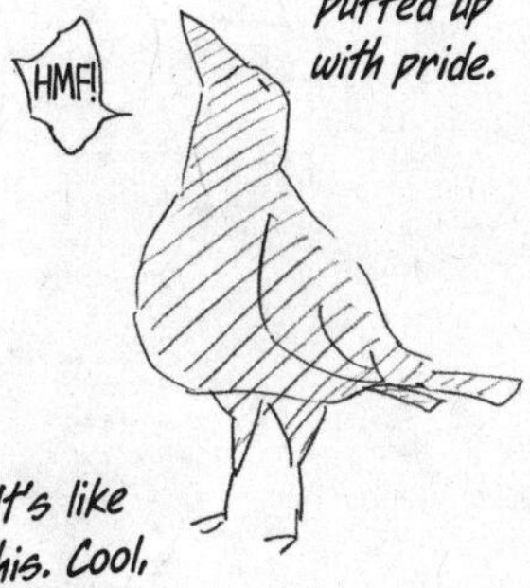
HMF!

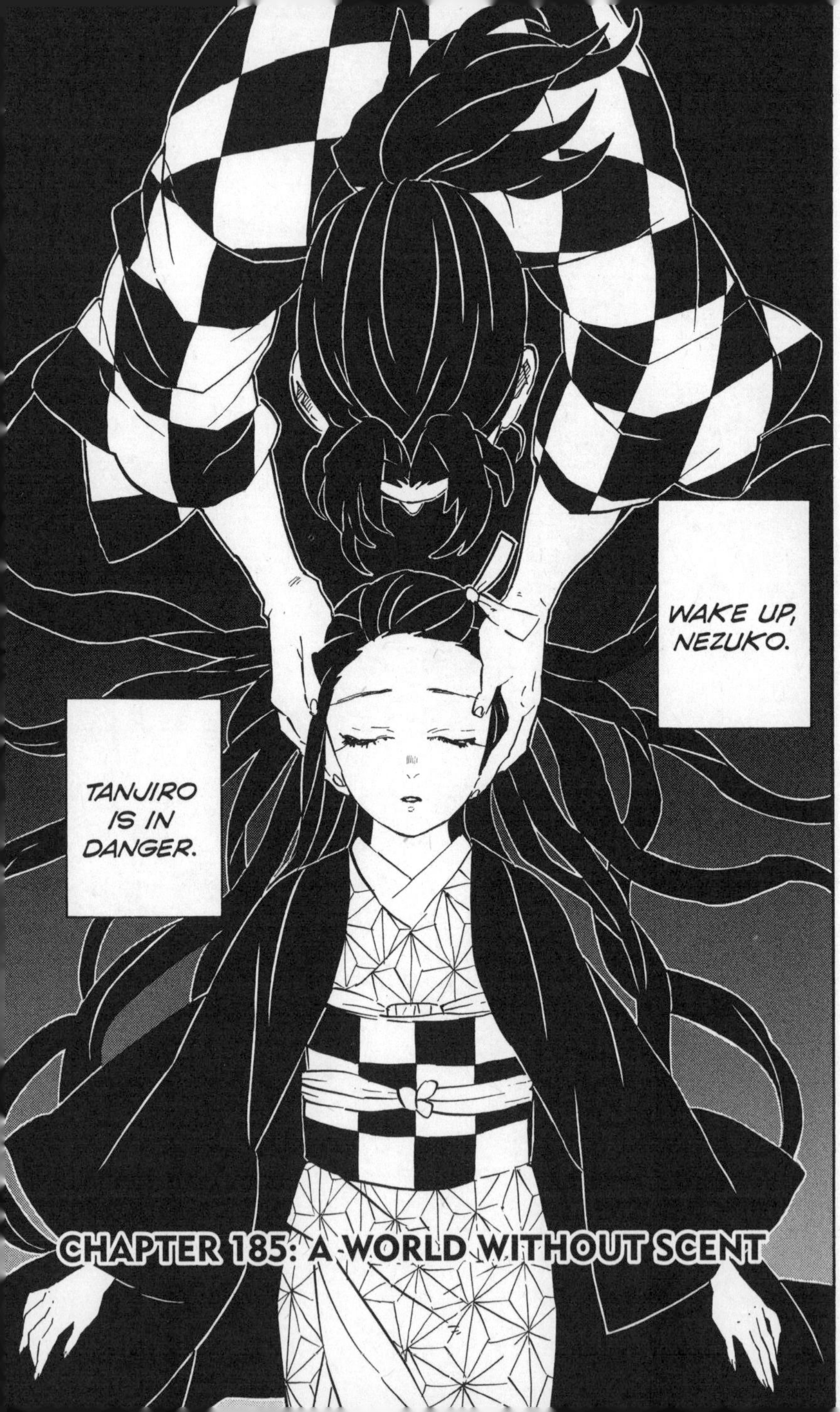
WAKE UP, NEZUKO.
TANJIRO IS IN DANGER.

CHAPTER 185: A WORLD WITHOUT SCENT

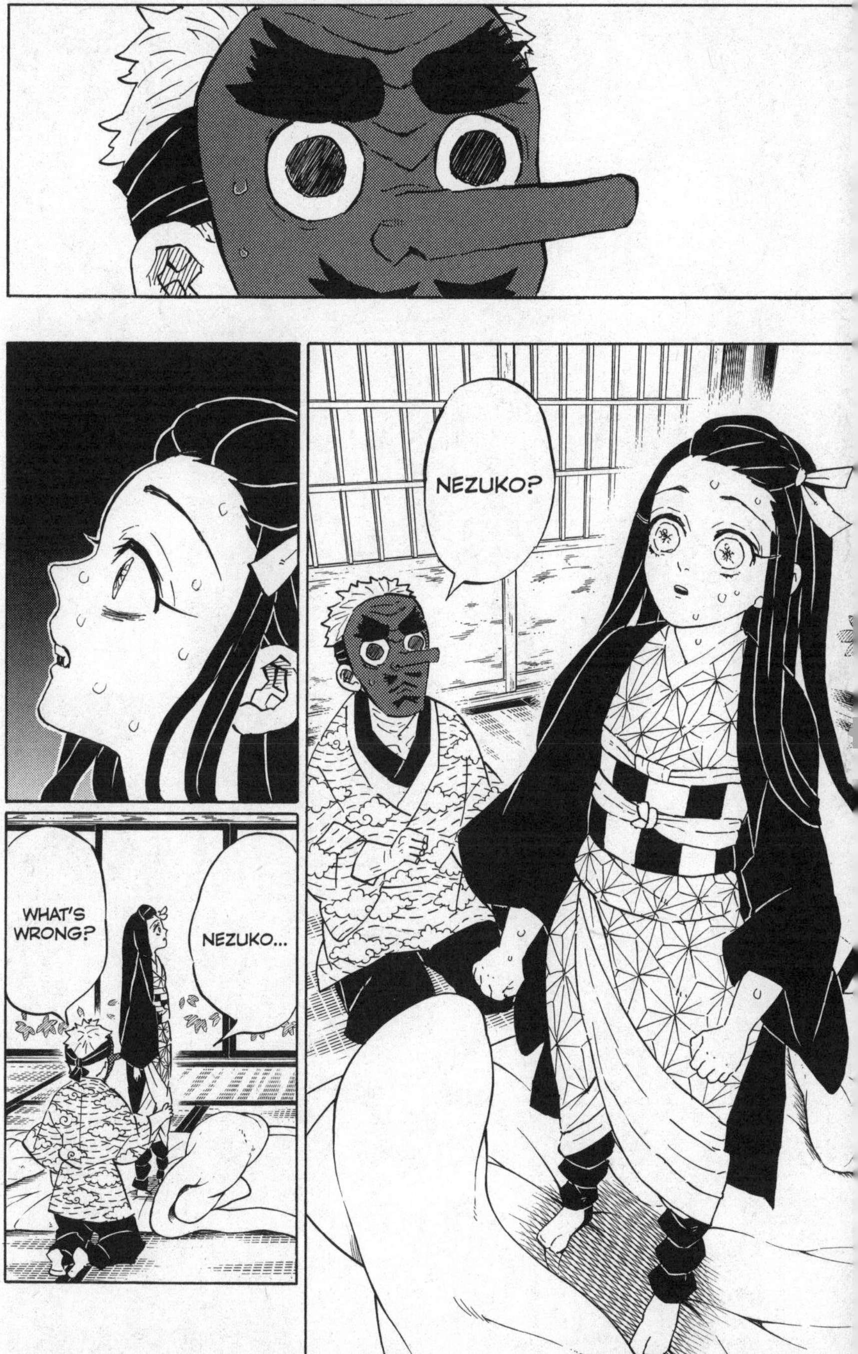
NEZUKO?
NEZUKO...
WHAT'S WRONG?

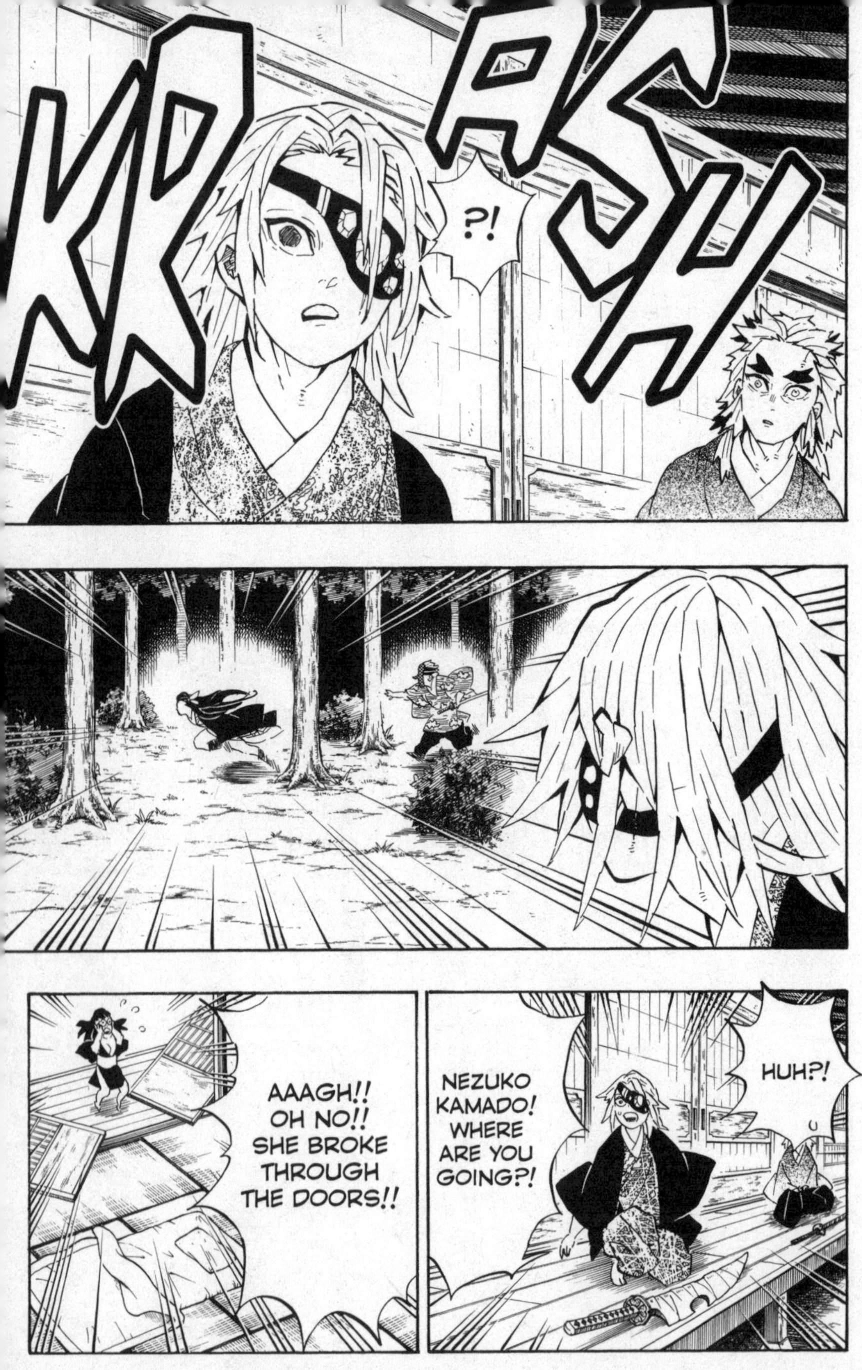
KRASH
?!
HUH?!
NEZUKO KAMADO! WHERE ARE YOU GOING?!
AAAGH!! OH NO!! SHE BROKE THROUGH THE DOORS!!

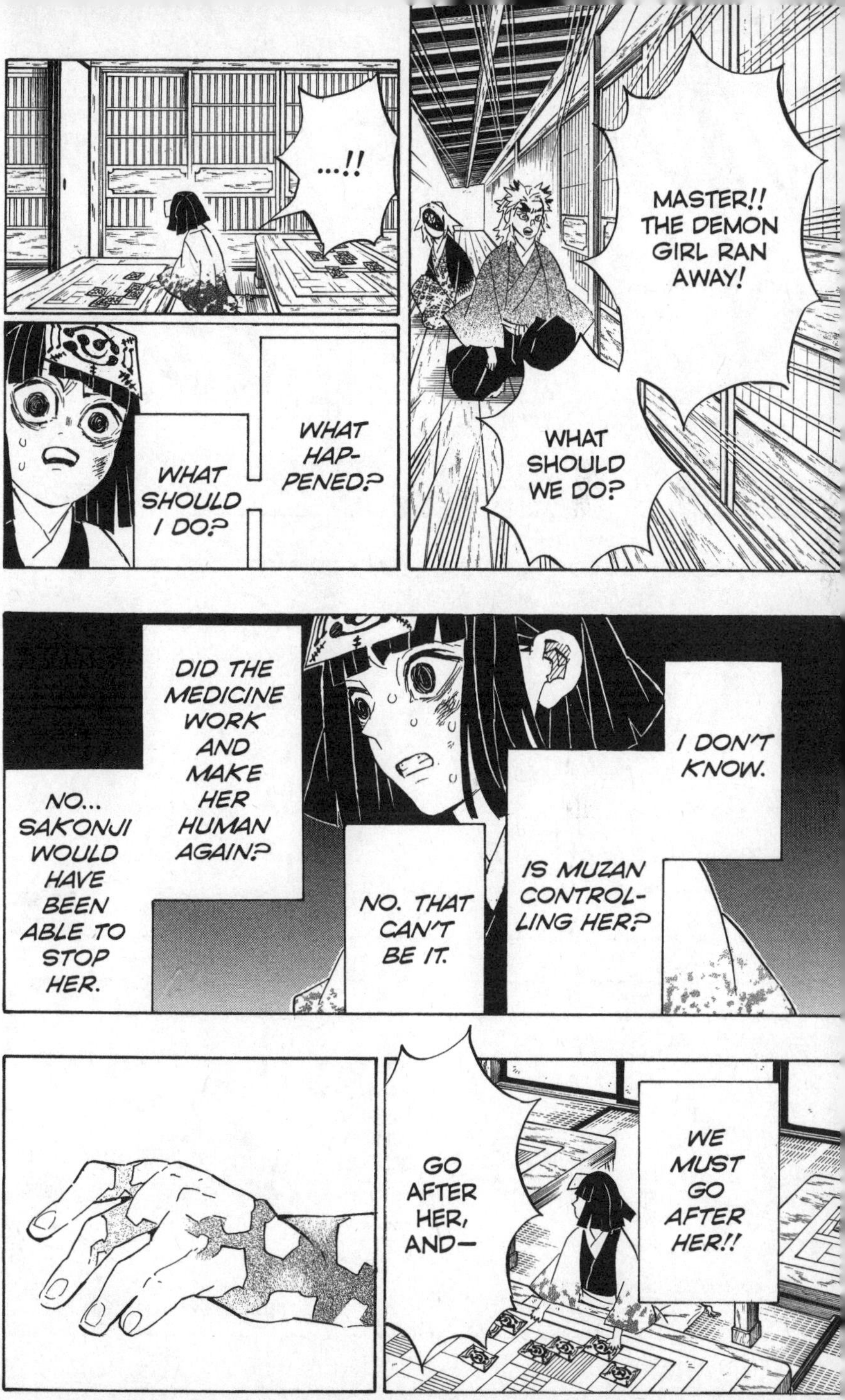
MASTER!! THE DEMON GIRL RAN AWAY!
WHAT SHOULD WE DO?
...!!
WHAT HAP-PENED?
WHAT SHOULD I DO?
I DON'T KNOW.
IS MUZAN CONTROL-LING HER?
NO. THAT CAN'T BE IT.
DID THE MEDICINE WORK AND MAKE HER HUMAN AGAIN?
NO... SAKONJI WOULD HAVE BEEN ABLE TO STOP HER.
WE MUST GO AFTER HER!!
GO AFTER HER, AND—

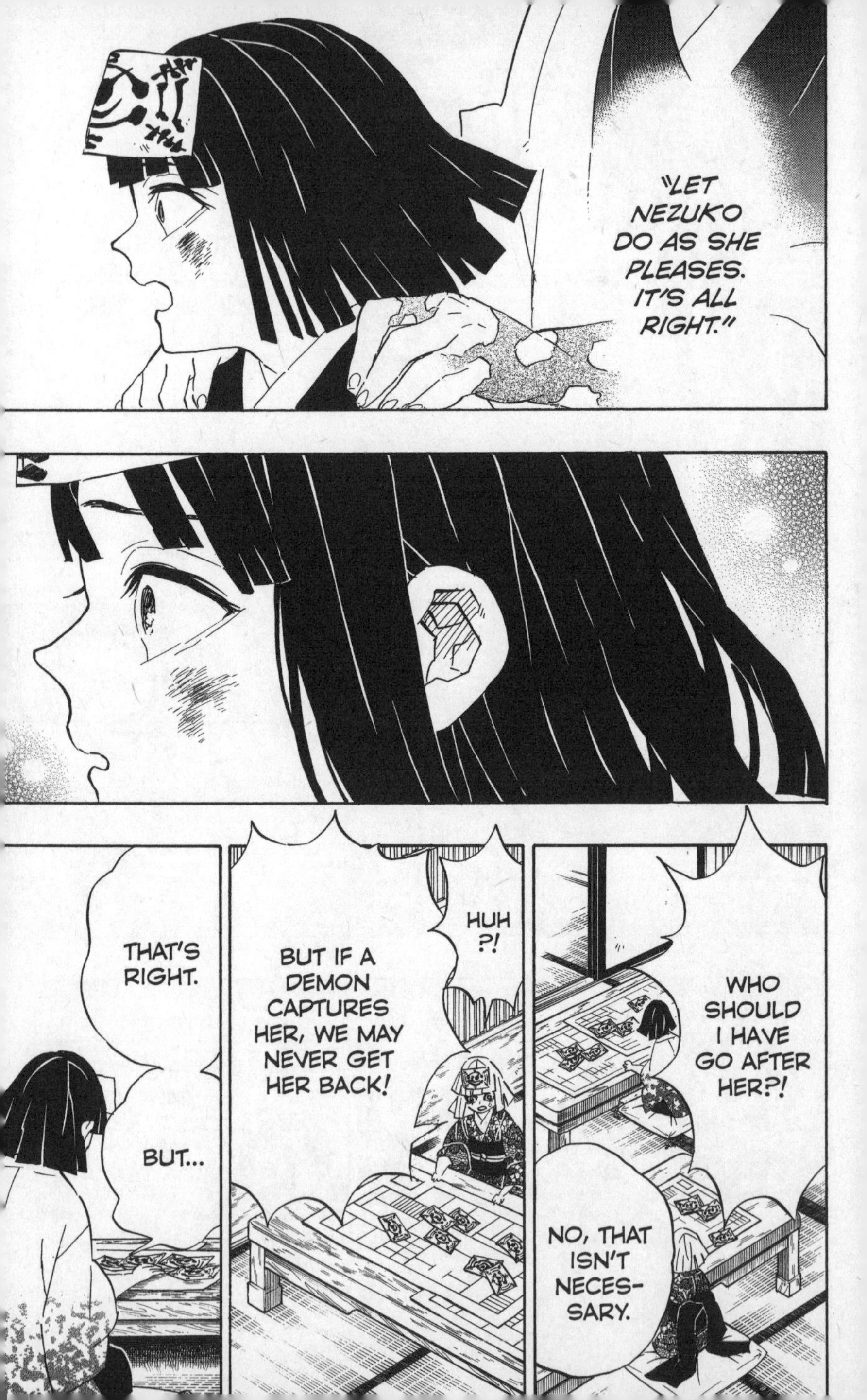
"LET NEZUKO DO AS SHE PLEASES. IT'S ALL RIGHT."
WHO SHOULD I HAVE GO AFTER HER?!
NO, THAT ISN'T NECES-SARY.
HUH ?!
BUT IF A DEMON CAPTURES HER, WE MAY NEVER GET HER BACK!
THAT'S RIGHT.
BUT...

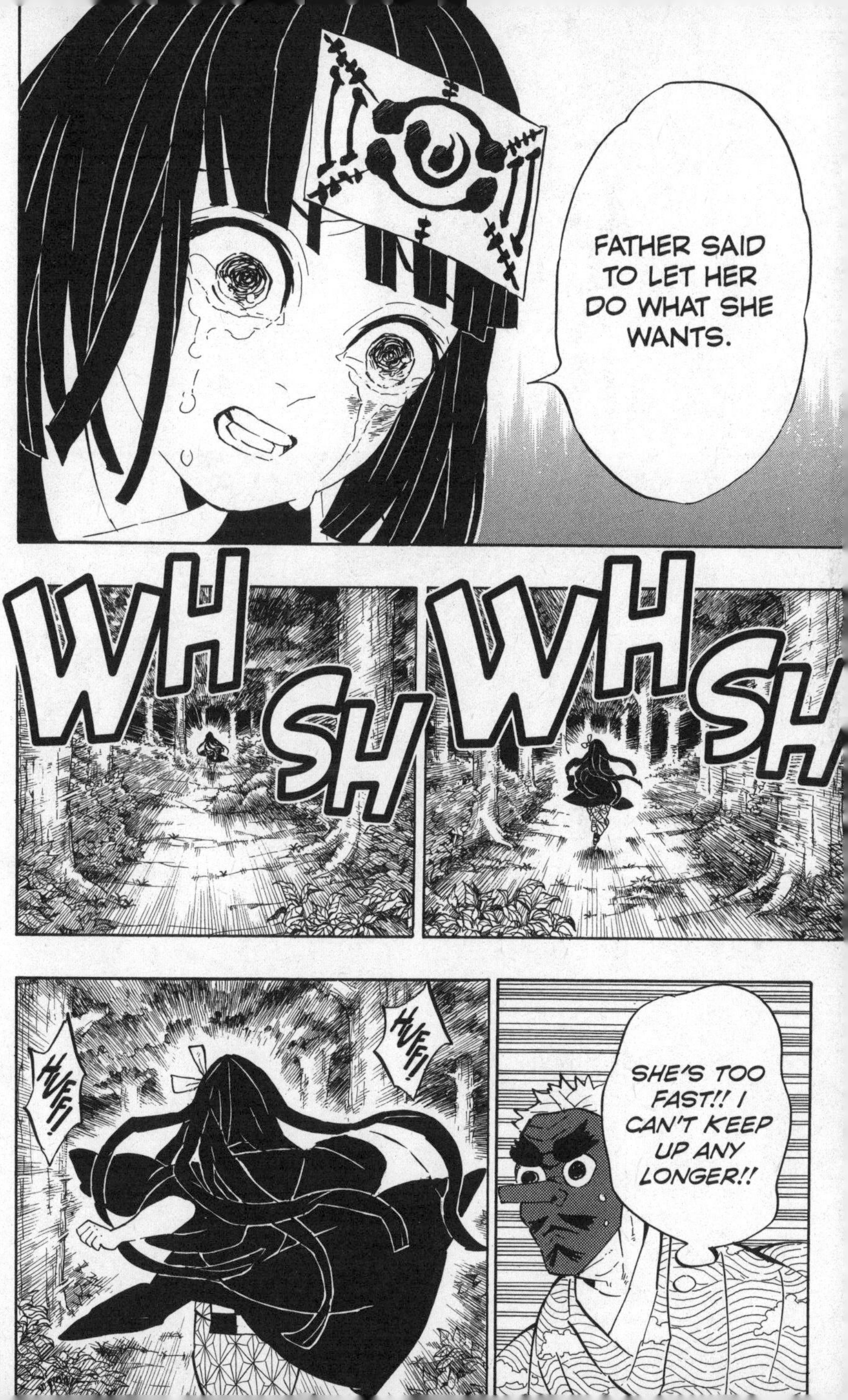
FATHER SAID TO LET HER DO WHAT SHE WANTS.
WHSH
WHSH
SHE'S TOO FAST!! I CAN'T KEEP UP ANY LONGER!!
HUFF!
HUFF!

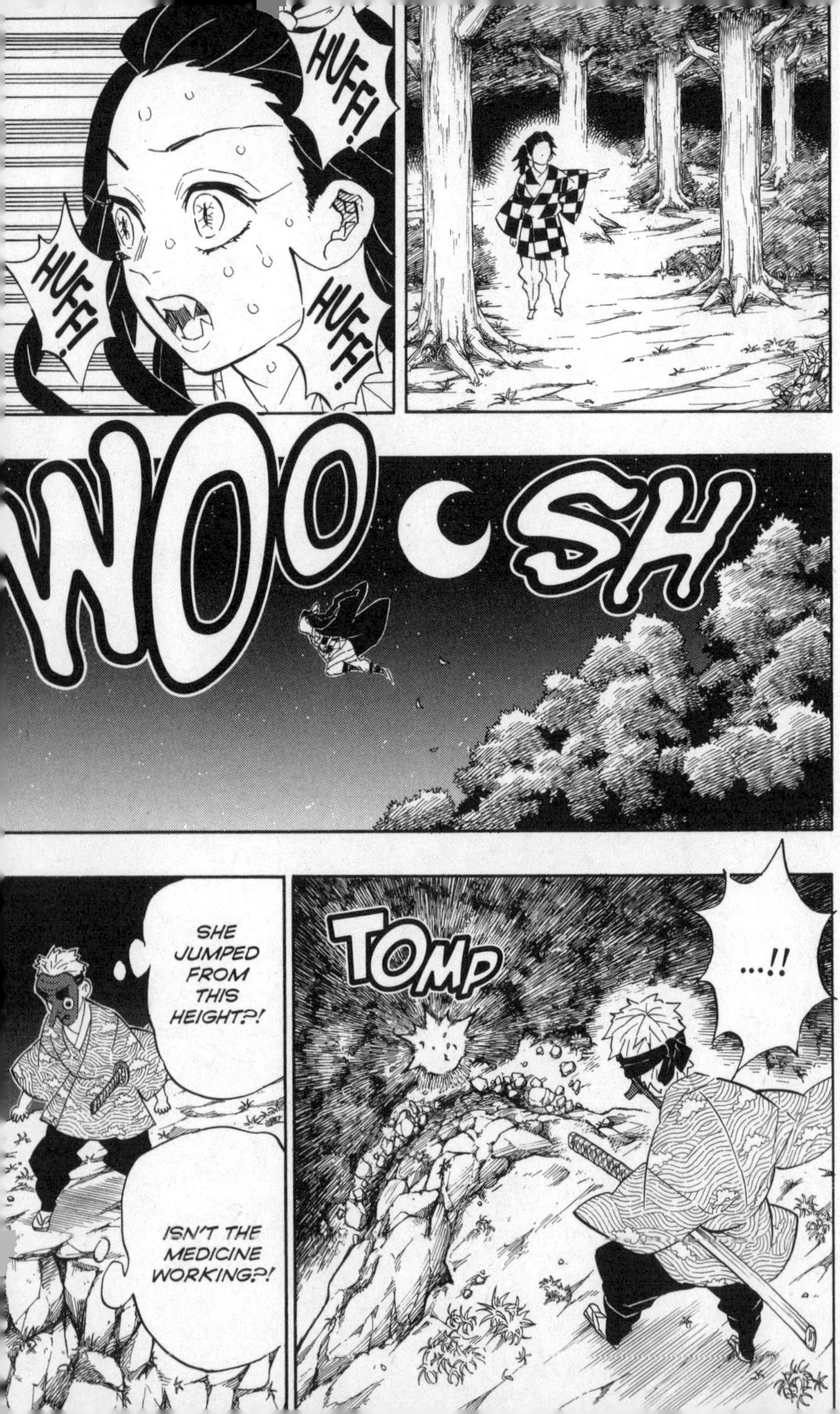
HUFF!
HUFF!
HUFF!
WOOSH
TOMP
...!!
SHE JUMPED FROM THIS HEIGHT?!
ISN'T THE MEDICINE WORKING?!

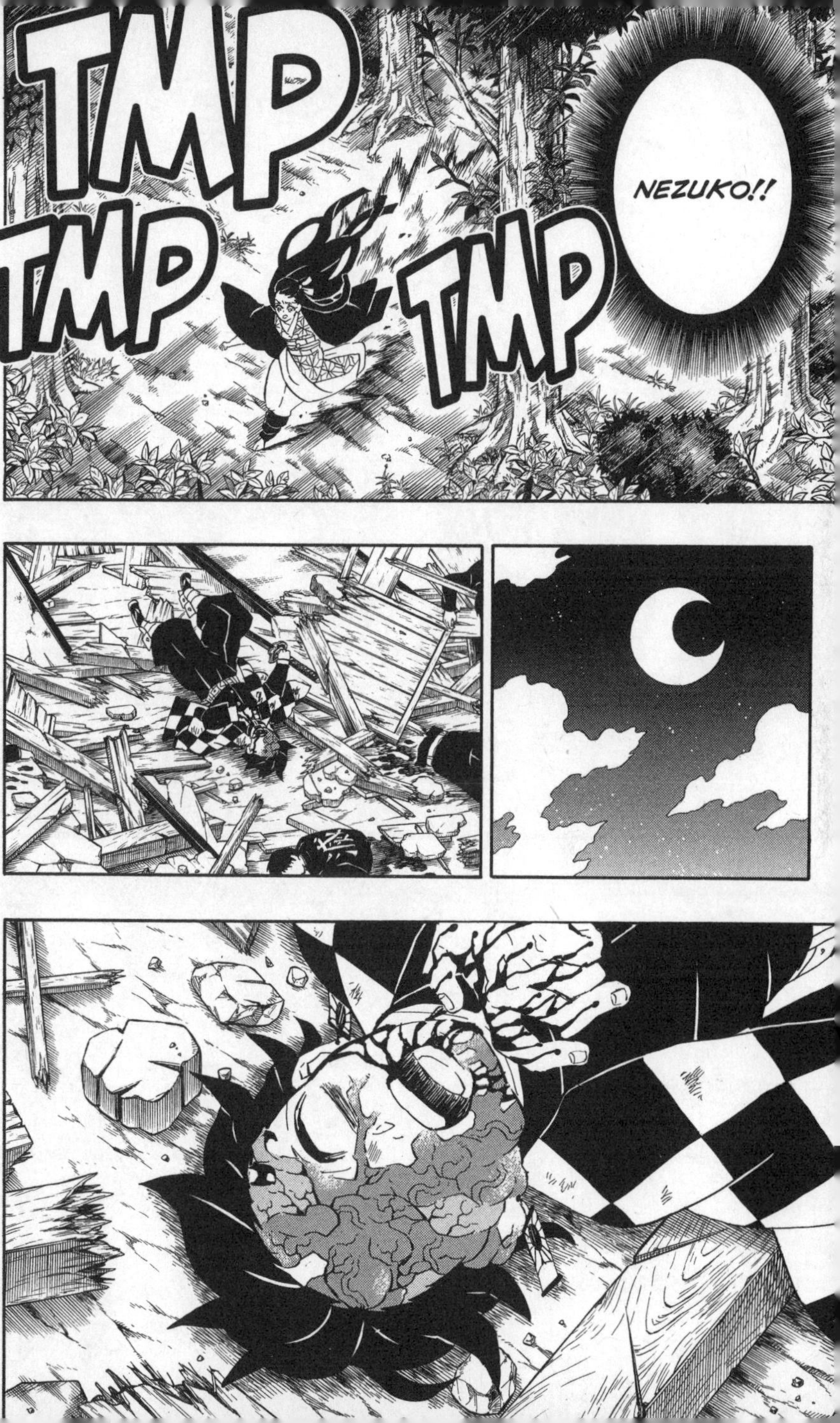
NEZUKO!!
TMP
TMP
TMP
TMP

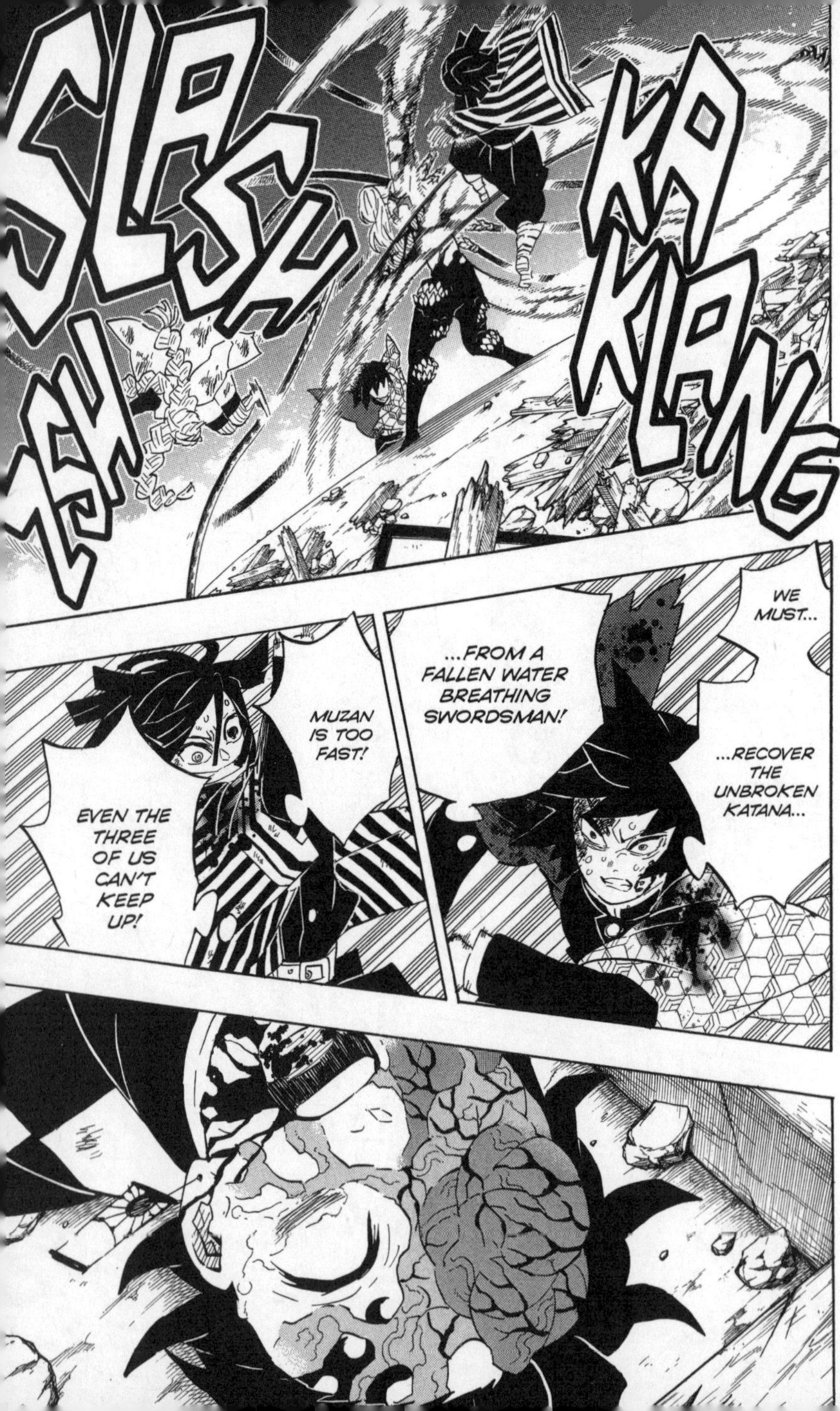
KA KLANG
SLASH
WE MUST...
...RECOVER THE UNBROKEN KATANA...
...FROM A FALLEN WATER BREATHING SWORDSMAN!
MUZAN IS TOO FAST!
EVEN THE THREE OF US CAN'T KEEP UP!

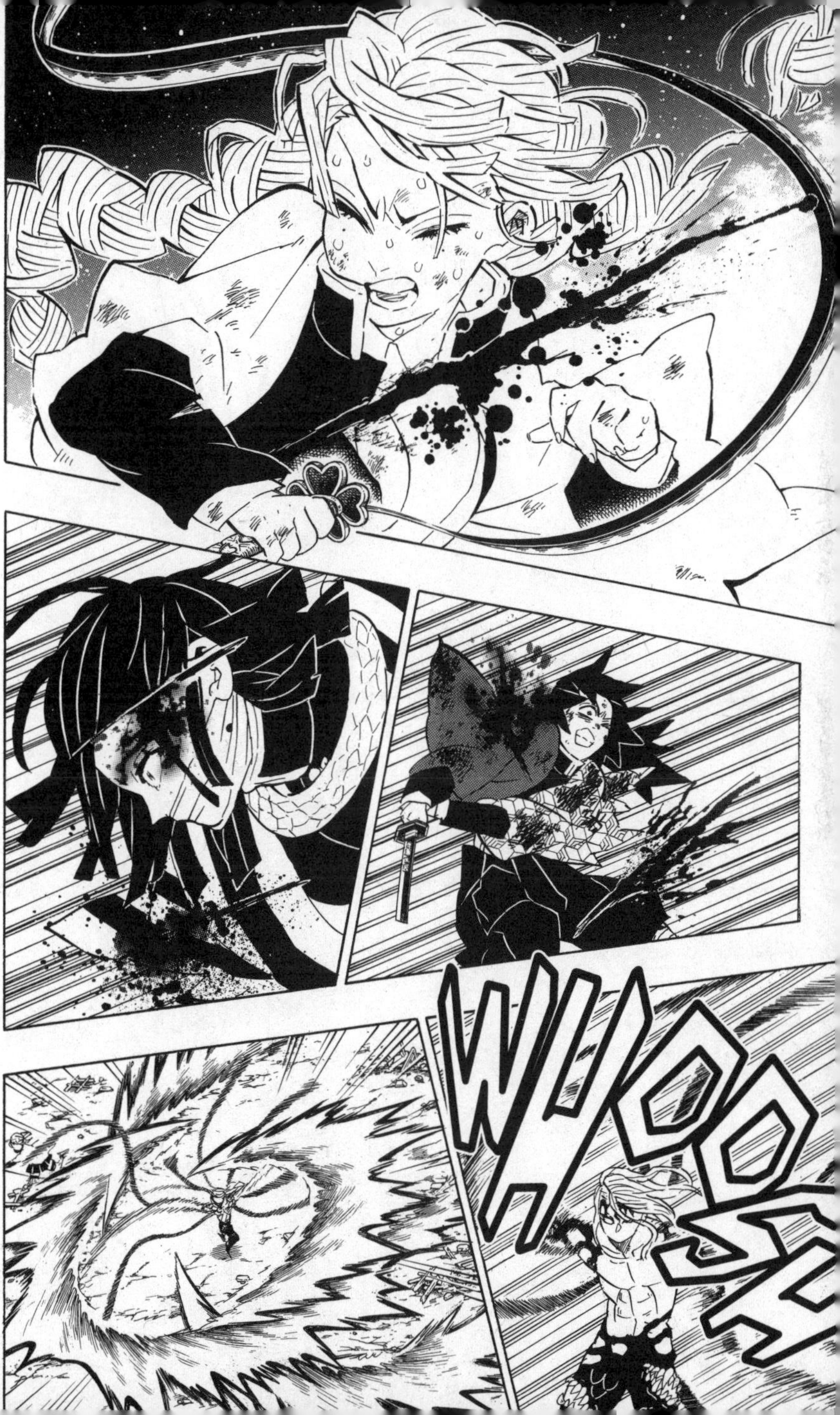
WHOOSH

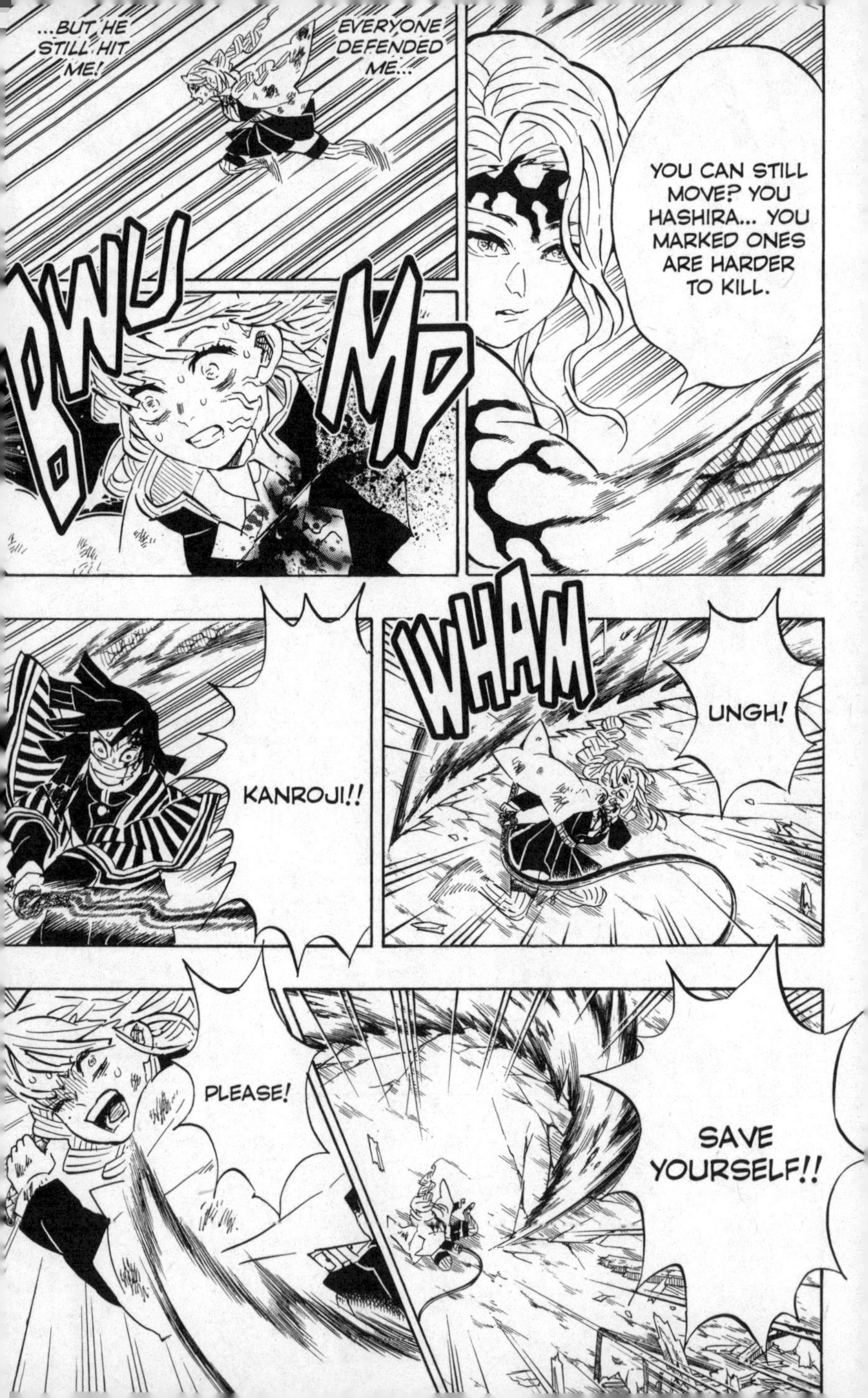
YOU CAN STILL MOVE? YOU HASHIRA... YOU MARKED ONES ARE HARDER TO KILL.
EVERYONE DEFENDED ME...
...BUT HE STILL HIT ME!
BWUMP
WHAM
UNGH!
KANROJI!!
SAVE YOURSELF!!
PLEASE!

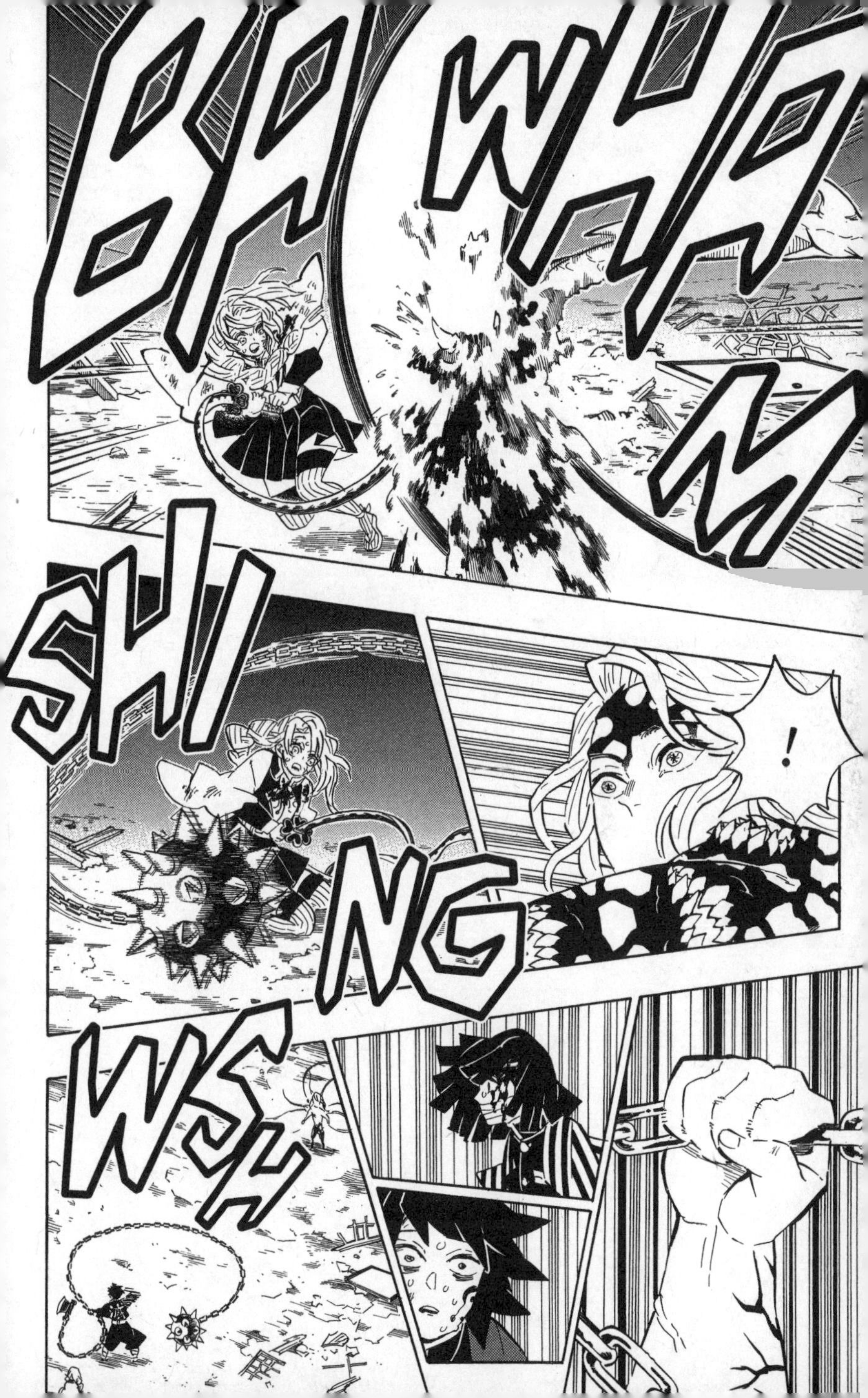
SHING
!
WSH

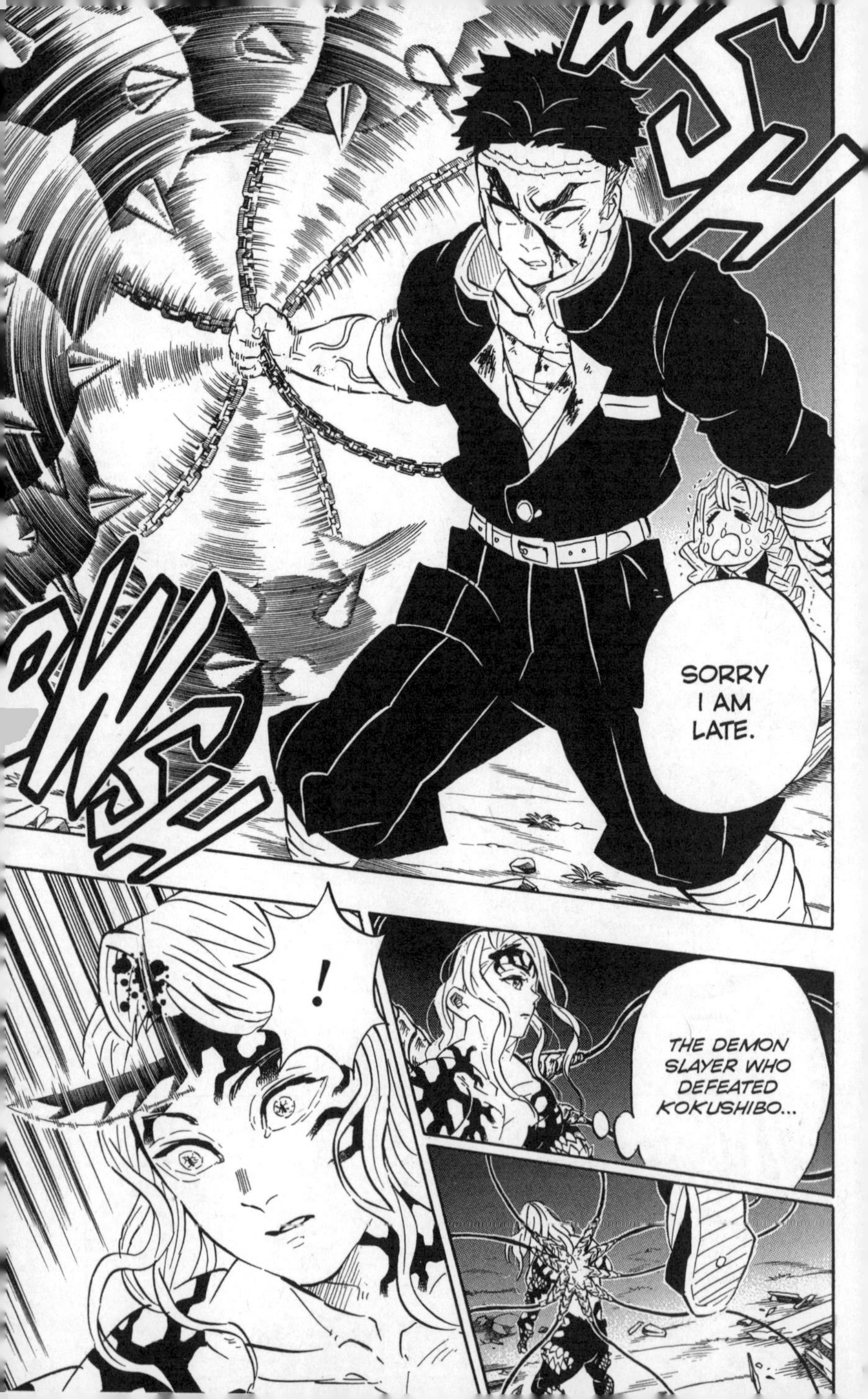
WHSH
SORRY I AM LATE.
WHSH
THE DEMON SLAYER WHO DEFEATED KOKUSHIBO...
!

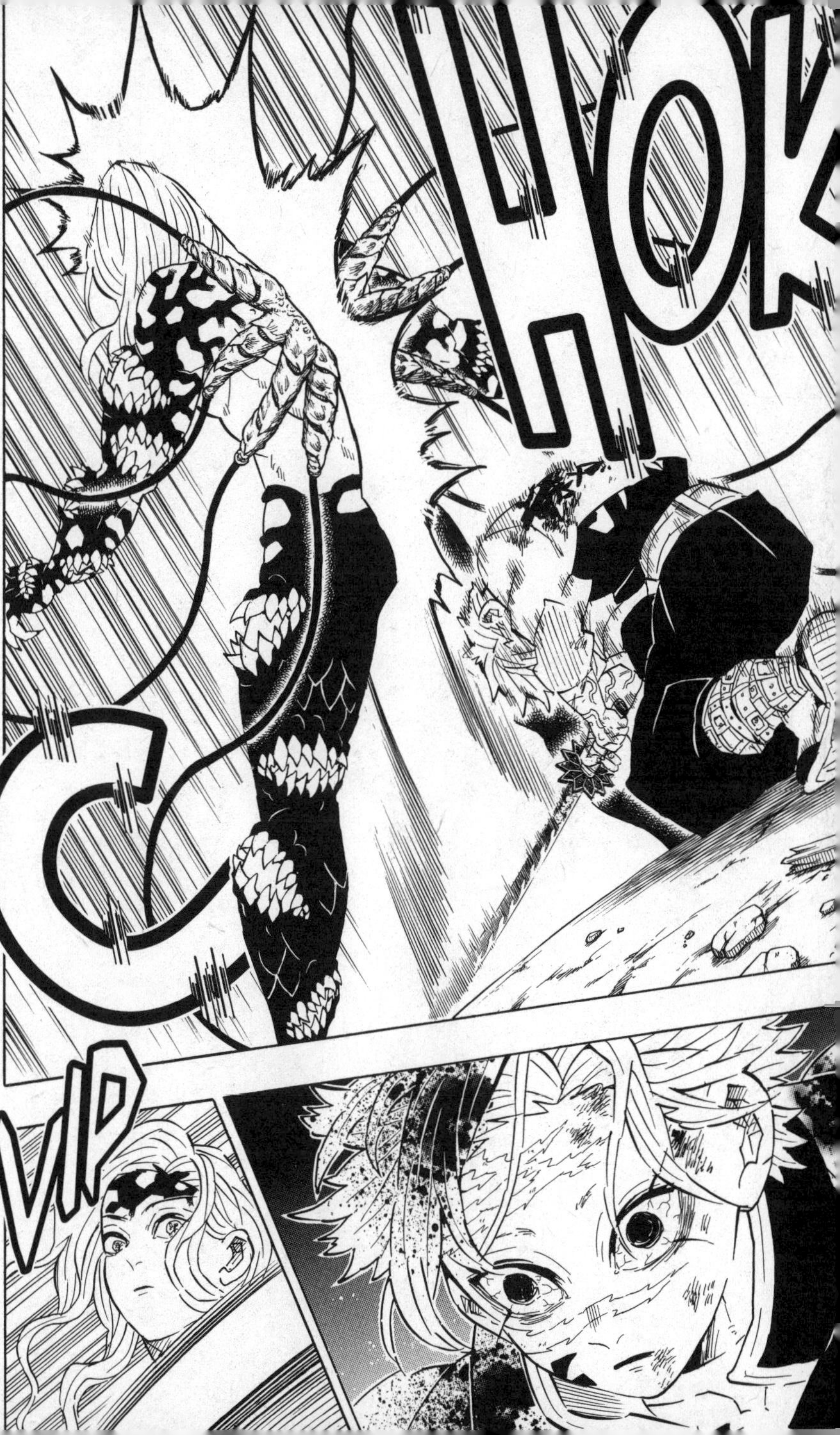
HOK
C
VIP

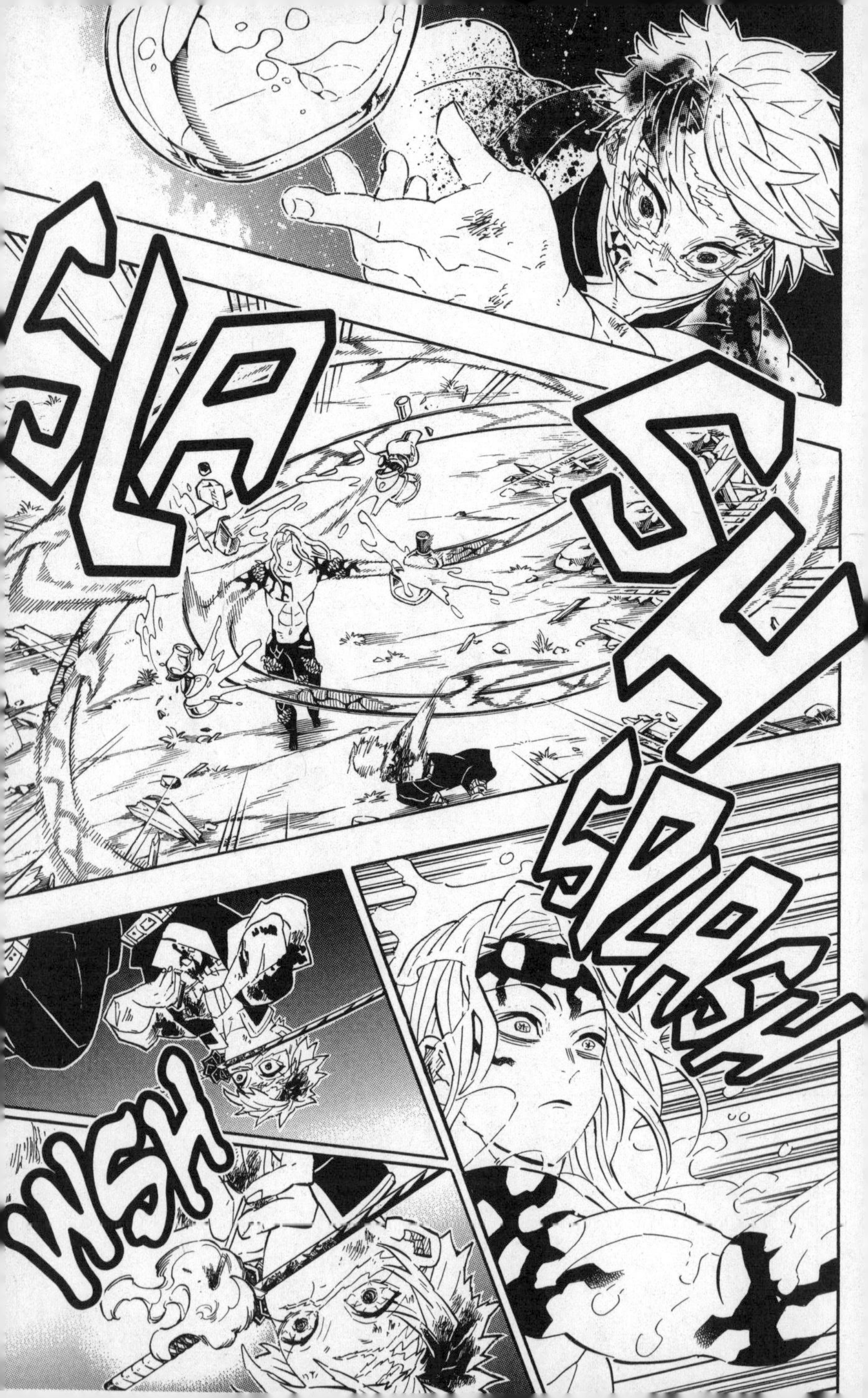
SLASH
SPLASH!
WSH

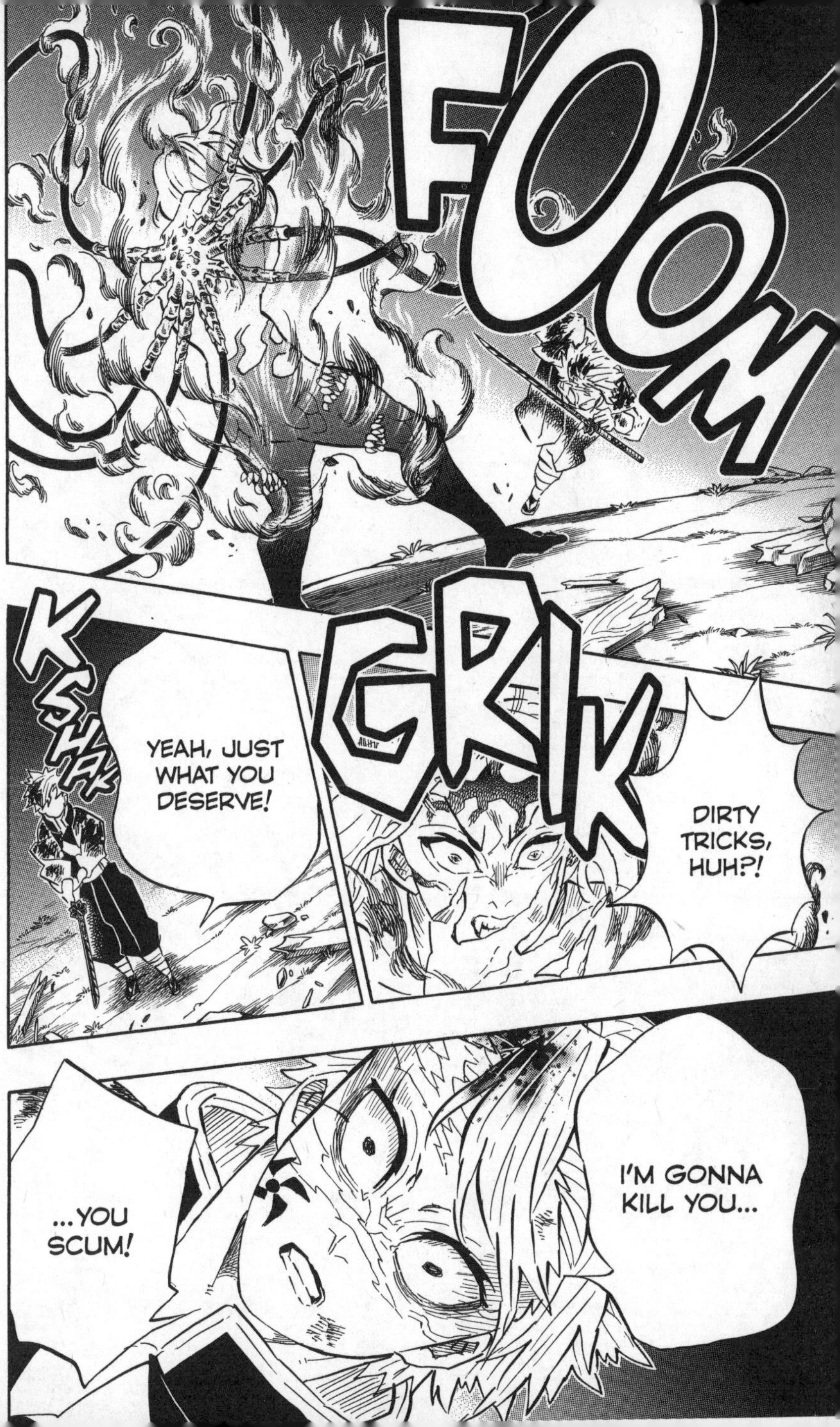
FOOM
CRIK
DIRTY TRICKS, HUH?!
K'SHAK
YEAH, JUST WHAT YOU DESERVE!
I'M GONNA KILL YOU...
...YOU SCUM!

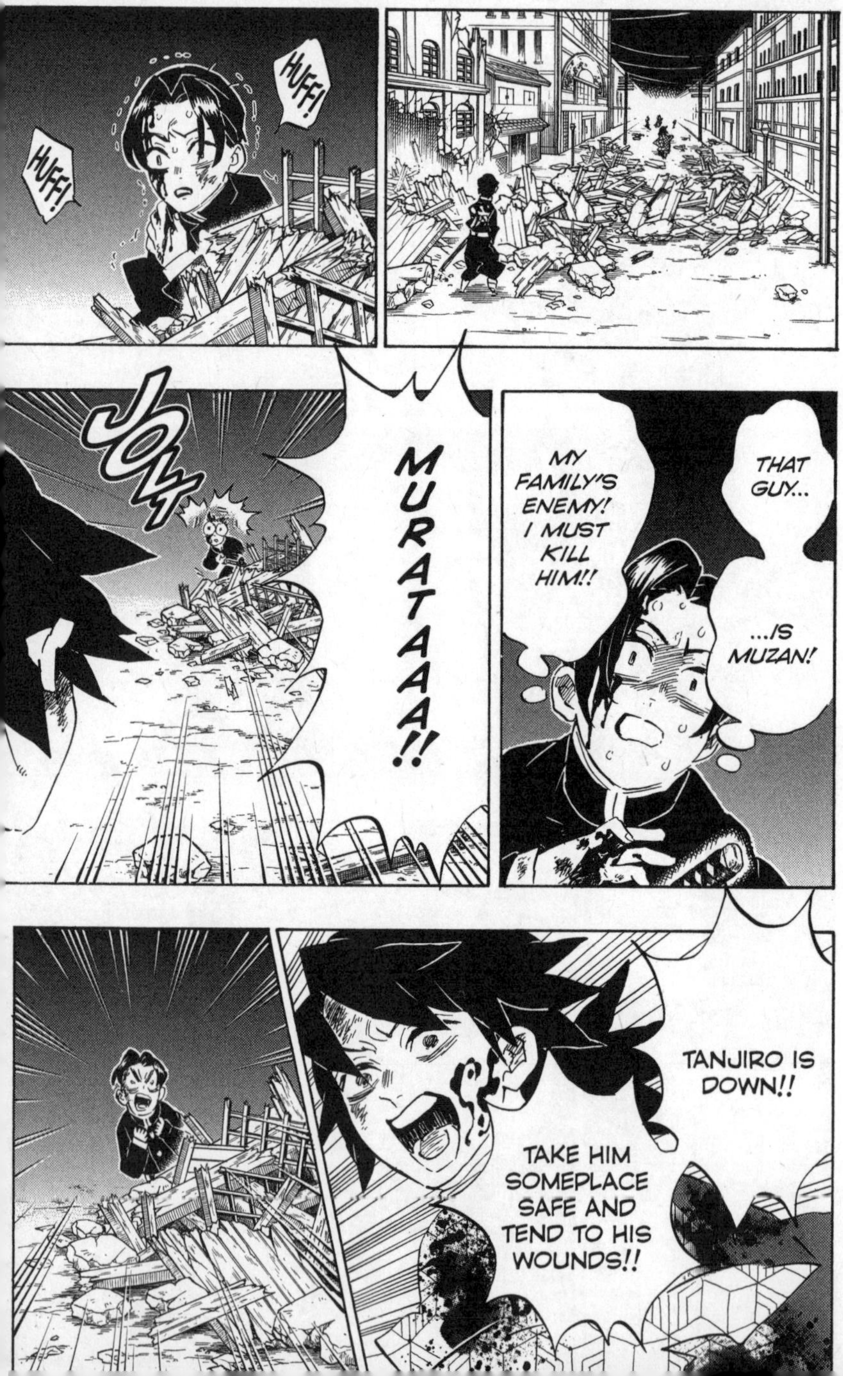
HUFF!
HUFF!
THAT GUY...
...IS MUZAN!
MY FAMILY'S ENEMY! I MUST KILL HIM!!
MURATAAAA!!
JOLT
TANJIRO IS DOWN!!
TAKE HIM SOMEPLACE SAFE AND TEND TO HIS WOUNDS!!

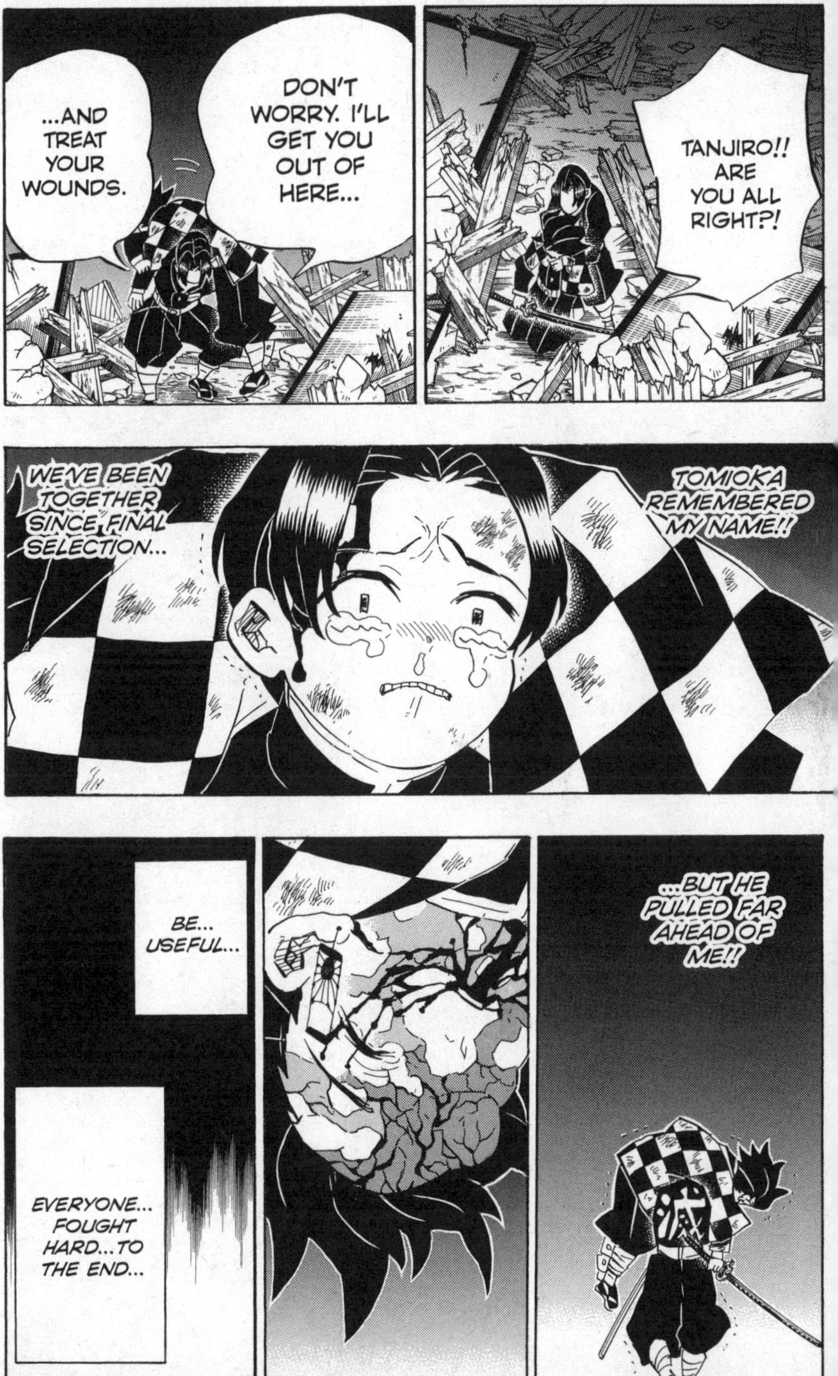
TANJIRO!! ARE YOU ALL RIGHT?!
DON'T WORRY. I'LL GET YOU OUT OF HERE...
...AND TREAT YOUR WOUNDS.
TOMIOKA REMEMBERED MY NAME!!
WE'VE BEEN TOGETHER SINCE FINAL SELECTION...
...BUT HE PULLED FAR AHEAD OF ME!!
BE... USEFUL...
EVERYONE... FOUGHT HARD...TO THE END...

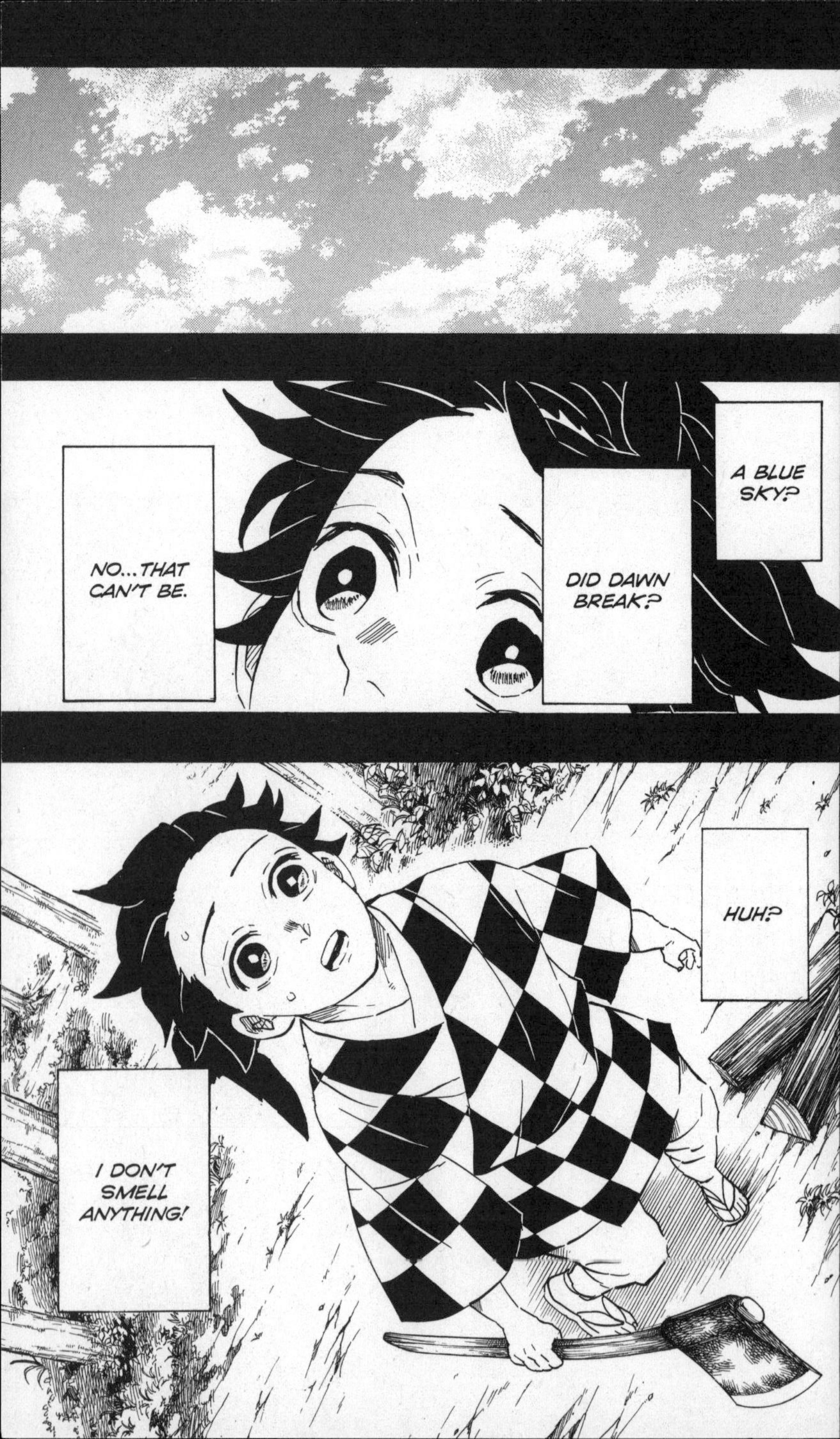
A BLUE SKY?
DID DAWN BREAK?
NO...THAT CAN'T BE.
HUH?
I DON'T SMELL ANYTHING!

Thank you, Tomioka! When this fight is over, let's go for a bite to eat! I'm so happy you remembered my name!

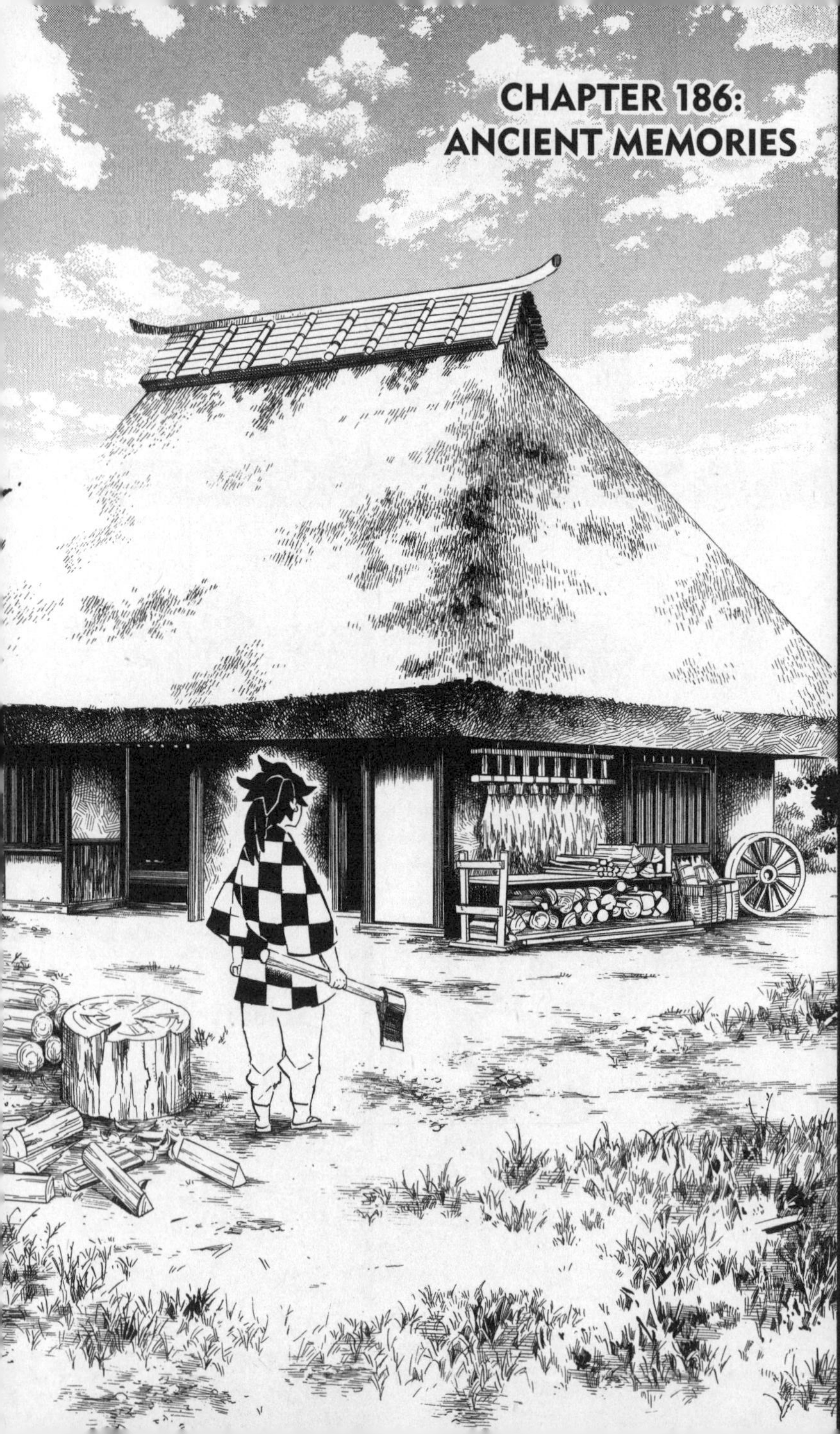
CHAPTER 186:
ANCIENT MEMORIES

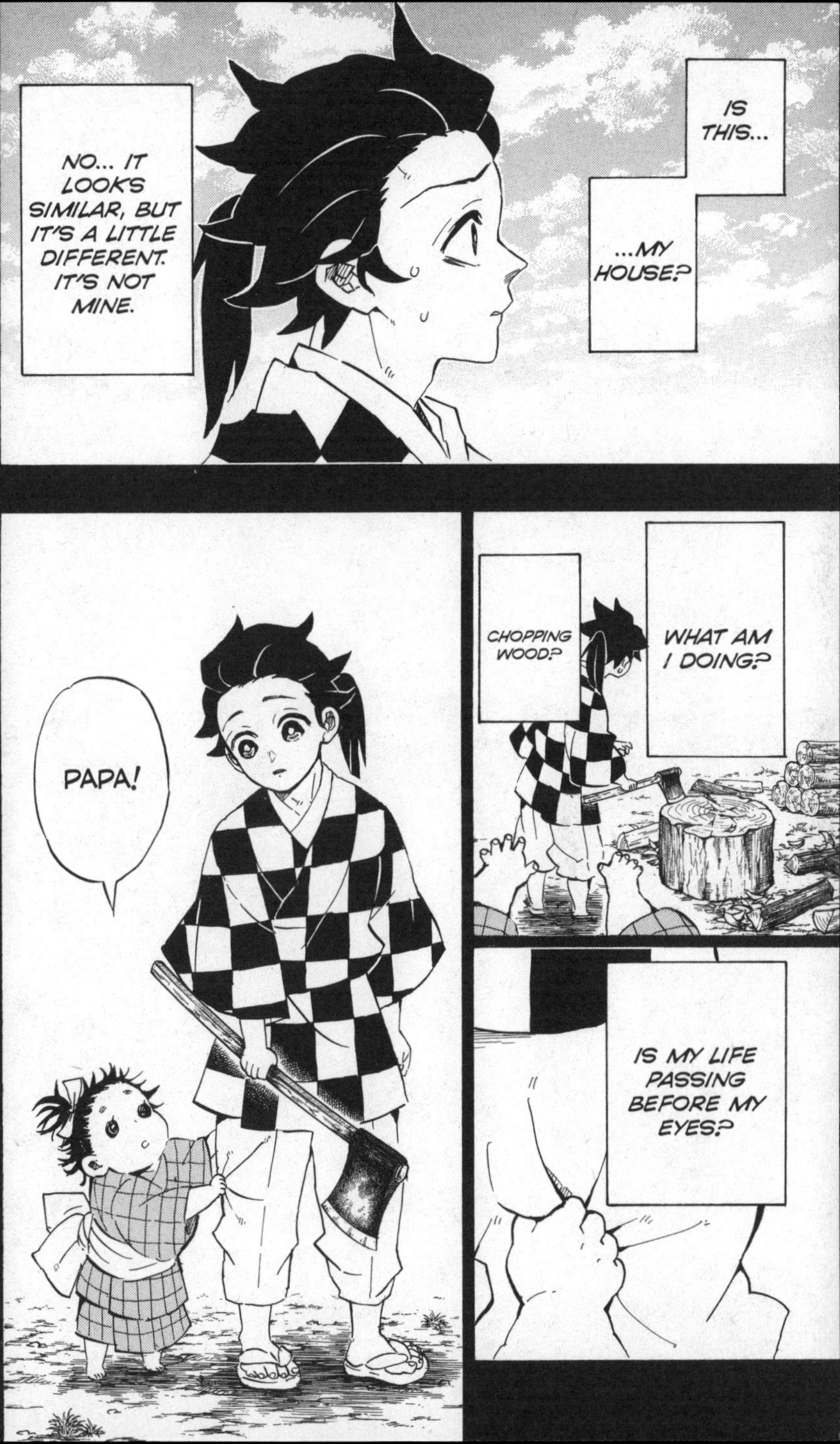
IS THIS...
...MY HOUSE?
NO... IT LOOKS SIMILAR, BUT IT'S A LITTLE DIFFERENT. IT'S NOT MINE.
WHAT AM I DOING?
CHOPPING WOOD?
IS MY LIFE PASSING BEFORE MY EYES?
PAPA!

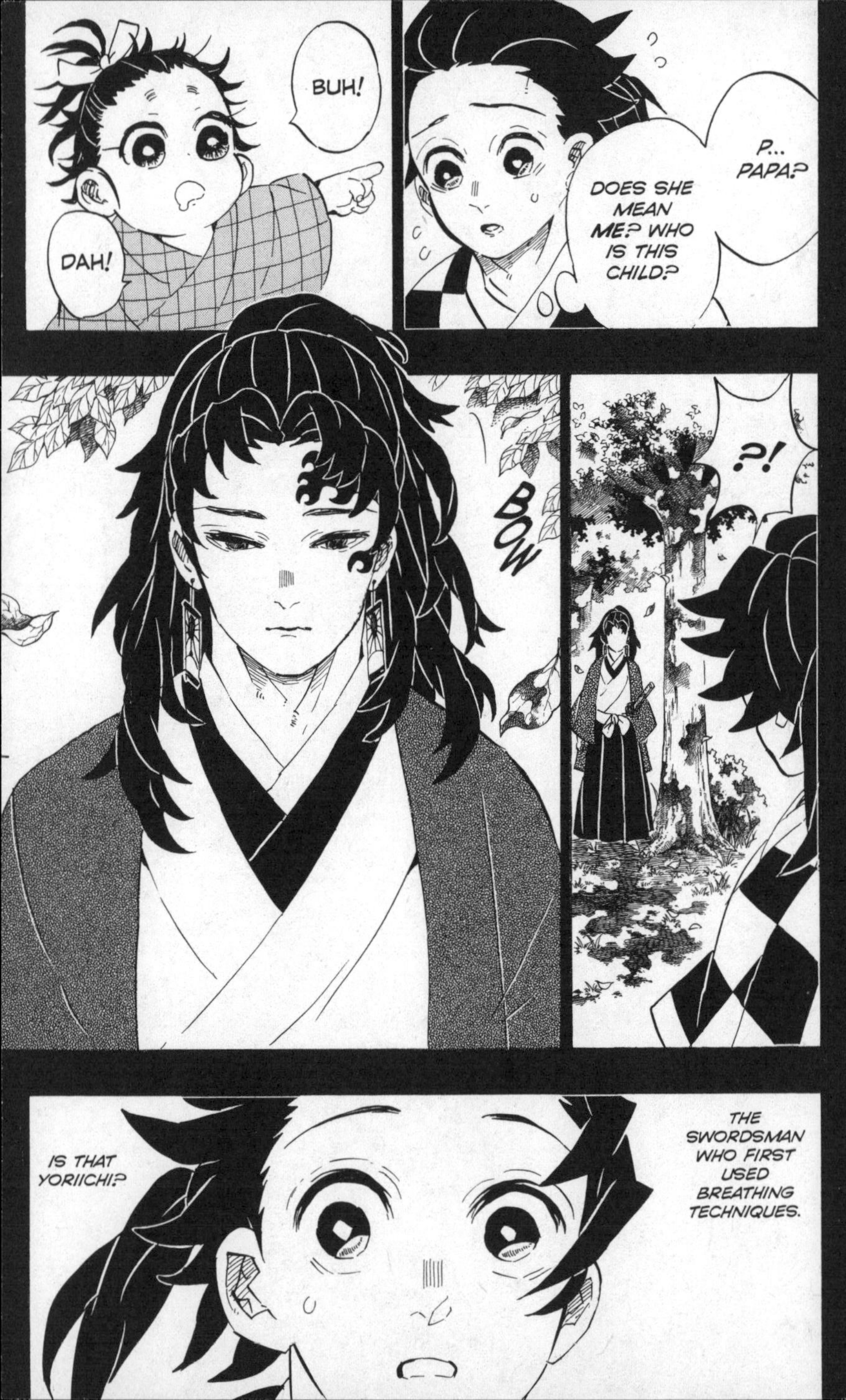
P... PAPA?
DOES SHE MEAN ME? WHO IS THIS CHILD?
BUH!
DAH!
?!
BOW
THE SWORDSMAN WHO FIRST USED BREATHING TECHNIQUES.
IS THAT YORIICHI?

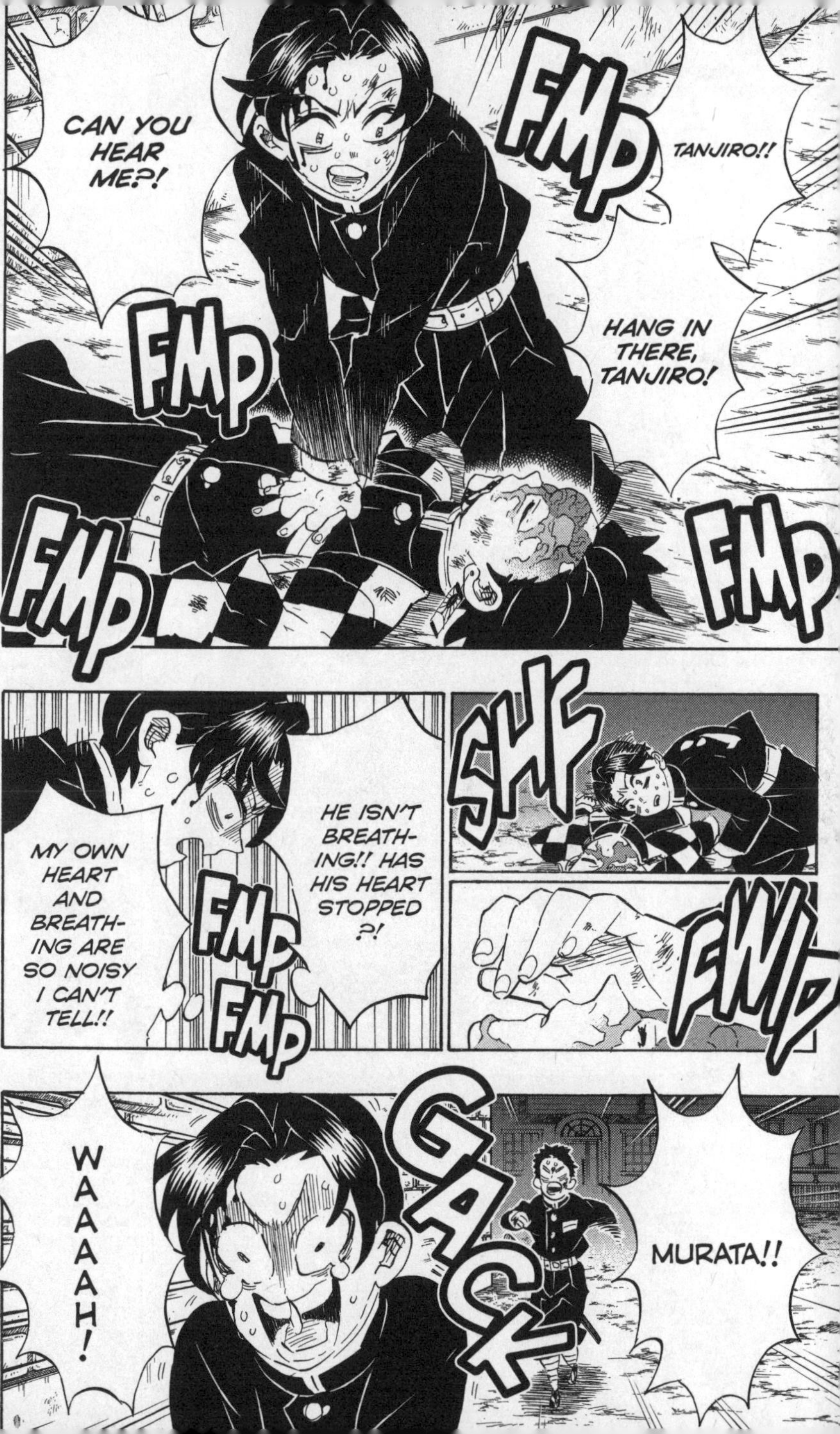
TANJIRO!!
FMP
CAN YOU HEAR ME?!
HANG IN THERE, TANJIRO!
FMP
FMP
FMP
SHK
FMP
HE ISN'T BREATHING!! HAS HIS HEART STOPPED?!
FMP
FMP
MY OWN HEART AND BREATHING ARE SO NOISY I CAN'T TELL!!
MURATA!!
GACK
WAAAAAH!

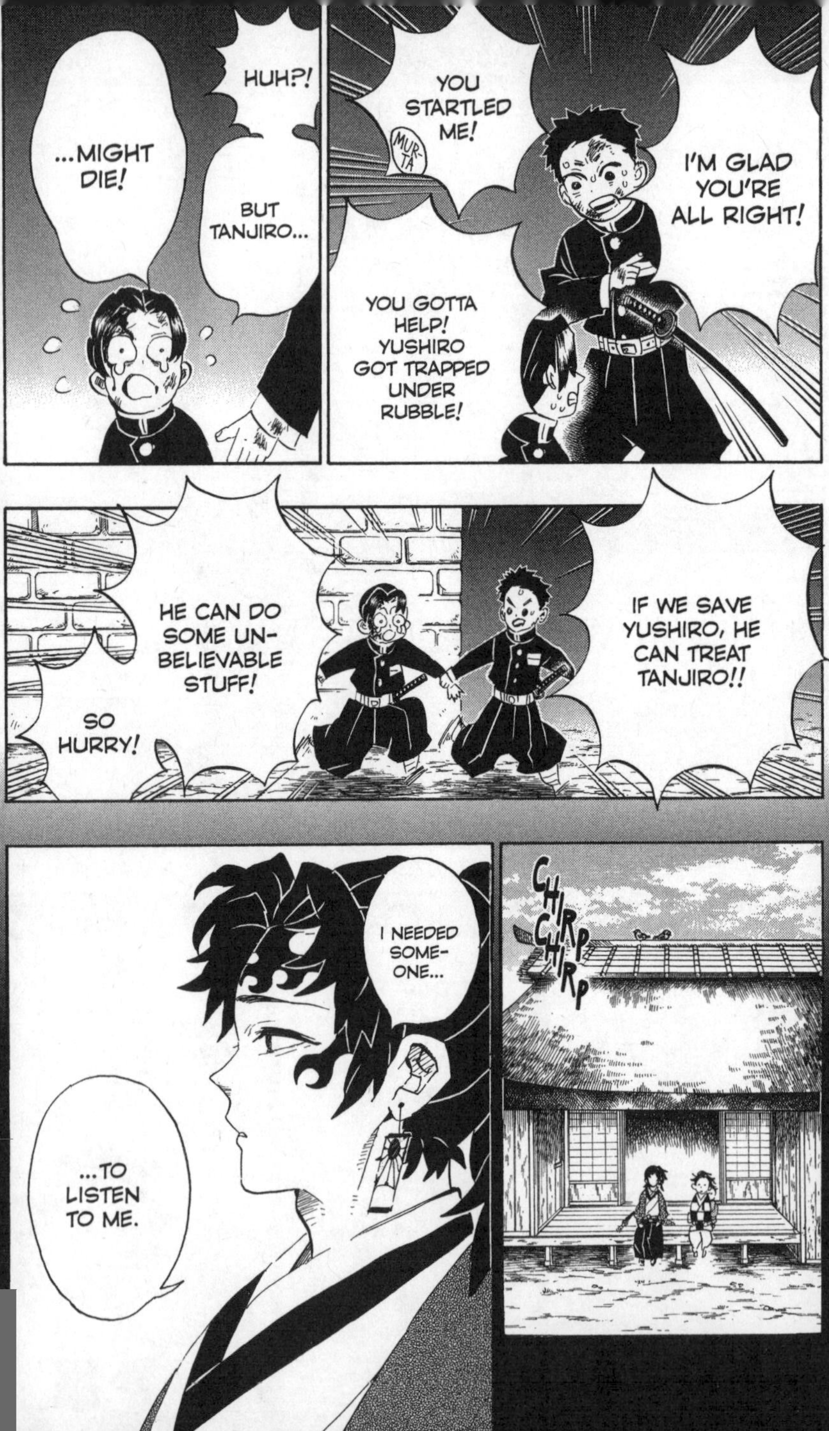
YOU STARTLED ME!
MUR-TA
I'M GLAD YOU'RE ALL RIGHT!
YOU GOTTA HELP! YUSHIRO GOT TRAPPED UNDER RUBBLE!
HUH?!
BUT TANJIRO...
...MIGHT DIE!
IF WE SAVE YUSHIRO, HE CAN TREAT TANJIRO!!
HE CAN DO SOME UN-BELIEVABLE STUFF!
SO HURRY!
CHIRP
CHIRP
I NEEDED SOME-ONE...
...TO LISTEN TO ME.

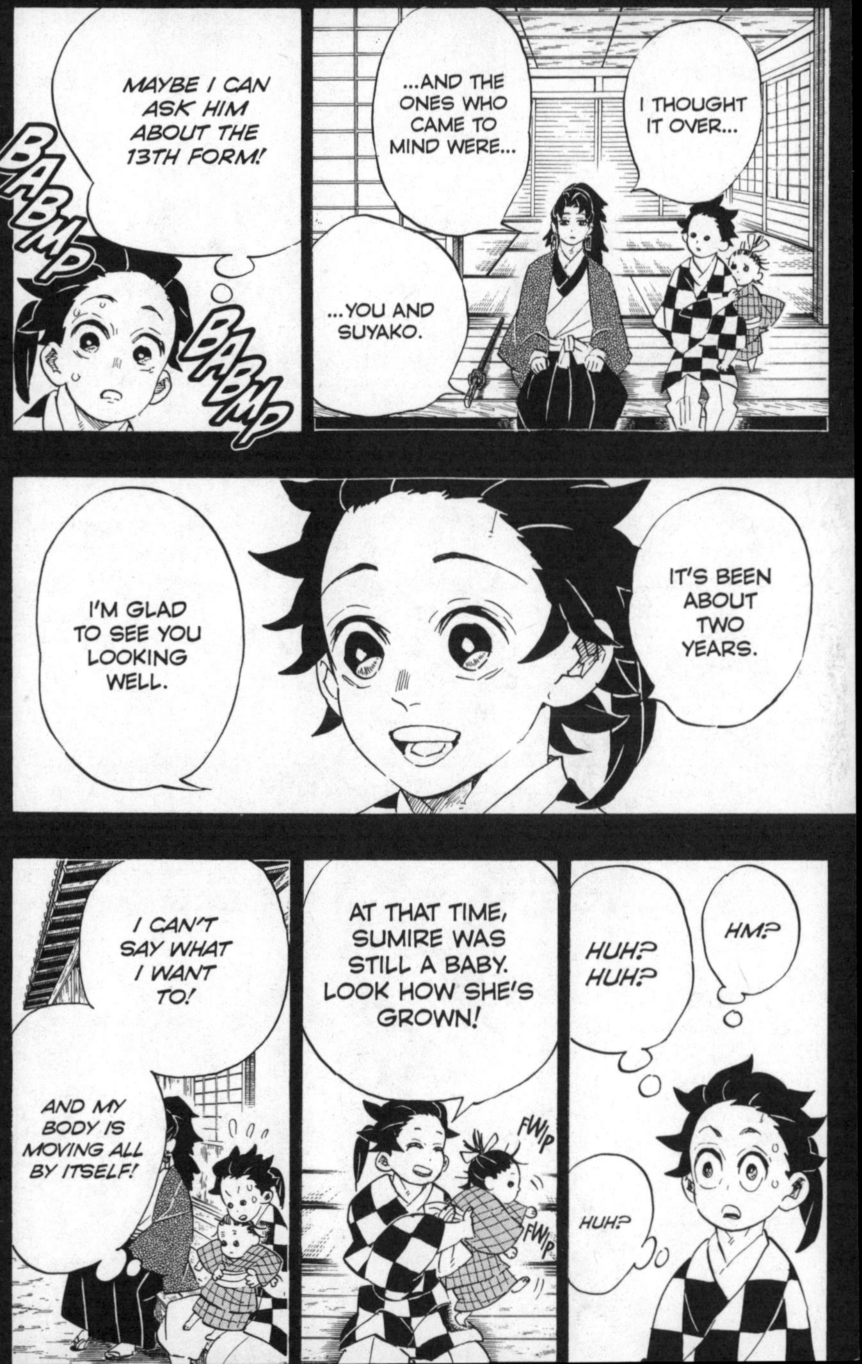
I THOUGHT IT OVER...
...AND THE ONES WHO CAME TO MIND WERE...
...YOU AND SUYAKO.
MAYBE I CAN ASK HIM ABOUT THE 13TH FORM!
BABMP
BABMP
IT'S BEEN ABOUT TWO YEARS.
I'M GLAD TO SEE YOU LOOKING WELL.
HM?
HUH? HUH?
HUH?
AT THAT TIME, SUMIRE WAS STILL A BABY. LOOK HOW SHE'S GROWN!
FWIP
FWIP
I CAN'T SAY WHAT I WANT TO!
AND MY BODY IS MOVING ALL BY ITSELF!

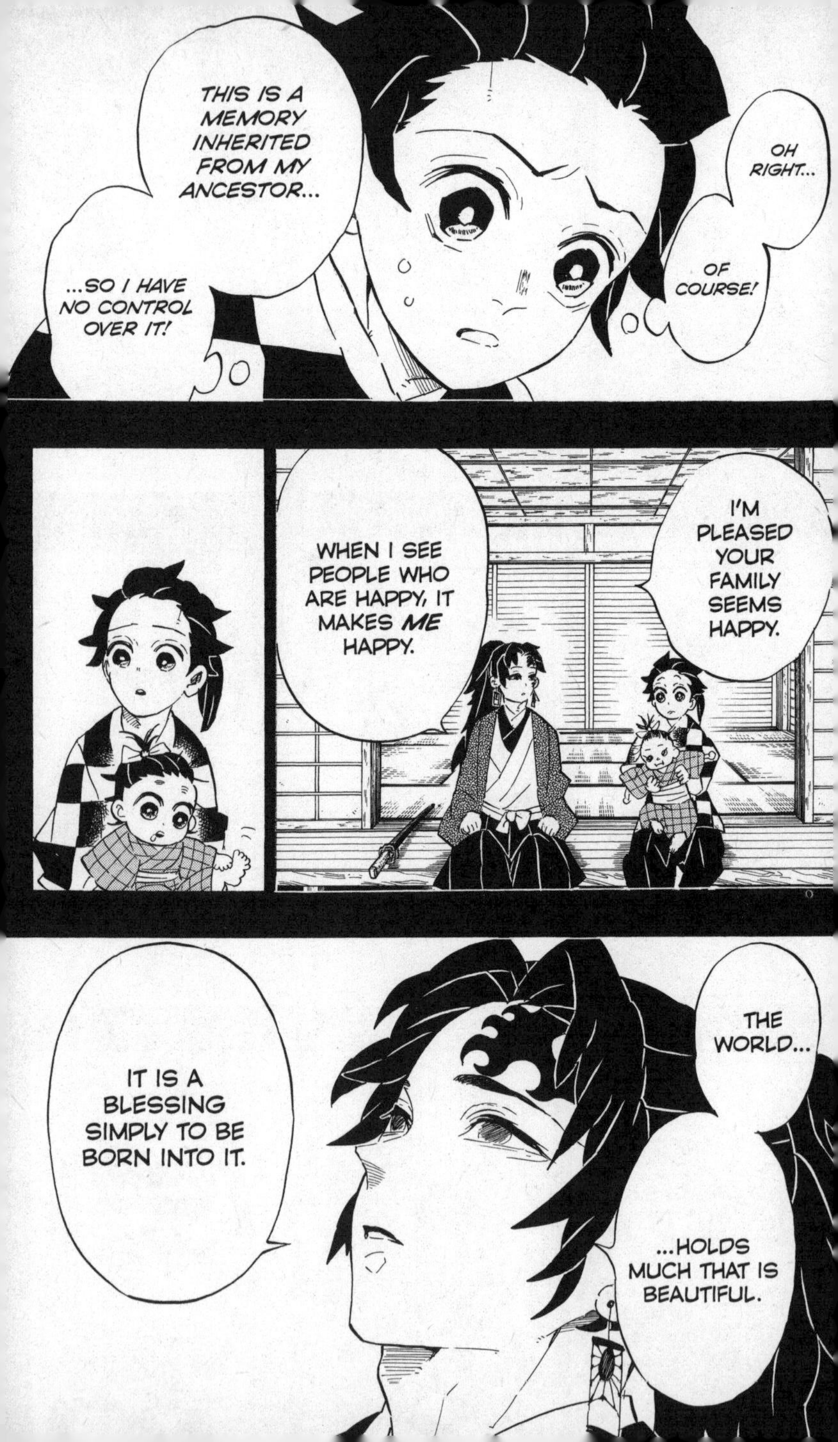
OH RIGHT...
OF COURSE!
THIS IS A MEMORY INHERITED FROM MY ANCESTOR...
...SO I HAVE NO CONTROL OVER IT!
I'M PLEASED YOUR FAMILY SEEMS HAPPY.
WHEN I SEE PEOPLE WHO ARE HAPPY, IT MAKES *ME* HAPPY.
THE WORLD...
...HOLDS MUCH THAT IS BEAUTIFUL.
IT IS A BLESSING SIMPLY TO BE BORN INTO IT.

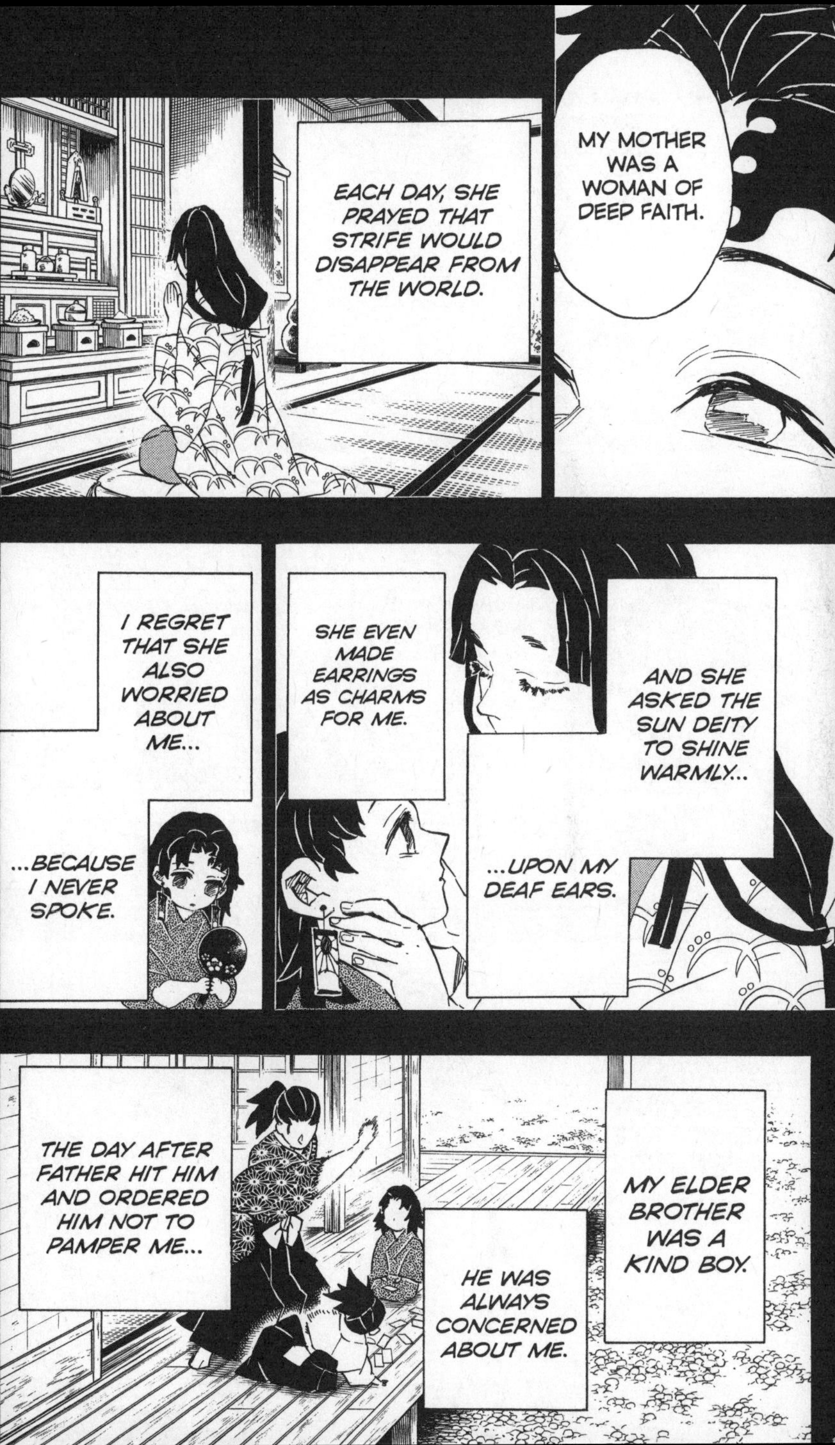
MY MOTHER WAS A WOMAN OF DEEP FAITH.
EACH DAY, SHE PRAYED THAT STRIFE WOULD DISAPPEAR FROM THE WORLD.
AND SHE ASKED THE SUN DEITY TO SHINE WARMLY...
...UPON MY DEAF EARS.
SHE EVEN MADE EARRINGS AS CHARMS FOR ME.
I REGRET THAT SHE ALSO WORRIED ABOUT ME...
...BECAUSE I NEVER SPOKE.
MY ELDER BROTHER WAS A KIND BOY.
HE WAS ALWAYS CONCERNED ABOUT ME.
THE DAY AFTER FATHER HIT HIM AND ORDERED HIM NOT TO PAMPER ME...

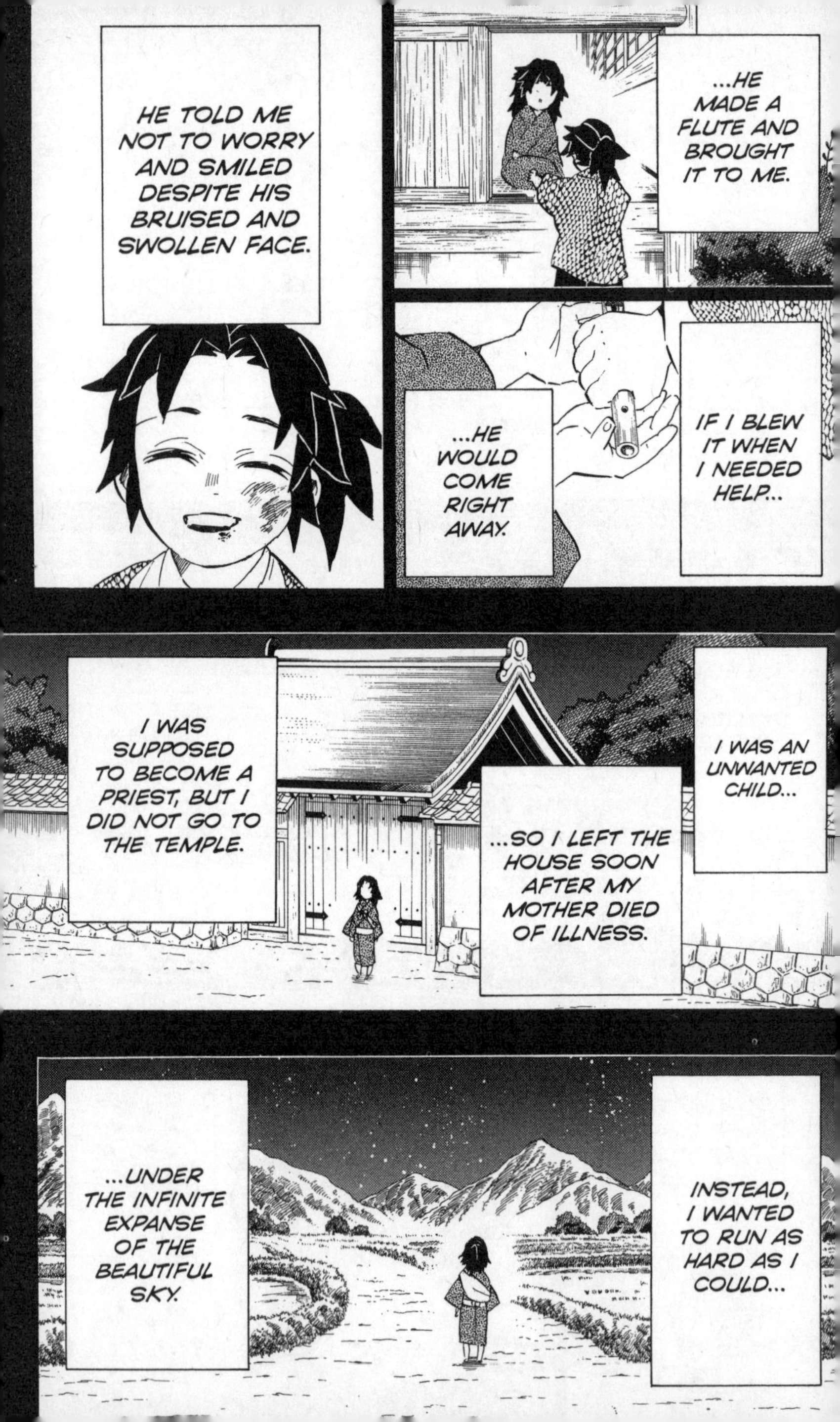
...HE MADE A FLUTE AND BROUGHT IT TO ME.
IF I BLEW IT WHEN I NEEDED HELP...
...HE WOULD COME RIGHT AWAY.
HE TOLD ME NOT TO WORRY AND SMILED DESPITE HIS BRUISED AND SWOLLEN FACE.
I WAS AN UNWANTED CHILD...
...SO I LEFT THE HOUSE SOON AFTER MY MOTHER DIED OF ILLNESS.
I WAS SUPPOSED TO BECOME A PRIEST, BUT I DID NOT GO TO THE TEMPLE.
INSTEAD, I WANTED TO RUN AS HARD AS I COULD...
...UNDER THE INFINITE EXPANSE OF THE BEAUTIFUL SKY.

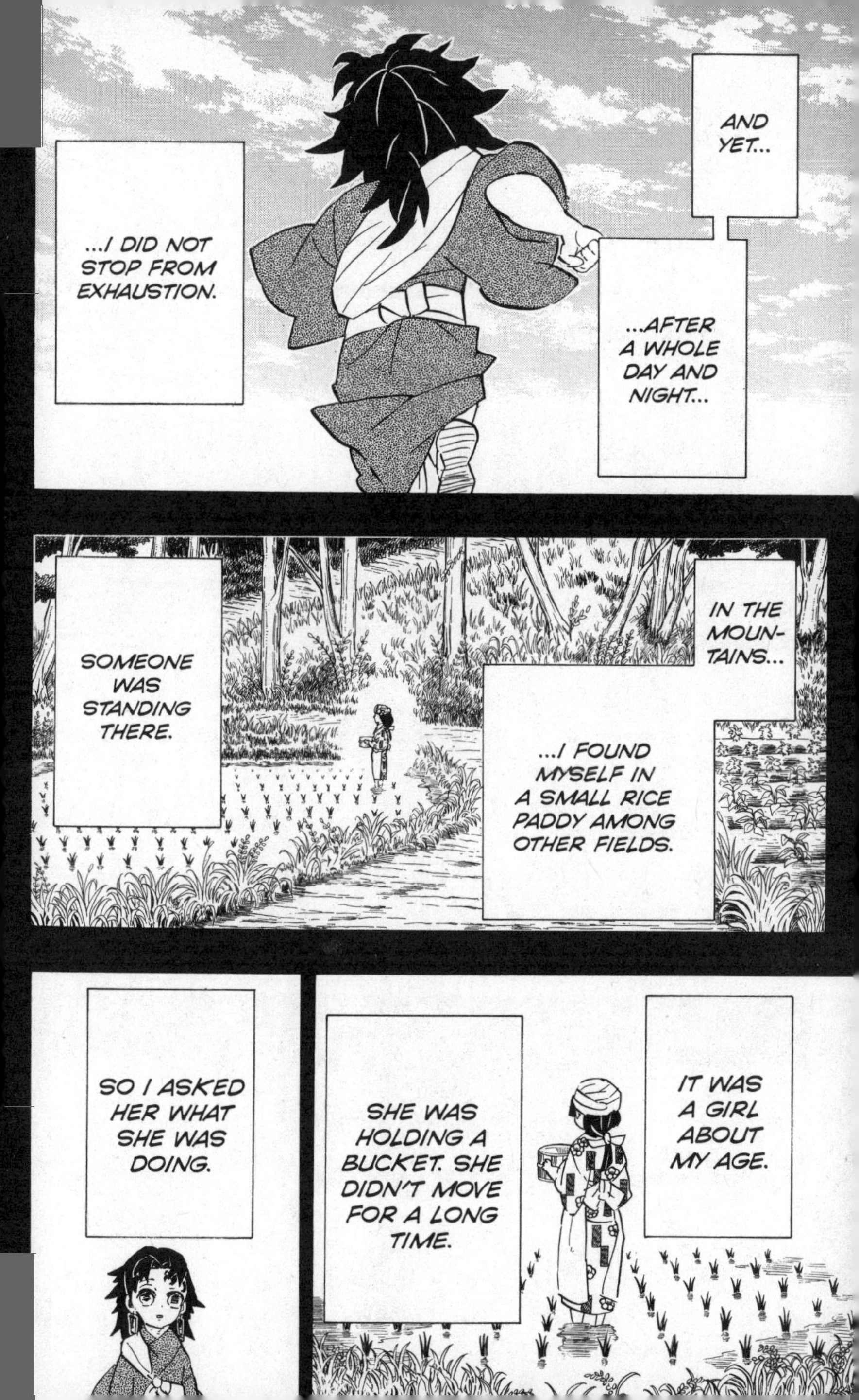
AND YET...
...AFTER A WHOLE DAY AND NIGHT...
...I DID NOT STOP FROM EXHAUSTION.
IN THE MOUN-TAINS...
...I FOUND MYSELF IN A SMALL RICE PADDY AMONG OTHER FIELDS.
SOMEONE WAS STANDING THERE.
IT WAS A GIRL ABOUT MY AGE.
SHE WAS HOLDING A BUCKET. SHE DIDN'T MOVE FOR A LONG TIME.
SO I ASKED HER WHAT SHE WAS DOING.

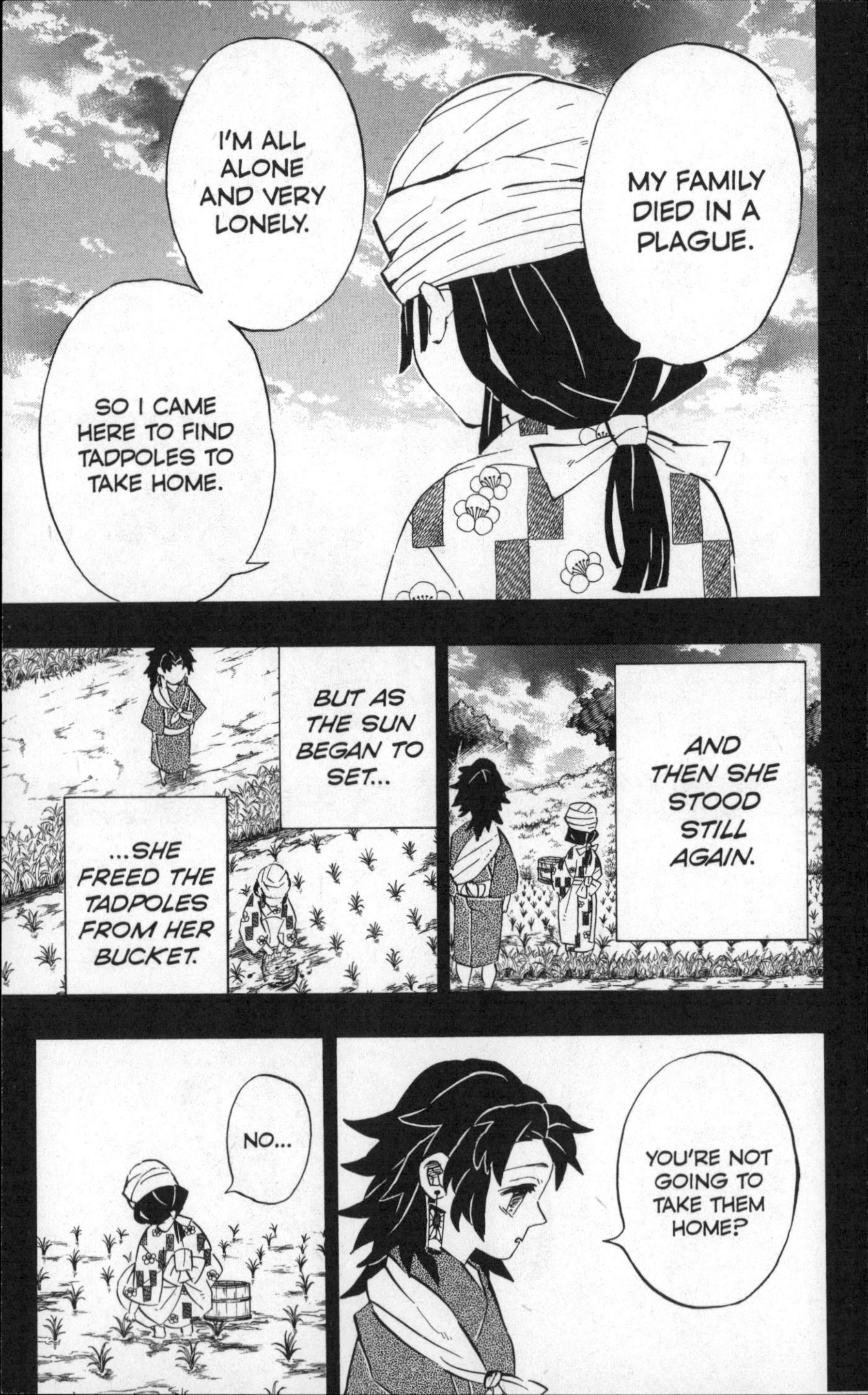
MY FAMILY DIED IN A PLAGUE.
I'M ALL ALONE AND VERY LONELY.
SO I CAME HERE TO FIND TADPOLES TO TAKE HOME.
AND THEN SHE STOOD STILL AGAIN.
BUT AS THE SUN BEGAN TO SET...
...SHE FREED THE TADPOLES FROM HER BUCKET.
YOU'RE NOT GOING TO TAKE THEM HOME?
NO...

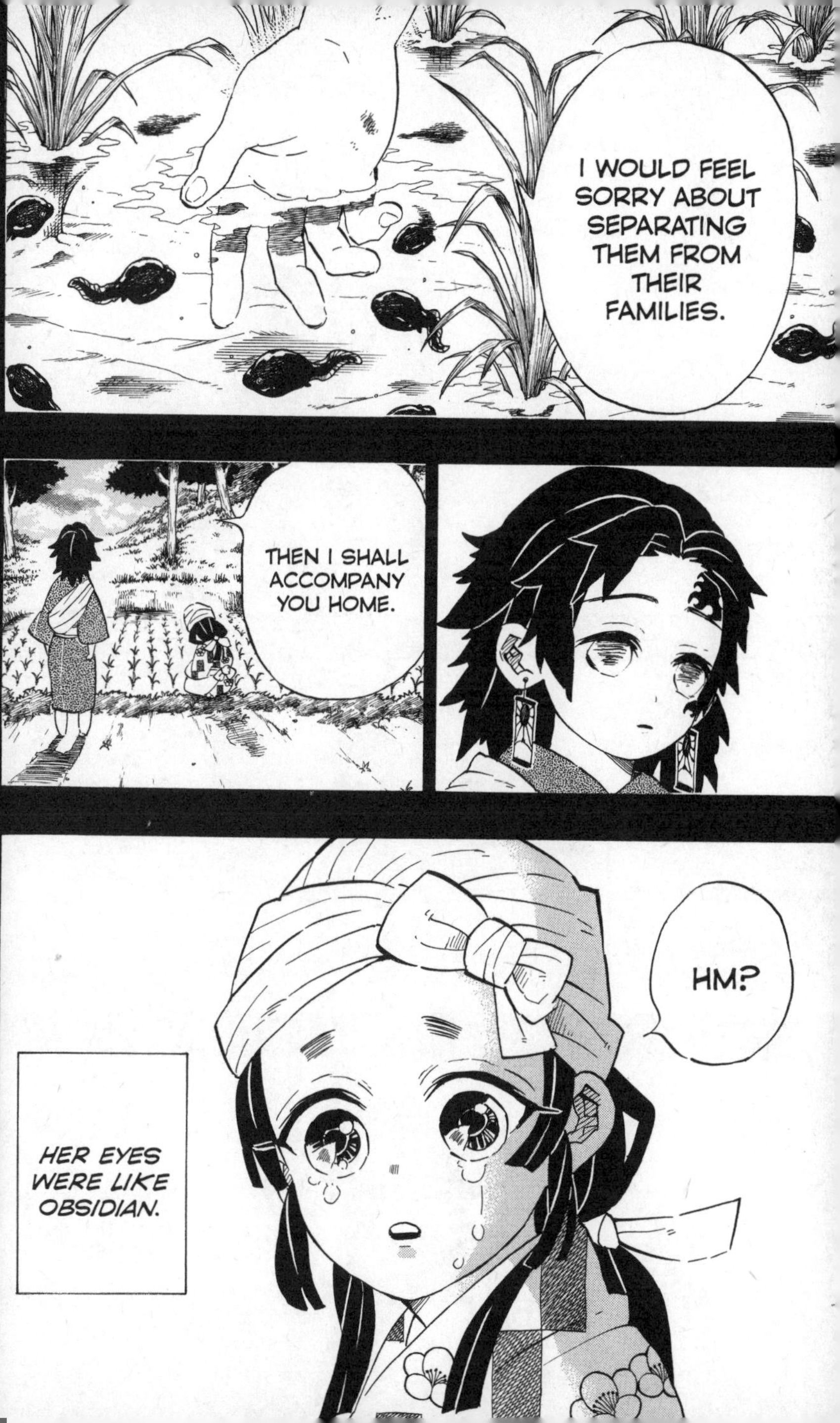
I WOULD FEEL SORRY ABOUT SEPARATING THEM FROM THEIR FAMILIES.
THEN I SHALL ACCOMPANY YOU HOME.
HM?
HER EYES WERE LIKE OBSIDIAN.

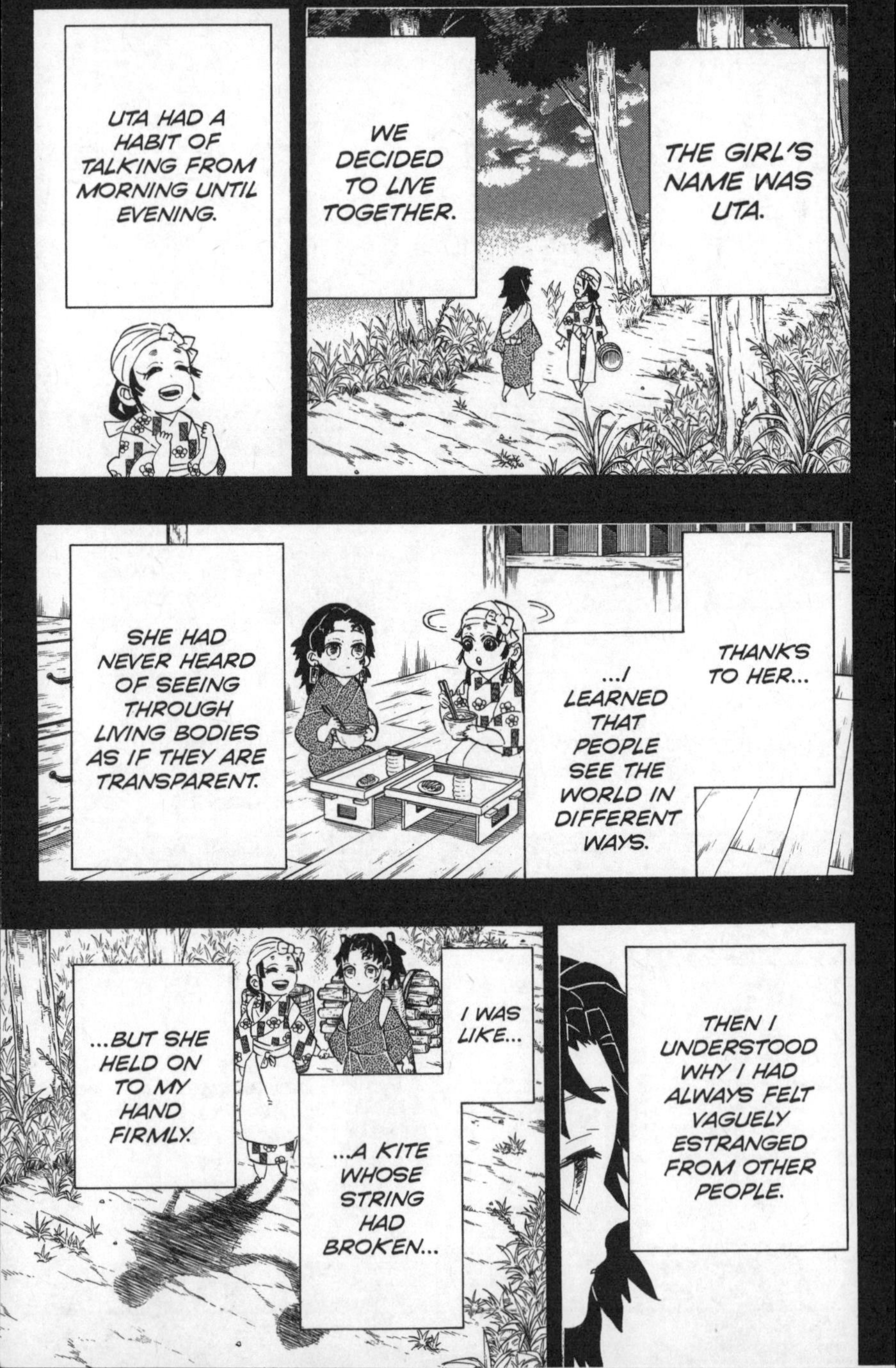
THE GIRL'S NAME WAS UTA.
WE DECIDED TO LIVE TOGETHER.
UTA HAD A HABIT OF TALKING FROM MORNING UNTIL EVENING.
THANKS TO HER...
...I LEARNED THAT PEOPLE SEE THE WORLD IN DIFFERENT WAYS.
SHE HAD NEVER HEARD OF SEEING THROUGH LIVING BODIES AS IF THEY ARE TRANSPARENT.
THEN I UNDERSTOOD WHY I HAD ALWAYS FELT VAGUELY ESTRANGED FROM OTHER PEOPLE.
I WAS LIKE...
...A KITE WHOSE STRING HAD BROKEN...
...BUT SHE HELD ON TO MY HAND FIRMLY.

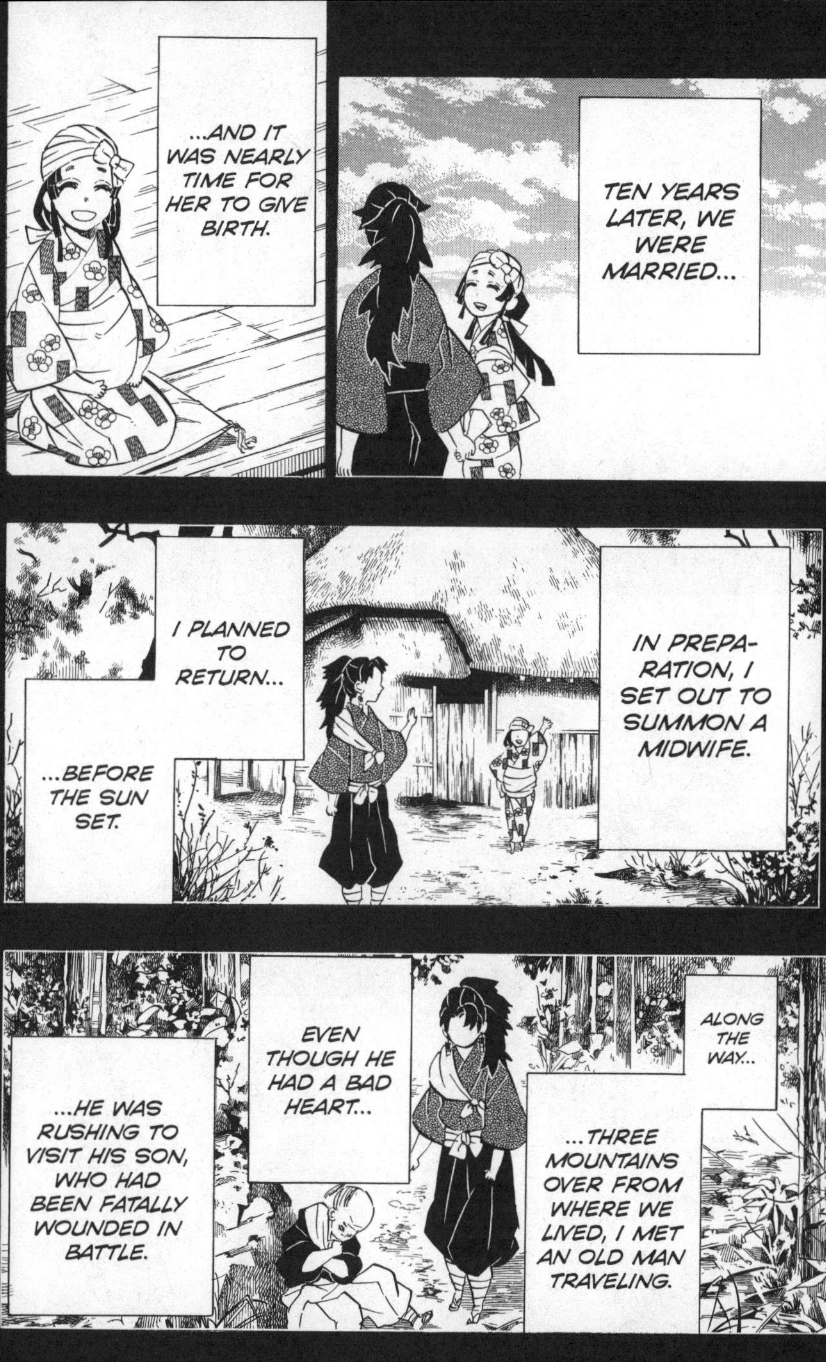
TEN YEARS LATER, WE WERE MARRIED...
...AND IT WAS NEARLY TIME FOR HER TO GIVE BIRTH.
IN PREPARATION, I SET OUT TO SUMMON A MIDWIFE.
I PLANNED TO RETURN...
...BEFORE THE SUN SET.
ALONG THE WAY...
...THREE MOUNTAINS OVER FROM WHERE WE LIVED, I MET AN OLD MAN TRAVELING.
EVEN THOUGH HE HAD A BAD HEART...
...HE WAS RUSHING TO VISIT HIS SON, WHO HAD BEEN FATALLY WOUNDED IN BATTLE.

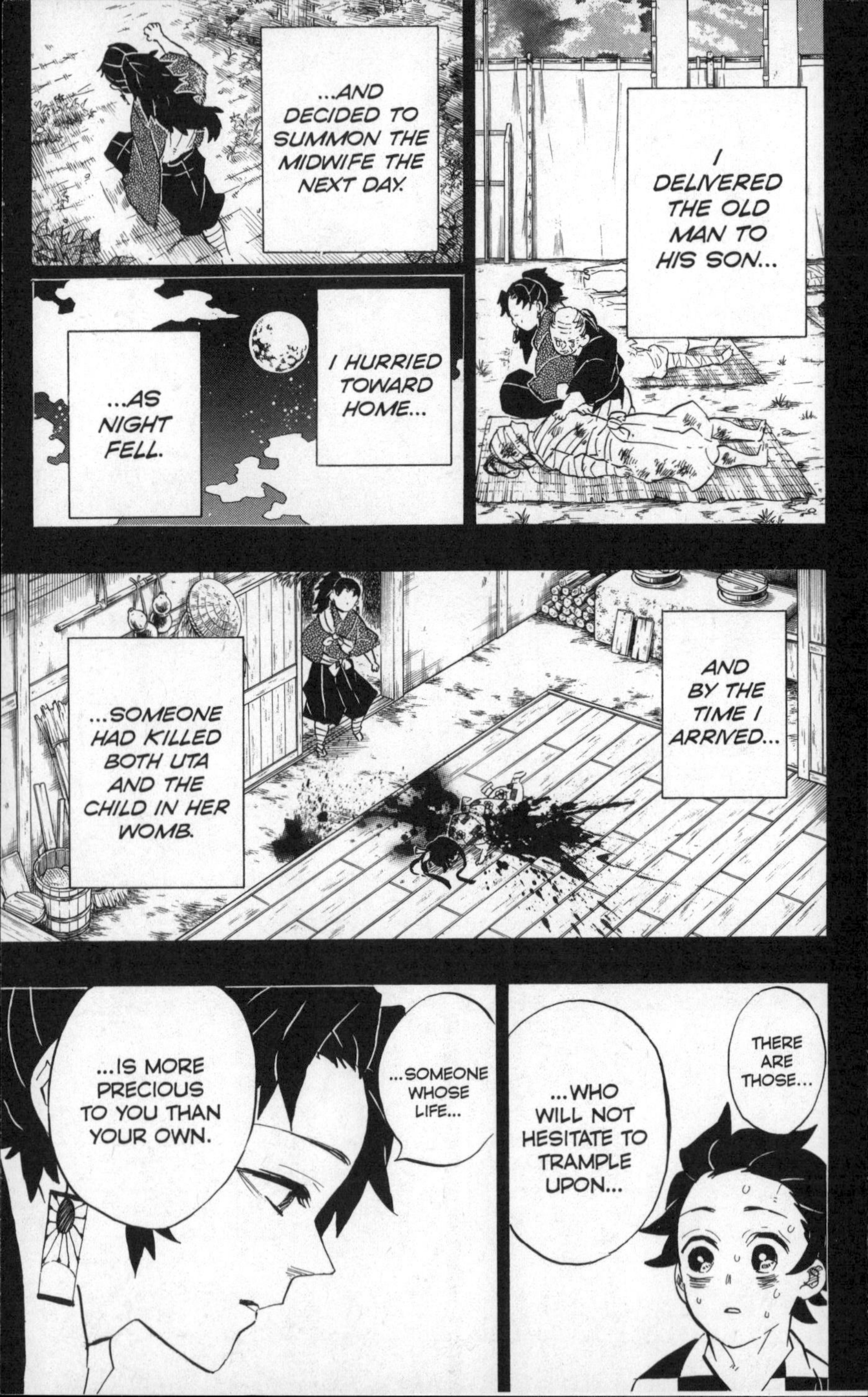

I DELIVERED THE OLD MAN TO HIS SON...
...AND DECIDED TO SUMMON THE MIDWIFE THE NEXT DAY.
I HURRIED TOWARD HOME...
...AS NIGHT FELL.
AND BY THE TIME I ARRIVED...
...SOMEONE HAD KILLED BOTH UTA AND THE CHILD IN HER WOMB.
THERE ARE THOSE...
...WHO WILL NOT HESITATE TO TRAMPLE UPON...
...SOMEONE WHOSE LIFE...
...IS MORE PRECIOUS TO YOU THAN YOUR OWN.

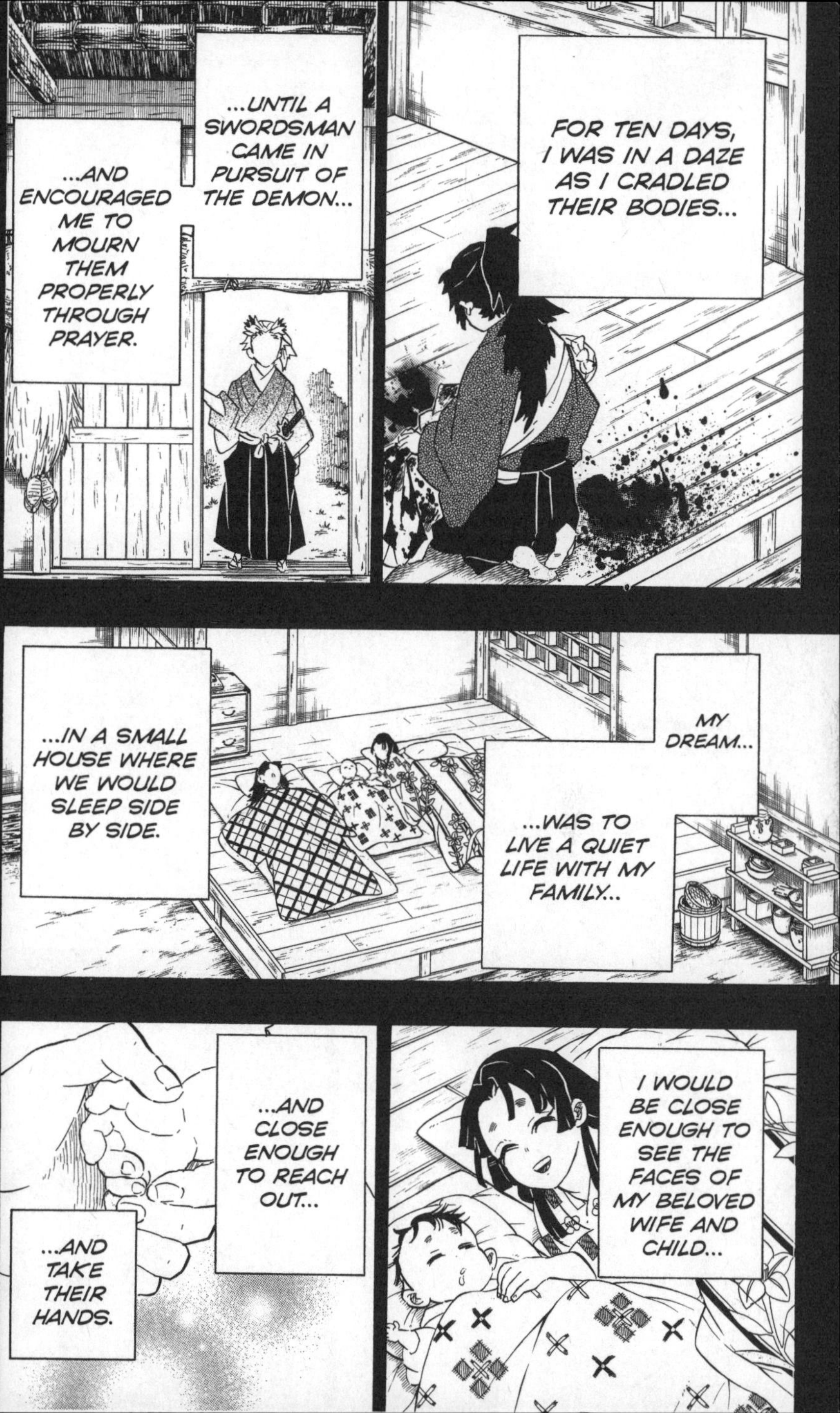
FOR TEN DAYS, I WAS IN A DAZE AS I CRADLED THEIR BODIES...
...UNTIL A SWORDSMAN CAME IN PURSUIT OF THE DEMON...
...AND ENCOURAGED ME TO MOURN THEM PROPERLY THROUGH PRAYER.
MY DREAM...
...WAS TO LIVE A QUIET LIFE WITH MY FAMILY...
...IN A SMALL HOUSE WHERE WE WOULD SLEEP SIDE BY SIDE.
I WOULD BE CLOSE ENOUGH TO SEE THE FACES OF MY BELOVED WIFE AND CHILD...
...AND CLOSE ENOUGH TO REACH OUT...
...AND TAKE THEIR HANDS.

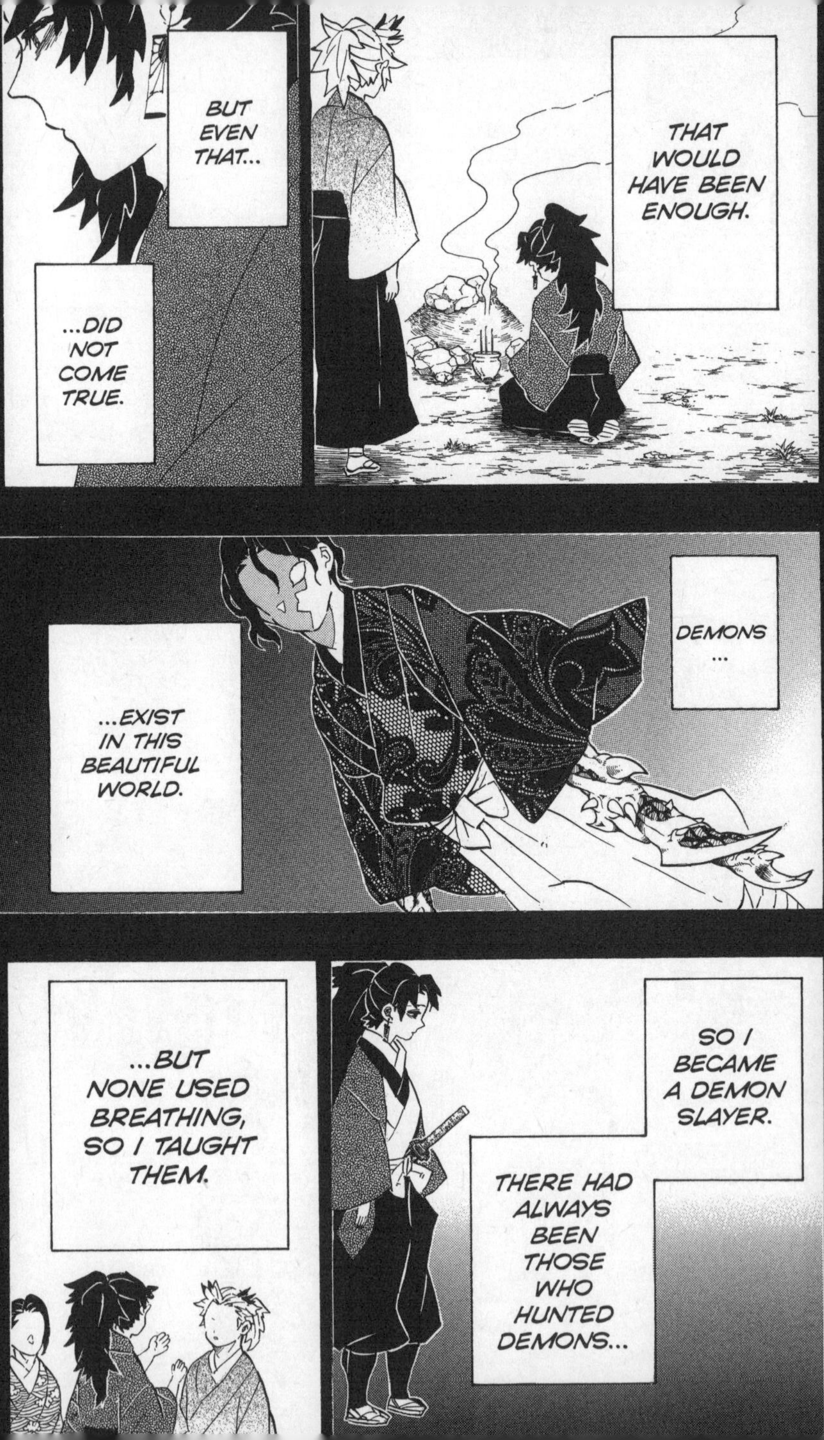
THAT WOULD HAVE BEEN ENOUGH.
BUT EVEN THAT...
...DID NOT COME TRUE.
DEMONS ...
...EXIST IN THIS BEAUTIFUL WORLD.
SO I BECAME A DEMON SLAYER.
THERE HAD ALWAYS BEEN THOSE WHO HUNTED DEMONS...
...BUT NONE USED BREATHING, SO I TAUGHT THEM.

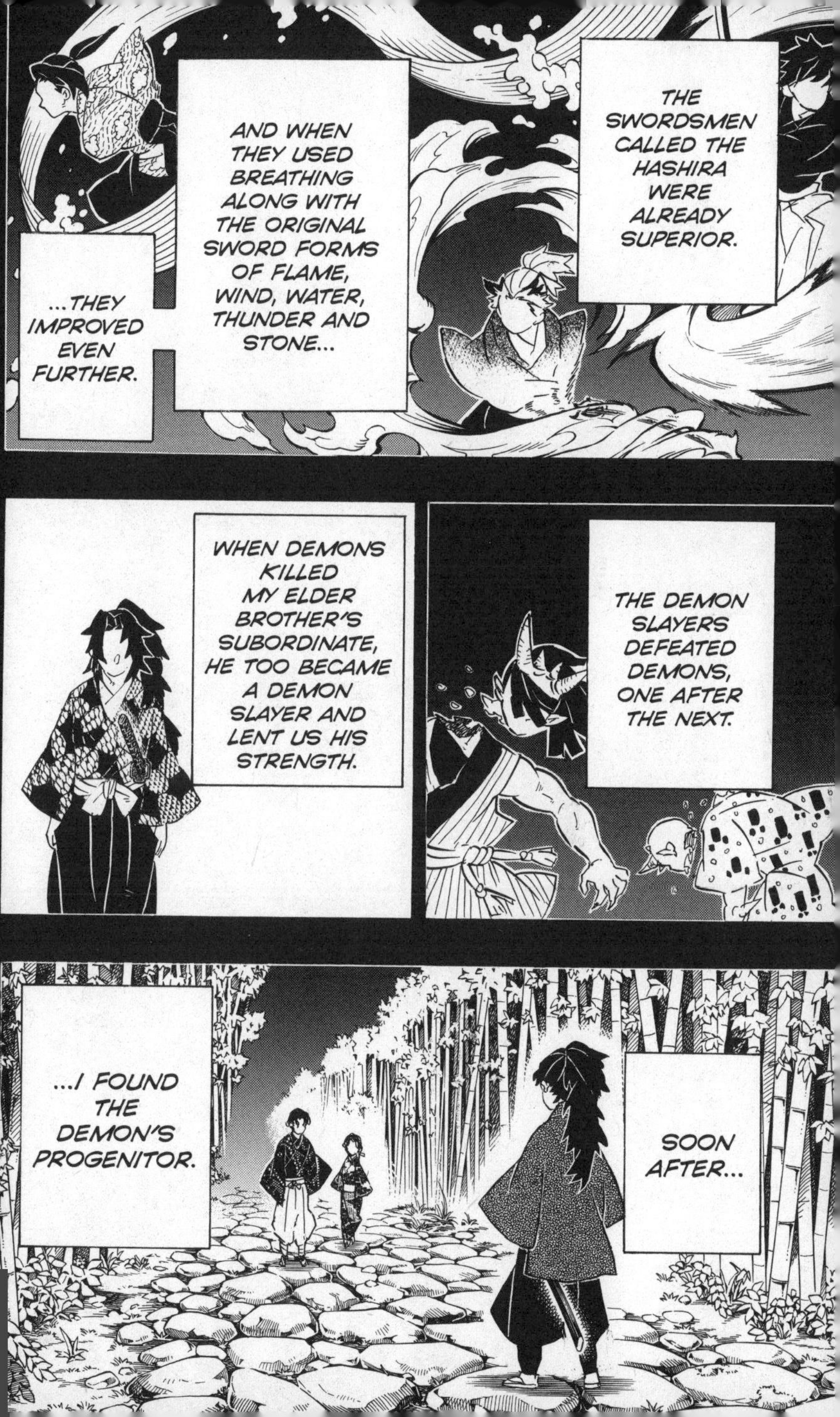
THE SWORDSMEN CALLED THE HASHIRA WERE ALREADY SUPERIOR.
AND WHEN THEY USED BREATHING ALONG WITH THE ORIGINAL SWORD FORMS OF FLAME, WIND, WATER, THUNDER AND STONE...
...THEY IMPROVED EVEN FURTHER.
THE DEMON SLAYERS DEFEATED DEMONS, ONE AFTER THE NEXT.
WHEN DEMONS KILLED MY ELDER BROTHER'S SUBORDINATE, HE TOO BECAME A DEMON SLAYER AND LENT US HIS STRENGTH.
SOON AFTER...
...I FOUND THE DEMON'S PROGENITOR.

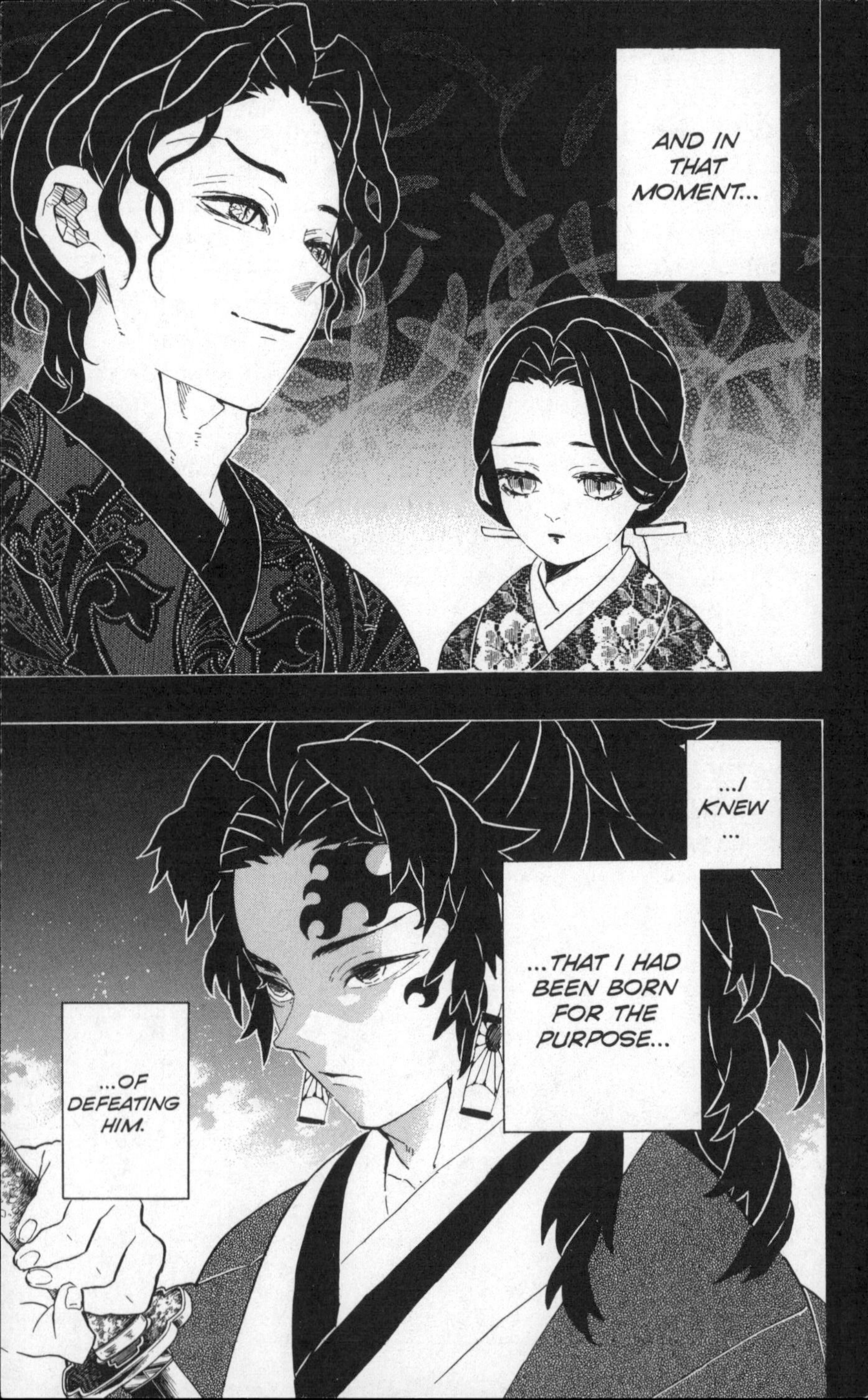
AND IN THAT MOMENT...
...I KNEW ...
...THAT I HAD BEEN BORN FOR THE PURPOSE...
...OF DEFEATING HIM.

SENGOKU WHISPERS

Yoriichi's attitudes and emotions are straightforward and simple, just as Sumiyoshi sensed they were, but he doesn't show his feelings on his face. Like his mother, Akeno, his personality is gentle and not given to conflict. Just because people aren't laughing out loud doesn't mean they aren't having a good time, and just because they aren't visibly shedding tears doesn't mean they aren't sad. Uta was able to sense changes in Yoriichi's emotions independent from his facial expressions, so even if Yoriichi's face didn't change much, they had no difficulty communicating.

Yoriichi's skill with a sword makes such a strong impression that the quiet side of his personality doesn't get enough emphasis. I doubt many people remember what kind of person Yoriichi was besides a good swordsman.

Uta thought of Yoriichi as a low-key person. He didn't even flinch when lightning struck, so there was a time when she thought he was the spirit of the divinity Jizo or a household spirit like Zashiki-warashi. Animals and insects are fond of Yoriichi. Uta loves it when birds, tanuki, foxes and other animals gather to eat from his hand.

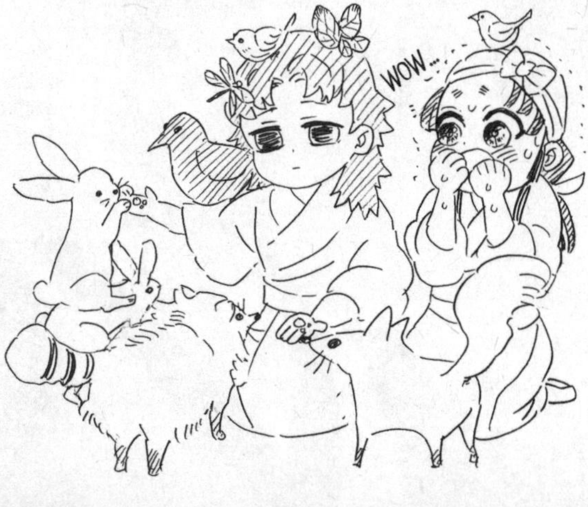
WOW...

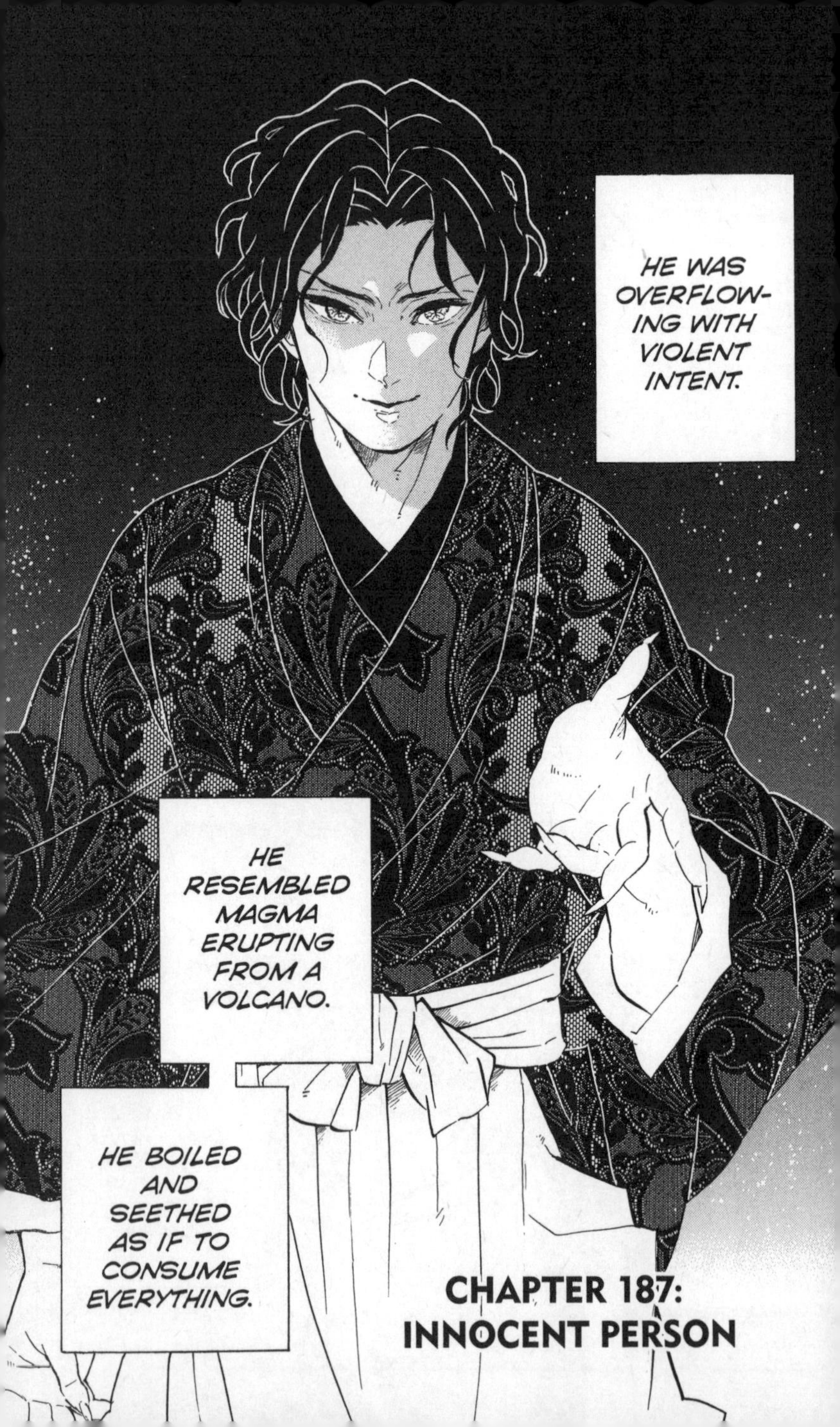
HE WAS OVERFLOWING WITH VIOLENT INTENT.
HE RESEMBLED MAGMA ERUPTING FROM A VOLCANO.
HE BOILED AND SEETHED AS IF TO CONSUME EVERYTHING.
CHAPTER 187: INNOCENT PERSON

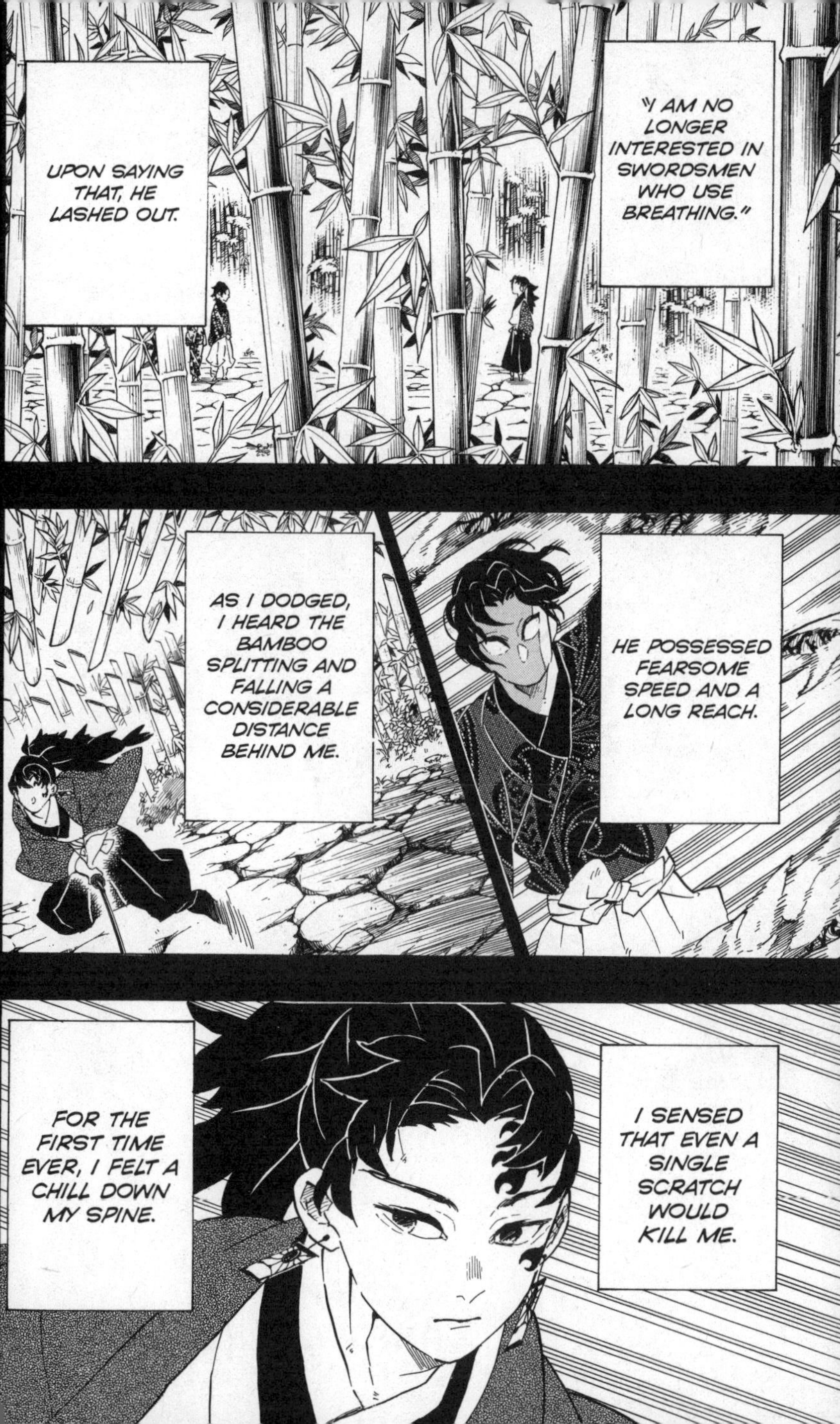
"I AM NO LONGER INTERESTED IN SWORDSMEN WHO USE BREATHING."
UPON SAYING THAT, HE LASHED OUT.
HE POSSESSED FEARSOME SPEED AND A LONG REACH.
AS I DODGED, I HEARD THE BAMBOO SPLITTING AND FALLING A CONSIDERABLE DISTANCE BEHIND ME.
I SENSED THAT EVEN A SINGLE SCRATCH WOULD KILL ME.
FOR THE FIRST TIME EVER, I FELT A CHILL DOWN MY SPINE.

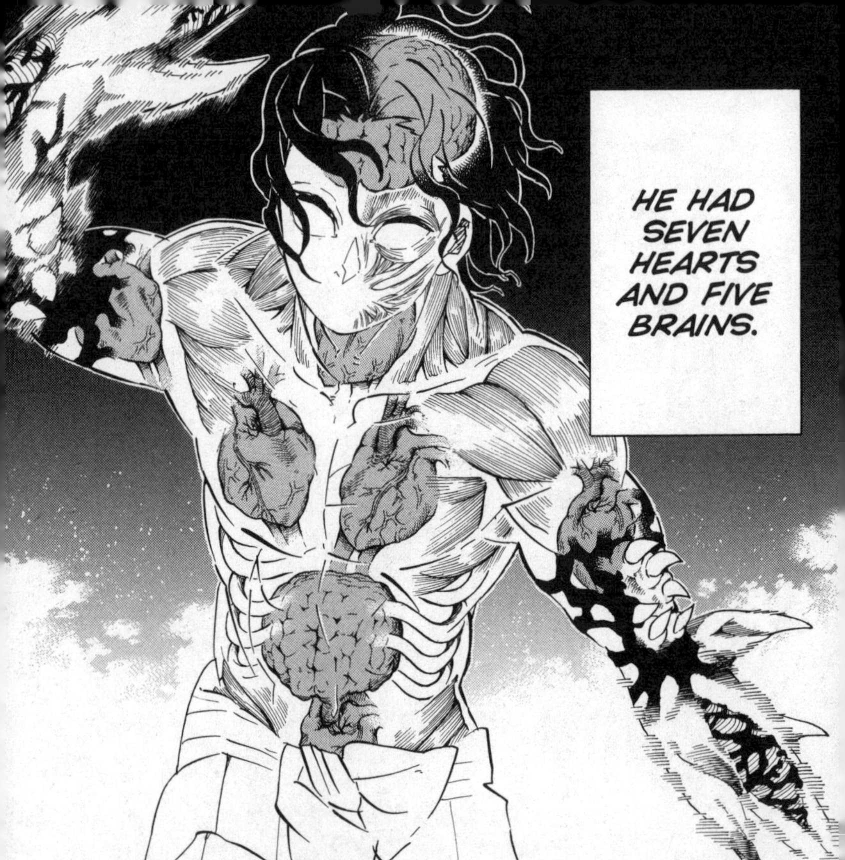
HE HAD SEVEN HEARTS AND FIVE BRAINS.

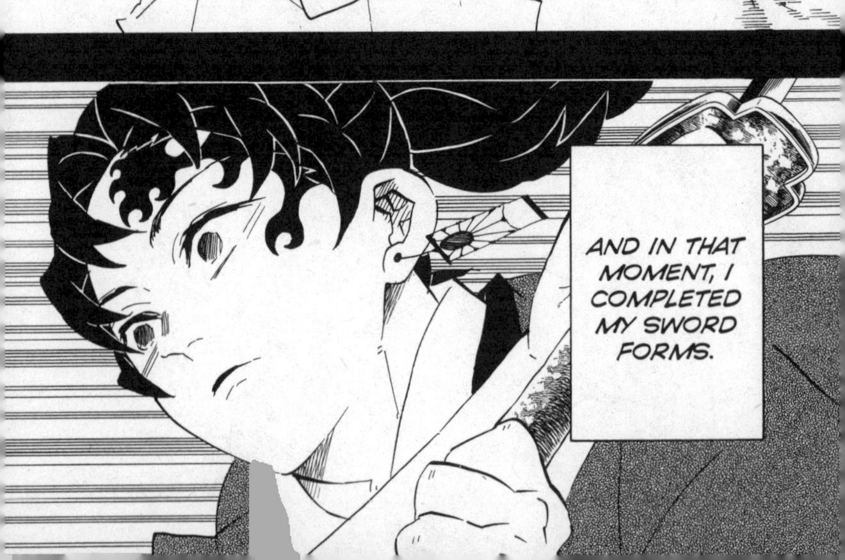
AND IN THAT MOMENT, I COMPLETED MY SWORD FORMS.

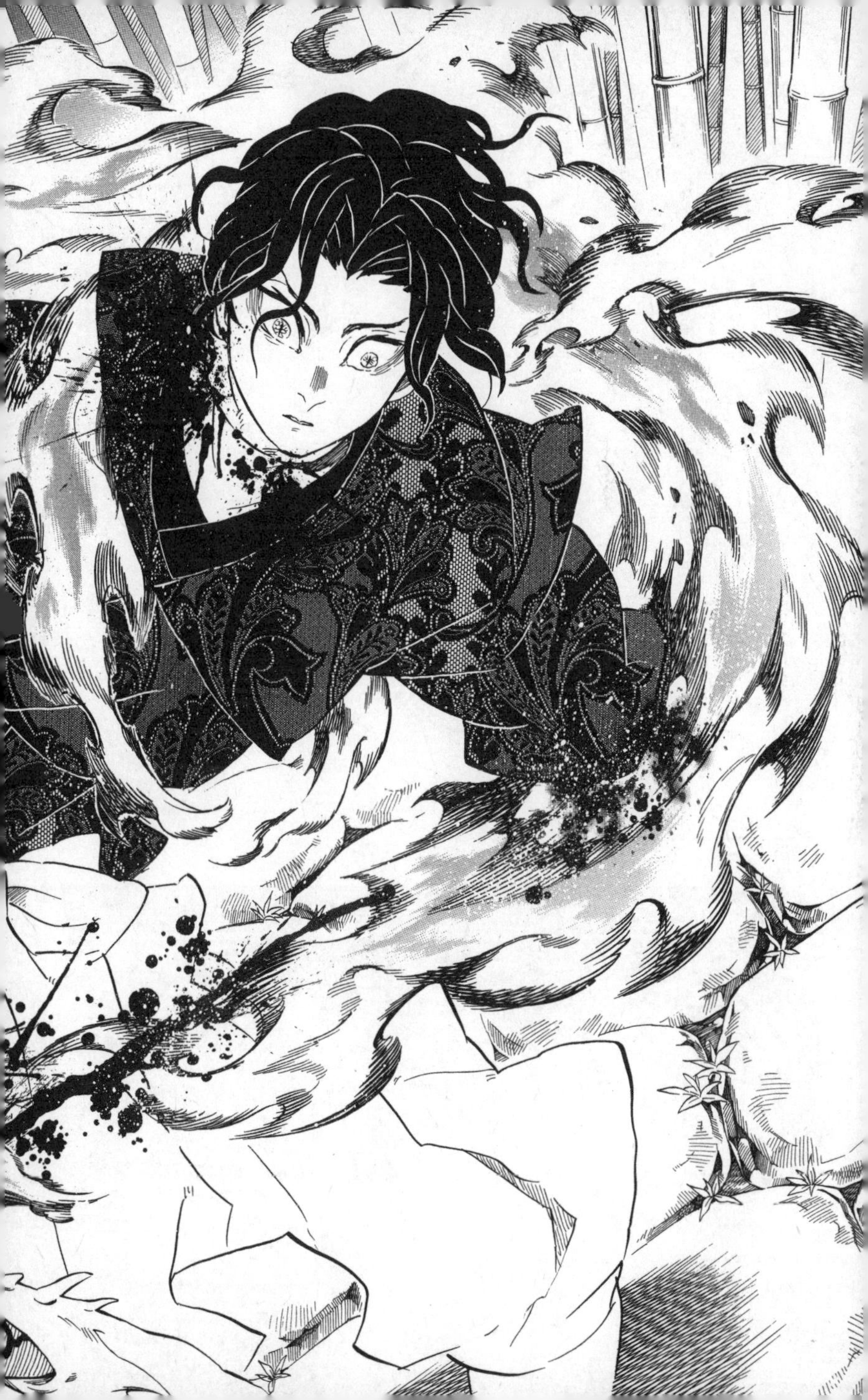

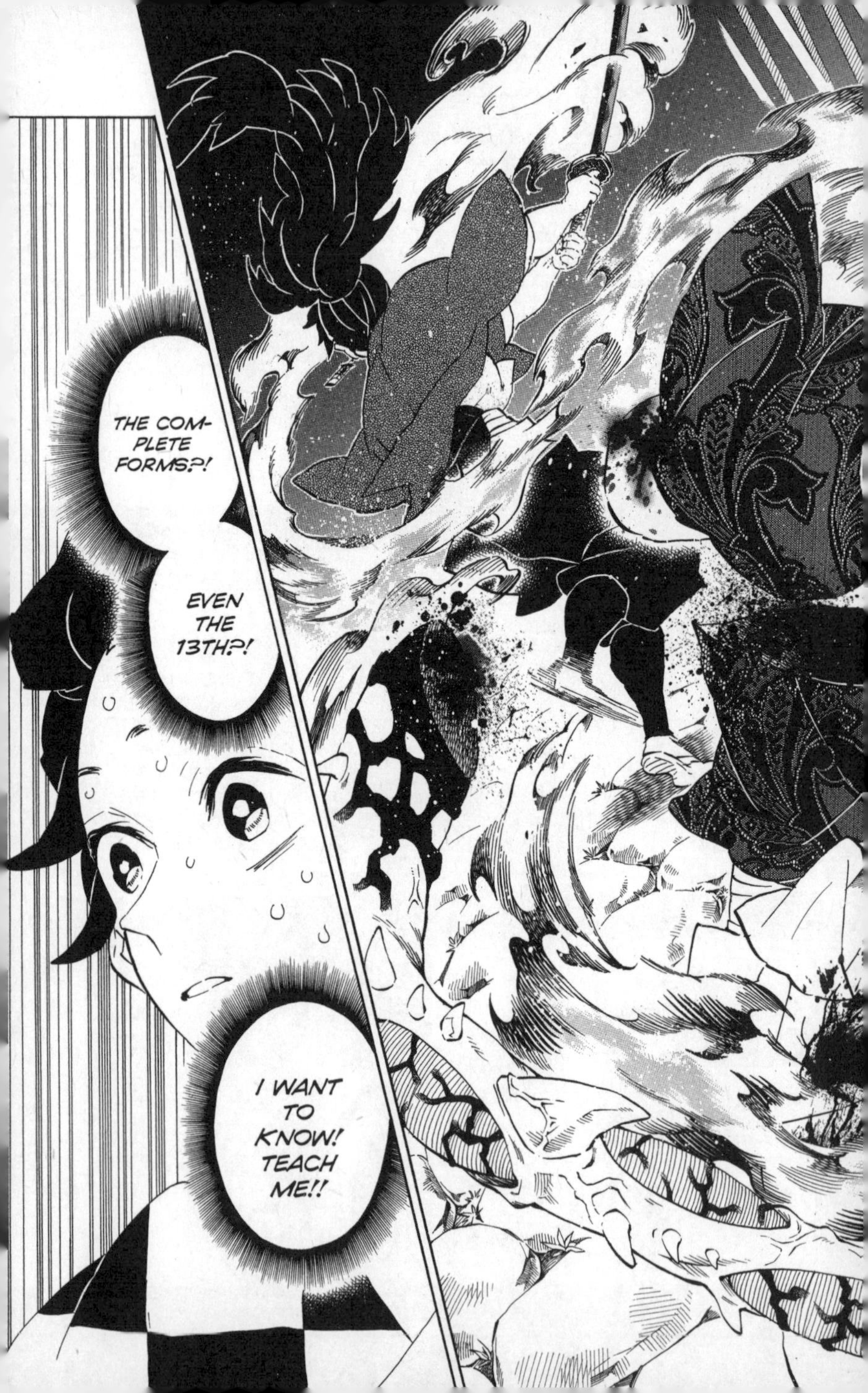
THE COMPLETE FORMS?!
EVEN THE 13TH?!
I WANT TO KNOW! TEACH ME!!

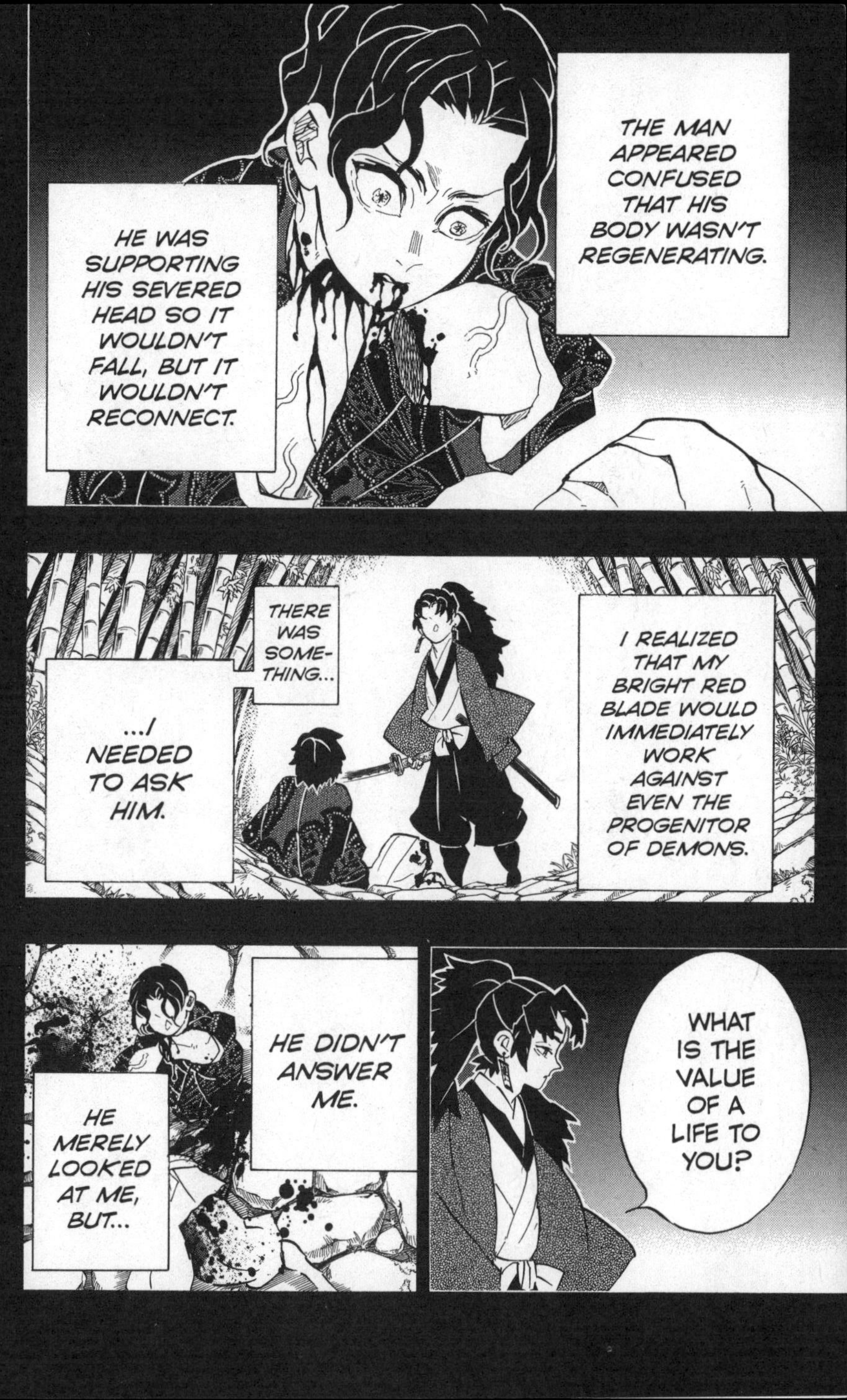
THE MAN APPEARED CONFUSED THAT HIS BODY WASN'T REGENERATING.
HE WAS SUPPORTING HIS SEVERED HEAD SO IT WOULDN'T FALL, BUT IT WOULDN'T RECONNECT.
I REALIZED THAT MY BRIGHT RED BLADE WOULD IMMEDIATELY WORK AGAINST EVEN THE PROGENITOR OF DEMONS.
THERE WAS SOME-THING...
...I NEEDED TO ASK HIM.
WHAT IS THE VALUE OF A LIFE TO YOU?
HE DIDN'T ANSWER ME.
HE MERELY LOOKED AT ME, BUT...

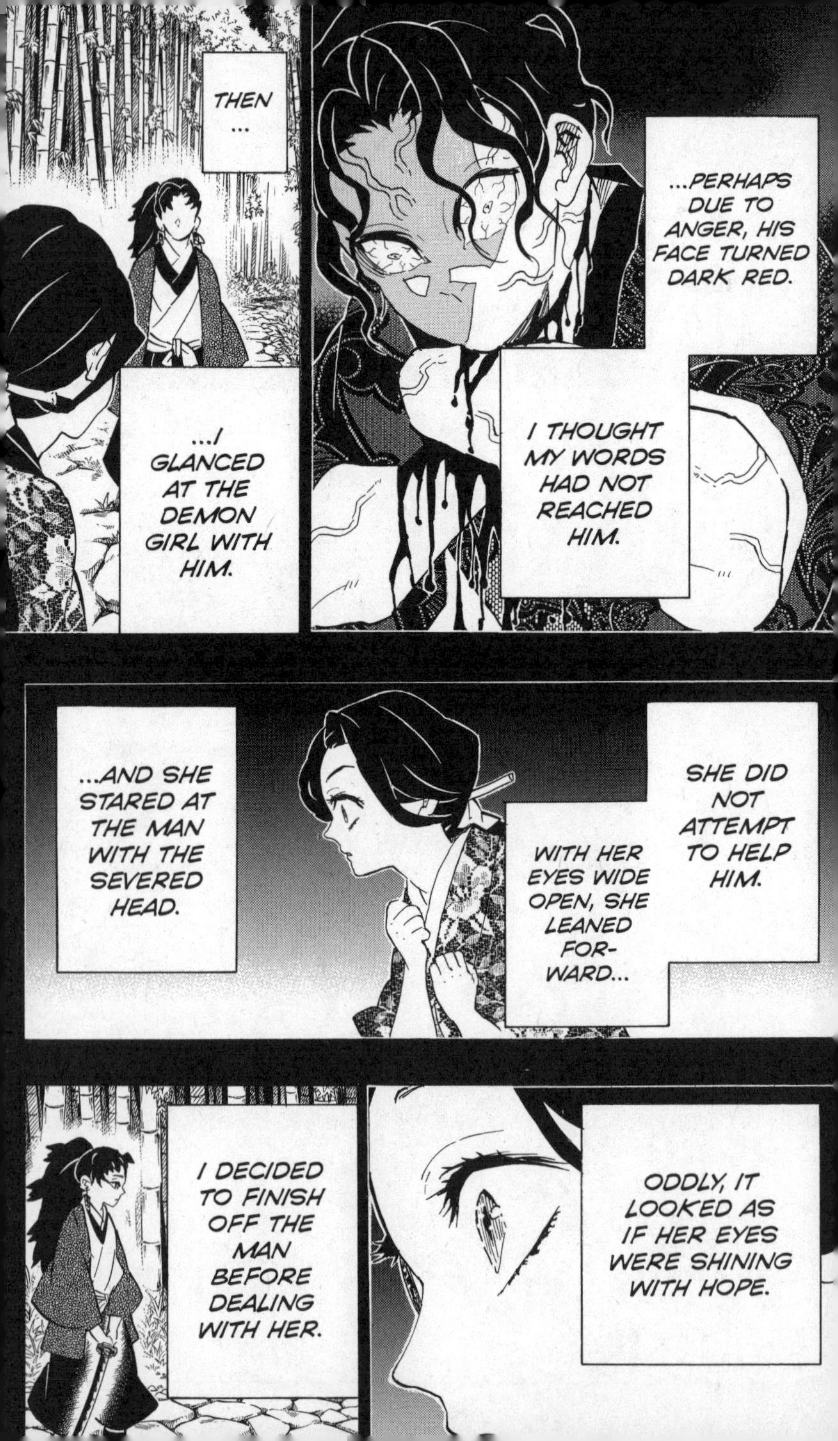
...PERHAPS DUE TO ANGER, HIS FACE TURNED DARK RED.
I THOUGHT MY WORDS HAD NOT REACHED HIM.
THEN ...
...I GLANCED AT THE DEMON GIRL WITH HIM.
SHE DID NOT ATTEMPT TO HELP HIM.
WITH HER EYES WIDE OPEN, SHE LEANED FOR-WARD...
...AND SHE STARED AT THE MAN WITH THE SEVERED HEAD.
ODDLY, IT LOOKED AS IF HER EYES WERE SHINING WITH HOPE.
I DECIDED TO FINISH OFF THE MAN BEFORE DEALING WITH HER.

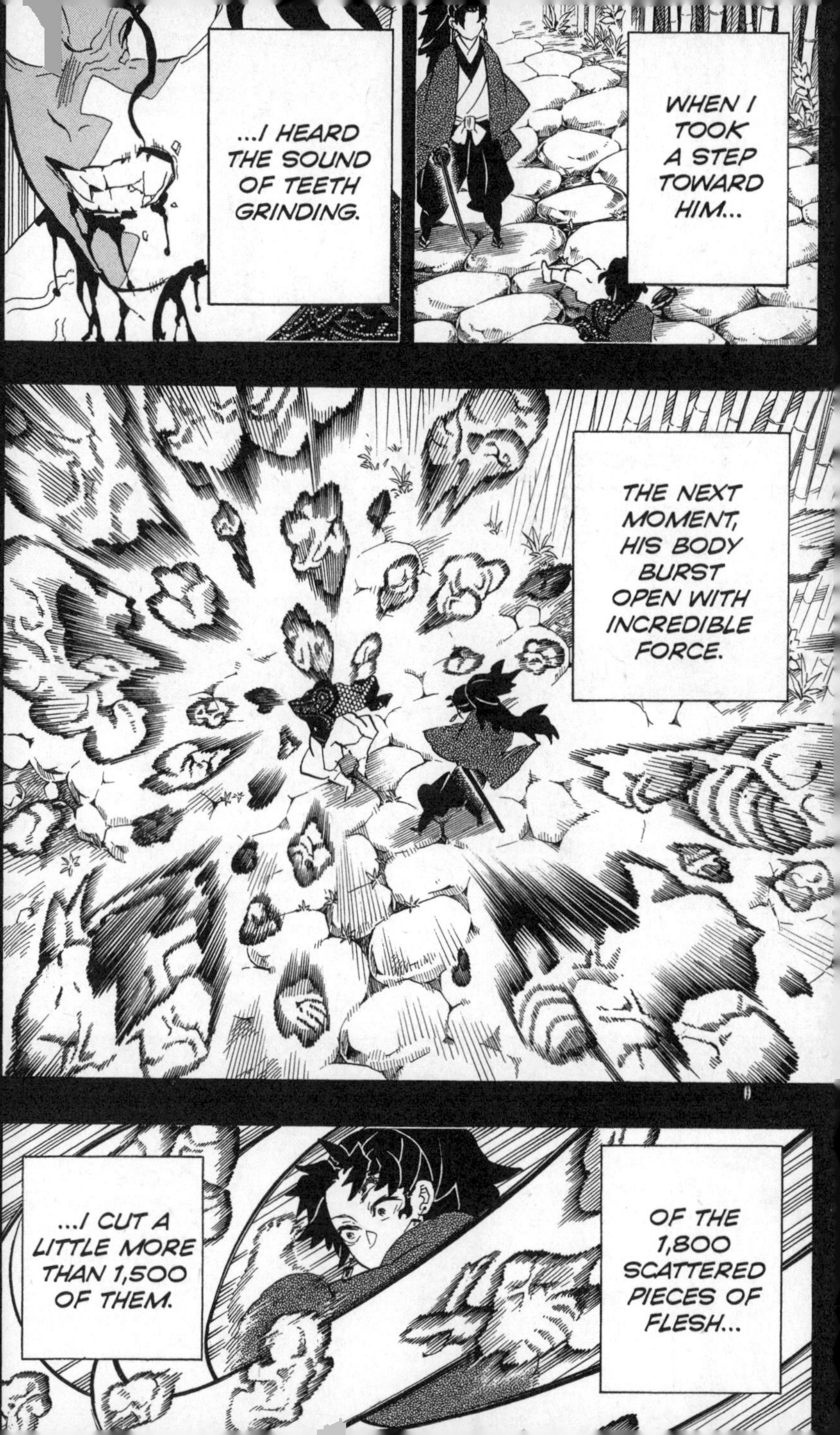
WHEN I TOOK A STEP TOWARD HIM...
...I HEARD THE SOUND OF TEETH GRINDING.
THE NEXT MOMENT, HIS BODY BURST OPEN WITH INCREDIBLE FORCE.
OF THE 1,800 SCATTERED PIECES OF FLESH...
...I CUT A LITTLE MORE THAN 1,500 OF THEM.

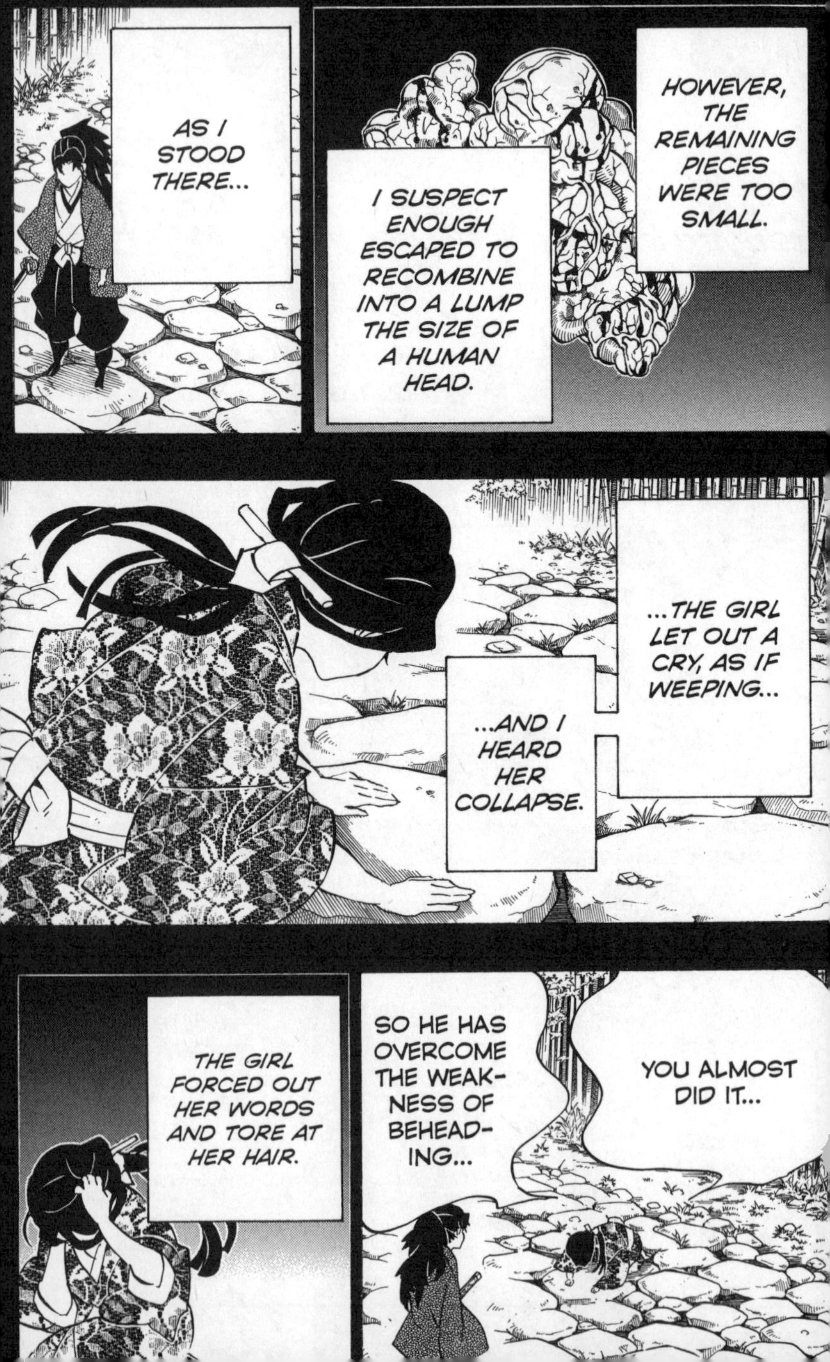
HOWEVER, THE REMAINING PIECES WERE TOO SMALL.
I SUSPECT ENOUGH ESCAPED TO RECOMBINE INTO A LUMP THE SIZE OF A HUMAN HEAD.
AS I STOOD THERE...
...THE GIRL LET OUT A CRY, AS IF WEEPING...
...AND I HEARD HER COLLAPSE.
YOU ALMOST DID IT...
SO HE HAS OVERCOME THE WEAK-NESS OF BEHEAD-ING...
THE GIRL FORCED OUT HER WORDS AND TORE AT HER HAIR.

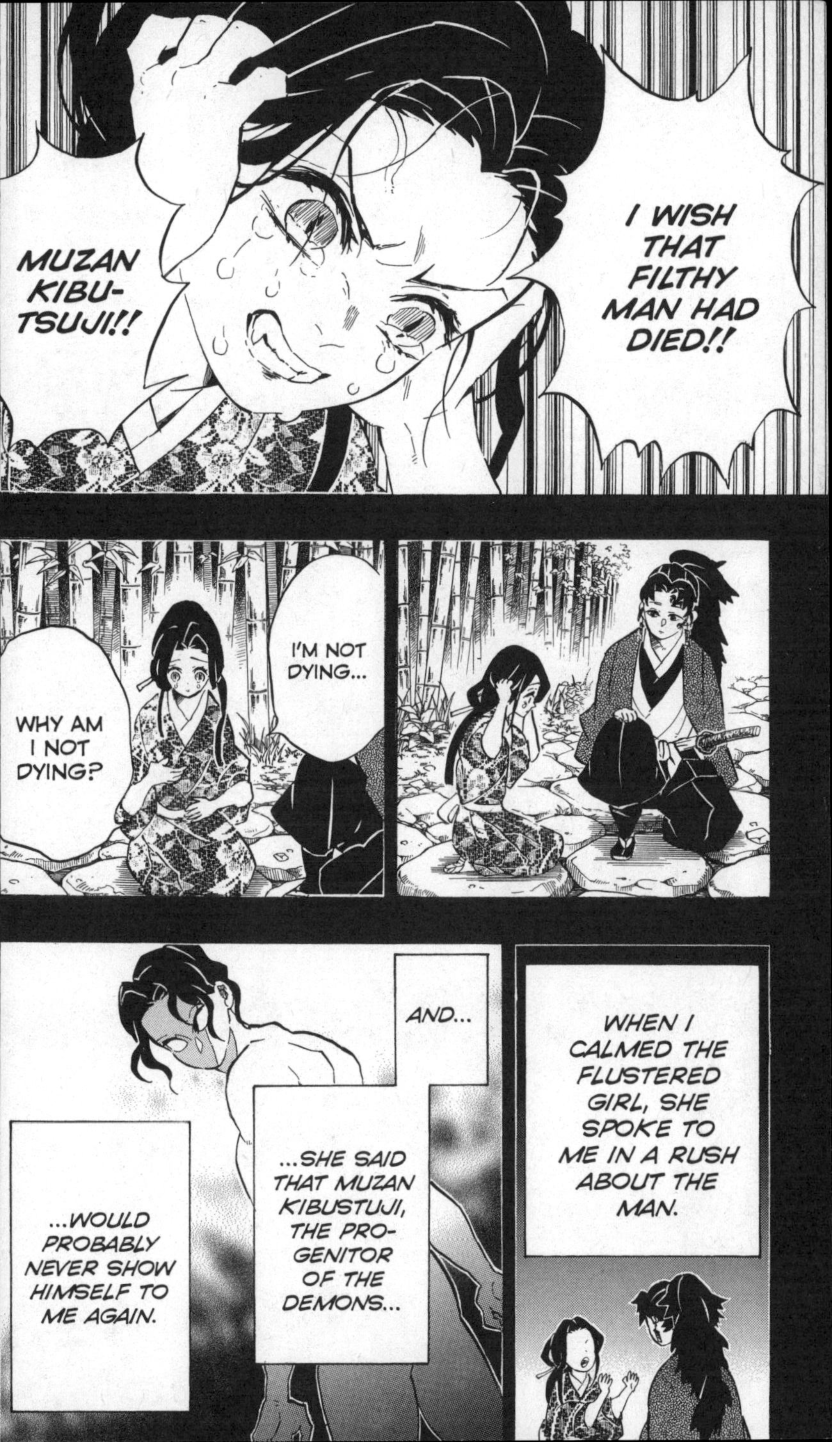
I WISH THAT FILTHY MAN HAD DIED!!
MUZAN KIBU-TSUJI!!
I'M NOT DYING...
WHY AM I NOT DYING?
WHEN I CALMED THE FLUSTERED GIRL, SHE SPOKE TO ME IN A RUSH ABOUT THE MAN.
AND...
...SHE SAID THAT MUZAN KIBUSTUJI, THE PRO-GENITOR OF THE DEMONS...
...WOULD PROBABLY NEVER SHOW HIMSELF TO ME AGAIN.

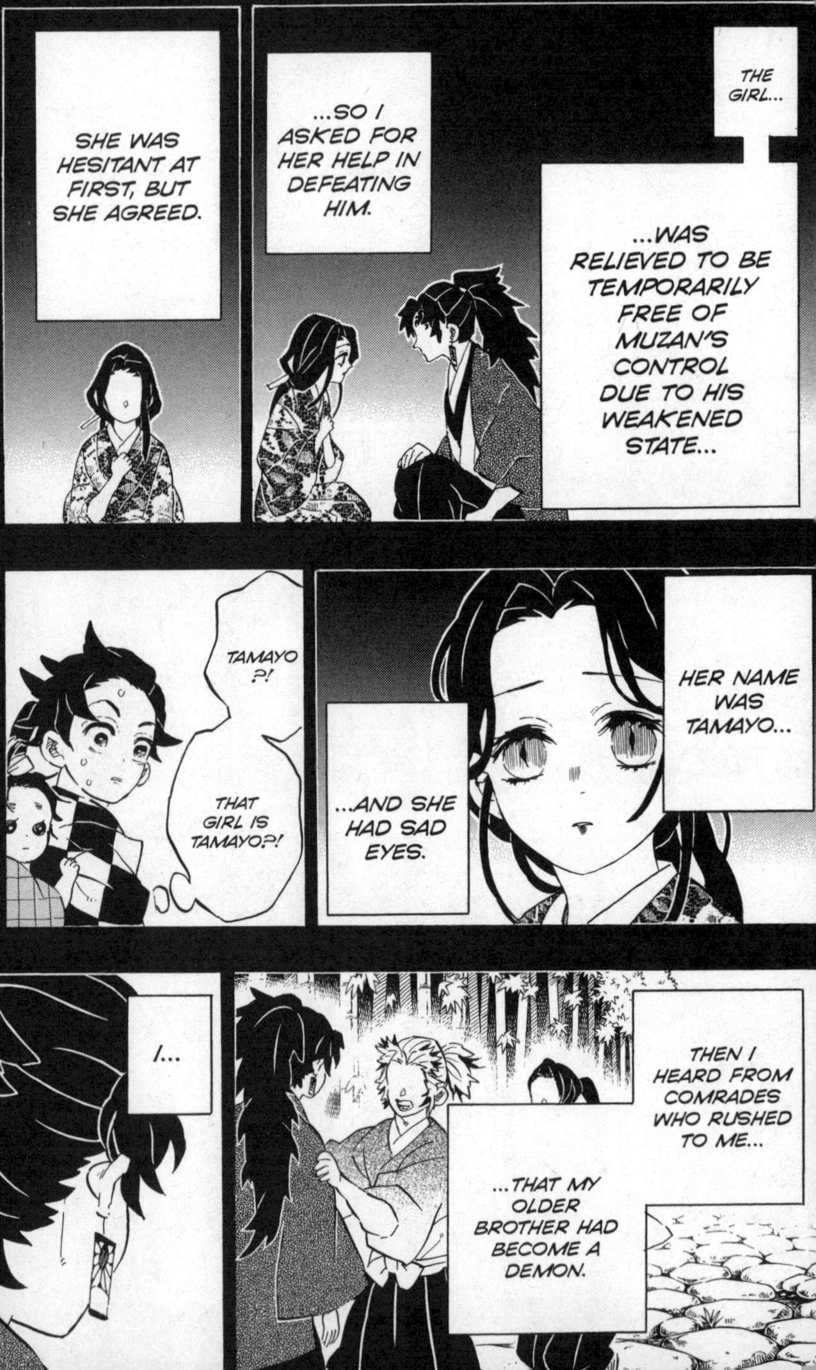
THE GIRL...
...WAS RELIEVED TO BE TEMPORARILY FREE OF MUZAN'S CONTROL DUE TO HIS WEAKENED STATE...
...SO I ASKED FOR HER HELP IN DEFEATING HIM.
SHE WAS HESITANT AT FIRST, BUT SHE AGREED.
HER NAME WAS TAMAYO...
...AND SHE HAD SAD EYES.
TAMAYO ?!
THAT GIRL IS TAMAYO?!
THEN I HEARD FROM COMRADES WHO RUSHED TO ME...
...THAT MY OLDER BROTHER HAD BECOME A DEMON.
I...

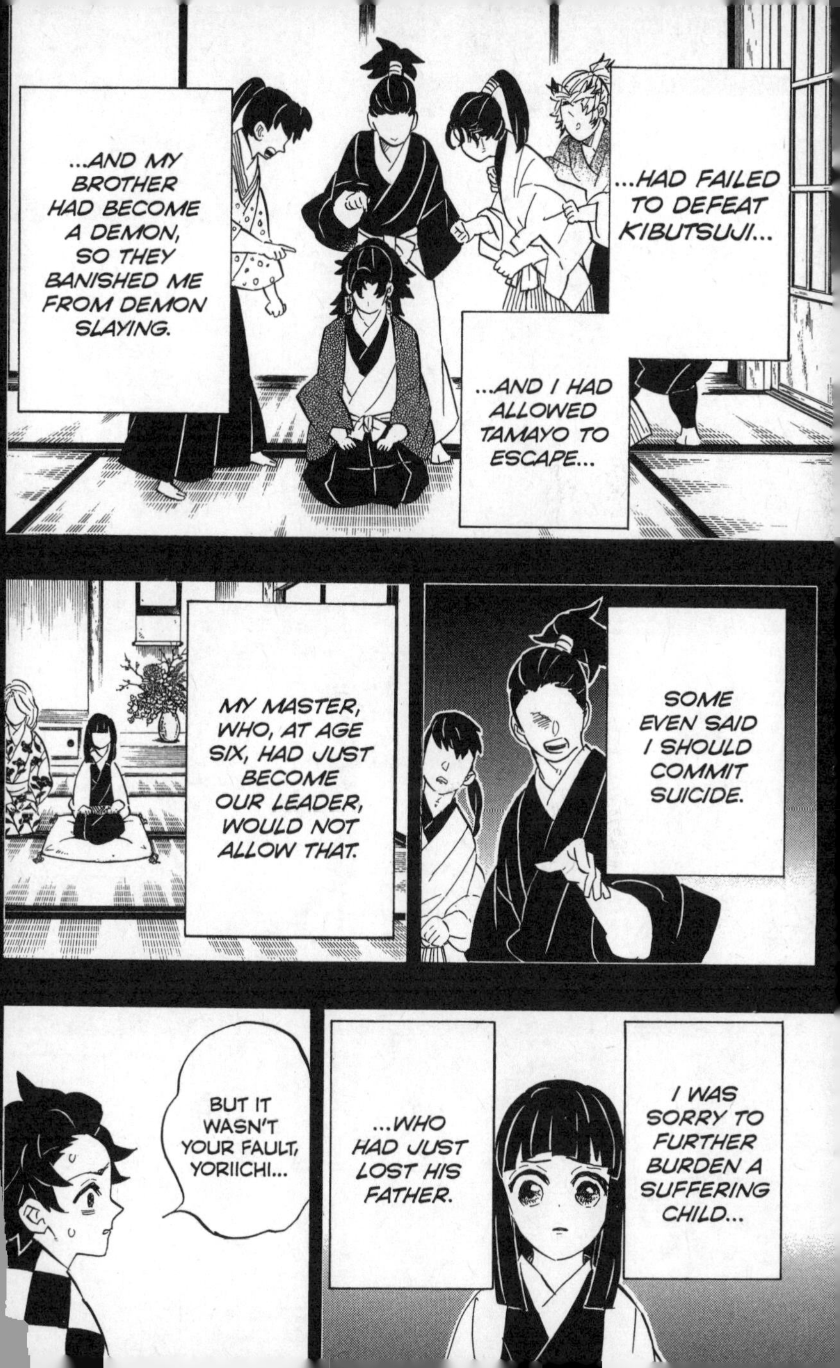
...HAD FAILED TO DEFEAT KIBUTSUJI...
...AND I HAD ALLOWED TAMAYO TO ESCAPE...
...AND MY BROTHER HAD BECOME A DEMON, SO THEY BANISHED ME FROM DEMON SLAYING.
SOME EVEN SAID I SHOULD COMMIT SUICIDE.
MY MASTER, WHO, AT AGE SIX, HAD JUST BECOME OUR LEADER, WOULD NOT ALLOW THAT.
I WAS SORRY TO FURTHER BURDEN A SUFFERING CHILD...
...WHO HAD JUST LOST HIS FATHER.
BUT IT WASN'T YOUR FAULT, YORIICHI...

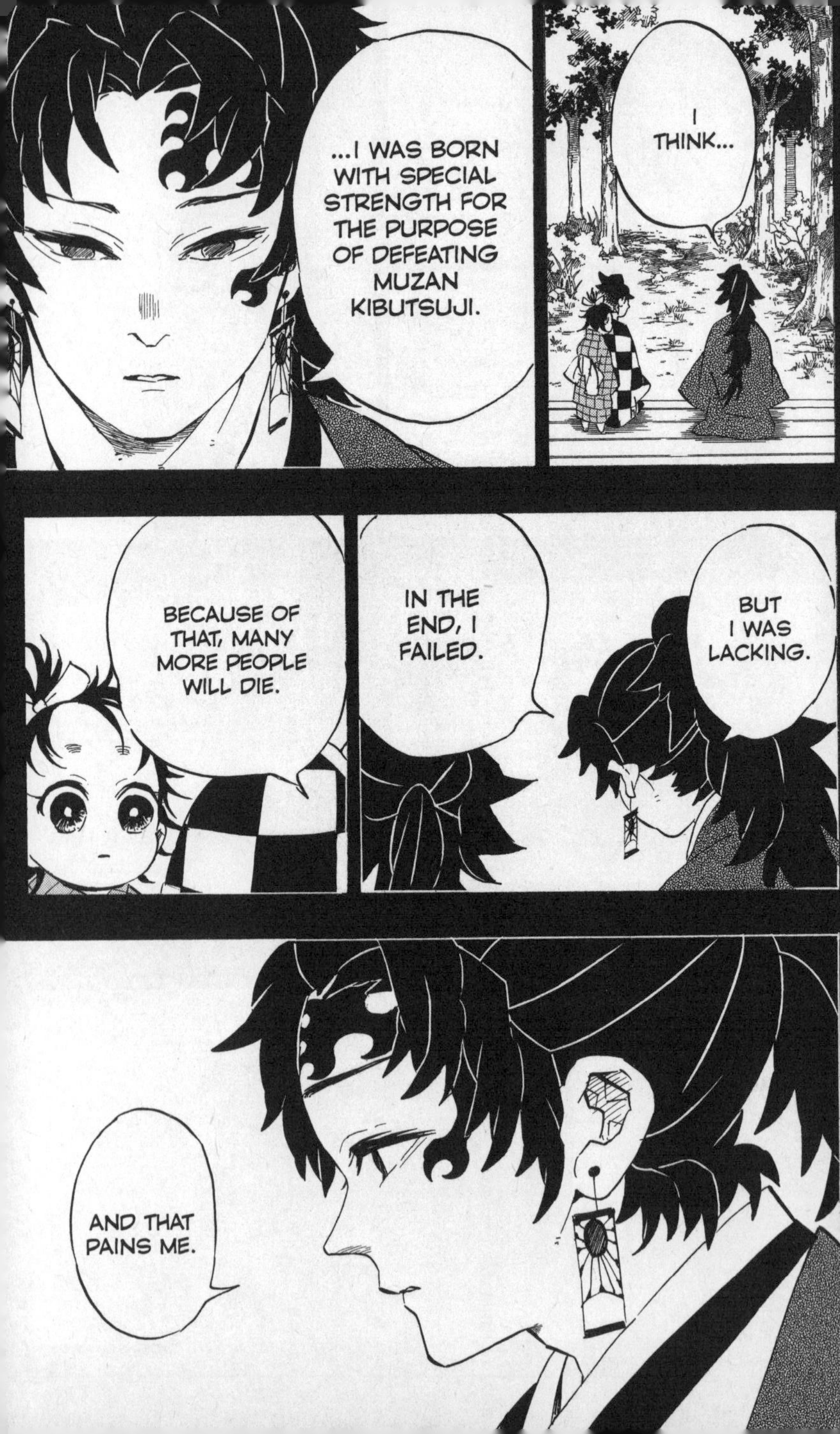
I THINK...
...I WAS BORN WITH SPECIAL STRENGTH FOR THE PURPOSE OF DEFEATING MUZAN KIBUTSUJI.
BUT I WAS LACKING.
IN THE END, I FAILED.
BECAUSE OF THAT, MANY MORE PEOPLE WILL DIE.
AND THAT PAINS ME.

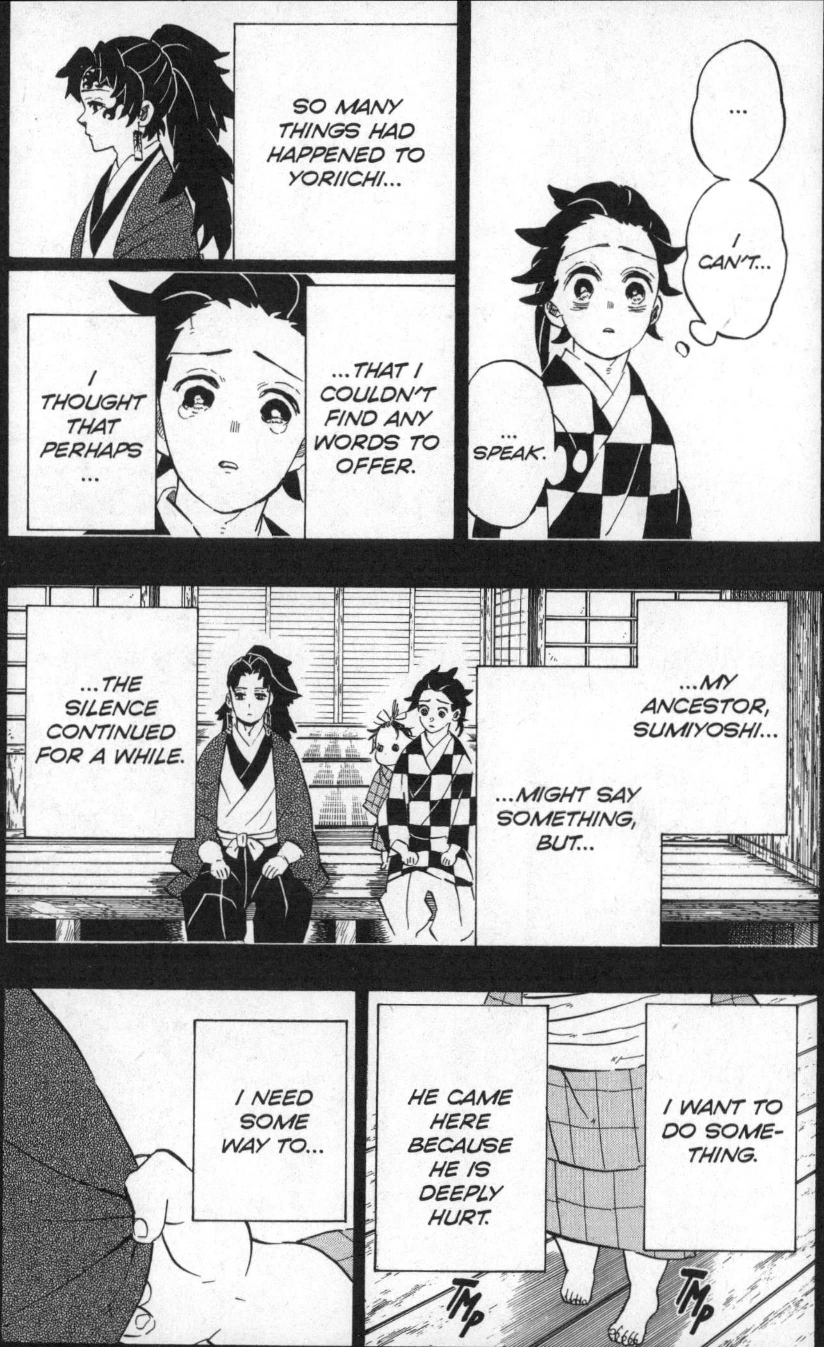

...
I CAN'T...
... SPEAK.
SO MANY THINGS HAD HAPPENED TO YORIICHI...
...THAT I COULDN'T FIND ANY WORDS TO OFFER.
I THOUGHT THAT PERHAPS ...
...MY ANCESTOR, SUMIYOSHI...
...MIGHT SAY SOMETHING, BUT...
...THE SILENCE CONTINUED FOR A WHILE.
I WANT TO DO SOME-THING.
HE CAME HERE BECAUSE HE IS DEEPLY HURT.
TMP
TMP
I NEED SOME WAY TO...

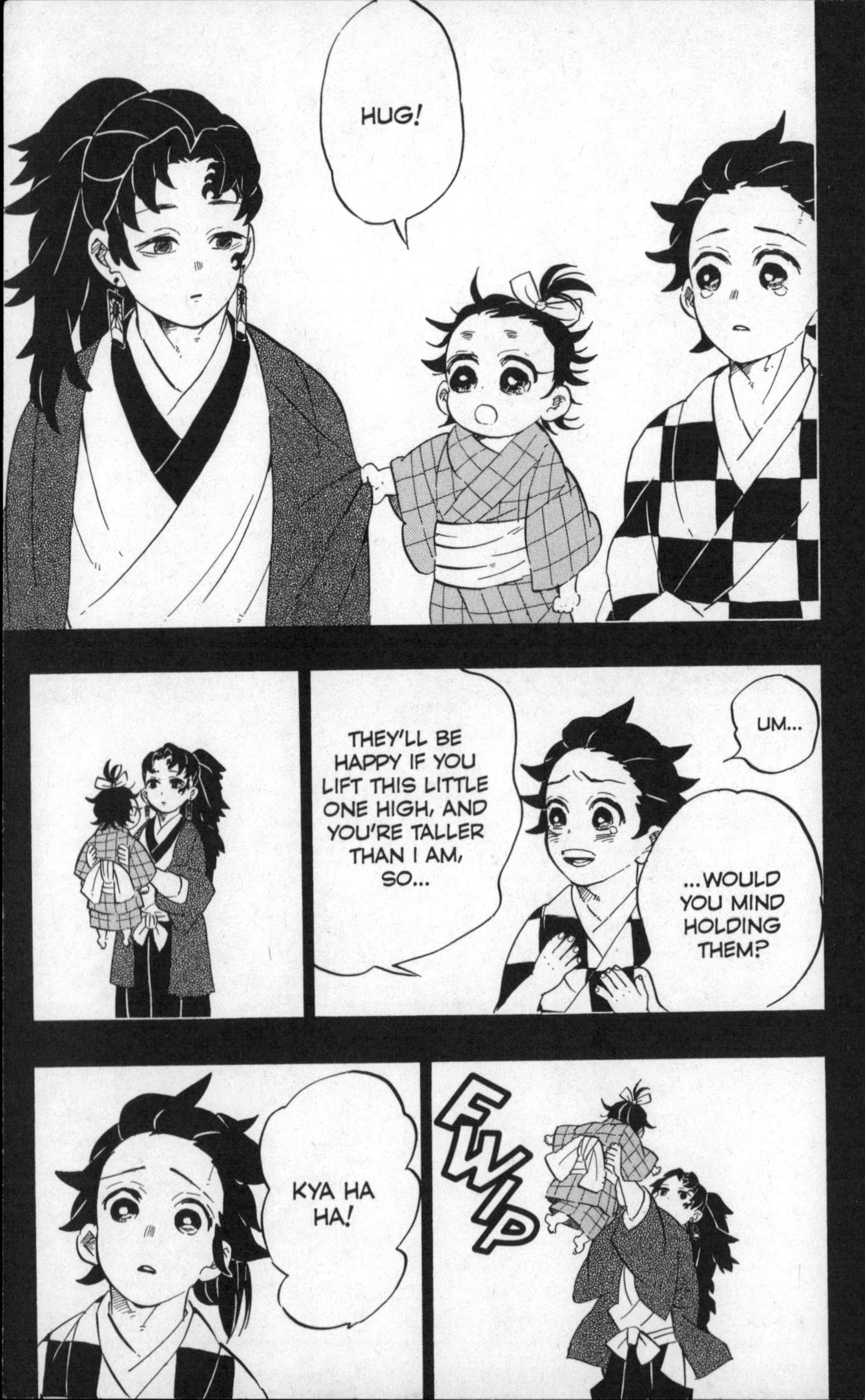
HUG!
UM...
THEY'LL BE HAPPY IF YOU LIFT THIS LITTLE ONE HIGH, AND YOU'RE TALLER THAN I AM, SO...
...WOULD YOU MIND HOLDING THEM?
FWIP
KYA HA HA!

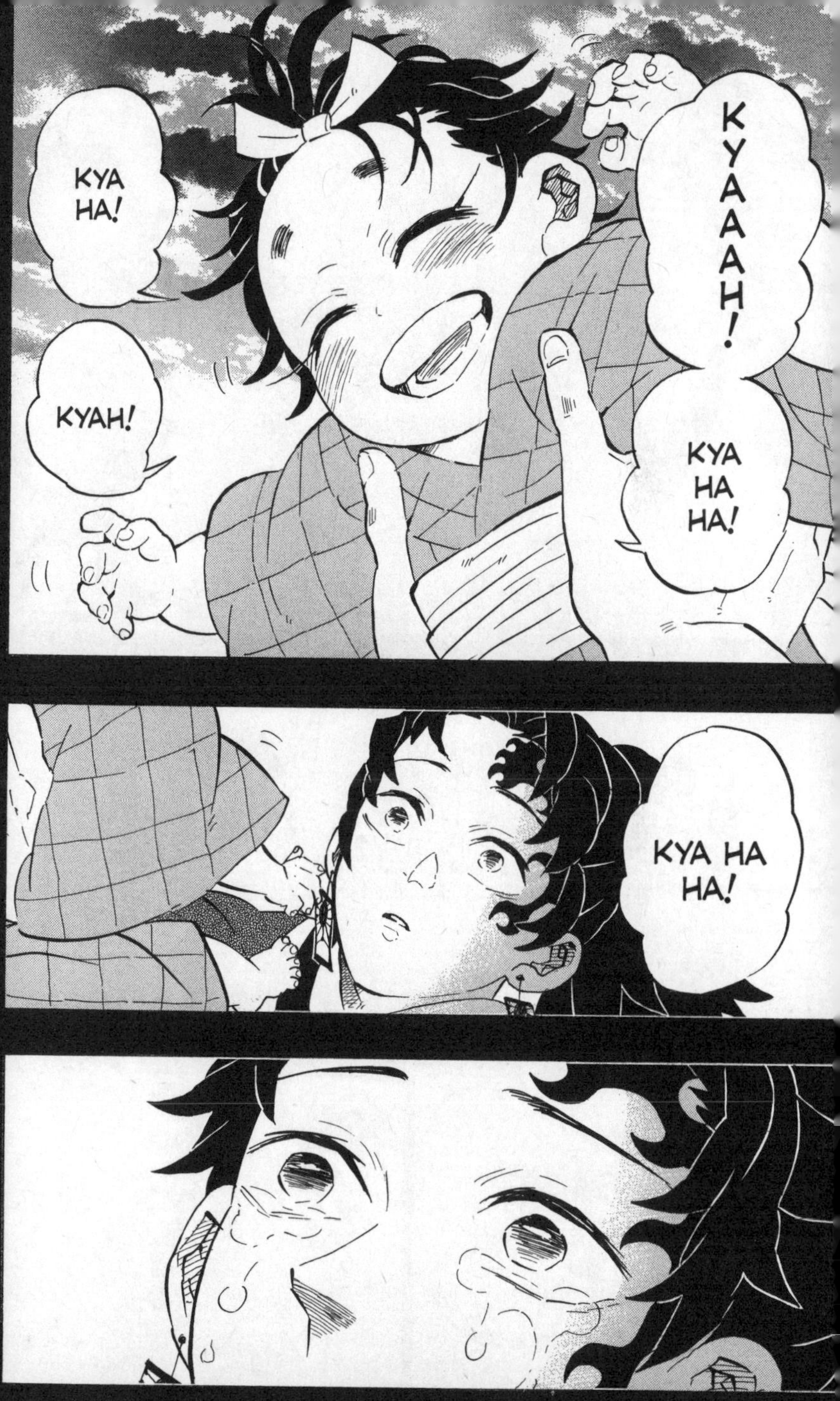
KYAAAH!
KYA HA HA HA!
KYA HA!
KYAH!
KYA HA HA!

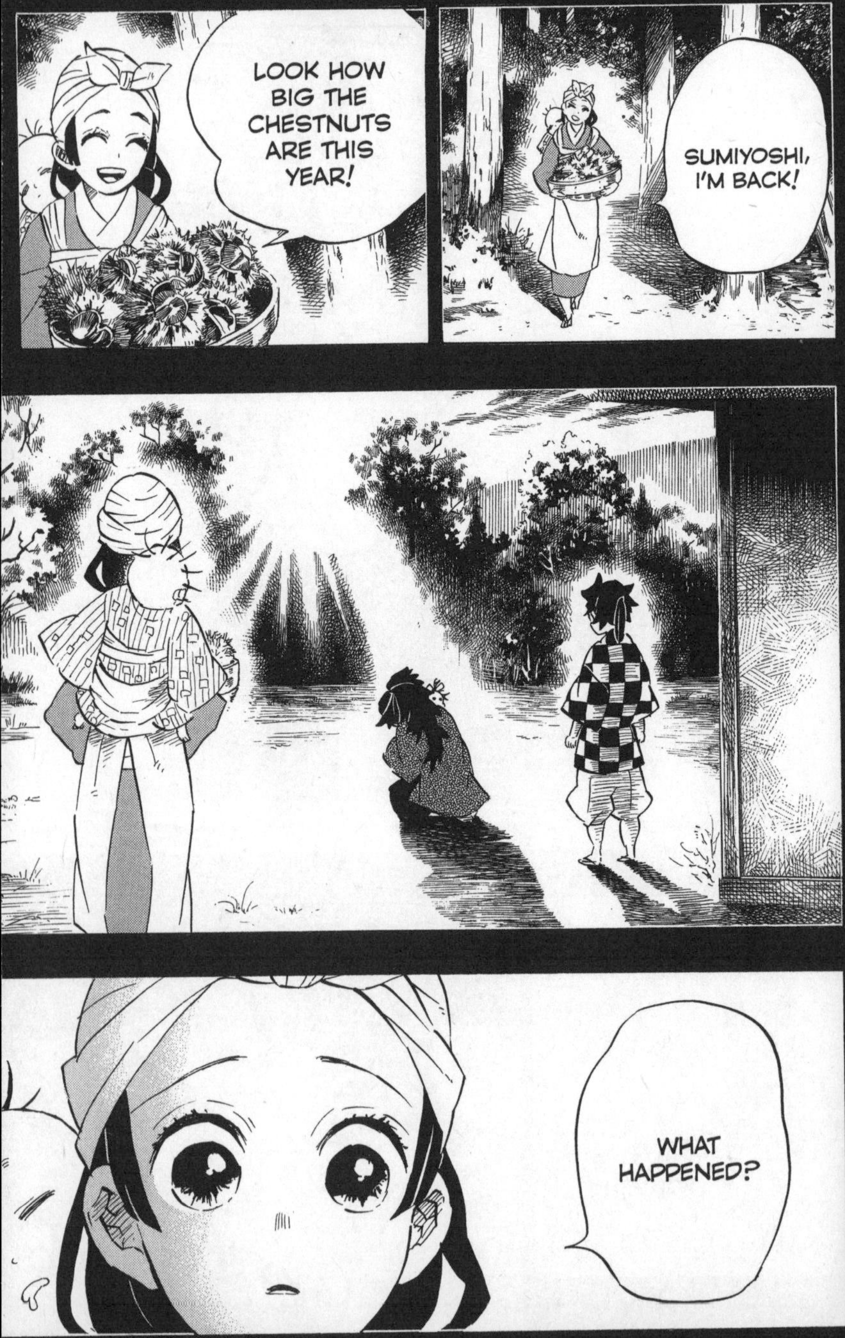
SUMIYOSHI, I'M BACK!
LOOK HOW BIG THE CHESTNUTS ARE THIS YEAR!
WHAT HAPPENED?

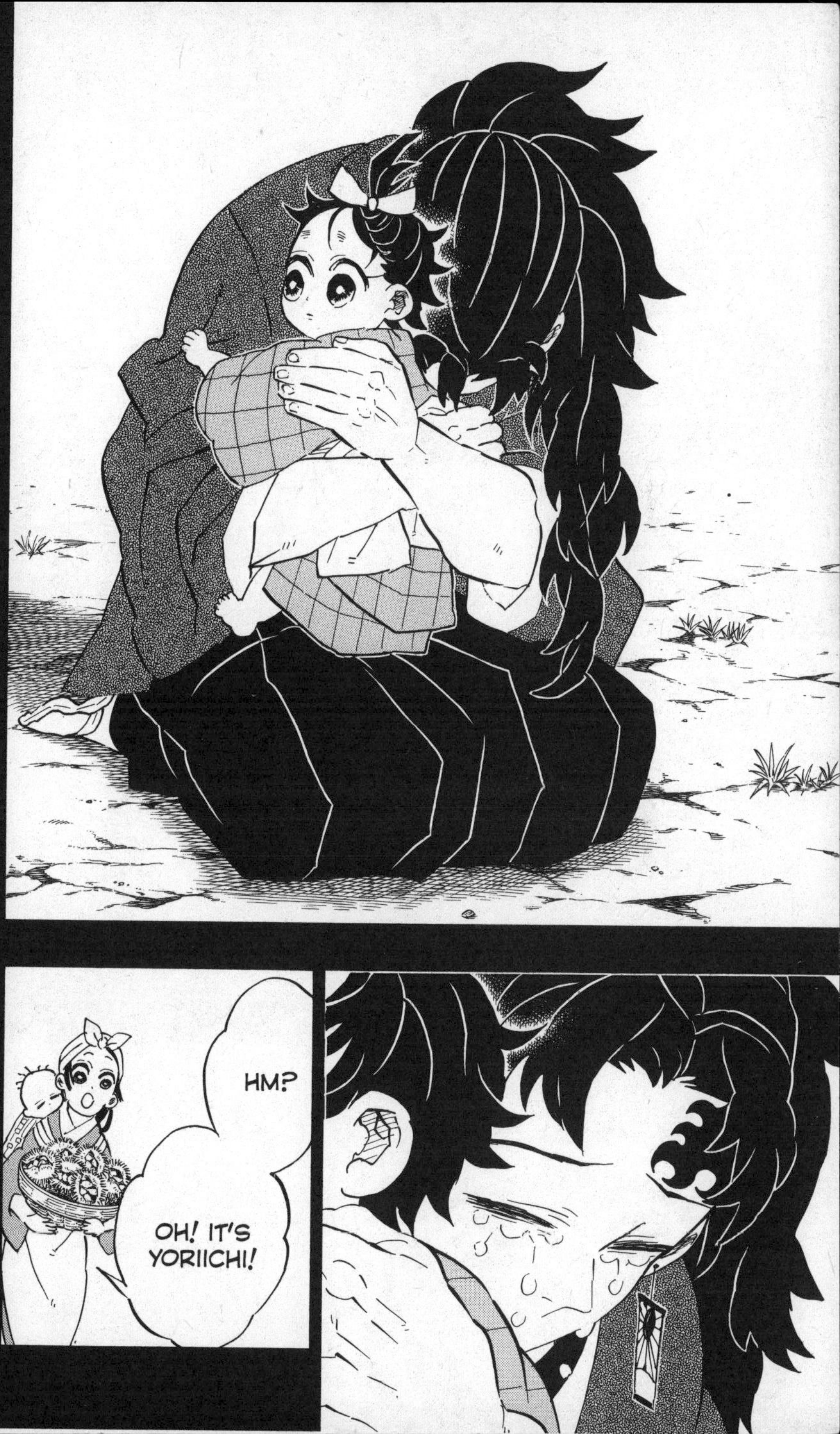
HM?
OH! IT'S YORIICHI!

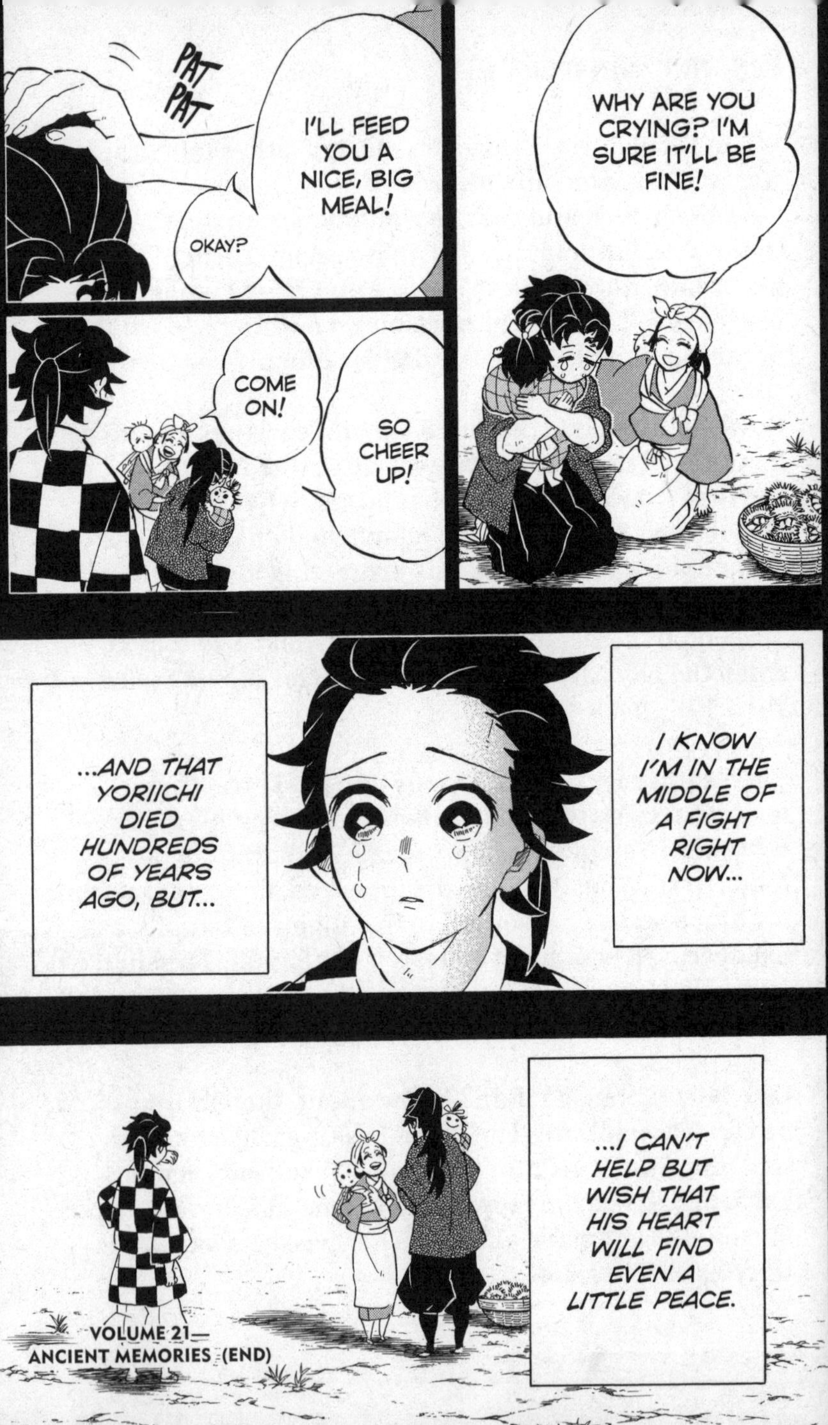
WHY ARE YOU CRYING? I'M SURE IT'LL BE FINE!
I'LL FEED YOU A NICE, BIG MEAL!
PAT PAT
OKAY?
SO CHEER UP!
COME ON!
I KNOW I'M IN THE MIDDLE OF A FIGHT RIGHT NOW...
...AND THAT YORIICHI DIED HUNDREDS OF YEARS AGO, BUT...
...I CAN'T HELP BUT WISH THAT HIS HEART WILL FIND EVEN A LITTLE PEACE.
VOLUME 21—
ANCIENT MEMORIES (END)

SENGOKU WHISPERS 1

When Yoriichi was two years old, his father told him he was an unwanted and unlucky child who never should have been born and that he would bring misfortune to the Tsugikuni family. For that reason, Yoriichi held his breath, didn't talk to anyone and tried to make his presence felt as little as possible so nothing bad would occur. He thought it was wrong for him to even be there.

However, when his mother gave him earrings as charms, he realized she thought he was deaf, so he spoke for the first time to show her that he could hear. Though he wouldn't tell her why he hadn't spoken before, she immediately realized he was protecting his father. Michikatsu and Yoriichi hurt inside because their parents often quarreled about them. The parents also fought when the boys' father hit Michikatsu for playing with Yoriichi.

Their father was superstitious and paid attention to feng shui, so he would do things like put on his right tabi sock first and begin his meals by eating certain foods first. When Yoriichi disappeared, he went looking for him because he wanted to live together happily as his deceased wife had requested in her will. They had quarreled incessantly, but he loved her from the bottom of his heart. After she passed away, he never remarried.

Like Michikatsu, he didn't know about Akeno's illness, so he clung to her body, crying and asking why she hadn't told him. Shock over his wife's death and concern for Yoriichi, who had disappeared, harmed his health. After Michikatsu got married, the father passed away in his thirties as if in relief.

SENGOKU WHISPERS 2

Yoriichi was very happy holding hands with Uta as they came and went along the path to and from the rice paddies and fields. After losing Uta and the baby, he remained single. The only woman he ever loved throughout his whole life was Uta. After becoming a Demon Slayer, he got along well with the Hashira of that time, so he began talking a lot.

Even after his banishment, he kept in touch with a few Hashira, which the master silently allowed. Michikatsu killed the previous master, the father of the master at that time, and presented the head to Kibutsuji. After that, the organization kept the master's residence in stricter secrecy than before. That's also about the time the Kakushi came into existence.

After Yoriichi died, Muzan made his move and killed all the sword wielders who had learned Sun Breathing from Yoriichi. During that time, the Demon Slayer organization fell into a disorganized state. The Flame Hashira recorded how the Demon Slayers gradually weakened after Yoriichi left, because no one remained who could teach them swordplay as skillfully as he could.

After Yoriichi let Tamayo escape, she fed on animals and human corpses to survive. Yoriichi had told her that he believed in her desire to defeat Muzan. She often recalled those words and resolved that no matter how much she suffered, she would never attack human beings.

I found some notes I made before, so I've recorded them here. I cut a large amount, but it's still quite a lot! (*Sweat*)

YOU'RE READING THE
WRONG WAY!

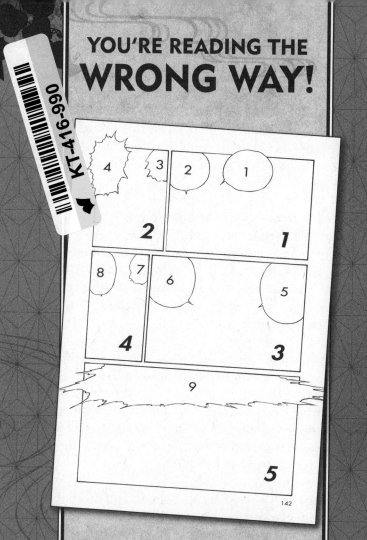

KT-416-990

142

DEMON SLAYER: KIMETSU NO YAIBA
reads from right to left, starting in the
upper-right corner. Japanese is read
from right to left, meaning that action,
sound effects and word-balloon order are
completely reversed from English order.